CONTRACTS

IN A NUTSHELL

FIFTH EDITION

By

CLAUDE D. ROHWER
Professor of Law
McGeorge School of Law
University of the Pacific

ANTHONY M. SKROKI
Professor of Law
McGeorge School of Law
University of the Pacific

WEST
GROUP

ST. PAUL, MINN.
2000

In memory of Gordon Duane Schaber

(1927–1997)

Lawyer, Professor, Dean, Community Leader,
Judge, Adviser, Scholar and Friend

*

PREFACE

PURPOSE

This Nutshell is intended to assist those who are attempting to learn and understand the basic principles of the law of Contracts and of Sales of Goods in the United States. The reader should appreciate that a work of this type is intended only as an additional supplemental resource to aid in the organization and understanding of the substantive law. As such, it could be used to acquire a preliminary overview of a specific area, or it could be used after one believes he or she has already acquired an understanding of the basics. It could also be used simultaneously and continually with other sources during the entire learning process. Whichever choice is made as to its use, we again emphasize that the materials as presented here are not intended as the primary source of acquisition of the knowledge and understanding of the substantive law and their underlying policies.

METHOD

There are no "quick and easy" methods or formulae for acquiring the knowledge and understanding of the policies of the law, nor for acquiring the ability to apply the law to the facts of a particular problem to reason to a logical conclusion. You will not "learn the law" from any one source, or even from any combination of sources, and "learning the law" is not the purpose of law school. You will acquire an ability to understand the law and the ability to explain and apply it only by your own consistent and persistent dedication of time and effort. Acquiring this ability of "self-learning" is a goal of law school because it is the basic requisite for the practice of law.

SEQUENCE

The sequence of materials as presented here may differ from the order or approach that the reader is utilizing for the study of the law of Contracts. For example, some Contracts courses may start with "Consideration", and others may start with "Remedies". Recognizing the diversity in approach, most chapters of this Nutshell have been written to be comprehensible regardless of the order of study. Therefore, the student should be able to focus upon individual chapters without immediate concern about continuity.

Issues related to modification of contracts have been presented as a separate body of material. Although this is not ordinarily done, contract modification raises a rather standard clutch of issues that we think can efficiently be taught and understood as a package.

Chapter 14 consists of questions and analyses that are intended to give the reader an opportunity for self-evaluation.

The last chapter consists of a short outline entitled "A Framework for Review". This is meant to be used after the study of the entire Contracts course is completed. It may assist in developing a manageable approach to the application of the extensive materials covered in the course. A student would be well-advised to self-test his or her own understanding of the course by evaluating why this "Framework" was put together as it was and whether the student could make improvements in it.

ACKNOWLEDGMENTS

The authors gratefully acknowledge the very capable assistance of Kim Horiuchi, class of 2001, and other student researchers who have made contributions to this and the prior four editions, as well as that of Professor Charles D. Kelso and Professor Phillip H. Wile.

Special acknowledgment and thanks are also given to our most efficient and patient administrative assistant, R.K. Van Every. Without her, this Nutshell would still be sitting amidst the piles of other papers on the desks of the authors.

*

OUTLINE

CONTRACTS

CHAPTER 1. INTRODUCTION

CHAPTER 2. CONTRACTS FORMA-TION

A. MUTUAL ASSENT TO A BARGAIN

OUTLINE

OUTLINE

B. PROMISSORY ESTOPPEL

CHAPTER 3. STATUTE OF FRAUDS

A. CONTRACTS WITHIN THE STATUTE

OUTLINE

CHAPTER 4.   CONTRACT INTERPRE-
TATION

A.   GENERAL INTERPRETATION PROB-
LEMS

B. PAROL EVIDENCE RULE

C. IMPLIED TERMS AND TERMS IMPOSED BY LAW

CHAPTER 5.   DEFENSES

A. DEFENSES AFFECTING ASSENT

OUTLINE

CHAPTER 6. EVENTS THAT EXCUSE PERFORMANCE

A. IMPOSSIBILITY OR IMPRACTICABILITY

B. FRUSTRATION OF PURPOSE

CHAPTER 7. CONTRACT MODIFICA-TION

CHAPTER 8. PERFORMANCE

A. PROMISES AND CONDITIONS

B. EXCUSE OF CONDITIONS

C. SALE OF GOODS

D. GOOD FAITH AFFECTING PERFORMANCE

OUTLINE

CHAPTER 9.   REMEDIES

A.   REMEDIES AVAILABLE AT COMMON LAW

B.   REMEDIES IN SALES OF GOODS

Page

CHAPTER 12. ASSIGNMENT OF RIGHTS AND DELEGATION OF DUTIES

A. ASSIGNMENT OF RIGHTS

B. DELEGATION OF DUTIES

CHAPTER 13. DISCHARGE

OUTLINE

CHAPTER 14.   CONTRACTS QUESTIONS

CHAPTER 15.   A FRAMEWORK FOR REVIEW

TABLE OF CASES

References are to Pages

TABLE OF CASES

TABLE OF CASES

*

CONTRACTS

IN A NUTSHELL

FIFTH EDITION

*

CONTRACTS

CHAPTER 1

INTRODUCTION

§ 1.1 Scope of this Nutshell—Contract Law and Sales Law

The Restatement, Second, Contracts (hereafter referred to as "Restatement") in section 1 states, "A contract is a promise or set of promises for the breach of which the law gives a remedy, or the performance of which the law in some way recognizes as a duty."

A promise is a commitment or an undertaking that some event will or will not occur in the future. A promise may be made by using express words or it may be implied from conduct or some combination of words and conduct.

Thus, any transaction in which one party makes or both parties make a legally enforceable promise is a contract.

There can be a sale of goods in which neither party makes a promise. For example: A buyer in a department store who picks out a bottle of perfume and pays cash for it at the register makes a purchase and the store makes a sale of the perfume but it would be difficult to find a contract between the store and the consumer. Most likely, neither party made any promises and there was no point at which either was bound to some future performance. There was a sale of goods and the seller may have impliedly warranted that the perfume is of merchantable quality, but no one made a promise so there is no contract.

The primary focus of this Nutshell will be just what the title states, "Contracts." However, the materials herein will cover not only the law of Contracts, but also some of the law applicable to the sale of goods (regardless of whether there was a contract formed). Materials relating to the law of restitution are also included in Chapter 10.

Contract law determines the enforceability of the promises of the parties and establishes the body of law for the formation, interpretation, and performance of the contract, as well as for the remedies in the event of the failure of a party to perform the promise(s) made. Freedom of contract, the freedom of individuals and enterprises to make their own economic arrangements with each other, is a fundamental prerequisite for a free society. This notion of contract law being a fundamental freedom is easily overlooked in a community in which this right is taken for granted. However, adoption and enforcement of laws permitting freedom of contract have been among the major necessities in countries that have been evolving from a command economy to a market economy in recent decades.

§ 1.2 Basis for Enforcement of Promises

Contract law is concerned with enforcing promises. All the principal legal systems in the world distinguish between those promises that create legal duties and those that do not. It seems to be accepted wisdom that we do not wish to enforce every promise made. Therefore, all legal systems have established standards for determining the enforceability of promises.

The most common basis for enforcing promises in the United States involves the concept of consideration. There is consideration for a promise if that promise was made as a part of a bargain or deal. The underlying principle is that the promise is being enforced because the promisee paid a price for that promise. Consideration involves the concept of exchange: the notion that the promise you are seeking to enforce was made in exchange for the act or promise of the person to whom the promise was made.

Consideration as a basis for promise enforcement is a concept that was developed in the common law courts in England. The common law has been generally adopted in those countries that were formerly British colonies. With the exception of Louisiana, the law of which has its roots in the French Civil Law, the courts in the United States follow the common law. Thus, courts in the United States will enforce a promise if it is made as a part of a bargained exchange for another promise or for the performance or forbearance of an act. The promising party may have been an offeror and the offeree may have given the consideration by either promising something in return or doing or forebearing from doing something in return. If the consideration was a return promise from the offeree, then the return promise will likewise be enforceable. The promises may be written or oral, resulting in what is sometimes called an express contract. The promises may be implied from the conduct of one or both of the parties, resulting in an implied-in-fact contract. Characterizing the manner of creation of the promise(s) or contract is legally insignificant as both express and implied contracts are enforceable.

§ 1.2.1 Enforcement of Promises Not Made as Part of a Bargain

There are certain promises that are enforced even though they are not supported by consideration. For example:

(a) A court may enforce a promise that induces a foreseeable and detrimental change of position by the promisee (promissory estoppel). The law may provide a remedy for the breach of a promise regardless of whether the promisor was seeking something in return (consideration) or whether the promise was gratuitous, if it was foreseeable that the promisee would detrimentally change position in reliance on the promise, and did so under circumstances that justice requires some remedy for breach of the promise. This concept, called promissory estoppel, was first recognized by courts in the western states around the start of the twentieth century and is now generally accepted by American courts. The original cases used promissory estoppel only as a basis for enforcing gratuitous promises when there was no contractual intent, but currently it is also being used in situations where there was contractual intent but the contract did not come into existence for some reason, perhaps because of a revocation of the offer prior to an effective acceptance.

(b) Courts may enforce promises that renew or restate a previous promise that was unenforceable.

(1) A promise to perform an obligation that was unenforceable when made because the promisor lacked legal capacity (such as a voidable promise of a minor) may be enforced without new consideration.

(2) A promise to pay preexisting obligations that were valid at one time but became unenforceable because the time permitted by law for bringing suit has expired (the statute of limitations has run) or because the debt has been discharged by bankruptcy. There are specific federal statutory limitations relating to renewing debts discharged in bankruptcy, and some states by statute restrict the revival of debts barred by the statute of limitations.

(c) There are statutes which make promises enforceable notwithstanding the absence of consideration. Examples of these include a promise modifying a contract for the sale of goods (Uniform Commercial Code § 2–209(1)), a release of a claim by a signed and delivered writing (U.C.C. § 1–107), and a written promise by a merchant not to revoke an offer (U.C.C. § 2–205).

(d) Some jurisdictions may still recognize that a signed writing under seal is enforceable without consideration. Most states have abolished the legal effect of a seal and the U.C.C. has abolished it for the sale of goods. The validity or invalidity of a sealed writing is subject to statutory limitations of the specific states and is not dealt with in this book.

§ 1.2.2   Quasi–Contract—Unjust Enrichment—Restitution

Under the law of Restitution, courts impose an obligation to pay for benefits conferred despite the absence of a promise. This **non-consensual** obligation imposed by law, is sometimes called an "implied-in-law contract" but it is not a contract. It has nothing to do with any promise, either express or implied, and therefore there is no promisor or promisee. It is premised upon the concept of avoiding unjust enrichment, and the authors would not be mentioning this term until the topic on restitution were it not for the fact that the concept of quasi-contract tends to appear early in some contract discussions. In some cases when the court cannot find a true contract based upon a manifested promise it will allow relief under a restitutionary theory to prevent unjust enrichment.

It is helpful from the outset to realize that this topic is made confusing in our law due to the absence of a generally accepted vocabulary. "Restitution" and "unjust enrichment" are synonymous. These terms are generally used to describe a separate branch of law (neither contract nor tort) in which people who are unjustly enriched at the expense of another are required to disgorge that enrichment.

"Quasi-contract" is a term that is used to describe a certain type of restitution case, that being a case involving imposition of a duty to pay for a benefit conferred through rendition of services or delivery of goods. The terms "quasi-contract" and "implied in law contract" are generally treated as synonymous. Each is the product of historical accident. They were developed to impose upon the defendant a liability similar to the liability that arises from a true contract. The critical point to remember is that these terms are used in cases where there is no contract. Without an express or implied promise, no contract can exist.

"Quasi-contract" is an accepted term today and no particular harm will result from its usage. One need only remember that the liability is in restitution, not contract. By contrast, the term "implied in law contract" almost inevitably leads to confusion. True contracts can be either express or implied. Thus, one form of true contract is properly called an "implied contract" meaning a contract where a person's promise is implied from that person's conduct ("implied in fact"). If one uses the term "implied in law contracts" to describe quasi-contracts, it is only a matter of time before one confuses "implied in fact" and "implied in law" and loses track of the basic subject being discussed. Use of the term "implied in law contracts" should be avoided.

One classic quasi-contract fact pattern involves an unconscious auto accident victim and the ambulance company called to the scene by the police, as well as the hospital and the various medical providers at the hospital. It goes without saying that an unconscious patient is not going to be signing agreements or orally promising to pay for medical services, nor is it reasonable to conclude that the failure of the unconscious patient to object to the emergency medical treatment is conduct implying a promise to pay for the services. There is no consensual undertaking on the part of the unconscious patient to pay and therefore there is no express or implied contract. The providers of the care are not doing so in return for a promise or in reliance upon a promise from the patient in their care. However, the law will hold the patient responsible for the reasonable value of the services provided. The basis for this is not contract. It is restitution.

The subject of restitution is discussed generally in Chapter 10.

§ 1.3 Sale of Goods and the Uniform Commercial Code

The Uniform Commercial Code (referred to herein as the U.C.C.) consists of numerous articles which deal with different areas of commercial law. Article 1 (in which all section numbers begin with

"1") contains general principles of law and definitions that apply to the entire U.C.C. unless inconsistent with the language of a later article. Article 2 (in which all of the section numbers begin with "2") applies to all "transactions in goods" other than transactions intended as security transactions (which are covered by Article 9) and leases (which are covered by Article 2A).

Transactions in goods are "security transactions" when the purpose of the transaction is to secure a loan or other obligation (U.C.C. § 2–102).

U.C.C. section 2A–103(1)(j) defines a "lease" to exclude a transaction in goods that may be referred to by the parties as a "lease" but which in fact is a sale with a reserved security interest in the "lessor." The so-called "lessor" in such a circumstance will be recognized as a "seller" and the "lessee" as a buyer and the entire transaction will be subject to Article 2 as well as Article 9.

Articles 3 through 9 deal with other aspects of what are usually commercial transactions. For example, Article 3 deals with the law relating to negotiable instruments (promissory notes, drafts, and checks). Article 3 would apply to any check written even though it may have been issued by Aunt Bernice as a birthday present to her nephew, Otto, hardly a commercial transaction as between them. These other articles of the U.C.C. have no direct bearing upon the study of the law of contracts except for certain portions of Article 9, which makes significant changes in the common law relating to assignments. (See Chapter 12.)

§ 1.3.1 Defining Goods

Because the U.C.C. makes important changes in the common law relating to contracts for the sale of goods as well as for the sale of goods, it is important to understand the definition of "goods." U.C.C. section 2–105(1) provides in part: " 'Goods' means all things (including specially manufactured goods) which are movable at the time of identification to the contract * * *" The "time of identification to the contract" can vary in different contexts and can include existing goods which may or may not be in the possession of the seller at the time the contract is made or goods not yet in existence but which come into existence and are identified at or before the time of performance. Frequently the key question is whether the contract involves tangible things that are movable when performance is to be rendered. "Things" do not include intangible rights such as contract rights, patent rights, or royalty rights, nor the money in which the price is to be paid.

A contract for a special machine to be designed and built by the seller and delivered to the buyer is a contract for the sale of goods. A "sale" is the passage of title for a price (U.C.C. § 2–106(1)). The machine would have come into existence and been "movable" when performance was due. Whether the contract is for the sale of goods could be determined by either the dominant nature of the transaction or alternatively by looking at the cause of the harm.

A contract may involve both goods and services in which case a court might focus upon which part is the dominant part of the transaction. A contract to change the oil and lubricate a car is probably a service contract because the goods (oil and grease), although necessary parts of the contract performance will be found to be incidental to the transaction. A contract for the sale of a new piano which the seller is to deliver and tune after it is moved is a transaction in goods because the services of delivery and tuning are incidental to the sale of the goods. A contract in which an artist is to paint a portrait of the family matriarch is probably a service contract. The artist is to deliver the completed painting which could be viewed as specially produced goods, however, the dominant nature of the contract is probably the service of the artist in painting the picture. But, buying an already completed painting displayed at the same artist's studio is a sale of goods.

Construction contracts involve the rendition of a service by the contractor. There is actually no sale of goods involved. Boards, nails and other goods delivered to the construction site are the property of the contractor who can remove them to another job and must replace them if they are stolen. When the board is nailed to something fixed to the foundation, the board and nail now belong to the owner, but they are no longer moveable items so they cease to be goods. The point at which the owner acquires a property interest is the same point at which the goods stop being goods and become part of the land. One side effect of this is that the owner does not have to pay sales tax for the price of the boards and nails. There has been no sale of goods to the owner.

In the case of defective materials in a construction project, it may be to the owner's advantage to find a sale of goods because such a sale would likely produce warranties such as a warranty of merchantability. In a minority of jurisdictions, courts have been willing to look at the specific portion of the contract that is the cause of the harm that brought the dispute before the court for resolution. For example, if the plaintiff is alleging that the plumber failed to perform the plumbing contract properly because the pipes were not properly tightened, the court would most likely conclude that the resulting water damage to the plaintiff's property was a result of the service portion of the contract and Article 2 would not be applicable. However, if the cause of the leak was a defective valve provided by the plumber, this portion of the contract, supplying the valve, could be treated as a sale of goods. These jurisdictions would apply U.C.C. Article 2 even though, had the dominant nature test been applied, the contract would have been characterized as a service contract and therefore not within Article 2.

A contract for the sale of minerals or the like or a structure or its materials to be removed from realty is a transaction in goods only if they are to be severed by the seller. If they are to be severed by the buyer, the contract should be subject to contract provisions that are applicable to the sale of an interest in realty and not Article 2. However, a contract for the sale of growing crops or timber (apart from the land itself) or other things attached to the realty (but which are not minerals or the like or a structure) are within Article 2 regardless of whether the severance is to be done by the buyer or seller provided that they can be severed without material harm to the realty. (See U.C.C. §§ 2–105 and 2–107 and comments.)

To the extent that the U.C.C. has not changed the law relative to transactions in goods, principles of common law and equity as well as other statutory provisions are applicable (U.C.C. § 1–103). In making reference to the U.C.C., the essence of certain sections will be summarized or paraphrased for the purpose of explaining their significance. Such summaries should not be treated as substitutes for your own careful reading of the actual statutory language.

§ 1.3.2 Merchants: Special Duties; Good Faith

The U.C.C., including Article 2, applies to all persons and entities. To emphasize, **Article 2 is not limited to transactions between merchants.** Article 2 will apply if it is a transaction in goods regardless of whether the buyer or seller or both or neither are merchants. A few sections and portions of sections are applicable only if both parties are merchants or only if just one party has merchant status. The term "merchant" is not defined in its ordinary sense, and whether a party is a merchant or not for application of a specific section may depend upon the particular portion of the transaction giving rise to the dispute. (U.C.C. § 2–104 and comment 2.) For example, a court could find that a law firm buying conference room furniture would be a "merchant" for purposes of U.C.C. section 2–201(2) but the firm would not be a "merchant" under U.C.C. section 2–313 if it were selling its used furniture to another party.

Whether a party has merchant status would also be important for determining the scope of the obligation of good faith. U.C.C. section 1–203 provides: "Every contract or duty within this Act imposes an obligation of good faith in its performance or enforcement." This "good faith" obligation can have substantive impact in many contract situations and should not be viewed as a simple iteration of honorable intentions. However, there are two different standards of "good faith." The general definition applicable to all parties is found in U.C.C. section 1–201(19) which provides: " 'good faith' means honesty in fact in the conduct or transaction concerned." Whereas, U.C.C. section 2–103(1)(b) provides: " 'good faith' in the case of a merchant means honesty in fact and the observance of reasonable commercial standards of fair dealing in the trade." These definitions should be analyzed with care. The standard created for non-merchants is said to be subjective and is sometimes referred to as "the pure heart and empty-head test." If the non-merchant is pure of heart, the reasonableness of the conduct is irrelevant. The standard of "good faith" for a merchant, however, includes not only the subjective honesty-in-fact requirement, but also that the merchant meet the objectively ascertainable "reasonable commercial standards of fair dealing in the trade."

§ 1.4 Contracts Which Constitute a Bargained Exchange

The primary basis for enforcing a promise in common law systems is because the promise was made as a part of a bargained exchange. This requires that there be a manifestation of intent to be bound by the promisor for which the promisee promises to do something or does something in return for the promise. This bargained exchange typically occurs as a result of there being an offer made by a person identified as the offeror and an appropriate and timely acceptance being made by the offeree, the person to whom the offer was made. The resulting agreement will be enforceable as a contract provided that the terms are sufficiently definite or certain so that a court can determine the extent of the parties' obligations and provide an appropriate remedy in the event of a breach of an obligation. Remember the definition of a contract, "A promise or set of promises for the breach of which the law gives a remedy * * * " (Restatement § 1).

It is not uncommon for parties to engage in a series of discussion in which various terms of what they desire are discussed or specified. Ultimately, the parties may shake hands, literally or figuratively, manifesting their assent to their respective undertakings. In such circumstances, an agreement will be found to have been reached without either party making a specific identifiable offer which the other accepted (Restatement § 22(2)). Realizing that one may not be able to find a specific offer and acceptance in every contract relationship that comes into existence, it is nonetheless best to approach the concept of contract formation by focusing upon the basic elements involved in the offer and acceptance interchange. (Restatement § 22(1).)

Although manifestations of intent to be bound can be communicated by words or conduct, we will focus upon verbal (oral or written) communications.

CHAPTER 2

CONTRACTS FORMATION

A. MUTUAL ASSENT TO A BARGAIN

1. OFFER

§ 2.1 Manifestation of Assent to Be Bound

An offer is a communication that creates in the offeree the power to form a contract by an appropriate acceptance. Section 24 of the Restatement provides that it must be a "manifestation of willingness to enter into a bargain, so made as to justify another person in understanding that his assent to that bargain is invited and will conclude it." Thus, the first element of an offer is a manifestation of intent to be presently legally bound. If there is such an intent and the terms can be determined, the offeror will have created the power of acceptance in the offeree.

The critical issue in the analysis of a communication is whether it is an offer (creating the power of acceptance in the offeror) or whether it is merely preliminary negotiations which is inviting further discussion or soliciting an offer from the other party. Restatement section 26 provides:

A manifestation of willingness to enter into a bargain is not an offer if the person to whom it is addressed knows or has reason to know that the person making it does not intent to conclude a bargain until he has made a further manifestation of assent.

Whether a communication is an offer or simply preliminary negotiations is a question of fact. If the recipient is aware that the proposal is also addressed to other parties and that the person making the proposal cannot perform to more than one person, the communication can not be an offer. It is clear that the person sending the communication has no intention to be presently bound to all of the people receiving the communication, therefore these communications cannot be offers. For example, a letter on its face addressed to two or three people indicating a desire to sell "my horse, Charley", would not likely be found to create a power of acceptance because each recipient should know that the sender does not intend to create in each of them the power to form a contract. There is only one Charley. However, if a recipient had no reason to know that the letter was also sent to others, and the letter was worded so as to create the power of acceptance, that is the recipient was justified "in understanding that his assent to that bargain is invited and will conclude it" (Restatement sec. 24), Charley's owner may be found to have entered into a contract with each of the recipients who accepted the offer. Of course, only one contract can be performed, but the offeror will be liable for damages caused by the breach of any other contract or contracts formed but not performed.

As will be discussed later, for a communication to be an offer, in addition to the requirement of intent to be bound, the communication must be sufficiently definite as to terms or empower the other person to specify terms to clear up any uncertainties. If intention to be bound is not clear, the more definite a proposal is, the more likely it is that the trier of fact will conclude that the communication is an offer. Conversely, the less definite a proposal is as to terms, the less likely will it be found to be an offer because the intention to be presently bound is less clear.

§ 2.1.1 Subjective and Objective Intent

Contract liability is primarily predicated upon the intention that a party objectively manifests even though that manifested intention may be inconsistent with that party's actual unexpressed intention. The actual but unexpressed or uncommunicated intention (referred to as subjective intention) of one party will not usually be considered in determining the existence of or terms of a contract if the other party had no reason to know of such uncommunicated intention. The focus is ordinarily upon what the person to whom the communication was directed should reasonably have understood.

In determining what legal effect should be given to a particular communication, the message is construed as a whole in light of all surrounding facts and circumstances including all of the prior communications and transactions between the parties. Common sense, upon which we believe the common law is founded, dictates that expressions which are later in time are controlling over inconsistent earlier expressions; that language added by the parties will take precedence over printed materials in a standard form; and that language is to be interpreted in light of any prior course of dealing between the parties and any custom or usage in the trade or community.

Because contract law is predicated upon a consensual relationship created by the parties' manifestations of assent, there are circumstances in which the subjective intentions of the parties are relevant. If the application of the objectively manifested intent standard were applied literally in every case, a contract could be found to exist based upon communications between parties when neither of them actually meant to be bound. If it is determined that neither party subjectively intended to be bound then there should be no contract found. Contract law is concerned with protection of the reasonable expectations of the parties and there is ordinarily no reason to enforce what appear to be manifestations of agreements if neither party actually intended or wanted a contract at the time the communications occurred.

The subjective intention of the parties is also considered when a mutual misunderstanding exists. No contract should be found to exist if each party knew or had reason to know of the different meanings intended by the other. Section 20 of the Restatement takes the position that there is no mutual assent if the parties attach materially different meanings to their manifestations and neither know or had reason to know of the meaning intended by the other (§ 6.6).

If both parties were jesting or for other reasons did not intend their words to have legal effect, then no contract results. This is true even if a third party observer would conclude that both parties intended their promises to be taken seriously. Contracts professors and students make many "agreements" in class which are nothing more than hypothetical bargains with no legally enforceable rights resulting. Countless real agreements are made in life relating to matters such as social dates or meetings with no intent that there be legally enforceable rights and duties. If the person to whom a proposal is made knows or should have known that the proposal is not meant to result in a legally enforceable bargain, then no contract exists.

In an effort to explain and inculcate the objective theory of contract intent, people sometimes make statements to the effect that contract law is concerned only with what intent was objectively manifested and has nothing to do with the subjective intention of the parties. This is clearly an overstatement. If a court finds that at the time the purported agreement was made, both parties shared the same subjective understanding as to their legal relationship, then that understanding will determine their legal rights.

§ 2.1.2 Agreements That Contemplate a Future Writing

If one or both parties manifest an intention that their agreement be reduced to a formal writing, this presents a question of fact whether they intended to be presently bound to a contract before the writing is executed or whether their intent was that no contract would exist unless and until a writing was signed.

It is not unusual for parties to enter into a contract in an informal manner, either orally or through an exchange of written communications, and also intend that at some time in the future they will memorialize their existing agreement by a more formal signed writing. The desire for a signed formal contract may be merely to lessen the risk of future misunderstandings as to their agreement. Perhaps documented proof of the existing contract is necessary to satisfy a third party, such as a financing institution.

If the parties intend a contract to exist presently, with the signed writing when it is created constituting a mere memorialization of the existing contract, then there is a contract in existence from the time of the initial agreement. If however, the parties have reached an agreement but their intent is that the agreement will not be enforceable unless and until there is a signed formal contract, then there will not be a contract unless and until the signed writing does come into existence.

There are no specialized legal rules to be applied in this situation. Recall that the assent necessary to create a contract is a manifested assent to be presently legally bound. All surrounding circumstances and communications between the partes must be analyzed to see whether such intent to be bound now, rather than later, has been manifested.

A related problem arises when a person executes an agreement with qualifying language such as "subject to the approval of my attorney." One interpretation of such language might be that the party has manifested intent to be presently bound with the stated condition relating only to an attorney's approval of the legal sufficiency of the documents . However, circumstances might justify a factual determination that the condition is more fundamental and manifests an intent to obtain advice and counsel concerning the wisdom of the transaction. For example, an attorney might advise against entering an agreement to sell property because of tax consequences. In this situation, depending upon the facts, the language may have indicated that there was to be no contract until there was approval by the attorney and therefore there was no intent to be presently legally bound.

§ 2.1.3 Letters of Intent

There are circumstances in which parties wish to have a writing that will provide a record of the negotiations that have taken place to date even though no contract has been reached. This is of particular importance in complex transactions in which the consent of many parties may be necessary to permit the deal to go forward.

For example, assume that Company S (Seller) wishes to sell a major part of its business including factories and distribution networks and has been negotiating with Company B (Buyer) concerning this potential sale. Of necessity, negotiations must proceed in detail on some issues before agreement is obtained on other issues. Terms must be settled specifically before either side can approach its board of directors or the banker's loan committee or the Justice Department lawyers who handle antitrust enforcement or the city planning commission. It is necessary to have a working document that describes the deal even though there is no deal yet.

There is no contract because neither party has assented to be presently legally bound. In this sense, a letter of intent is not worth much. However, the signed document evidences the tentative agreements that have been reached on a number of matters which is important in itself. It is also a document that can be shown to various parties to determine how they will react if the terms are eventually adopted by both parties as a binding agreement. Thus, for example, a bank could commit to loan a given sum of money to Buyer to finance the purchase if it is carried forth on the terms specified in the letter of intent. With bank financing assured, Buyer's board of directors could decide whether to authorize the officers to consent to the agreement.

It has been accepted law that no one is bound in a letter of intent and everyone knows that. While terms may be very detailed, neither party has manifested an intention to be presently bound. Letters of intent typically contain language such as "this is not a binding agreement" and "any reliance upon this agreement by either party is at that party's sole risk and expense." However, people do incur expenses and otherwise rely upon these letters and when one of the parties gets a better proposal from a competitor and abandons the negotiations, this can produce bitter feelings and may result in a law suit. Since no one made a binding promise, the only argument is that the parties each had a duty to continue in good faith to pursue a bargain with each other. While a few courts have found such an obligation, there are serious problems with the legal theories involved as will be seen in section 2.43.

§ 2.2   Certainty of Terms in the Offer

To have an enforceable contract, the parties must manifest their assent to a bargain that is sufficiently definite and certain to enable a court to determine what the respective rights and obligations of the parties are. This is necessary so that the court can determine if there has been a breach and what an appropriate remedy for the breach might be.

It is the contract and not the offer which must contain the required certainty as to terms. This can be so even for a term as important as subject matter. For example, an offer may propose the sale of either a certain roan horse or a certain chestnut horse with specific terms stated for each. The offer leaves to the offeree the choice of which horse is desired. Until this selection is made, the offer itself is uncertain as which of the horses the seller will be obligated to sell and the buyer obligated to buy. To accept this offer, the buyer must exercise the choice by designating which horse the buyer wishes. Therefore, it does not matter that the offer is uncertain because when the buyer makes an appropriate acceptance choosing one of the horses the resulting contract will be specific.

In many cases, contract disputes do not develop until after the parties have been performing the contracts for a period of time. Courts can and do look to the course of performance of the contract to find the parties' intentions as to terms. Thus even if an agreement was too vague or indefinite to be enforced when it was first made, it might become an enforceable contract after the parties have rendered and accepted some performances and thereby manifested what they in fact both intended their agreement to be.

Older court opinions state that the agreement must contain all of the "essential" terms of the contract. Many of these opinions contain statements to the effect that the function of courts is to enforce contracts or provide remedies for their breach, not to write contracts for the parties.

Recent decisions are more likely to focus upon the question of whether the contract is sufficiently definite to permit the court to grant the relief the

plaintiff seeks. If the plaintiff seeks money damages, the court must be able to determine whether
the contract was breached and what damages were
caused. If the plaintiff seeks a court order to compel
performance, more certainty may be required as the
court is being asked to order the defendant to do
something and the judge will want a clear picture of
what it is the defendant agreed to do.

It is sometimes stated that the essential terms
include the parties, price, subject matter and time
for performance. The identity of the parties is usually obvious and seldom a problem. The time for
performance, even if not specified, can be found by
the court to be a reasonable time in many cases.
Subject matter and price will be important in transactions such as land contracts, but there are situations, for example, an oral contract for the plumber
to replace the water heater in your mountain cabin,
in which the price and subject matter may not be
specifically agreed upon, but a contract can be
found regardless. The parties may have intended for
the price to be a reasonable price, including the
"usual" labor charges for the area, and that the
plumber will choose a replacement water heater of
the requisite type (gas or electric) and size (30
gallon, 40 gallon, 50 gallon) as the prior heater and
of a brand the plumber carries or deems appropriate. To fill the gaps regarding terms on which the
parties failed to agree, a court can substitute a term
that is reasonable such as the market price at the
time of delivery, provided of course that the parties

intended to be bound notwithstanding the lack of agreement as to terms.

Rather than attempting to create a list of "universal" material terms, one should appreciate that the essential terms will vary from transaction to transaction. In a cash transaction, interest rates have no significance, but a provision that the price will be paid over a period of 10 years at an interest rate to be agreed upon may make the entire agreement unenforceable due to uncertainty. The interest rate is subject to many variables including the creditworthiness of the buyer, the value of any collateral given to secure the loan, whether there are any guarantors, the volatility of the financial market, and the likelihood of success of the enterprise.

The degree of certainty or definiteness which is required for an enforceable contract varies with the subject matter and complexity of the transaction. For example, in real property transactions, the parties typically proceed with due care and deliberation, setting forth their agreement in specific detail. Much significance is also attached to the transfer of ownership of real property, and aggrieved parties often seek the remedy of specific performance which requires particular certainty of terms. It is therefore more likely a court will deny enforcement of a contract for the sale of realty for lack of certainty of terms than would be the case if it were a goods transaction.

An analysis of common law decisions in contract cases leads to the generalization that more certainty of terms is required in land contracts than is required in service contacts such as employment or construction contracts. Common law decisions involving transactions in goods generally required even less certainty. The practice of the market place often involved making agreements with the intent to be presently bound despite the absence of terms on matters which could be rather important. This common law approach to more liberal rules of formation in goods transactions is carried forward by the U.C.C. as discussed in the next section.

Restatement section 33, takes the following position on the subject of certainty:

(1) Even though a manifestation of intention is intended to be understood as an offer, it cannot be accepted so as to form a contract unless the terms of the contract are reasonably certain.

(2) The terms of a contract are reasonable certain if they provide a basis for determining the existence of a breach and for giving an appropriate remedy.

(3) The fact that one or more terms of a proposed bargain are left open or uncertain may show that a manifestation of intention is not intended to be understood as an offer or as an acceptance.

There is a definite relationship between certainty of terms and manifestations of intent to be bound. If parties have reached some agreement but there are significant terms to be settled, a court might properly find that the parties have not yet manifested their intent to be presently bound but have expressed only an intention to continue to negotiate and will not consider the deal done until they have reached agreement on the remaining terms. Where intent to be bound is a close call, missing terms may tip the scale to a conclusion that there was no such intent manifested yet. Conversely, the more terms that are agreed upon the more likely it is that a court would conclude that there was an intent to be bound.

§ 2.2.1 Certainty of Terms Under the U.C.C.

Under the U.C.C., in a sale of goods, the most common question is whether the parties manifested an intent to be bound. If they did, one can usually find a way to establish any terms not expressly agreed upon. This is also the modern trend in common law decisions involving subject matter other than goods.

U.C.C. section 2–204(3) provides:

(3) Even though one or more terms are left open a contract for sale does not fail for indefiniteness if the parties have intended to make a contract and there is a reasonably certain basis for giving an appropriate remedy.

There are other sections such as 2–207(1) and (3) which direct a court to enforce a contract where the parties have expressed by words or conduct their intention to be bound despite the fact that one or more terms are the subject of disagreement. Sections 2–204 and 2–207 can both apply to a problem and they are to be interpreted together.

Unspecified terms can also be supplied by looking to the course of performance of the parties under the contract before the dispute arose as well as their course of dealings in prior transactions and the usage of the trade or industry. (See U.C.C. §§ 1–205 and 2–208.) The U.C.C. assumes that any course of performance, course of prior dealings and trade usages applicable were intended to be included in any agreement between the parties.

U.C.C. section 1–201(3) provides in part as follows:

> (3) "Agreement" means the bargain of the parties in fact as found in their language or by implication from other circumstances including course of dealing or usage of trade or course of performance as provided in this Act (§§ 1–205 and 2–208)....

To facilitate enforcing contracts despite terms that may not have been expressly agreed upon by words, conduct, course of performance, course of dealing or trade usage, the code also provides what are called "gap filling" provisions in sections 2–304 through 2–311 to assist the court in fashioning an appropriate remedy. These provisions will apply only of there is intent to be bound and the parties have not "otherwise agreed," essentially making them "default" provisions. For example, if there was intent to be bound and time for payment was not established by words, conduct, or trade usage, the U.C.C. will provide that the time for payment will be at the time at which the buyer is to receive the goods (U.C.C. § 2–310(a)). Notice that these "gap fillers" will be resorted to only if the parties have not "otherwise agreed" and that "agreement" as defined above includes course of performance, course of dealing, and trade usage.

§ 2.2.2 Effect on Intent To Be Bound if There is a Failure of External Standards Used to Establish Terms

A contract may leave terms of performance to be established by external standards. For example, a contract for the sale of goods may provide for a price equal to the price on a certain date of comparable goods on a given commodity market, or interest on an obligation may be fixed at one percent over the prime rate established by a designated bank or the average of a group of banks.

A problem is presented when the external standard fails, e.g., the commodity market closes or the designated bank ceases the practice of establishing or publicizing a prime rate. Some common law decisions demonstrated a reluctance to "rewrite" the contract for the parties. Thus, if an alternative standard is not provided for in some manner in the contract terms, the contract would fail for lack of certainty. If the subject matter is goods, U.C.C. section 2–305(1)(c) directs that where an external price standard fails, the court shall substitute a reasonable price at the time of delivery, but again only if the court finds that the parties intended to be bound notwithstanding the failure of the external pricing mechanism (U.C.C. § 2–305(4)).

The approach taken in transactions in goods had an influence on the common law of contracts. Where there is a failure of the formula or device selected by the parties to fix the price or another contract term, modern decisions frequently focus upon the question of whether the parties intended to be bound in the event the formula failed. If it is found that they did intend to be bound, the court can be expected to substitute reasonable alternative terms and enforce the contract.

The parties may fix quantity in terms of requirements of the buyer or the output of the seller. The principles applied to these contracts are discussed in section 2.32.

Contracts may also provide that one or the other of the parties shall specify a term of performance. The term that the party specifies will be enforced so long as the specification was made in good faith. This principle was recognized at common law and has been codified in the U.C.C. (§ 2–311) which specifies that the exercise of discretion must be in good faith and "within limits set by commercial reasonableness."

§ 2.3 Advertisements, Mass Mailings, and Price Quotations

An advertisement typically indicates a willingness, even an eagerness, to enter into a bargain.

One is thus tempted to label such an advertisement as an offer. However, one must remember that for a communication to be an offer it must justify another person's understanding that his assent is invited and "will conclude the bargain." This latter element is typically lacking in advertisements. Advertisers seldom manifest an intention to be bound to sell or buy potentially unlimited quantities to all who might see or hear the ad. Absent particular language and facts, persons who see or hear the advertisement should know that the advertiser does not intend to give all such people the power to "accept" and bind the advertiser without any further expression of assent from the advertiser. Anyone receiving the ad should know the advertiser would be incapable of performing to all the potential recipients of the advertising.

The terms which are generally found to be lacking in the typical advertisement are those pertaining to quantity and the identity and number of intended offerees. If these terms can be satisfied without further communication by the advertiser, a valid offer may be found. For example, an ad that identified an item with sufficient specificity as to subject matter and price and limited the offer to the "first person who shows up" at a particular place and time, may be found to have created the power of acceptance in the "first person who shows up" and tenders the required price. However, the typical ad which offers items such as lawn chairs for a stated price is usually treated as an invitation to contact the advertiser if one is interested in purchasing lawn chairs. Such an ad could be called an "invitation to make an offer."

Courts have concluded that merchants are not contractually bound to the terms stated in their ads unless some further assent is given. This may offend one's sense of justice in our consumer-oriented society. However, concerns regarding prevention of deceptive advertising and improper sales tactics such as "bait-and-switch" can be more effectively addressed by consumer protection legislation. Such legislation can provide for meaningful "civil penalty assessments" or even criminal sanctions with enforcement entrusted to consumer fraud units of local or state law enforcement agencies or even actions for civil penalties brought by the aggrieved consumer. Suing the local grocer in contract for damages resulting from refusal to sell a quart of mayonnaise at the price listed in the newspaper is simply not an efficient remedy.

Advertisements that promise a reward for a certain act can be found to be offers. If the reward is for the return of "my lost dog Barfy", there can be only one person to whom the owner will be liable, and there is only one "Barfy" that can be returned. The concerns about "quantity" and number of intended offerees are not typically present in reward situations. And, although the reward offer was in fact made to anyone who may have learned of it, the power of acceptance is limited to the first person to find and return Barfy. (See Restatement, sec. 29 and sec. 36, comment b.)

Mass mailings are typically treated the same as advertisements in the media. A communication which expresses a willingness to sell a specific item of property and which is sent to a large number of persons ordinarily would not exhibit an intention to be bound to all of them or even any one of them without further assent from the originator of the mailing. To treat the mass mailing as "offers" would expose the seller to multiple contracts to sell a single item or limited supply item, and a reasonable recipient of the mailing would not attribute such an intention to the sender. Assuming that the material sent is of such a nature that the fact of wide distribution is readily apparent, the recipients are not justified in assuming that their assent alone will conclude the bargain.

Distributions of catalogues, price lists, and the like, ordinarily are only solicitations of orders from the public with the orders constituting the offers. People in business frequently use the term "price quote" which ordinarily implies that there is no present intention to be bound. However, a catalogue, price list or "quote" which is sent in response to a buyer's specific request for a price for goods is more likely to be found to manifest an intention to be presently bound and therefore an offer. The buyer's request reasonably manifested to the seller an immediate and specific interest in purchasing the designated goods. If the goods are unavailable or not for sale, the seller has an opportunity to say so. By responding with a price quotation, the seller may be seen to be expressing a willingness to be presently bound to supply the goods at that price.

To determine what intent a party has manifested, it is necessary to consider all of the facts. Mailing a price list in one situation may be a mere solicitation and in another circumstance the same act may be an offer. One must avoid conclusionary phrases such as "price quotes are not offers" and must instead consider the facts and what inferences can be drawn from them in each case.

§ 2.4 Receipt of the Offer

Restatement section 23 provides: "It is essential to a bargain that each party manifest assent with reference to the manifestation of the other." Contract law is primarily concerned with protecting reasonable expectations created by the promises of others. Offers cannot create expectations until they are "communicated" to the offeree, with "communicated" here being defined as having been received and resulting in the offeree having actual knowledge of the offer at the time of the purported acceptance.

Assume that X places a reward offer in the newspaper. Y performs the requested act without knowledge of the offer. No bargained exchange has occurred and no contract results. Y had no expectation to be protected or fulfilled unless Y knew of the existence of the offer at the time he performed the requested act. Most cases will permit a person who learns of the offer after rendering part of the requested performance to accept by completing the performance with the intention of accepting the offer. (See Restatement § 51.) Rewards posted by governmental entities have been recognized as creating rights or entitlements in the persons who perform the requested acts even though without knowledge of the reward, but such rights are properly characterized as bounty rights or statutorily or administratively created entitlements rather than contract rights.

Assume that X sends an offer to Y by mail. Y mails an identical offer to X. The offers cross in the mail. No contract results from the sending and receipt of these offers as neither party gave a promise in exchange for that of the other. It should be noted that there are now two offers outstanding and either party may accept the offer of the other. Conduct by either or both may manifest such an acceptance. If the parties proceed with performance based upon these "cross-offers," an acceptance will be found and a contract will exist.

§ 2.4.1 Communication in the Intended Manner

A person should not be held to manifest an intent to be bound by a communication unless that person is responsible for having made and sent the communication. Therefore, a message is not effective as an offer unless it was communicated in a manner intended by the offeror. If X learns from Z that Y has mailed an offer to X, X would not have any power to accept until the mailed offer was received by X. Of course, if Z was an agent of Y with authority to communicate Y's offer to X, then the rule would be satisfied upon the communication by Y's agent to X.

However, if Y, the offeror, inadvertently but volitionally communicated the offer to X, the offer would nonetheless be effective so long as X was unaware of the lack of intent of Y. For example, assume that Y prepared and signed a letter addressed to X that would manifests an offer to X but Y then decided not to mail it. If Y inadvertently mailed the letter, the offer would be effective when it was received by X. Remember, contract law protects the reasonable expectations of a party which are created by the objectively manifested words or actions of another. Y's lack of subjective intent to contract under this fact pattern would be irrelevant.

An offeror who publicizes a reward offer is assumed to intend that the offer receive the widest possible dissemination. It is expected that people will talk about it and tell other people, and the offeror is assumed to assent to this secondary communication. Thus, any person with knowledge of a public reward offer is assumed to be an offeree authorized to accept.

§ 2.4.2 Assignment of Offers; Who May Accept an Offer

Since an offer is intended only for the person to whom it is communicated by the offeror, an offer is not assignable or transferable to another. It is sometimes stated that "An offer is personal to the intended offeree." This is for the protection of the offeror, and recognizes the rights of parties to contract with whom they choose because many times all the offeror would have by way of assurance of return performance would be the promise of the chosen offeree. To allow an offeree to transfer the power to accept to a stranger would leave the offeror in a contractual relationship with a person not of the offeror's choosing and without any recourse against the original offeree.

An exception to this rule involves an offer that is made as part of an option contract. An option contract involves an offer (e.g., a promise to sell Greenacre on stated terms) and an additional promise by the offeror that the offer will not be revoked. If the offeree has paid a price for the promise not to revoke, then that promise is supported by consideration and the promise not to revoke is thus enforceable. The option contract is the bargain between the offeror in which the offeree agrees to pay a price (ordinarily a sum of money) in exchange for the offeror promising not to revoke his offer. Because the offeree has paid for the promise not to revoke, the power and right to accept the offer are considered to be enforceable rights in the nature of a property right in the offeree. Absent contrary agreement between the parties, the original offeree's right to accept the offer will be assignable as is the case with most property rights. However, the option contract terms could expressly limit the power of acceptance only to the offeree and this limitation could prevent the transfer of the power of acceptance.

§ 2.5 Duration of an Offer

Because the offeror is the creator of the offer, the offeror can determine virtually every characteristic of the offer if the offeror so chooses. Therefore, if the offer has a stated time for its duration, the offer will terminate at the end of the time stated. Any attempted acceptance after that time is merely a counter-offer from the offeree.

The usual inference is that the time for acceptance of an offer begins to run when the offer is received. If S mails an offer on July 1 which states that B has "ten days to accept" or that the offer is "good for ten days", and the letter arrives in the normal course of mail on July 3, the inference is that the offer will lapse at the end of the day on July 13.

If there is a delay in communication and the offeree knows or should know of this fact, then the reasonable inference is that the offeror intended the time for acceptance to begin to run from the date on which the offer would ordinarily have been received. If the above-described letter were postmarked on July 1 and would ordinarily be delivered in two days, the offer will lapse on July 13, even if it is delivered on July 12. If it is not delivered until July 14, the offer has already expired and there was never an offer that the recipient could accept. However, if the offeree does not know or have reason to know that the letter was delayed, his reasonable expectations which are created from reading the letter will be protected, and he will have ten days from receipt to accept.

If no time is stated in the offer, it can be assumed that the offeror intended the offer to remain open for a reasonable time. The duration of a reasonable time is a question of fact, and dependent upon the nature of the proposed contract, business usages, and other circumstances of which the offeree either knows or should know. The nature of the subject matter, e.g. a commodity with a rapidly fluctuating price, and the mode of communication, e.g. electronic transmission, are important in that they may indicate a degree of urgency connected with the transaction. In some cases, twenty-four hours or even two hours may be beyond a reasonable time. The controlling question is what are the offeree's reasonable expectations arising from the offeror's communication.

In face-to-face or telephone communications, most court decisions result in a factual determination that an offer made in the course of conversation lapses when the conversation is terminated. The offer would remain open if there was some reasonably clear indication that the offeror intended for it to continue beyond the conversation. However, even if the parties were to agree that the offeree should "get back" to the offeror soon, it might well be found that the intent of the offeror was that the offer had lapsed when the conversation ended and that there would be new negotiations if and when the offeree called back.

It is sometimes stated that an acceptance must be seasonably made. The word "seasonable" is used to mean within the time permitted. This would be the time fixed by the offeror or a reasonable time if no time was set by the offeror, and before the occurrence of an event or communication that would terminate the offer (§§ 2.5.3–2.5.7).

§ 2.5.1 Termination of the Offer by Death or Insanity

Death or insanity of the offeror terminates the offeree's power of acceptance, and despite the objective theory of contracts, notice to the offeree of these events is not necessary. The termination is premised upon the assumption that there cannot be a contract without two parties in existence and the lack of the physical or mental presence of the offeror precludes the mutual assent required for formation.

Death or insanity of the offeree also ends the prospect of forming a contract, not because the offer is terminated but because only the intended offeree has the power of acceptance and when the offeree dies or becomes incapacitated acceptance of the offer becomes impossible.

The above rules do not apply if the offer is irrevocable due to the existence of an option contract. Neither death nor incapacity of the offeror or offeree would terminate an offer if an option contract existed or if the offer was irrevocable for other reasons.

§ 2.5.2 Termination of the Offer by Death or Destruction of a Person or Thing Essential to Performance

An offer will terminate by operation of law if prior to acceptance there is death of a person or destruction of a thing essential for the performance of the proposed contract. An offer by Dad to Photographer to have Photographer cover Daughter's wedding would terminate if Daughter died prior to acceptance of the offer by Photographer. If S offered to sell or B offered to buy a specific classic automobile, destruction of the automobile by a force other than the offeror would terminate the offer. An attempted acceptance after the destruction would have no legal effect.

If the automobile had been destroyed before the offer was made and B "accepted" the offer prior to either party acquiring knowledge of the destruction, S could seek to raise the defense of mistake (§§ 6.5–6.5.5). If the automobile was destroyed after acceptance but before delivery and before the risk of loss had passed to B, the contract would have been formed but S could seek to be excused from performance on the basis of impossibility (§§ 7.1–7.2). If the automobile had been destroyed after the contract was formed and while the vehicle was en route to B's museum, the effect on the already formed contract would be determined by rules governing risk of loss. If the risk of loss had already passed to B, the contract would not be discharged and B would have to pay the contract price for the vehicle (U.C.C. §§ 2–509, 2–510 and 2–709).

§ 2.5.3 Termination by Rejection by the Offeree

A rejection by the offeree terminates an offer and it cannot be revived thereafter by the offeree's attempted acceptance. An offer is rejected when the offeror is justified in inferring from the words or conduct of the offeree that the offeree does not intend to accept the offer nor take it under advisement. Under the majority view, a rejection is not effective until it is received by the offeror. Thus, the offeree's power to create a contract by acceptance is not terminated merely by sending a rejection. Sending a rejection may, however, affect the time when an attempted acceptance is effective because most cases find that when the offeree has sent a rejection, a contract will be formed only if the acceptance arrives before the rejection.

If the offer is irrevocable because it is an option contract, the usual rule is that the offer will also survive a rejection. The logic is that the offeree paid to have the offer held open for a given period and is entitled to that time.

§ 2.5.4 Termination by Counter-offer

The making of a counter-offer impliedly manifests a rejection of the offer and therefore terminates the offer. Consider the following:

(1) S offers to sell Greenacre for $500,000 to B. B replies: "I will pay you $200,000 cash and give you a one-year note at 10% interest for the balance." Absent contrary facts, the offer would be interpreted to require payment in cash at the

time the deed is delivered, and since B's response changes that term, it would be a counter-offer and rejection of S's offer. The counter-offer/rejection would be effective upon receipt by S.

(2) S makes the same offer as above. B replies: "I will try to raise the $500,000 as you ask and will accept your offer promptly if I am successful. But, if you would be willing to take $200,000 cash and a one-year note at 10% interest for the balance, I could have it to you immediately." This communication manifests a desire to keep the offer open and whether it contains a counter-offer as well or simply an inquiry as to possible alternative terms, it negates any implication of a rejection.

The significant point is that the making of a counter-offer ordinarily communicates to the offeror that the offeree does not wish to accept the offer. When the offeree manifests an intention not to reject the offer, a rejection should not be found simply because the offeree proposes or suggests an alternative bargain.

§ 2.5.5   Termination by Revocation

Offers are revocable prior to an effective acceptance. Exceptions to this general rule exist if there is an option contract (§ 2.6.1), if there is detrimental reliance by the offeree upon a promise not to revoke the offer or reliance upon the offer itself (§ 2.6.2), or, in the case of an offer for a unilateral contract, when the offeree has begun to perform the requested act (§ 2.6.4), or a statute precluding revocation from having legal effect (e.g., U.C.C. § 2–205). In the absence if one of these exceptions, an offeror may revoke prior to acceptance even when a promise had been made to keep the offer open for a stated period of time.

Offers may be revoked by words communicated to the offeree which indicate that the offeror no longer wishes to be bound by the terms of the offer. The offeror need not use any specific words of revocation, such as "I revoke." It is sufficient if the offeror simply indicates that he no longer intends to be bound by the offer. For example: "You have missed a wonderful opportunity," or "I have decided not to sell Greenacre."

§ 2.5.6 Revocation by Indirect Communication of Facts Inconsistent With Intent to Be Bound

An offer will also be deemed revoked if an offeror takes definite action inconsistent with intent to be bound and the offeree acquires reliable information of this fact. For example: the offer would likely be revoked if the offeree observes that the offeror has begun to build a building on the property that was offered for sale as a bare plot of land. An offer to sell a parcel of land would be terminated if the offeree learned from a reliable source that the offeror had sold the land to another, even without any communication from the offeror to the offeree. The offeree under these circumstances should know that the offer no longer intends to be bound to the offer to the offeree and therefore the offeree has no expectations deserving of protection.

Note that it is not the sale of the land that destroys the power of acceptance in the offeree. It is the fact that the offeree learned of the sale that terminates the offer. If the offeree had not learned of the sale, the offer would not have terminated and if the offeree makes a timely acceptance, the offeror will have entered into two contracts for the sale of the same piece of land. While the seller cannot perform both contracts, a court can enforce one contract and grant a judgment for damages to the aggrieved buyer for breach of the other contract.

§ 2.5.7 Time When Revocation Is Effective

Since the law is concerned with protecting the reasonable expectations of the parties, the offeree is not charged with knowledge of any attempted revocation that has not yet been received. Since a revocation must be received before it will terminate the offer, an acceptance that becomes operative prior to the receipt of the revocation will create a contract.

Under early nineteenth century common law, an offer was considered revoked when the offeror changed his mind even though such fact was not communicated to the offeree. This was the product of emphasizing a subjective "meeting of the minds" theory which was rejected later in the nineteenth century. This requirement of the coincidence of both parties' subjective intent is no longer the law, and the phrase "meeting of the minds" is misleading and should be avoided.

A few states (including California, Montana, North Dakota, and South Dakota) have statutes which provide that revocations are to be treated in like manner as acceptances. The implication of these statutes is that a revocation might be effective when sent. At least one of these states (South Dakota) has so interpreted this statutory language.

§ 2.6 Irrevocability of Offers

It is interesting to note that under most of the world's legal systems, offers are treated as generally irrevocable for a stated period of time or a reasonable period of time. An offeror can avoid this result by expressly reserving the right to revoke. By contrast, the common law starts with the beginning premise that all offers are revocable. If the offeror elects to revoke the offer before acceptance, the burden is upon the offeree to establish some reason why this particular offer should be treated as irrevocable. Even if the offeror promises to keep an offer open, this simple promise not to revoke the offer is not enough. In the absence of consideration or some other basis for promise enforcement, a simple promise not to revoke an offer will not be enforced (§§ 1.2 and 1.2.1).

§ 2.6.1 Irrevocability by Virtue of Option Contracts

An option contract is created when the offeree gives consideration for the offeror's promise not to revoke the offer. The power of acceptance is owned by the offeree for the time stated because it has been "bought and paid for." The promise not to revoke is enforceable and is usually held to affect not only the offeror's right to revoke but also the power to revoke. Therefore an attempted revocation of an offer contained in an option contract will not terminate the offer. Likewise the power of acceptance created by an option contract is not terminated by rejection, counter-offer, or the subsequent death or insanity of the offeror or offeree.

Assume that S offers to sell Blackacre to B for $350,000 and that B pays S $100 in exchange for S's promise not to revoke this offer for 90 days. These facts give rise to an option contract. One month later, B advises S that B has turned his attention away from real property and will not accept S's offer. The prevailing view is that there is no termination of the offer by virtue of this rejection because B has paid for and owns a right to accept the offer for a period of 90 days.

The only exception that exists to protect the offeror would be based upon the concept of estoppel. If S had reasonably and foreseeably changed position to his detriment in reliance upon B's stated intention not to accept the offer, then B should be estopped from denying that his rejection terminated his power of acceptance.

§ 2.6.2 Irrevocability Due to Reliance on Promise Not to Revoke

An express or implied promise not to revoke an offer will be enforced in most jurisdictions in cases in which the offeror could foresee that the offeree would rely to his detriment upon the promise not to revoke and the offeree does in fact so rely. This concept is analogous to an option contract. Instead of a bargained for option contract with consideration, here there is a promise not to revoke which was gratuitous but the promise not to revoke is enforced because of the foreseeable reliance which in fact occurred.

Restatement, Second, section 87(2) provides:

An offer which the offeror should reasonably expect to induce action or forbearance of a substantial character on the part of the offeree before acceptance and which does induce such action or forbearance is binding as an option contract to the extent necessary to avoid injustice.

Note that sec. 87(2) does not expressly require that the court find a promise by the offeror not to revoke the offer. However, if the offeror does not at least impliedly promise not to revoke, it is hard to justify a finding that the offeror should reasonably foresee that the offeree would rely upon the offer prior to acceptance.

§ 2.6.3 Irrevocability by Statute

Various states have adopted statutes which make certain types of offers irrevocable. When a merchant makes an offer to buy or sell goods in a signed writing which by its terms gives assurance it will be held open, the offer is irrevocable for the stated period of time or for a reasonable time if no time is stated. (U.C.C. § 2–205). By its terms, section 2–205

limits the period of irrevocability to a maximum of
three months, but ordinarily the stated time or
reasonable time would be far less than three
months. Numerous jurisdictions provide that bids
(offers) made to public agencies are irrevocable for
stated periods. There are a few state statutes which
make other types of offers irrevocable if the offeror
has made a promise not to revoke. For example,
New York General Obligations Law section 5–1109
provides for enforcement of signed written promises
not to revoke despite the absence of consideration.

§ 2.6.4 Irrevocability of Offers for Unilateral Contracts

If an offer is interpreted to be one for a unilateral
contract, once an offeree has begun to perform, the
offeror may not revoke but must give the offeree
the amount of time stated in the offer, or, if no time
is stated, a reasonable time to complete the requested performance. The offeror is bound to permit the
offeree to complete the requested act even though
the offeree is not obligated to do so.

At least three theories have been used to prevent
revocation of an offer for a unilateral contract after
performance has begun.

(1) Beginning of performance constitutes an acceptance and the contract is formed at that time
with the offeror's duty of performance being conditional upon the offeree completing the requested act
or forbearance within the appropriate time. (Compare U.C.C. § 2–206.) Application of this theory
leads to the question: once the offeree has begun to

perform, is he obligated to finish? If the contract is unilateral, then by definition there is a promise by only one of the parties. This must be the offeror. Thus, the offeree makes no promise and cannot be bound. On the other hand, if a contract is created when the offeree begins to perform, one might find that this contract assumes a bilateral character with both parties being bound from that point forward.

(2) The offer for a unilateral contract carries with it an implied promise not to revoke if the offeree begins performance. Thus the beginning of performance is the acceptance of and consideration for the implied promise not to revoke and an option contract is created under which the offeree has the option of completing and forming the contract or ceasing to perform and allowing the offer to lapse. The option contract prevents the offeror from revoking the principal offer and the offeree has the appropriate time to complete performance. (See Restatement § 45.)

(3) By beginning performance, the offeree in fact promises to finish and the contract thus assumes a bilateral character. In this situation, one might conclude that the offer was not really one for a unilateral contract but rather an offer for a bilateral contract that could be accepted either by a return promise or by beginning performance (Restatement § 62(2)).

Cases draw a distinction between mere preparation to perform by the offeree and the beginning or tendering of the actual performance invited by the offer. Only the beginning of actual performance will result in the offeror losing the power to revoke. It matters not how minimal the performance is by the offeree if it in fact is some performance or tender of performance.

If it is found that the offeree has merely commenced preparations for performance, there is no resulting option contract in favor of the offeree based upon the principle of Restatement section 45. Preparation may be substantial and costly, but the rule noted above protects only the offeree who has made some start on the actual performance requested. Careful analysis of the language of the offer to determine precisely what acts the offeror requested is necessary to determine whether the offeree has engaged only in preparation or has actually commenced to perform the requested act.

However, if the offeree's preparations, though not constituting performance, are substantial, it is possible that a court might still find an option contract making the offer irrevocable, but will limit any recovery to the offeree to an amount necessary to avoid injustice. (See Restatement § 87(2).)

Assume that X offers to pay $250,000 to the first person who flies across the English Channel in a human-powered aircraft before a fixed date. Several interested parties, including Y spend substantial time and money on research, development and training for the attempt. X revokes the offer and thereafter Y performs the act prior to the date fixed. Y probably has no rights under Restatement section 45 because Y had not begun to perform the requested act prior to the revocation by X. Y would have no right to the "prize money". However, Y might prevail under Restatement section 87(2) on the theory that Y detrimentally relied upon X's implied promise not to revoke and the court might allow recovery in an amount "necessary to avoid injustice."

2. ACCEPTANCE

§ 2.7   Offeror's Control Over Manner and Medium of Acceptance

The offeror as the creator of the power of acceptance has the right to dictate not only the terms of any resulting contract but also the manner of, and medium by which the offeree can exercise the power of acceptance.

"Manner of acceptance" as used here relates to whether the offeree can accept by making a return promise or by performing or tendering performance of the act that the offeror is seeking to have done. If the offeror has empowered the offeree to accept by returning a promise, the offer can be characterized as an offer for a bilateral contract. If the offeror has empowered the offeree to accept only by full performance of the requested act the offer can be characterized as an offer for a unilateral contract.

"Medium of acceptance" as used here refers to how the acceptance is to be communicated, mail, facsimile, hand-delivered, etc:

Matters relating to medium of acceptance can raise two quite distinct questions. Will acceptance by an inappropriate method result in no contract, or will sending the acceptance by an inappropriate method simply result in the acceptance not being effective until it is received by the offeror?

It is possible for an offeror to dictate a particular medium required for an acceptance to be effective and communicate the intention that there will be no contract unless the offeree complies. This is not commonly done, and a court would not be eager to find such an intention. However, it is within the offeror's power to make such an offer. For example, a corporate officer might state in the offer: "If you wish to accept this offer, you must hand-deliver your written acceptance directly and personally to Ms. Shirley Black in our San Antonio office." Given this specific directive, it is unlikely that the offeree can properly exercise the power of acceptance and form a contract by communicating to a different corporate official or a different location. It might even be found that the offeree could not accept by mailing a letter to Ms. Black. Assuming that the offeror's directive was clearly expressed, a court could be expected to respect the instruction and find that acceptance can be effected only by hand-delivery to Ms. Black.

The problem discussed in the preceding paragraph occurs with some frequency in Contracts classes but is seldom encountered in real life. The usual problem that arises under the heading of "authorized medium of acceptance" relates to the precise time when the attempted acceptance will be legally effective. An acceptance that is sent by an authorized medium will be effective when sent and both parties will be bound at that time even though the offeror does not yet know that acceptance has occurred. The acceptance that is sent by an unreasonable or inappropriate medium will not have legal effect until it is received. Under U.C.C. section 2–206, an authorized medium is defined as "any medium reasonable under the circumstances."

Given the risks of an offer being revoked or rejected or otherwise lapsing or being terminated while an acceptance is being transmitted, it can be quite important to determine the precise time at which the acceptance has legal effect. Timing is also important if the acceptance is lost or delayed in the course of transmission.

It may be helpful to consider the fact that if parties deal by mail, whatever event is fixed to determine when a contract is formed will inevitably place upon one party the burden of being bound despite the fact that he does not know this fact. If an offeror makes an offer and impliedly authorizes acceptance by mail, it does not seem unreasonable that this burden be placed upon that offeror. Since the offeror is the master of the offer, the offeror is free to provide that no acceptance will be effective until it is received. There is nothing unfair or improper about such changes in the general rules. If the offeree does not like it, the offeree can make a counteroffer and provide that acceptance will not be effective until received. If neither party can agree on this issue, then they can both go contract with someone else.

§ 2.8 Medium of Acceptance: Electronic Communications

Contract formation issues will arise in a context in which communication was by electronic means. To the extent that this removes delays attendant with the use of mails, this can eliminate some of the problems involving timing. One can also foresee different problems that are going to arise. As we move from telex to facsimile to e-mail to the net to direct communication between computers (even without human intervention) and on to yet unknown methods, the new technology will create new problems. Absent specialized statutory enactments such as the revisions proposed for Article 2, and the new Article 2B of the U.C.C., courts are going to resolve these new problems using established rules and focusing particularly on the reasons for these rules.

Some general observations might be helpful.

Many people who communicate with each other by electronic means have an established pattern of conduct by which the communications occur. They may have worked this out between themselves (which will be referred to as a course of dealing) or it may have been established by some network or group to which these parties belong or adhere (which is referred to as a usage of trade). This course of dealing or usage of trade will be binding upon them unless specific language in the current communication indicates a different intention.

Use of an electronic medium to communicate an offer may connote some measure of urgency and will likely induce expectations or understandings that prompt responses to the communications are required. Where no time for acceptance is specified in the offer, the duration of the offer may be relatively short.

Where problems arise due to a breakdown in communications caused by equipment failure, courts may take into account various factors. If neither party has yet relied upon a contract being formed, it may be tempting simply to find no contract existed. However, court decisions in recent decades seem to have found renewed respect for protecting the expectations of the parties. An offeree who accepts in an authorized manner and medium has expectations which should be protected even if the offeror did not receive the message. Perhaps this is analogous to a properly mailed acceptance that never arrives. Perhaps the risk of non-receipt should be placed on the party who is in the best position to determine if the electronic acceptance was received and to determine the cause for any non-receipt. In many cases this will be the sender, and unless the recipient is responsible for the non-receipt, perhaps the risk of non-receipt of an acceptance should be on the offeree even if the offer does not so expressly provide.

Most troublesome could be the problems that can arise when contracts are being made between computers without human intervention or awareness of the specific transactions. The computers will ordinarily react as they are programmed, but many challenging issues can be forecast. For example, what should be the result if the seller's computer adds to the proposed standard contract provisions a clause disclaiming certain warranties. Must the seller's computer send a message that will alert the buyer (or the buyer's computer) to the change of terms in order to comply with a legal requirement that the exclusion of warranties must be part of the "dickered" terms and "conspicuous?"

As lawyers and judges prepare to argue and resolve these new issues, it will be most important that they focus upon the reasons for the rules that have been developed in the common law and existing statutes.

§ 2.9 Manner of Acceptance (by Promise or by Conduct): Alternative Approaches

In the first half of the twentieth century the formal structuring of the law of contracts was in vogue. It was considered necessary to divide all offers into one of two categories. There were offers that could be accepted by performance and offers that could be accepted by a return promise.

Those offers that could be accepted only by performance resulted in unilateral contracts. No contract would be formed until full performance had been rendered by the offeree and therefore at the instant of creation there was only one party with any unperformed promises. This contract which had performances owing only by one side was dubbed a unilateral contract.

Those offers that could be accepted by a return promise would result in a contract upon the giving of the promise by the offeree in return for the promise by the offeror. Therefore at the moment of creation, both sides had unperformed promises. This contract was dubbed a bilateral contract.

The offer for a unilateral contract could be accepted only by conduct (performance of the requested act or forbearance) by the offeree. The offeree may act or forbear as requested, but he cannot be sued in contract for failing to perform or even abandoning performance once commenced because the offeree has not made any promises. When the contract is formed by the offeree's completed performance, only the promise(s) of the offeror remained unperformed.

If the offeror promised to do something or not do something in exchange for a promise by the offeree to act or refrain from acting in a certain way, the proposed contract is bilateral, because if the offeree accepts by making the requested promise there will be unperformed promises on both sides at the time of formation of the contract. The bilateral contract is the more common type of contract in business transactions.

The modern approach to the nature of the contract recognizes that many offers do not clearly indicate whether acceptance is to be effected by making a promise or by performing or commencing to perform. U.C.C. section 2–206 and Restatement, Second, section 30(2) provide that unless otherwise indicated by the language or circumstances, an offer invites acceptance in any manner and by any medium reasonable under the circumstances. Thus acceptance either by making a return promise or by commencing performance is appropriate unless the offeror has manifested a requirement to have one or the other.

§ 2.9.1 The Traditional Approach: Bilateral and Unilateral Characterization

The Restatement, First applied the traditional structure in which every offer is either an offer for the formation of a unilateral contract or a bilateral contract. As stated in the preceding section, this requires that one characterize the nature of the contract that the offeror proposes in order to determine whether the offeree must give a return promise or perform the requested act to create a contract.

Virtually all offers seek to induce the offeree to act or refrain from acting in a certain way so that the offeror can get the ultimate desired result. However, the critical question for formation purposes is what the offeror desired the promisee to do in order to form (as compared to perform) the contract. Did the offeror want the promisee to promise to act or forbear at some time in the future (and thus have a promise of future performance from the offeree)? If so, the return promise by the offeree would constitute the acceptance thus making a bilateral contract. Or did the offeror want merely the act or forbearance itself from the offeree? In this case, the acceptance would be the act or forbearance by the offeree (not a promise) at which time the contract would be formed.

The position of the Restatement, First, is that offers which are uncertain as to the manner of acceptance should be treated as offers for bilateral contracts.

By way of example, consider the following:

(1) The offer states: "If you will meet me at the airport and drive me home when I return next Thursday at 11:00 p.m., I will pay you $20." Certainly, the offeror desires the performance of the act on Thursday at 11:00 p.m. But it would be reasonable to conclude that the offeror wants a promise from the offeree in advance of Thursday at 11:00 p.m. which obligates the offeree to perform the act. This should properly be construed as an offer for a bilateral contract.

(2) The offer states: "I will sell you my book for $25 at the end of this semester. If you want to buy it, wave your hat at me in class." The waving of the offeree's hat is an act, but it is not performance of the thing that the offeror wanted in return for the offeror's performance. The offeror wanted $25. The waving of the hat is an act that the offeror invited the offeree to do to communicate the offeree's promise to pay the $25. If the

offeree seasonably waves the hat, it will be conduct manifesting a promise to pay $25 in exchange for a promise to deliver the book, thus resulting in a bilateral contract, the performance of which is not due until the end of the semester.

(3) The offer states: "I will pay you $500 if you will swim across San Francisco Bay from Alcatraz Island on January 1." Absent other language or circumstances, this is most likely an offer that can be accepted only by performance of the act and thus is an offer for a unilateral contract. However, there is always a possibility that the circumstances are such that the offeror wants a commitment from the offeree, perhaps as part of a staged "publicity stunt" for whatever reason. If so, the offeree is expected to accept by a return promise within the appropriate time prior to January 1, and failure to do so would result in termination of the offer by lapse of time.

If the matter is in doubt, the preferred interpretation is to treat the offer as one for a bilateral contract. There are some offers which clearly seek a return promise as an acceptance. And, although there are many business offers which at first glance appear to be seeking performance as acceptance, there really are very few that are truly offers for unilateral contracts. For example, an offer to pay $3,000 "if you will re-paint the interior of my office by the time my tenants are due to take possession on March 10," is most likely an offer for a bilateral contract. The offeror is reasonably found to be seeking a return promise because the offer manifested a need for assurance that the act of painting will be performed.

Common examples of offers for unilateral contracts include reward offers and transactions in which a party is invited to put money in a vending machine or in a fare collection box.

§ 2.9.2   Effect of Traditional Unilateral–Bilateral Determination Upon Attempted Acceptance

If the court determines that an offer is one for a bilateral contract, then the appropriate manner in which the offeree may accept is by making the requested return promise. This might effectively be done by a written or oral expression or by conduct which communicates to the offeror an implied promise by the offeree that performance will be rendered. However, if the offeree misconstrued the offer (for a bilateral contract), believed it was an offer for a unilateral contract, and failed to make the required return promise, no contract would exist. If the offeree simply began to perform the requested act, the offeree might be protected if the offeror was aware of the offeree's conduct and acquiesced in this manner of communicating an implied promise to perform. But if the offeror was unaware of the offeree's activities, the rendering of part performance would not create a contract because the offeree failed to communicate the return promise necessary to form the bilateral contract.

If the determination of the court is that an offer was one for a unilateral contract, then the appropriate manner of acceptance was to perform or forbear as required by the offer. If the offeree mistakenly assumed that the offer was one for a bilateral contract and attempted to accept by communicating a return promise, no contract would be formed thereby.

The characterization by the court of the offer as having been one for a bilateral or unilateral contract occurs after the actions of the parties with respect to formation. The court is called upon to determine what a reasonable person in the position of the offeree should have understood to be the intention and desire of the offeror as to the manner of acceptance based upon the manifestations of the offeror and the surrounding circumstances. The court knows how the offeree did in fact interpret the offer. Unless it is apparent that the offeree was reacting unreasonably in the face of clear requirements by the offeror as to the manner of acceptance, the court will be disposed to interpret the offer as the offeree interpreted it. This is not to say that offers are interpreted as offerees read them. It is nothing more than concluding that when an offeror did not think enough about the manner of acceptance to indicate with some degree of clarity what was sought as acceptance, the court will likely follow along with whatever manner of acceptance the offeree reasonably concluded was appropriate. To be sure, each court will reach its determination for the stated reason that it so interpreted the objective manifestations of the offeror. The traditional common law decisions did not indicate that the offeree had an option as to the manner of acceptance.

A fundamental criticism which can be made of the traditional approach is that many offerors are rather unconcerned about whether the offeree is to accept by communicating a promise or by simply rendering the requested performance. While notice of what is transpiring may be significant, the offeror might be quite indifferent as to the manner of acceptance. Thus, while the law should preserve the right of an offeror to specify a manner of acceptance, there is little purpose to be served by the court showing a greater concern for the manner of acceptance than the offeror exhibited.

§ 2.9.3 Modern Approach to Manner of Acceptance

The U.C.C. and the Restatement, Second divide offers into three categories rather than two.

(1) Offers that unambiguously communicate a requirement for a return promise will be treated as offers for bilateral contracts and a contract will result when the offeree complies by making the promise required.

(2) Offers that unambiguously communicate a requirement for performance as acceptance (without any return promise being sought) will be treated as offers for unilateral contracts and will require acceptance by performance and not by the making of a return promise.

(3) Offers that do not clearly communicate what the offeror requires will be interpreted as empowering the offeree to accept in any reasonable manner as the offeree chooses.

Restatement, Second section 32 provides: "In case of doubt an offer is interpreted as inviting the offeree to accept either by promising to perform what the offer requests or by rendering the performance, as the offeree chooses." Both the U.C.C. and the Restatement, Second, avoid the use of the terms "bilateral" and "unilateral". However, many courts continue to use these terms as they remain useful labels to describe offers that invite or require acceptance by return promise (resulting in bilateral contracts) and offers that invite or require acceptance by performance (resulting in unilateral contracts).

§ 2.10   Acceptance by Promise or by Performance; When the Parties Are Bound

In the case of an offer for a bilateral contract unambiguously requiring an acceptance by promise, acceptance must be by a return promise that unequivocally manifests an intent to be bound. It is effective when sent by the offeree or when received by the offeror as described in sections 2.7 and 2.19. If the offeree begins to perform without communicating an express promissory acceptance, there will not be a contract formed unless the offeror acquires knowledge of the beginning of performance and acquiesces in this informal manner of attempted acceptance. At such time both parties are bound, the offeror by the promise contained in the offer and the offeree either by the promise contained in the verbal acceptance or the implied promise to complete performance manifested by the beginning of performance.

In the case of an offer unambiguously seeking formation of a unilateral contract, acceptance forming the contract will not be found to occur until the offeree has completed the requested performance. As the Restatement, Second indicates, a return promise from the offeree may be worthless to the offeror or the circumstances may make it unreasonable for the offeror to expect a firm commitment from the offeree to complete the requested act. For example: The offer states, "I will pay $100 for the return of my dog, Barfy." Neither the promise that "I accept. I will search for you dog." nor the commencement of a search for the dog will constitute an acceptance. If it truly was an offer for a unilateral contract, the offeree does not become contractually bound to complete the requested performance even though performance is begun.

However, in the case of an offer for a unilateral contract, if the offeree does in fact commence any performance of the requested act (however slight), or if the offeree foreseeably, reasonable, and substantially changes position in reliance upon the offer, the offeror may be precluded from revoking the offer. (See § 2.42 and Restatement, Second, §§ 45 and 87(2).) The offeree may be given the time permitted by the offer to complete performance and be entitled to the promised performance upon timely completion, or in the alternative the offeree may be entitled to recover some or all of the losses incurred in reliance upon the offer.

If the court finds that an offer is one that invites acceptance either by a promise or by performance, then the offeree can accept in either manner. Communicating a verbal (oral or written) promissory acceptance will form the contract. The beginning of performance will also communicate an implied promise by the offeree to complete the performance, thereby forming a bilateral contract. This is the likely result without regard to whether the offeror is aware of the commencement of performance.

For example: Assume you left an offer on the windshield of the car of Ned, your 18 year old neighbor which read, "I'll pay you $20 if you cut my grass by noon tomorrow." Assume further the following alternative events.

Example #1: You receive a phone call from Ned in which he says, "I accept your offer."

Example #2: At 8:00 a.m. while you are still in bed, you hear the lawn being cut, look out the window and see Ned doing the mowing. You promptly go back to sleep.

Example #3: After you placed the note on Ned's windshield, you left town for the weekend. When you returned two days later you found:

(a) Ned had mowed the entire lawn.

(b) Ned had mowed about one-third of the front lawn and quit for no good reason.

It could be safely predicted that a court would find the offer to be one capable of being accepted either by a return promise or by performance. Therefore, Ned's reply in Example #1 would result in a bilateral contract when you received Ned's phone call.

As to Example #2, since Ned could also accept by performance, his beginning of performance would be an appropriate acceptance and carry with it an implied promise to complete. Therefore a bilateral contract was formed binding both you and Ned as of the time Ned began to perform.

As to Example #(3)(a), Ned could accept by performance even without your knowledge.

As to Example #(3)(b), Ned could accept by performance and the beginning of performance was an implied promise to finish. You as the offeror are bound despite your lack of knowledge of the beginning of performance. Because Ned's conduct of beginning performance contained an implied promise to finish performance, thus forming a bilateral contract, Ned appears to be in breach.

Additional discussion concerning any requirements of notice of acceptance is contained in the following section.

Consider this unusual offer.

Ned. You are undoubtedly the least dependable person I have ever met. I have never known you to see anything through to completion. You have promised me before that you would mow my lawn and you never did, or if you started you never finished. This time, I want no promises from you. I will pay you $20 only if you will mow my lawn completely, finishing no later than noon tomorrow.

It would be difficult to conclude that Ned could accept by a verbal promise or that Ned's conduct of beginning to perform would be an implied promise to finish. Therefore Ned would never be bound to any contract to mow the lawn, and if he started to mow, could stop part way through without being in breach. Upon commencement of mowing, the offeror would be barred from revoking the offer, and if Ned completed the task by noon, a unilateral contract would be formed and the offeror would owe Ned $20.

§ 2.10.1 Notice of Acceptance

Unless dispensed with by the offeror expressly or impliedly, the offeror is entitled to notice that the offer has been accepted. In many circumstances, notice is not an issue because the offeree's return promise is made directly to the offeror or the performance is rendered in the offeror's presence. However, where the acceptance is accomplished in some other manner, the offeree is required to use reasonable diligence to notify the offeror unless the offeror has manifested that such notice is not required.

The offeror controls how acceptance is to be effected and may expressly provide that no contract will be created until the offeror has received notice of acceptance. Absent such directive, a contract can be formed before the offeror has received notice or before any notice is even sent. The effect of failure to notify the offeror within a reasonable time is that the offeree loses the right to enforce the contract.

These rules are summarized in Restatement sections 54 and 56 as follows:

Sec. 54. Acceptance by Performance; Necessity of Notification to Offeror

(1) Where an offer invites an offeree to accept by rendering a performance, no notification is necessary to make such an acceptance effective unless the offer requests such a notification.

(2) If an offeree who accepts by rendering performance has reason to know that the offeror has no adequate means of learning of the performance with reasonable promptness and certainty, the contractual duty of the offeror is discharged unless

(a) the offeree exercises reasonable diligence to notify the offeror of acceptance, or

(b) the offeror learns of the performance within a reasonable time, or

(c) the offer indicates that notification of acceptance is not required.

Section 56 provides that except for acceptance by silence and situations in which notice is waived, " * * * it is essential to an acceptance by promise either that the offeree exercise reasonable diligence to notify the offeror of acceptance or that the offeror receive the acceptance seasonably."

A similar requirement is imposed by U.C.C. section 2–206(2) which provides:

(2) Where the beginning of a requested performance is a reasonable mode of acceptance an offeror who is not notified of acceptance within a reasonable time may treat the offer as having lapsed before acceptance.

§ 2.11 Non–Promissory Offers (Reverse Unilateral Contracts)

An offer may be made in which the offeror's performance is completed when the offeree accepts the offer.

Example 1: X's horse is being boarded at Y's stable. X states: "If you will promise to pay me $1,000 for that horse, he is yours as of now." Y is already in possession of the horse and it is assumed that there is no documentation needed to be completed by X. Since there is no need for delivery or tender of the horse by X, the only obligation left under the contract as of the time of its formation is that of the offeree, Y, to pay the money.

Example 2: R fills out an application form for a one-year term life insurance policy and submits it along with a check for the premium for the year. The company's acceptance of R's offer creates the contract and R's performance is already completed. The contract is unilateral because only the offeree insurance company has made a promise.

Restatement sections 1 and 55 take the position that a non-promissory offer which requests an act from the offeree is not a contract because a contract is a promise or set of promises for the breach of which the law gives a remedy. Thus, an exchange of performances is not a "contract". While this may be a valid point, it should be observed that many of the legal results that we tend to associate with contract law may still be present. For example, an offer for a reverse unilateral contract in which a merchant offers to let a customer keep the goods already in the customer's possession upon payment of a sum of money will be treated as a sale of goods for purposes of implying a warranty of merchantability (U.C.C. § 2–304). Of course, one could find a "sale" to have occurred despite the finding of no "contract," however, the basic standards which must be met to satisfy the warranty are defined in terms of the "contract description." One would also assume that other basic principles of contract law such as mistake, misrepresentation, duress, lack of capacity, and undue influence would also be applicable to make the transaction voidable.

Bargained exchanges of performances (rather than promises)may properly be categorized as not being contracts but much of the law of contracts and certainly of sales will be applied to such transactions.

§ 2.12 Common Law Requirement that an Acceptance Must Conform to the Terms of the Offer

The common law requires that an acceptance must be unequivocal and must comply with the terms of the offer as to the return promise to be made or the performance to be rendered. The offer constitutes a manifestation of intent by the offeror that he is willing to be presently bound to the terms proposed subject only to the condition that the offeree accept. The offer creates in the offeree the power to accept and thereby form a contract but that power is limited to the terms proposed by the offeror unless the offeror manifests a willingness to leave some choices in the offeree. The traditional common law position is that any communication made by the offeree in an attempt to exercise the power of acceptance but which adds a term or attempts to change a term of the offer will not operate as an acceptance.

A purported acceptance which requires the offeror to assent to terms which are additional to or different from those offered is not an acceptance but a counteroffer. Such a communication does not result in a contract, but is a continuation of the negotiation process. It manifests the offeree's intent to be presently bound but not on the offeror's terms and therefore the consent of the offeror to the offeree's new terms will be needed before the contract will be formed. Thus, it is a counteroffer and the original offeror is now the party who has the power to form a contact by accepting in the appropriate manner.

§ 2.12.1 Acceptances Which Merely Suggest or Propose New Terms

An acceptance in which the offeree agrees to be bound to the offeror's terms is effective to form a contract on the offeror's terms even though the offeree may at the same time be requesting a change to those terms. The offeree is assenting to a contract and seeking the offeror's assent to a modification of that contract, as distinguished from making a counteroffer in which the offeree is manifesting the intent that there will be no contract unless the offeror assents to the counteroffer. So long as the response from the offeree is not made dependent upon the offeror agreeing to some changes or additions, it is effective as an acceptance.

The parties who make a contract are free to modify that contract in the absence of some intervening third party's rights. There is no theoretical or practical problem with an offeree accepting an offer, thus concluding the contract, and in the same communication proposing a modification of the contract just formed. So long as there is an unequivocal acceptance of the offeror's terms, the contract is formed.

For example, assume that the offeror's terms for the proposed sale of corporate stock include a requirement that the offeree pay cash on delivery of the shares of stock. The offeree's response is unequivocal, "I accept your offer and will pay cash on delivery, however, if you can see your way clear to wait about 10 days for payment, I would really appreciate it. Please let me know." The contract has been formed. Unless the offeror agrees to an effective modification, payment will be due on delivery.

§ 2.12.2　Impact of the U.C.C. Upon Acceptances that Contain Terms Additional or Different From Those Found in the Offer

Section 2–207 of the U.C.C. was designed to change the common law rules relating to responses to offers that purport to be expressions of acceptance but contain different or additional terms. While common law cases were not consistent on the subject, most court decisions held that a response by an offeree that varied the terms of the offer did not operate as an acceptance but as a counteroffer (§ 2.12.1). If a prospective buyer sent an order for goods requesting shipment on Monday, a response that purported to be an acceptance (e.g., "We are pleased to accept your order") would likely be held not to operate as an acceptance if it indicated that shipment would not be made until Tuesday. In actual practice, the two parties might consider themselves to be bound, but if the seller failed to perform, the seller's attorney could defend on the grounds that no contact had been formed. The variance of terms made the "acceptance" a counteroffer.

Under the common law, the potential for "surprises" to the unwary offeror were many. For example, assume that the buyer on March 1, had submitted an offer to buy 1,000 grade A widgets for delivery no later than June 20. The buyer's offer was silent as to the manner of dispute resolution. Assume further that the seller responded on March 2, with a communication with definite words of acceptance such as, "Your order has been accepted and will be shipped as requested." The seller's form also provides that any disputes shall be resolved by arbitration rather than litigation and that the seller reserves the right to ship refurbished (meaning used) grade B widgets. The buyer's clerk looked over the seller's form, checked the price and delivery date and placed the form in a file.

The following results could occur under common law rules.

(1) June 20 has come and gone. The price of widgets has increased significantly since March. Seller never shipped the widgets and does not intend to. Buyer has no cause of action for breach because all that existed was an offer from the buyer and a counteroffer from the seller which was never accepted by the buyer.

(2) The goods were shipped timely and received by buyer. Buyer did not notice that what was shipped were refurbished Grade B widgets as the only way to tell them from new Grade A widgets would be to disassemble the widgets and this is not customarily done. Buyer has paid for the widgets and installed them in his assembly line equipment. After six months, the widgets fail to function properly solely due to the fact that they are Grade B widgets. Buyer has no claim against Seller. Seller's form was a counteroffer due to the variance in terms. Buyer's conduct of taking possession of the widgets and paying for them was conduct by Buyer which constituted an implied in fact acceptance of Seller's coun-

teroffer. Therefore neither party was bound until Buyer took and paid for the goods at which time there was a contract on Seller's terms. That means the dispute would be arbitrated and Buyer would lose.

The intent behind section 2–207 was to alter this result. Subsection (1) of 2–207 provides that a definite and seasonable (meaning timely) expression of acceptance operates as an acceptance even though it contains terms additional to or different from those offered. (Subsection (1) also deals with written confirmations that are sent following the making of an oral contract, but that is a separate problem which will be discussed in section 2.14.

Professor Karl Llewellyn and his wife Professor Soia Mentschikoff, who were Chief Reporter and Associate Chief Reporter for the U.C.C., did a thorough job of reversing the common law result of finding a counteroffer if there was an added or changed term in the communication which contained words of acceptance.

The common law conclusion was that "A purported acceptance that contained terms additional to or different from the terms of the offer had the legal effect of a counteroffer." The result was that up to that point in time no contract was formed. And as indicated above in the hypothetical, if the buyer took possession of the goods and used them, such conduct would be the acceptance of the counteroffer and the resulting contract would be formed on the terms of the offeree.

Section 2–207(1) results in just the opposite conclusion. "A definite expression of acceptance" even though it contains terms additional to or different from the terms of the offer will have the legal effect of an acceptance. This means that a contract will be found to be formed as a result of the offeree's response and, at the time of formation, it will be formed on the terms proposed by the offeror. (There can be an exception to this result in jurisdictions that apply the knock-out rule. See § 2.13.2.)

The key phrase in section 2–207(1) is "definite expression of acceptance", a term that is not defined in the Code and that had no established meaning at common law. To have a "definite expression of acceptance," one must find that the offeree has used language of acceptance manifesting on its face an intent to conclude a bargain. It might be best understood if it is distinguished from an "expression of counteroffer" which also manifests an intent to be bound but requires further assent by the offeror before a bargain is concluded. If the offeree expressly conditions his assent upon the offeror agreeing to the different or additional terms contained in the offeree's response, then a contract is not yet formed. This response would be a counteroffer because it requires assent by the offeror to complete the bargaining process.

Professor Llewellyn was asked to comment upon the application of subsection 2–207(1) while testifying before the New York Law Revision Commission in 1954. He is quoted as saying:

We were attempting to say, whether we got it said or not, that a document which said "This is an acceptance only if the additional terms we state are taken by you" is not a definite and seasonable expression of acceptance but is an expression of a counteroffer.

"Expression of acceptance" must be interpreted more broadly than the term "acceptance". If it were synonymous with "acceptance", then subsection (1) would end up providing that "an acceptance * * * operates as an acceptance." Such an interpretation would make subsection (1) meaningless. "Definite expression of acceptance" should be interpreted as referring to the apparent intention of the words used whereas "operates as an acceptance" refers to the legal effect, which is the formation of a contract.

Therefore, no longer will an offeree be permitted to use "words of acceptance" and then hide behind the absence of identical terms in the offer and the response to assert that the "words of acceptance" did not form a contract. An offeree who desires not to be bound to a contract unless the contract is formed on the offeree's terms can obtain this result by not making a "definite expression of acceptance." Further, the offeror will no longer be misled into believing a contact has been formed by words of acceptance only to discover that the "acceptance" contained a term at variance with the offer and therefore the "acceptance" was a counteroffer. Now the "expression of acceptance" will form the contract on the offeror's terms. Professor Llewellyn accomplished this result with a remarkable brevity

of words: "A definite * * * expression of acceptance
* * * will operate as an acceptance even though it
states terms additional to or different from those
offered * * * ." Compare this to the common law
rule which is still the general rule in non-goods
transactions: Under the common law, even a definite expression of acceptance will operate as a counteroffer if it states terms additional to or different
from those offered.

Subsection (1) has a final clause that requires
attention. It is the language "unless acceptance is
expressly made conditional on assent to the additional or different terms." This language is probably redundant. From Professor Llewellyn's testimony and from the plain language of the subsection it
should be evident that any response by an offeree
which adds or changes terms and expressly requires
that the offeror assent thereto before the offeree is
willing to be bound could not be a "definite expression of acceptance," but rather would be an expression of counteroffer.

For example, assume the following reply from the
offeree: "Confirming acceptance of your offer we
will ship as requested, however our acceptance is
expressly conditioned on your assent to our terms
contained herein." What may have started out like
a definite expression of acceptance cannot be so
interpreted when the offeree is manifesting intent
to be bound only upon the offeror assenting to the
offeree's terms. This requirement for further assent
makes the offeree's response a counteroffer.

When attempting to resolve the issue of whether a response by an offeree is or is not an acceptance under the Code, the inquiry should focus upon whether the response is a definite expression of acceptance. The inquiry should not focus upon whether that response adds terms or changes terms as compared to the offer because that fact does not preclude the response from "operating as an acceptance" and thereby forming a contract. Of course, if the response is expressly conditioned upon the offeror agreeing to those different or additional terms, it is not an expression of acceptance.

A response by an offeree may be found to be an expression of acceptance and thus form a contract even if it proposes an addition or change which is material. One must be very careful not to read into subsection (1) any requirement that the additional or different term be non-material. Or said another way, there is nothing to indicate that subsection (1) is limited to expressions of acceptance with only non-material additional or different terms. There is no implication of such a requirement or limitation in subsection (1) and subsection (2)(b) would be rendered meaningless if subsection (1) only permitted formation of contracts if the additional or different terms in the offeree's "expression of acceptance" were not material.

Another common student error in interpretation is to try to read into subsection (1) the requirement that it be applied only to transactions between merchants. Subsection (1) applies to all transactions in goods regardless of whether both parties or either of them is a merchant.

If a contract is found under subsection (1) it would be formed immediately upon the "definite expression of acceptance" having legal effect which in most cases would be when the acceptance was deposited in the mail (§ 2.8). Except in jurisdictions applying the knock-out rule (§ 2.13.2), the terms of the resulting contract should be the terms as proposed by the offeror. Some students find that they can accept this statement as accurate in the abstract or in theory but have difficulty in applying it to an actual fact situation. The simple fact is that as soon as we embrace a rule of law that directs us to find a contract despite the fact that the offer and acceptance do not contain the same terms, it is absolutely inevitable that one party or the other is going to be bound to a contract that contains terms to which that party did not agree.

Assume that X offers to sell a generator to Y for a stated price. Y responds stating: "We accept your offer for the generator but we also need the installation hardware to install it in our power plant as the generator is useless to us without the hardware." If it is concluded that this is a definite expression of acceptance (and it is certainly not "expressly conditioned" on the offeror's assent to include the installation hardware), a contract is formed. The terms of the contract are those terms contained in the offer which include the sale of a generator for the stated price. The already formed contract does not include any terms relating to installation hardware.

Finding a contract that ignores the clearly expressed needs or desire of the offeree is a hard result for some to accept. How can an offeree be bound to purchase a generator without installation hardware when the reply clearly stated that this was what was needed. The answer is simple. Offerees should not use "definite expressions of acceptance" if they don't intend an acceptance. If they intended an acceptance then a contract should be formed and the only question left is which of the two parties' terms should be used to determine the terms of the contract.

If one remembers that the offeror is the person who created the power of acceptance in the offeree, then the offeree can have no greater power than that which the offeror created. The offeror created power to accept on the offeror's terms. The offeree made a "definite expression of acceptance" or we would not be worrying about which parties will get "their terms". The result is a contract on the offeror's terms. If the offeree is displeased with this result, the offeree is free to make a counteroffer instead of expressing his acceptance of the offer.

Subsection (1) of 2–207 does nothing more than recognize that a "definite expression of acceptance * * *" not "expressly conditioned on the offeror's assent to the additional or different terms" forms a contract. Subsection (1) makes no attempt to resolve the looming issue of whose terms are going to ultimately control, but as we shall see, we start with the conclusion that at the time of formation, the terms of the contract are as proposed by the offeror. And it should be rare to find that those terms should be taken away or new terms foisted upon an offeror without the offeror's clearly manifested assent to modify the existing contract.

§ 2.13 Contract Terms Following Acceptance with Additional or Different Terms

Additional Terms

When an offer is accepted by an expression of acceptance which states a term additional to those contained in the offer, subsection (2) must be applied to determine whether this additional term becomes part of the contract found to be in existence because of the application of subsection (1). It should be noted that subsection (2) is never applicable in any fact situation unless a contract has been found pursuant to subsection (1). Any attempt to incorporate subsection (2) factors such as materiality or merchant status into subsection (1) determinations is inappropriate.

Subsection (2) has nothing to do with formation, or the lack thereof. The only reason for the existence of subsection (2) is for a resolution of whose terms are going to apply. One must beware not to fall into the trap of concluding that "because the proposed additional term was material and the offeror did not assent to it, subsection (2) would result in no contract being formed." This is erroneous. The contract was already formed under subsection (1) or you would not be in subsection (2). The sole function of subsection (2) is to provide a "yes" or "no" answer to the question: "Was the contract which was formed under subsection (1) modified by adding the terms which the offeree proposed to add?"

The first sentence of subsection (2) provides as follows: "The additional terms are to be construed as proposals for addition to the contract." This is another beautifully simple Llewellyn sentence. It means that at the time of the subsection (1) "definite expression of acceptance" there is a contract formed and it has been formed **on the offeror's terms.** What else would "proposals for addition to the contract" mean if it did not mean the **contract that is already in existence.** The offeree therefore has done what we have seen offeree's do before-manifest assent to be bound to the terms of the offer thus forming a contract on the offeror's terms and at the same time proposing additional terms for the offeror to accept or reject. If the offeror assents to the offeree's proposed modification, the contract will be modified. If the offeror does not assent to the proposed modification, the existing contract will continue unmodified and the contract remains as the offeror proposed.

Notice that there is no limitation in this first sentence of subsection (2) as to the status of the parties as merchants or non-merchants. Therefore, it applies equally to all and if the offeree manifests assent to the proposed modification, the contract will be deemed to be modified. Likewise, there is no reference to materiality or non-materiality as to the terms of the proposed modification. Therefore, the first sentence of subsection (2) applies to proposed additional terms which may be material or non-material and whether the parties are merchants or not. Pursuant to section 2–209(1), no consideration is needed for any modification assented to by the parties.

The second sentence of subsection (2) is applicable only if both parties have the status of merchants. As will be seen with other areas of the UCC (such as sec.2–201(2)), this second sentence is predicated upon the assumption that merchants are supposed to read their mail and object to things that do not suit them. This second sentence provides that the offeror's silence in the face of the proposed modification will operate as assent by the offeror to modify the existing contract but only if both parties are merchants and it is found that:

a) the additional terms do not materially alter the contract,

b) the offeror had not already indicated that he objects to this addition or to any addition to the contract, and

c) the offeror failed to give notice of objection within a reasonable time after the expression of acceptance is received.

Although 2–207 has been subject to much criticism, its premise is simple and its application should be uncomplicated both as to formation under subsection (1) and as to addressing proposed modifications under subsection (2).

As to subsection 2–207(1):

1. The offeror is in control of the offer.

2. The offer is what creates the power of acceptance in the offeree.

3. The offeree is free to exercise that power or not but cannot expand the terms of the offer to affect the offeror. Any "acceptance" forms a contract on the terms of the offer. The offeree cannot "cram down" any additional terms against the offeror's assent. (An exception will be seen in jurisdictions that apply the knock-out rule to different terms. See § 2.13.2.)

4. If the offeree uses words that constitute a "definite expression of acceptance" a contract will be formed regardless of additional or different terms in the offeree's response to the offer.

5. The contract will be on the offeror's terms. See 2 and 3 above.

As to subsection 2–207(2):

1. The offeree has simultaneously accepted on the offeror's terms and has proposed a modification of the existing contract.

2. The existing contract will be modified to include the offeree's additional terms only if the offeror in some manner manifests assent to the proposed modifications.

3. If the parties are not both merchants, silence on the part of the offeror will not constitute implied assent of the offeror to add any terms to the existing contract. The contract will continue in existence on the offeror's terms.

4. Even if both parties are merchants;

(a) it is not reasonable for the offeree to assume that the offeror in remaining silent is manifesting assent to the proposal by the offeree that would materially alter the contract.

(b) it is not reasonable for the offeree to assume that the offeror in remaining silent is manifesting assent to a term that the offeror in some manner has already indicated would not be assented to.

Therefore, once the contract has been formed under subsection (1), it is formed on the offeror's terms. Any additional terms contained in the acceptance are mere proposals to modify the existing contract. Upon receipt by the offeror of the proposed modification, the offeree is entitled to interpret the offeror's silence as consent to modify the contract only if both parties are merchants, and the proposals are not material, and the offeror has not previously indicated an objection to the attempted modification.

One might be tempted to conclude that by performing or accepting performance from the offeree, the offeror was manifesting assent to the additional terms proposed by the offeree. However, since the expression of acceptance formed a contract on the offeror's terms, the fact that the offeror proceeds with the performance of the contract, as he has a right and duty to do, does not in any way manifest assent to the additional terms which the offeree wished to add. Of course, if the offeror actually performs in accordance with the proposed additional term, this conduct could manifest assent to add that term to the contract.

Different Terms

The above discussion all relates to additional terms contained in the acceptance. If the offeree's expressions of acceptance contained different terms as distinguished from additional terms, a serious problem of Code interpretation is presented. Subsection (1) expressly refers to both additional and different terms but Subsection (2) expressly applies to "additional" terms and makes no mention of "different" terms. One might conclude that this is simply a drafting error or oversight. The conclusion that the authors meant to include "different" terms in subsection (2) finds support in comment 3 to section 2–207 which begins: "Whether or not additional or different terms become part of the agreement depend upon the provisions of subsection (2) * * * ." In addition, comment 4 gives examples of materiality and these examples include terms that seem to be properly classified as "different" rather than just "additional." Materiality can only be an issue if one is analyzing a problem within subsection (2). It might also be noted that the first sentence of subsection (2) would logically apply equally to terms that are different as well as additional. However, when the state of Wisconsin and later the state of North Carolina attempted to "cure" the apparent oversight by adding "or different" in subsection (2), these modification were disapproved by the Permanent Editorial Board for the U.C.C. with the following comment:

Reason for Rejection: The stated purpose is to conform the language of subsection (2) with that of subsection (1). The change is harmless as it affects the first sentence of subsection (2), but "different terms" as distinguished from "additional terms," do not become part of the contract under the second sentence of subsection (2), since they have already been objected to. See subsection (2)(c) and Comment 6. Moreover it is the express policy of the subsection that an offeror is not subjected to the hardship or surprise of terms which are "different" in that they materially alter the original bargain.

This issue was addressed albeit by dicta in a footnote in *Steiner v. Mobil Oil Co.* (Cal. 1977). The court concluded that while writers were in disagreement as to what to do with different terms, the question whether different terms were to become part of the contract should properly be decided by applying subsection (2). Since the offeror had not expressly consented to the different terms, the first sentence of subsection (2) did not resolve the problem. Because the transaction in that case was between merchants, the court applied the second sentence of subsection (2) and concluded that the different terms were not accepted by the silence of the offeror for two reasons: a) the change was material, and b) since the offeror had expressly discussed his desires on the subject with an employee of Mobil Oil and had stated specific terms different from that inserted by Mobil Oil in the acceptance, the offeror had already given notice of objection to the term proposed by Mobil. Using this logic, it becomes evident that if different terms are analyzed under subsection (2), they will seldom if ever become part of the contract unless the offeror expressly consents to them. While the California Supreme Court did not cite and perhaps was unaware of the comment of the Permanent Editorial Board quoted above, it should be noted that the Board accurately predicted the result that would be reached if subsection (2) was applied to different terms. It stated that different terms "have already been objected to" and that they "materially alter the original bargain."

§ 2.13.1 Contract Terms if Offeree's "Different" Terms Are Not to be Analyzed Under 2–207(2)

If one were to conclude that different terms should not properly by analyzed under subsection (2), the obvious problem is determining where else to turn to determine what to do with the proposed change of terms desired by the offeree.

Based upon the Permanent Editorial Board comment and the analysis above, it would appear that a second approach would be that there is just no need to do any kind of analysis as to when the offeree's proposed different term would ever take the place of term already in the contract. The answer would be that unless the offeror expressly or by very specific conduct assents to the different term, the different term will never become part of the existing contract. The offeree should have no expectation of having his terms prevail over the already existing inconsistent term desired by the offeror.

§ 2.13.2   The "Knock–Out" Rule

There is an alternative approach applied by a few courts and purportedly based on the belief that Professor Llewellyn was trying to "level the playing field" in regard to 2–207. In a misguided effort to accomplish this goal, these courts hold that when an exchange of communications results in a contract despite the fact that each parties has proposed different terms, then neither party should get its terms. This has been termed the "knock-out rule" because it results in the different terms in each party's communication knocking out the other party's desired terms on the same subject.

There is no obvious statutory basis for the knock-out rule. One can start with the fact that subsection (2) refers to additional terms but does not include different terms. If different terms are not to be handled under subsection (2), where does one go with them?

Some believe that the source for the knock-out rule is found in subsection (3) of 2–207. However, it is difficult to apply subsection (3) to this problem given its language which provides: "Conduct of both parties which recognizes the existence of a contract is sufficient to establish a contract for sale although the writings of the parties do not otherwise establish a contract. In such case, the terms of the

particular contract consist of those terms on which
the writings agree, together with any supplementa-
ry terms incorporated under any other provisions of
this Act."

On its face, subsection (3) would appear to apply
to two situations. The first would be one in which
the parties exchanged communications that discussed terms but did not manifest an intention to
be presently bound following which they both proceeded with performance. (Section 2–204 discusses
contract formation and can also be applied to this
problem.) The second situation to which subsection
(3) applies is one in which an offer is made to which
the offeree responds with an "expression of counter-offer" perhaps by making an "acceptance" but
making it "expressly conditioned on the offeror's
assent to the additional or different terms." Thereafter the parties proceed to perform as if they had a
contract. For an example of this second situation,
see *C. Itoh v. Jordan Int. Co.,* (7th Cir. 1977).
(Subsection 3 will be discussed in § 2.15.)

The knock-out rule was applied in *Southern Idaho Pipe & Steel v. Cal–Cut Pipe & Supply, Inc.,*
(Idaho 1977). This court found support for the
knockout rule in comment 6 to section 2–207 despite the fact that this comment appears to apply to
confirming memoranda sent by both parties after
an oral contract has been formed. (This would be a
situation in which there was an existing contract on
terms not in dispute, but subsequent to formation,
each side sent a confirmation of the contract and
each proposed terms in their confirmation different

from that proposed in the other's confirmation. Application of the knock-out rule here makes sense.)

The following examples show the working of the knock-out rule. Assume that a backpacking outfitter is ordering a tent from a supply company. Consider these alternatives.

1) Offer: I will pay you $750 for a Model X tent.

Acceptance: We accept your offer but the tent will be sold as is without any warranties.

2) Offer: I will pay you $750 for a Model X tent. Payment shall be due in sixty days with a 2% discount if paid within 20 days.

Acceptance: We accept your offer. Our terms require that you pay cash in full on delivery.

3) Offer: I will pay you $750 for a Model X tent which you must expressly warrant to be made without any artificial fibers.

Acceptance: We accept your offer but the tent we deliver will be sold as is and will not be warranted in any fashion.

4) Offer: I will pay you $750 for a Model X tent. Any disputes arising out of this sale shall be arbitrated in Sacramento, CA.

Acceptance: We accept your offer. Any disputes arising out of this sale shall be arbitrated in Denver, CO.

The result of the knock-out rule is that when the terms in the offer and acceptance are different, the party who sought a term different from that contained in the default rules of the Code is going to lose.

In hypothetical #1 above, the offer is made without any special terms other than description of goods and price. The offeror does not propose any variation from the default rules of the Code. In the acceptance, the offeree attempts to vary the standard Code terms. The offeree will lose out.

Since the offer proposed a sale of goods by a merchant, the offer is properly interpreted as an offer to buy goods that are impliedly warranted to be merchantable (U.C.C. § 2–314). The offeree attempted to change this with a different term. The different terms contained in the offer (with implied warranty) and in the acceptance (without implied warranty) will knock each other out. In their place, the court will supplement the contract with terms found in Article 2. This means that the court will find an implied warranty of merchantability under section 2–314. The offeror will prevail because the Code will supply the term that the offeror wanted.

In hypothetical #2, the offeror sought a credit transaction with a discount for prompt payment. The offeree has requested a different term, cash on delivery, so under the knock-out rule, these different terms will cancel each other out. In place of the canceled terms, the court will substitute the default rule under the Code. The default rule in the Code provides for payment in cash at time of delivery (U.C.C. §§ 2–307 and 2–310(a)). Thus the offeree (seller) will prevail getting a contract on the terms sought by the seller.

This hypothetical #2 demonstrates the flaw in the knock-out rule. The buyer offered to buy if the buyer could buy on credit and obtain a discount for payment within 20 days. By virtue of the seller's response, the buyer is now bound to pay cash with no discount, a term to which the buyer never consented. There is no practical way for an offeror to avoid this result.

Any time an offeror requests something different from what is provided by the default rules of the code, the application of the knock-out rule permits the offeree to bind the offeror to a contract that does not contain this particular term that the offeror requested.

In hypothetical #3, we again see an offer that includes a specific term (an express warranty) that is not found in the default rules of the Code. The offer also includes an implied warranty of merchantability for the reason discussed under hypothetical #1 above. In the acceptance, the offeree changes two terms. The offeree denies any express warranty and also disclaims the implied warranty of merchantability. Here we will see a split decision. The terms regarding both express and implied warranties are different and thus will all cancel each other out. The court will look to the U.C.C. to fill the gaps. Since the U.C.C. supplies an implied warranty of merchantability in the case of a sale by a merchant who deals in goods of that kind

(§ 2–314), the contract has that implied warranty. Since the Code does not provide for an express warranty unless it is found in the terms of the contract (§ 2–313), there will be no express warranty regarding artificial fibers. One should note that as in hypothetical #2, application of the knock-out rule results in the term that the offeror specifically requested (express warranty regarding materials) being deleted from the contract without any opportunity for the offeror to object. The offeror has no practical way to prevent this from happening.

In hypothetical #4, both parties agreed to arbitrate disputes. Thus that clause should survive and become part of the contract. Each party proposed different terms regarding the place of arbitration, so those terms cancel out and the court would order arbitration at a site selected by the court.

One last hypothetical might be informative.

Offer: I will pay you $750 for a Model X tent.

Acceptance: We accept your offer. You are advised that our price for the Model X has been increased to $800.

It is not clear that there is a contract here. That question must be resolved under subsection 2–207(1). If the response is found to be an expression of acceptance, then one should find a contract. (It is not expressly conditioned on assent to the different term.) If a contract is found and the knock-out rule is applied, then the different price terms proposed by the two parties will knock each other out. The result is a contract with no price. Under U.C.C. section 2–305, the court will supply a reasonable price which one would hope would be found to be no less than $750 nor more than $800.

§ 2.14 Effect of Confirming Memoranda Sent After an Informal Contract is Formed

Every student of contracts understands that U.C.C. section 2–207(1) applies to issues regarding offer and acceptance by communication. What is not so clear is that 2–207(1) also was intended to provide rules to clarify terms when two parties entered into an informal contract (either an oral contract or a contract writing with incomplete terms) following which one or both parties sent a confirming memorandum which contained additional terms or terms different from those already agreed upon. This latter situation is quite distinct. When a party sends a confirming memorandum, the parties already have a *valid* contract. Even if it is within the statute of frauds, it may well be enforceable. (See U.C.C. § 2–201.) There may be a sufficient writing or part performance or admission by the defendant or other basis for enforcement.) Since there is a valid contract, the remaining issue under section 2–207 relates only to finding what are the terms of that contract.

Assume that Buyer and seller enter into an oral contract and thereafter Seller sends a confirming memorandum that adds a term not orally agreed upon or that changes a term in the oral agreement.

(This confirming memorandum is a sufficient writing to satisfy the statute of frauds even though it misstates the terms of the oral contract. See the last sentence of § 2–201(1).) The question is what effect this writing has upon the terms of the oral contract that the parties had already concluded. Section 2–207(1) refers to this problem in a very inartful and indirect manner ("or a written confirmation which is sent within a reasonable time," referring to a reasonable time after the making of the oral contract). It is difficult to find a precise meaning in subsection (1), but it is apparent that courts are directed to look to subsection (2) to determine whether additional terms in a written confirmation (or confirmations if sent by both parties) become part of the contract that the parties had already orally concluded. Whether a court should look to subsection (2) or subsection (3) to determine what to do with a term in a confirmation which is different from the orally agreed upon terms could be analyzed as discussed in the preceding section.

It is important to realize that since the parties in fact have a valid (although perhaps unenforceable due to the statute of frauds) oral contract, no party should be permitted to "knockout" any term of that contract by sending a written confirmation which contains a different term than that already agreed upon. That party has already agreed to be bound by the terms of the oral contract and should not be permitted unilaterally to change or "knockout" any of those terms. Of course if both parties send a confirmations and each confirmation contains a term which is different from a term contained in the other's confirmation, then the knockout rule should be applied to those terms in the confirmations which are different from the others. See comment 6 to section 2–207. It is suggested that this is the only situation to which the knock-out rule should properly be applied.

§ 2.15 Application of U.C.C. Section 2–207(3)

Subsection (3) can be applied when the parties have exchanged communications that did not result in a contract. Perhaps the offeror made an offer and the offeree did not make a "definite expression of acceptance" and instead made a reply that was "expressly conditional" on the offeror's assent to the additional or different terms. There would then be only an offer and counteroffer in existence and no contract. Or whatever the communications may have been, they did not result in a contract.

The seller, perhaps believing there is a contract on its terms, ships the goods and the buyer, perhaps believing there is a contract on its terms, takes possession of the goods and uses them. There was no contract formed under subsection (1) of 2–207, but subsection (3) of 2–207, as well as section 2–204, recognize that the conduct of the parties can result in a contract. When this occurs, there is a need to determine the terms of the contract. Subsection (3) of 2–207 does this in a simple manner.

As to the terms that are identical in the seller's communication and the buyer's communication, there can be no dispute as to their intentions and there is no need to look elsewhere for alternative terms. The terms on which the writings of the parties agree are part of the contract.

As to the terms in communications that are additional to or different from the terms in the other party's communications, none of those terms are part of the contract as initially formed by the conduct of the parties. For example, assume the following:

Buyer's terms as stated in the offer were:

100 widgets @ $10 each ($1,000), the widgets to be backed by Seller's express warranty that the widgets will function at below freezing temperatures, the $1,000 payment due 60 days after delivery. (Because Seller is a merchant there will also be an implied warranty of merchantability pursuant to § 2–314.)

Seller sends a response that adds and changes terms and is expressly conditioned upon Buyer's assent and is thus a counteroffer. It provides:

100 widgets @ $10 each ($1,000), the $1,000 payment due 10 days after delivery. The counteroffer has conspicuous language purporting to exclude all warranties including a disclaimer of the implied warranty of merchantability (see § 2–316). The counteroffer provides for arbitration of any disputes between the parties.

Despite the fact that there is no contract yet, Seller shipped the widgets which were timely received by Buyer on September 1. Buyer resold the widgets to Buyer's customer (X) on September 10. On December 1, X made claim against Buyer because the widgets are not functioning in cold weather.

What are the terms of the contract between Buyer and Seller?

Subsection (3) of 2–207 would apply because the writing between the parties did not result in a contract but the parties by their conduct have consummated a contract for the sale of the goods. Note that neither of them should have any "favored" status as an offeror who has received a "definite expression of acceptance" that may have misled them. Both are equally responsible (culpable) for the fiasco, as each could have avoided formation at any time notwithstanding the exchange of communications. This is where the "playing field should be leveled" giving neither party the benefit of any terms that have not been agreed upon.

Therefore, what are the terms?

1. "100 widgets @ $10"—These terms are in both parties' communications. Had Seller shipped fewer or Buyer tried to pay less, the other could enforce the terms as stated in both writings. The parties should be bound to the terms that they both apparently intended. There is no need to look elsewhere to supply quantity or price.

2. Buyer requires an express warranty re: "freezing". Seller did not "accept the offer" and propose a modification. Seller made a counteroffer which did not include an express warranty re:

"freezing." It might be tempting to say Seller's exclusion of warranties "knocked out" Buyer's requirement for the warranty, but that is not necessary and it is not what subsection (3) provides. Subsection (3) states that the contract formed by conduct will contain those terms on which the writings of the parties agree. Seller's response did not "agree" as to the express warranty and therefore Buyer's term regarding functioning in below freezing temperatures will "drop out". And this would have been the result even if Seller had not attempted to exclude any express warranty. It does not matter if the response of the other party contains an additional as compared to a different term. Regardless of which it is, because there will be no "match" in the other party's communication, additional terms as well as different terms will "drop out." Any term in one writing that does not correspond to a matching term in the other writing will drop out.

3. Buyer's offer did not state a willingness to make the purchase without the implied warranty of merchantability. Seller's language excluding the implied warranty of merchantability will "drop out".

4. Buyer's form provided for payment in 60 days. Seller's form did not agree to this time period. The "60 days for payment" provision drops out. Seller's form provided for payment in "10 days". Buyer did not "agree" to this term. Seller's term requiring payment in "10 days" drops out because there is no corresponding term in Buyer's writing.

5. Arbitration was called for by Seller's form but is not "agreed" to as a term in Buyer's form. The arbitration provision will drop out.

What are the terms that will be provided by the code and the court as to those that are in dispute? The "playing field" has been leveled but what terms should be found to be "fair to impose upon the parties" who are equally innocent or blameworthy?

The terms needed to resolve any dispute will be found by looking first to the parties course of performance, course of prior dealings and trade usages, (in that order) if they exist and can be established. If such exist, they will be used. If such do not exist, then the court will look to the "default" provisions of the code, sometimes called the "gap-fillers."

Application of the "gap fillers" will result in the following:

Freezing: Because there is no code provision that would create an express warranty regarding freezing, Buyer will not have such a warranty. Seller got what it wanted by "default". The U.C.C. tips the playing field in favor of the standard terms that are provided in the Code. Since Buyer was seeking additional protection not provided for in the Code, the result is going to favor Seller as Seller never assented to this additional responsibility.

Implied warranty of merchantability: The implied warranty of merchantability will be supplied by section 2–314. Buyer got what it wanted by "default." The U.C.C. tips the playing field in favor of the terms that are supplied by the Code. When a seller seeks to disclaim warranties provided for in the Code, this seller is going to lose unless the buyer has assented. In general, the terms provided for in the Code are more favorable to a buyer than the terms that a typical seller will wish to substitute. Thus, gap filling provisions tended to tip the balance in favor of buyers.

The time for payment (assuming there was a dispute) will be supplied by section 2–310 and will be found to have been due when buyer received the goods. Neither party got what it wanted but the U.C.C. favors prompt payment to sellers. This result is anomalous. Even Seller was willing to extend credit to Buyer, yet since they each selected a different period of time, the Code would appear to require payment on delivery. One might anticipate that a judge would reach out for a solution that would give Buyer ten days to pay as Seller proposed.

Regarding arbitration, the U.C.C. has no gap filler stating that in the absence of agreement, the parties will arbitrate their disputes. Therefore dispute resolution will be through litigation (again absent an established and applicable course of performance, course of prior dealing, or trade practice).

§ 2.16 Acceptance by Conduct under U.C.C. Section 2–206

U.C.C. section 2–206(1)(a) allows an offeree to accept an offer in any manner and medium reasonable under the circumstances, unless the offeror unambiguously indicated otherwise. Thus, where the manner of acceptance is not specified, the offeree can accept by return promise or by commencing performance if either manner of acceptance is reasonable under the circumstances. Unless the offeror has specifically indicated otherwise, any medium of acceptance such as mail, facsimile or other electronic means is permitted if it is reasonable under the circumstances.

Many common law decisions refer to the offeree being permitted to respond in any medium "authorized" by the offeror. Section 2–206(1)(a) refers to any medium reasonable under the circumstances. There is probably no substantive distinction and if so, 2–206(1)(a) is not a departure from the common law. However, consider the following hypothetical and compare the common law result with that which would occur under 2–206(1)(b).

Buyer ordered Grade A widgets for prompt shipment. Seller shipped Grade B widgets which are similar in appearance to Grade A widgets. Buyer did not notice the difference, took and used the goods, and paid for them. Subsequently Buyer discovered the fact that the widgets were Grade B.

At common law, Seller is in a position to argue that if Seller did not ship what Buyer ordered, then Seller did not accept Buyer's offer. When Seller shipped non-conforming goods in response to Buyer's offer, Seller was making a counteroffer to sell Grade B widgets on the terms proposed by Buyer.

Buyer's taking possession and use of the goods constituted an implied-in-fact acceptance of the counteroffer and therefore the contract terms were those of the counterofferor which included the fact that the subject matter was Grade B widgets. Therefore there was no breach by Seller. This is a most unhappy and unfair result for Buyer.

Professor Llewellyn also desired to avoid placing the risk of such occurrence on buyers and did so by the use of two words in section 2–206(1)(b) which provides: "(1) Unless otherwise unambiguously indicated by the language or circumstances . . . (b) an order or other offer to buy goods for prompt or current shipment shall be construed as inviting acceptance either by a prompt promise to ship or by the prompt or current shipment of conforming *or non-conforming* goods, but such a shipment of non-conforming goods does not constitute an acceptance if the seller seasonably notifies the buyer that the shipment is offered only as an accommodation to the buyer." (Emphasis added.)

Adding the words "or non-conforming" had a similar effect on the common law as did section 2–207(1) in requiring the seller to be accountable for communications, whether by words or conduct, that create the appearance of an acceptance. Thus, under our hypothetical above, the shipment by Seller of Grade B widgets, without further communication from Seller, would be an acceptance of Buyers's offer for Grade A widgets. The contract would be formed by the shipment of Grade B widgets but the subject matter would be Grade A widgets. The seller has simultaneously agreed to a contract calling for Grade A widgets and at the same time breached it by shipping Grade B widgets. See comment 4 to section 2–206.

Sellers can avoid forming a contract by shipping non-conforming goods "if the seller seasonably notifies the buyer that the shipment is offered only as an accommodation to the buyer." If such notice is given, the shipment will be a counteroffer which the buyer is free to accept or reject.

Subsection 2–206(2) provides that where acceptance is made by beginning performance, Seller will lose the right to enforce the contract if notice of acceptance is not given to the offeror within a reasonable time. This simply confirms the common law rule that one who accepts an offer by performing must take reasonable steps to attempt to notify the offeror if the offeror has no convenient way of learning whether the act is being performed.

§ 2.17 Impact of U.C.C. Upon Common Law Rules of Contract Formation

Common law changes over time. These changes are made by courts often following able argument by counsel. Changes in contract law are motivated by the courts' perceptions of changed circumstances and attitudes in our commercial world and social life. The U.C.C. was drafted after wide participation by various constituencies in this country. Its acceptance is evidenced by its overwhelming adoption by the various states and by Congress for the U.S. Territories and the District of Columbia. It has had

significant influence on international commercial
law treaties and upon some domestic law in foreign
countries. It should not be surprising that some
rules found in the U.C.C. have been incorporated
into the common law of the federal system and the
various states. This is evidenced by numerous individual court opinions and by some of the black
letter law and commentary found in the Restatement Second of Contracts which was drafted and
adopted after the U.C.C. had been adopted by most
states.

Students of contract law must always recognize at
the beginning that Article 2 of the U.C.C. by its
express terms applies only to transactions in goods
(§ 2–102). Having noted that fact, it is proper to
advance the argument that a particular provision
found in Article 2 should be applied by analogy as
the common law rule controlling contracts of other
types. The force of this argument will depend in
substantial part upon the degree to which one can
convince the court that the U.C.C. rule is a good
one that has worked well in actual practice and that
the common law contract before the court is sufficiently similar to a transaction in goods that the
Article 2 rule could properly be borrowed and applied to it.

Focusing specifically upon the U.C.C. rules relating to contract formation, one finds that some rules
have already been accepted into the common law
while others have been less warmly greeted.

Common law contract decisions from the early part of the twentieth century were often predicated upon a high degree of formalism. To convince a court that a contract existed, counsel had to establish precisely which communication was an offer and precisely when and how the offeree accepted that offer to create a contract. All essential terms were provided by the parties or there would be no contract. Court opinions often stated that it was the task of the courts to enforce contracts made by the parties, not to make contracts for them. If an offer was arguably one for a unilateral or a bilateral contract, the existence of a contract would be dependent upon proving to the court which type of contract the offer proposed and proving that the offeree in fact accepted in the "proper" fashion.

Article 2 has various rules that relax these highly structured rules. Rereading sections 2–204, 2–206 and 2–207(3) will demonstrate a philosophy quite different from that described in the preceding paragraph. If offers are unclear as to the manner of acceptance, offerees can accept by a return promise or by commencing performance. If parties intended to have a contract, it is the court's job to figure out what terms they agreed to and patch together the rest of the terms from gap-filling sections of Article 2 and other available sources. If parties act like they have a contract, courts are instructed to find a contract even if one cannot tell exactly when or how it was made. As a general principle, one could conclude that the collection of rules on contract formation in Article 2 focus upon what the parties really intended rather than upon compliance with formalisms.

To the extent that parties commonly enter into service contracts with a degree of informality similar to that found in sales of goods, the formation rules of Article 2 discussed above can appropriately by borrowed or applied by analogy in common law cases. To the extent that transactions involving real property are generally handled with more structure and formalism, courts may be somewhat less eager to relax traditional common law rules.

Section 2–207(1) has been the subject of a great deal of confusion and in the opinion of many, it has led to some results that are difficult to justify. For very good reasons it is the target for substantial revision in the proposed rewriting of Article 2. In its present form, one would not anticipate judges reaching out to embrace this subsection as a solution to offer and acceptance problems in common law cases. While Restatement Second section 59, comment "a" appears to provide a tentative opening for courts to adopt the substance of 2–207(1) and incorporate it into the common law of contracts, there does not appear to be any groundswell of movement in that direction.

§ 2.18 Prospective Amendments to U.C.C. Article 2: Focus Upon 2–206 and 2–207

In the summer of 1999, a revised version of U.C.C. Article 2 which had been approved by the American Law Institute was presented to the National Conference of Commissioners on Uniform State Laws. Approval by that body would be the final step before submission of the revised draft to the various states for adoption. The revised draft of Article 2 was not acted upon. The members of the drafting committee resigned and new members were appointed with instructions to "try again."

One proposed revision of Article 2 that is likely to be adopted eventually is the new term "record." As defined in proposed U.C.C. section 2–102(a)(33):

"record" means information that is inscribed on a tangible medium or that is stored in an electronic or other medium and is retrievable in perceivable form.

As part of the proposed modifications of Article 2, the word "record" is substituted where the term "writing" was previously used. It is evident that with the adoption of this change, the term "record" may come to replace the term "writing" generally in our law and would be more inclusive than most court interpretations of the term "writing" is today. The term "record" has already been utilized with the same definition in the new version of Article 5 (sec. 5–102(a)(14)).

The new draft of Article 2 will undoubtedly include substantial revision of what is presently covered by section 2–207.

§ 2.19   Time When Communications Are Effective

Offers are effective when received. An offer creates the power of acceptance in the offeree and an offeree cannot intend to exercise that power if he has no knowledge of its existence. Therefore, an offer is not effective until it is actually received by and thus made known to the offeree.

Acceptances may be effective when sent or when received. The offer may specify the time when an acceptance will be effective. For example, an offeror could simply provide that "no acceptance will be effective until it is actually delivered to me." If this is the case, the acceptance will not be effective unless and until it is delivered to the offeror.

In the absence of such a specification, a properly dispatched acceptance which is sent by an authorized medium is effective when sent and a contract is formed at that time regardless of whether the acceptance is ever received by the offeror.

A reminder: One must be careful to distinguish an offer which specifically requires a particular medium for acceptance (prohibiting any other), from an offer which invites (suggests, authorizes) a medium for acceptance, but does not prohibit others from being used.

For example, if the offer stated, "Any acceptance must be made by a signed writing and must be sent to me only through the U.S. Postal Service." If the offeree signed the acceptance and sent it via any other service other than the U.S. Postal Service, the question would not be whether the acceptance was effective when sent or only when received. The initial question would be whether there was an acceptance at all as it did not comply with the requirements of the offer. The offeree's power to accept was limited and to be effective at all it must comply with all of the requirements of the offeror. (See Restatement, Second § 60.) It is quite likely that a court would find the "acceptance" even though timely sent and timely received would not form a contract if it were not sent via U.S. Postal Service. It most likely would be found to be a counteroffer from the offeree.

If the offer had stated, "If you choose to accept, please fax me a copy of your signed acceptance no later than Friday at 5:00 p.m." Notice that the offeror did not require a fax and did not prohibit other means of transmitting the acceptance. If the offeree received this offer on Monday and mailed·a signed acceptance on the same day, the issue would be when (not whether) the mailed acceptance should be deemed to have legal effect as an acceptance, when sent or only when received. The Restatement section 67 refers to the mailed acceptance as an acceptance dispatched by an "uninvited means."

Where an acceptance is sent by other than an authorized medium, it is ordinarily effective when received. (Ordinarily one would not interpret an instruction or request by the offeror to mean that this is the only method by which the offeree can accept and form a contract. See § 2.7.)

It is generally held that an acceptance of an offer made irrevocable because it is an option contract is not effective until received. The apparent reason for this rule is that the offeree has "bought and paid for" a given period of time and must get the acceptance to the offeror within that period. Therefore, if the offeree posts an acceptance the risk of loss or delay is on the offeree and the offeree remains free to revoke the acceptance prior to receipt of the acceptance by the offeror. The parties are of course free to agree as to how and when an acceptance will be effective and such an agreement will control.

In the absence of special circumstances which are known to the offeree, an offer that does not expressly mandate a medium of communicating acceptance may be interpreted as impliedly authorizing the same medium as was used to communicate the offer, or a medium "customary in similar transactions at the time and place the offer is received." (See Restatement § 65.) Section 2–206 provides that "unless unambiguously indicated by the language or circumstances" an acceptance may be made by "any medium reasonable in the circumstances." Most courts, when deciding that an acceptance should be effective when sent would interpret the rule as requiring the acceptance to be sent by the same medium or better, meaning faster.

Common law decisions have proceeded on the premise that acceptances are effective at a specific point in time. If sent by an authorized medium with proper postage and correct address, they are generally effective on dispatch. If sent by a different medium or if improperly dispatched, they are effective when received. The Restatement, Second suggests a different approach in section 67 which provides:

> Where an acceptance is seasonably dispatched but the offeree uses means of transmission not invited by the offer or fails to exercise reasonable diligence to insure safe transmission, it is treated as operative upon dispatch if received within the time in which a properly dispatched acceptance would normally have arrived.

Application of this section can avoid some technical problems in the acceptance process. If the offeror expressly requests response by wire and the offeree sends a letter, the letter will have to be received before there can be any acceptance but if received within the required time period, the contract will be deemed to have been formed as of the time the letter was sent. If the letter is lost in transmission or is delayed for an extended period, no contract will result. But if the acceptance arrives within the time in which a properly dispatched wire would have been received, the acceptance will be deemed to have occurred as of the time of dispatch. Thus, an intervening revocation would not defeat the formation of a contract.

Section 67 will also avoid the issue that can arise when a communication is not properly dispatched, due to an incomplete or inaccurate address or inadequate postage. Such a communication will not be effective unless received in a timely fashion, but if it is received within the time contemplated, it will be operative as of the time of dispatch.

REVOCATION

Revocations are not effective until received by the offeree. Thus an acceptance that becomes legally effective prior to receipt of a revocation forms the contract. Statutes in some jurisdictions may have the effect of making a revocation effective when sent (§ 2.5.7).

REJECTION

A rejection is effective when received by the offeror. The dispatch of a rejection followed by the dispatch of an acceptance by an authorized medium creates the potential for problems. It has been held that the acceptance is still effective when sent (if sent before the rejection is received) and a contract is formed. However, if the offeror receives the rejection first and changes position in reliance thereon, the offeree can be estopped from enforcing the contract.

Restatement section 40 adopts a different approach to this problem. It provides that the sending of a rejection takes from the offeree the power to have his subsequently dispatched acceptance become effective when sent. The result is that the rejection and the subsequently dispatched acceptance will have legal effect only when received. If the acceptance arrives first, there will be a contract. If the rejection arrives first, there will be no contract. In this case the later received acceptance acts as a counter-offer.

Problems can also arise if the offeree has dispatched an acceptance that would be effective when sent and then attempts to reject the offer. The Restatement in section 63 calls this an attempt on the part of the offeree to "revoke the acceptance". The attempted revocation of the acceptance will not have any effect on the contract which was already formed by the dispatch of the acceptance. However, if the rejection/revocation of acceptance is received first and the offeror relies upon it, the offeree may be estopped from trying to enforce the contract. Depending on the circumstances, the offeror may choose to treat it as an offer to rescind the contract or perhaps as a repudiation of the contract.

§ 2.20 What Constitutes "Receipt" of Communications

Because some communications are deemed effective only on "receipt" it is necessary to establish what is meant by that term. Restatement section 68 provides:

A written revocation, rejection, or acceptance is received when the writing comes into the possession of the person addressed, or of some person authorized by him to receive it for him, or when it is deposited in some place which he has authorized as the place for this or similar communications to be deposited for him.

There is no requirement that the communication be read or that the recipient even have actual knowledge of the existence of the writing for it to be deemed "received". Sections 1–201(26) and 1–206(27) should be consulted for communications coming within that Code.

"Receipt" of an offer is a different matter in that one cannot accept an offer of which you are unaware. Therefore, there is no reason to analyze or discuss any concept of constructive receipt of an offer such as by delivery to a business. If the offeree does not have actual knowledge of the existence of an offer, then the offeree cannot intend to accept it.

§ 2.21 Acceptance by Silence

The basic rule in all legal systems is that silence does not constitute an acceptance. The common law has recognized limited exceptions.

One situation involves parties who have had prior dealings in which the offeree has led the offeror reasonably to understand that the offeree will accept all offers unless the offeree sends notice to the contrary. Of the few court decisions that have found a contract in this fashion, almost all have involved a situation in which the offeree, ordinarily the seller, has established a price, advised the buyer as to available quantities and invited the buyer to make an offer. The established practice between the parties is that the seller will accept the offer to buy by "filling the order" unless the order/offer is expressly rejected. With this established practice, another offer made in the same circumstances will be deemed accepted if the offeree/seller does not respond. The court opinions that have applied this rule have involved an offeree engaged in a business.

The Restatement Second section 69 recognizes silence could result in an acceptance under the above facts as well as in another situation. This is "where the offeror has stated or given the offeree reason to understand that assent may be manifested by silence or inaction, and the offeree in remaining silent and inactive intends to accept the offer." In this case the offeror has expressly indicated that the unmanifested subjective intention of the offeree to accept the offer will be sufficient to form a contract. If the offeree follows these instructions and subjectively intends to accept the offer, the offeror can hardly complain that its specific instructions were followed.

The second sentence of section 2–207(2) also provides limited circumstances in which there can be acceptance by silence of an offer to modify a contract.

§ 2.22 Acceptance by Exercise of Dominion and Control Over Goods or by Receipt of Benefits or Services

One who receives goods with knowledge or reason to know that they are being offered for a price is bound by the terms of the offer if he exercises dominion and control over the goods or does any act inconsistent with the offeror's ownership. The abuse of this common law rule by the senders of unsolicited merchandise has led to statutes in many jurisdictions which avoid placing contractual liability upon the recipient. One form of statute simply provides that the receipt of unsolicited merchandise is conclusively presumed to be a gift. In the absence of such statutes, however, the common law rule is still applicable.

One can visualize an awkward situation in which unordered goods are piled up on a party's loading dock and the sender does not respond to requests to remove them. The problem is aggravated if the goods are perishable, or seasonal or otherwise likely to decline in value.

The unwilling recipient must guard against conduct that can be interpreted as accepting an express or implied offer to sell. The recipient must also guard against conduct that might be interpreted as tortious conversion of the property of another. If there has been a prior course of dealing between the parties, the possibility exists that the recipient may owe some duty of good faith or other minimal duty to protect the property or even dispose of the property on behalf of the owner. The solution to this uncomfortable situation is to induce the sender to advise as to the desired disposition of the goods. Failing in that, the recipient might propose a specific course of conduct, such as disposition by sale, advising the sender that it will be followed if no contrary instructions are received.

One who knows or has reason to know that services are being offered with the expectation of compensation is liable for the reasonable value or stated value of such services if he takes the benefit of them under circumstances in which there was a reasonable opportunity to reject. This is not properly characterized as acceptance by silence. Standing by while services are performed for your benefit is a form of conduct.

§ 2.23 Auctions: Finding the Offer and Acceptance

Auctions With Reserve

An auction is with reserve unless otherwise stated. "With reserve" means that the owner has reserved the right to refrain from holding the auction or to interrupt the auction and terminate it or withdraw any item even after the bidding has begun. The owner may likewise make a bid and buy his own property in an auction with reserve. However, unless the right to do so has been announced, he may not "run up" a legitimate bidder and thereby inflate the price. Where the owner has bid without announcing the right to do so, the successful bidder has the right to enforce a contract at the price of the last legitimate bid which was made before the owner improperly entered the bidding. The U.C.C. gives the successful bidder under these circumstances the alternative remedy of avoiding the sale (§ 2–328(4)).

In an auction with reserve, the auctioneer solicits offers from the potential bidders. The bids are offers. The fall of the hammer or other customary words or action by the auctioneer constitutes the acceptance. Prior to acceptance, the bid or offer may be revoked. The auctioneer may reject all offers or may reject a particular offer, usually because it is not a sufficiently large increase over the prior bid. When the auctioneer recognizes a higher bidder, e.g., by saying: "I now have $300," he communicates a rejection of the previous bid. Thus, the revocation of a bid by the bidder does not reinstate a prior bid that had been surpassed.

Auctions Without Reserve

The term "without reserve" or "every item will be sold" or comparable language is used to manifest a promise by the owner that the auction will be held, the property in question will be sold to the highest bidder and nothing will be held back or withdrawn from sale. This promise is customarily made in advertising to encourage attendance and bidding. At the time it is made, it is a bare promise and is unenforceable. However, it might reasonably be interpreted by a potential bidder to be a promise for a unilateral contract which commits the offeror to hold an auction without reserve if the prospective bidder will attend the auction. Thus, the failure to hold or to proceed with an auction which has been advertised as without reserve could be a breach of this collateral contract.

U.C.C. section 2–328(3) provides:

In an auction without reserve, after the auctioneer calls for bids on an article or lot, that article or lot cannot be withdrawn unless no bid is received within a reasonable time.

The interruption of an auction without reserve by the owner and his refusal to complete the sale gives rise to an action by the party who made the highest bid before the auction was interrupted. By the terms of the collateral contract, the owner was legally obligated to accept the highest bid. Thus, the court can find a contract between the parties at that price. Where the owner refuses to start the auction, it is more difficult for a frustrated potential bidder to find a cause of action. Section 2–328 does not cover this situation No individual can prove that he would have been the successful bidder nor can one prove what the successful bid would have been. There is no reasonably certain basis for specifically enforcing a contract or for giving damages for the loss of the expectancy of the bargain. There is a theoretical basis for awarding reliance damages in such situations to compensate the frustrated bidder for costs reasonably incurred in attending the auction or otherwise preparing to bid.

The structure of the sales contract in the auction without reserve can be analyzed in the same manner as in an auction with reserve. The bids are offers. They may be withdrawn before acceptance. The acknowledgment of a higher bid impliedly rejects a prior bid. The fall of the hammer is the acceptance which terminates the bidding and forms the contract.

There is another less satisfactory theory that is sometimes applied to auctions without reserve. Some courts have held that in an auction without reserve, the owner makes an offer to sell and each bid is an acceptance which forms a contract subject to the condition that this contract will be terminated if a higher bid is made. The courts and writers who discuss this approach also take the position that bidders can still revoke their bids before the auctioneer "accepts" by the fall of the hammer.

This is, of course, inconsistent with the notion that the bid is an acceptance which creates a binding contract of sale subject to a higher bid.

The source of confusion which gives rise to this latter theory would appear to be the fact that some courts fail to define with care the offer which the seller makes by advertising an auction without reserve. It is mistakenly assumed that the seller's offer is an offer to sell as distinguished from a promise to be bound to accept the highest bid. Once this error is made, several problems arise. Each bid becomes an acceptance forming a contract but the "offeror" is still free to continue to offer the property to others in hopes that they will "accept" for a higher price. Also, despite the existence of a contract, the bidder can withdraw the "acceptance" before the fall of the hammer by which the auctioneer "accepts." It is a badly flawed theory that employs analysis and vocabulary that finds a "contract" for sale at a time when neither party is yet bound to the stated terms and that requires an offeror to "accept" an offeree's "acceptance."

There are many states that have specific statutes governing the conduct of auctions and there is a significant body of case law pertaining to possible misconduct at an auction. For instance, in a situation in which the owner has reserved the right to bid, the owner may be limited to making only one bid and the use of a shill or shills in the audience would be improper. The sanctions imposed by the statutes could include punitive damages and attorneys' fees. Even in the absence of an express provision for such recovery, such conduct could be found to give rise to a cause of action in tort for fraud with the possibility of punitive damages being awarded.

When you have completed your study of offer and acceptance, you may wish to analyze questions 1–10 at the end of this book and compare your analysis with the one given there.

3. CONSIDERATION

§ 2.24 Consideration: An Introduction

Every legal system makes distinctions between promises that are deemed to be legally enforceable and other promises that are not. In a common law jurisdiction, one who seeks to enforce a promise must affirmatively establish a basis for finding the promise to be enforceable. There are three possibilities: 1) the promise was made as part of a bargain for valid consideration; 2) the promise reasonably induced the promisee to detrimentally rely upon the promise (§ 2.41); or, 3) the promise comes within a statute which makes it enforceable despite the absence of consideration. (E.g., § 2–209(1).)

The primary basis for enforcing a promise in the common law system is that it was made as part of a bargained exchange as compared to being gratuitous. While there are special rules which will permit enforcement of certain gratuitous promises, the first inquiry should be to determine whether a promise was given in return for something or whether it was gratuitous.

In drawing lines of distinction between promises that are made as a part of a bargain and promises which the law deems to be gratuitous, common law courts have generally followed a formalistic approach. If there is any legal detriment incurred by the promisee that can be viewed as a bargained exchange for the promisor's promise, that is sufficient. In addressing the existence or non-existence of consideration, courts have not concerned themselves with the adequacy or fairness of the consideration but only with finding the presence of some legal detriment incurred as part of a bargain. Conversely, if there is no legal detriment or no bargain, courts will ordinarily find no consideration despite what might be viewed as the equities of the situation.

The application of this approach produces some results that are difficult to justify when viewed from a broad perspective of justice. Unlike the French system which asks whether there is proper *cause* to enforce a promise and which invokes issues of morality and common business practices to determine the presence or absence of such *cause*, the common law decisions usually turn on the technical question whether some legal detriment and bargain are present. Consider a promise by an employer to pay a retirement pension to an employee who has already worked for the company for 30 years. Under French law there is good *cause* to make such a promise and it is therefore enforceable. Under American law and the law of other common law systems, the question that must be answered is whether this promise to pay a pension was made as part of a bargain.

A promise to pay a pension is supported by valid consideration if it is made as part of the employment contract. Thus, if the employee is required to work for an additional period of time in exchange for the promised pension, there is a bargain. However, the same promise made to the employee after she retires is not supported by consideration because the employee is incurring no detriment as a bargained exchange for the promise. The required bargain may consist of a promise by the employee. (The company promises to pay a pension in exchange for employee's promise to work for an additional period of time such as a week or a month or ten years.) The required bargain may consist of an act by the employee. (The company promises to pay a pension if the employee actually works for some additional period of time such as six days or six months or six years.)

Because a formal requirement such as consideration may produce results that are viewed as unfair, a number of special rules have been developed and some court opinions bend the rules to get to what the judges consider a proper result. The role of an attorney or law student is first to understand the basic requirements of the law of consideration so that one will be fully aware of situations in which it presents a problem. When this has been accomplished, the second task is to identify the situations in which the law has recognized exceptions or in which a given court might be induced to interpret the facts in such a way as to find the requirement to be satisfied.

§ 2.25 Requirement of a Bargained Exchange

First, a point of clarification. There are always going to be at least two parties to a contract. Up until now the parties have typically been described as the offeror and offeree. To resolve a problem involving consideration, the issue is enforceability of a specific promise and the focus is upon whether the promisee gave any consideration for that promise. We are not concerned with offeror and offeree but rather with promisor and promisee. In the case of a unilateral contract, the likelihood of confusion is slight; there is only one promisor as the other has already fully performed. However, in the case of a bilateral contract, both parties are promisors and promisees, and it is critical that one first identify which party's promise is being sought to be enforced. That party will be the promisor for any analysis of consideration and the party seeking to enforce that promise will be the promisee.

Restatement section 71(1) provides: "To constitute consideration, a performance or a return promise must be bargained for." The term "bargained for" does not require a bargaining process involving offers and counter-offers such as might take place in a flea market. It does not require "haggling". To be "bargained for," the performance, or the return promise to perform, must merely have been given in exchange for the promise which is being sought to be enforced.

The law does not ordinarily concern itself with actual motive or inducement in resolving consideration issues. If a wealthy individual teaches contract law because it is the most pleasant activity in the world, the rendition of this service is sufficient consideration to support the school's promise to pay even if in fact the pay was neither the sole or primary motive or inducement to perform. Restatement section 81(2) provides:

> The fact that a promise does not of itself induce a performance or return promise does not prevent the performance or return promise from being consideration for the promise.

Assume that a parent wishes one of her children to have a valuable painting that hangs in her home. The simple method to accomplish this objective is to give the painting to the child. If the painting is delivered to the child with the intention of passing title, the gift is completed. Under the law of property, the painting now belongs to the child. No promise has been made and there is no issue regarding promise enforcement, therefore contract law is not involved.

However, suppose that the parent wishes to retain possession of the painting for a period of time but wishes the child to have an enforceable right to receive the painting at some time in the future. The parent knows that a bare promise to give the painting to the child will not be enforceable because of the absence of consideration. To avoid this result, she offers to sell the painting to the child for $100 and the child accepts this offer by either promising to pay the money or by paying it. Unless the sum is known by both to be a mere pretense of a bargain, the parent's promise would be enforceable.

Restatement section 81(1) provides:

> The fact that what is bargained for does not of itself induce the making of a promise does not prevent it from being consideration for the promise.

Restatement section 71(2) provides:

> A performance or return promise is bargained for if it is sought by the promisor in exchange for his promise and is given by the promisee in exchange for that promise.

It is helpful to observe precision in use of vocabulary when analyzing consideration issues. Distinguish carefully between "adequate" consideration and "sufficient" consideration. "Adequacy" refers to whether there was a fair bargain involving an exchange of equal values. "Sufficiency" refers to whether the consideration is legally sufficient to enforce a promise, and this requires only that there be some legal detriment incurred as a bargained exchange for the other party's promise.

Equality of values is not a prerequisite in determining whether sufficient consideration exists. Thus, in common law cases consideration need not be "adequate" in the sense of being sufficient in amount. In contrast to common law rules, courts of equity historically denied equitable relief for breach of contract if the consideration was not fair and reasonable or "adequate." This requirement of adequacy of consideration remains in our law today but applies only to preclude the plaintiff from obtaining an equitable remedy such as specific performance (§§ 9.1 and 9.6). The contract is still enforceable at law.

Legal sufficiency of consideration does not require that the exchange be fair, but it does require that some bargained exchange actually exist. Returning to the hypothetical above, assume that the parent offered the valuable painting to her child in exchange for the child's worn out, worthless shoe. The transaction appears to be a sham, and it is probable that a court will treat it as such and find consideration wanting. It would be erroneous to characterize this result as being predicated upon the old shoe not being the actual motive or inducement of the parent to make her promise, as actual motivation or inducement is not required. However, where the purported consideration is obviously without any value and the purported bargain is a sham, enforcement of the promise may be denied.

The exchange for which a promise is bargained may be either a return promise or a performance. The performance may consist of an act, a forbearance, or the creation, modification, or relinquishment of a legal right or relationship. Digging a ditch would be an act which could be the bargained consideration for a promise. Refraining from engaging in the shoe business in the City of Buffalo for one year would be a forbearance which could be a bargained consideration. Relinquishing the right to use the name "Shogun Restaurant" is the modification or relinquishment of a legal right which could serve as consideration for a return promise.

Most students have no difficulty in seeing that the actual performance of an act or the actual refraining from a particular course of conduct could operate as consideration. However, many contracts are formed by the exchange of promises and it is this exchange of promises that serves as the consideration for the bilateral contract. Therefore, promising to dig the ditch, promising to refrain from engaging in the shoe business, promising to refrain from the right to use the name "Shogun Restaurant" would also operate as consideration for the other party's promise. If it were true that no contract could be formed until the performance in fact occurred, the only type of contract that would be recognized would be a unilateral contract. Obviously, this is not the case. In the offer and acceptance scenario, the offeror may empower the offeree to accept either by performance or by a promise to perform. If the latter, the giving of the promise by the offeree would be the consideration for the offeror's promise. The contract is formed upon the exchange of the promises even though neither party's performance may be due until quite some time into the future.

§ 2.25.1 Detriment, Benefit and Preexisting Legal Duty

Analysis begins by determining what promise someone is attempting to have enforced and identifying which party made this promise (the promisor) and to whom it was made (the promisee).

Consideration requires a bargain in which each party incurs a legal detriment. A traditional formulation of the consideration requirement is that the promisee's act or forbearance which purports to be the bargained exchange must involve a legal detriment to the promisee or a legal benefit to the promisor. In all the cases in which there is a legal benefit to the promisor there will also be a legal detriment to the promisee. However, a legal detriment to the promisee can exist with no apparent benefit to the promisor. Therefore, the focus should be upon the presence or absence of legal detriment to the promisee.

A legal detriment is doing or promising to do that which one was not previously obligated to do, or forbearing or promising to forbear from doing that which one had a legal right to do. "Legal detriment" is not synonymous with harmful. Refraining or promising to refrain from smoking is a legal detriment assuming one has a lawful right to smoke.

If one promises to do or does that which one was already legally obligated to do, this action is not sufficient to fulfill the consideration requirement. This concept has been labeled the preexisting duty rule, but it is not a separate rule. It is simply the logical result of applying the basic definition of "legal detriment."

A few examples will assist in exploring the reach of this concept.

(a) X is contractually obligated to construct a building for Y for $200,000. X requests or demands additional money for this work, and Y agrees to pay $210,000. X would be seeking to enforce Y's promise to pay the additional $10,000, thus identifying Y as the promisor. X, the promisee of that promise, incurred no detriment in doing or promising to do that which X was already legally obligated to do, thus there was no consideration to make Y's promise to pay the additional sum enforceable.

(b) P has a nasty habit of firing his rifle at birds in F's backyard in violation of a city ordinance. F offers to pay P $100 if P will refrain from this activity for a period of one year. F's promise to pay P $100 is not supported by consideration because P, the promisee, was already legally obligated to forbear from engaging in this activity. Since P did not refrain or promise to refrain from doing anything that P had a legal right to do, there was no detriment to P.

(c) R, an on-duty police officer, apprehends a criminal for whom a reward has been offered. R has a preexisting duty to perform this activity and has incurred no legal detriment. R cannot enforce the promise.

(d) R, an off-duty policeman vacationing in a neighboring jurisdiction, apprehends a criminal for whom a reward has been offered. Assuming R was aware of the reward offer, consideration is present because R has incurred a legal detriment by doing an act which he had no legal obligation to perform.

R's knowledge of the offer is necessary because there can be no bargained exchange between the promisor and promisee unless the promisee performed the act with the intention of accepting the offer made by the promisor. One can define an offer as a proposal to enter into a bargain and an acceptance as words or conduct that manifest assent to that proposed bargain. Reflection upon this point will cause one to understand that offer, acceptance and consideration relate to a single concept. That concept is: the common law enforces bargains to which parties have manifested their assent. Everything that you have read in this book thus far relates to this single concept.

(e) X has a contract with C whereby C is obligated to pave a dusty road. Wishing to make certain that the road is paved, a neighbor, N, promises to pay C an additional $1,000 if C will pave the road, and C performs the requested act. There has been considerable conflict among the courts and the writers as to the correct result and the proper rationale.

Under the given facts, C is a party to a valid enforceable contract with X. Thus, C has a legal duty to pave the road. A further promise to pave or the act of paving is not a legal detriment in that C is only doing that which he was already legally obligated to do. This leads to the conclusion that there is no consideration to support N's promise to pay $1,000 to C, and the promise cannot be enforced.

There are several avenues of assault upon this analysis. One position suggests that if C made a promise to N to pave the road, then N has the right to enforce C's promise, and in the event C defaults, N has a legal remedy. Thus N is obtaining a legal benefit and C may incur additional legal detriment which can be the basis for finding consideration. This theory is the product of circular reasoning in which the presence of a valid contract is assumed for the purpose of determining whether a valid contract exists.

Another approach is to inquire into the potential for a rescission of the C–X contract. If in fact C and X might have mutually agreed to rescind their contract, then it could be found that N was bargaining for C to forego this legal right to negotiate a rescission agreement. C has given up a legal right and has incurred a detriment.

If the C–X transaction was simply an offer for a unilateral contract made by X to C, then C would have no preexisting legal obligation owing to anyone since only C's performance would conclude the bargain. If N made an offer to C for a unilateral contract, the performance by C of the act of paving the road could be a valid acceptance of both offers and there would be consideration to support each promise.

The most sweeping assault upon this phase of the preexisting duty problem would be to exclude from its application duties owing to third persons. Only a legal duty owed to the promisor would constitute a preexisting duty which would preclude a new promise or an act from constituting consideration. This is the position which the Restatement, Second, has taken. Section 72 provides: "Except as stated in Sections 73 and 74, any performance which is bargained for is consideration." The portion of the referenced sections which is relevant to this discussion is in section 73 which provides in part: "Performance of a legal duty owed to a promisor which is neither doubtful nor the subject of honest dispute is not consideration...."

The comments in the Restatement indicate that "legal duty owed to a promisor" includes legal duties owed to an individual as a member of the public by public officials. This Restatement rule would reach the same results described above in the hypotheticals involving police officers collecting reward offers. Presumably "legal duties owed" would include the duty to refrain from committing a tort or engaging in criminal activity that harms the person or property of the promisor. Thus, there would be a legal duty owing to the promisor not to fire a rifle in his backyard in hypothetical (b) above, and the same result (promise unenforceable) would be reached under the Restatement. However, as to the road, there was no legal duty owed by C to N, and therefore the paving or promising to pave by C would be consideration for N's promise to pay the $1,000.

§ 2.26   Compromise of Disputed Claims

From the principles outlined in the preceding sections, it should be apparent that a mutual agreement to compromise a disputed claim is supported by consideration. If P has properly asserted against D a tort claim for damages to P and D agrees to pay $50,000 for the settlement of P's negligence action, P's dismissal of the suit or release of P's claim is a legal detriment. This detriment is being incurred as a bargained exchange for D's promise to pay.

So long as there is a valid claim that is being compromised, no novel issues are presented. Problems arise if P brings an action to enforce D's promise to pay $50,000 that was made to settle a claim that may have been invalid. Assume that D seeks to defend by proving that under the facts and the applicable law, D could not have been liable for negligently causing P's damages. Assume further that D seeks to prove that P knew that there was no valid action for negligence against D or that P did not have a good faith belief that there was a valid action. The problems presented here require analysis of different policy considerations.

If P knows he has no claim, the solution is easy. P does not have a right to bring a claim that P knows is invalid. Therefore, forbearing or promising to forbear from bringing such a claim would not be legal detriment. P is not refraining from doing that which P has a legal right to do. One could also say that P would be deemed to be under a pre-existing duty not to bring such a claim.

A more difficult problem is presented if P had an honest belief or good faith belief that he had the right to sue, but D now seeks to prove that P would have lost. There are strong public policy factors supporting the voluntary settlement of disputes. It is bad policy to place impediments in the path of persons seeking to compromise their differences. One must also note that in claims in which liability is disputed because of uncertainty as to the facts or the law, it is self-evident that there is a possibility that the defendant is not liable. If the odds in favor of finding liability are no better than 50–50, one might expect to find P settling what is reasonably considered to be a $200,000 loss for $100,000. If liability is tenuous, P might be willing to settle a $200,000 loss for $25,000. Once a settlement agreement is reached, P should be able to enforce the promise to pay the $25,000 settlement amount without having to prove the validity of the underlying claim, otherwise P would have no motive to enter into a bilateral settlement agreement. If the resolution of disputes by voluntary settlement is to be fostered, it is apparent that contract law must accommodate the enforcement of proper settlement agreements.

To accommodate these policy concerns within the rules of consideration, courts hold that the surrender of a validly disputed claim or the release of a validly asserted defense is sufficient consideration for a return promise. A claim is validly disputed if there is factual or legal uncertainty as to its merits. If the known facts and the law establish that the

claim is definitely without foundation, some jurisdictions still treat the release of the claim as valid
consideration so long as the person who asserted
the claim had a good faith belief in its validity.
Court opinions sometimes state that this "good
faith belief" must have some foundation in fact or
law.

Legal detriment can also be found from the surrender of a defense if the same tests of good faith or
minimal foundation in law or fact are met. Legal
detriment can likewise be found from the surrender
of a claimed legal right. For example, assume that
Father died with a will disinheriting his children
and leaving his sole asset, a farm, to his friend
Jane. Assume further that Jane promised to pay
$5,000 to each child in exchange for the children
relinquishing any claim they might have to the
farm. Assuming that the children had a good faith
belief that they had the right to challenge Father's
will, giving up that claim is a legal detriment. This
provides consideration for Jane's promises to pay.

§ 2.27 Partial Payment in Exchange for a Discharge (Payment or Promise to Pay a Lesser Sum In Discharge of a Claim to a Greater Sum)

If D has a present undisputed duty to pay C $100,
C's agreement to discharge the entire $100 in ex-
change for D's payment or promise to pay $75 is not
supported by consideration. Promising to pay or
paying the lesser amount is not a legal detriment
because the party is simply doing that which he is

already legally obligated to do. Fulfilling a portion of a duty of immediate performance cannot provide consideration for the creditor's promise to release the balance. It was a holding to this effect in the English case of *Foakes v. Beer* (H.L. 1884), that is credited with providing the modern case law foundation for the preexisting duty concept. The *Foakes* case involved an agreement by which a judgment debtor paid the principal amount owing on the judgment in exchange for the creditor agreeing to forego her right to collect the interest then due. The court held that the creditor's promise to forego interest then due was unenforceable because the debtor incurred no legal detriment in paying the principal amount because that was something the debtor was already legally obligated to do. The debtor had an uncontested present legal duty to pay the entire amount and promising to pay or paying only a portion of such an amount is not legal detriment to the debtor.

The principle of the *Foakes* case remains the law in almost all jurisdictions. It is an excellent example of the manner in which the common law begins with a basic premise, in this case the rule that one cannot obtain legal rights under a promise unless one incurred a legal detriment in exchange for it, and then applies this rule rationally to all fact situations without regard to the fairness or economic efficiency of the results reached.

The result of the *Foakes* case does not comport with economic realities nor with everyday notions of what is a "benefit" and what is a "detriment."

Faced with an overdue account of uncertain collectibility, most creditors would be delighted to accept a proposal that the debtor will produce the necessary cash to pay the full amount of the principal owed in exchange for the creditor forgiving interest on the debt. This solution is certainly beneficial to the creditor. It is vastly superior to using the services of an attorney or collection agency. Payment of the principal is not a "legal detriment" to the debtor as we have come to define that term, but in economic reality it does involve the debtor doing more than a lot of other debtors we have come to know in our lives. The settlement that was reached in *Foakes* would be an economically efficient solution to the problem but it will not be utilized if debtors are not permitted to assert the agreement as a defense against a claim for the amount that the creditor agreed to discharge.

The quandary created by the preexisting duty rule is a recurring problem in the common law. The rule is clear. The rule leads to an obvious result. The result in many cases is not acceptable. Thus we must invent exceptions to the rule or interpret the facts in some imaginative manner to avoid the rule. When the exceptions become sufficiently great in number, the situation is ripe for some imaginative judge to declare that the rule is gone having been swallowed up by the exceptions, but until that happens, lawyers and law students must learn to operate within the existing situation. This requires that one know the basic common law rule and how it has been applied; know the reason for the rule that has produced these results; and understand the techniques that have been used or that might be accepted in future cases to avoid inappropriate results.

By statute or otherwise various exceptions have been recognized to avoid the principle that partial performance of an undisputed obligation cannot serve as consideration for discharge of the obligation.

(a) If the obligation in question is not yet due and owing, pre-payment of a lesser sum is sufficient consideration to support an agreement to discharge the whole. Payment at a place other than the place where payment is due has also been suggested to be a performance different from the duty that was owing and thus can serve as valid consideration. By paying early or paying at a different place, the debtor is doing (or promising to do) something that the debtor was not previously obligated to do, thus there is detriment incurred by the debtor in exchange for the promise of the creditor to discharge the unpaid balance. Note in this regard, however, that Restatement section 73 provides in part: " ... a similar performance is consideration if it differs from what was required by the duty *in a way which reflects more than a pretense of bargain.*" (emphasis added.)

(b) If the matter arises out of a transaction in goods, U.C.C. section 2–209(1) permits good faith modification of contracts without new consideration. This would appear to permit a seller of goods to agree to take a lesser sum in satisfaction of a greater sum that was due so long as the modification was made in good faith.

(c) Some states have statutes in addition to the U.C.C. which permit contract modification without new consideration in all types of transactions. Some statutes are more limited in scope providing that payment of a smaller sum can support a discharge of a greater sum that is presently owing. Some provide that a written release by a creditor needs no consideration to be binding. U.C.C. section 1–107, which would apply to any transaction within the Code (not just Article 2 relating to goods) provides that, "Any claim or right arising out of an alleged breach can be discharged in whole or in part without consideration by a written waiver or renunciation signed and delivered by the aggrieved party."

(d) All jurisdictions recognize that an existing contract can be mutually rescinded by the parties and a new contract can thereafter be formed. The fact that the new contract is identical with the old one but for one party assuming an added burden or being relieved of a burden does not raise a preexisting duty issue. Some states have used this rescission and new contract reasoning in situations where the facts do not support it. A few courts simply purport to find a rescission despite the absence of any factual basis. Other courts admit that they are using a legal fiction to accomplish what they consider to be a just result.

(e) All jurisdictions recognize that while a gratuitous promise may be unenforceable, a completed gift is irrevocable. This opens a door to finding that one party gratuitously released the other from his preexisting duty and that the gift is complete.

(f) There is authority for the proposition that a debtor who is insolvent and contemplating bankruptcy may incur a legal detriment by foregoing his right to seek a discharge of his obligations in bankruptcy. In some jurisdictions this has been found to serve as a bargained exchange for a creditor's promise to accept a lesser sum in satisfaction of a larger debt presently due and owing.

(g) At least one state supreme court has simply announced, albeit by way of dicta, that *Foakes v. Beer* will not be followed. (*Rye v. Phillips* (Minn. 1938).)

(h) If one creditor agrees to take less than what is due in satisfaction of the whole obligation in consideration for other creditors agreeing to do the same, then consideration is present in what is called a composition of creditors. (See Restatement Second § 80, comment c.) Likewise, a promise to pay or payment by X to C of a portion of the obligation owing from D to C in exchange for C's agreement to release the balance of the obligation is sufficient consideration. X and C are each incurring a legal detriment.

§ 2.28 Condition to Gift and Bargained Exchange Compared

A gratuitous promise may be conditioned upon the promisee doing something to place himself in a position to receive the gift.

If a professor wished to give a hornbook to a student, the professor might state: "Come to my office after class, and I will give you a copy of Farnsworth on Contracts." This communication contains a promise and a request that the promisee perform an act. The act of the promisee certainly involves legal detriment in the technical sense of the term because the student is being required to walk to the professor's office, an act that the student was not previously legally obligated to do. However, there is no consideration because there is no bargain. Coming to the office to pick up the book is simply a reasonable means to make it possible to complete the gift.

Assume that a professor needs the copy of Farnsworth on Contracts which she left in her office. The professor states to a student: "Go to my office and get my Farnsworth on Contracts, and I will give it to you after class when I am finished using it." This communication also contains a promise and a request that the promisee perform an act. The act again involves legal detriment as the student is being asked to walk to the professor's office, an act that he was not previously legally obligated to do. While the legal detriment is no different from that in the preceding hypothetical, here a court would likely find a bargain.

When a transaction involves legal detriment to the promisee but has gratuitous overtones—the appearance of being a gift—Professor Williston suggested some questions which one can ask to determine whether a court is likely to find a bargain. Is the act which was requested of the promisee something which was necessary or merely convenient to facilitate making a gift from the promisor to the promisee? Will the promisor benefit from the promisee's act?

Assume that a party with an empty house says to a relative: "Move here. You can stay in my empty house for a few years." Without additional facts, this appears to be a gift, and moving and staying in the house are simply conditions to that gift. Moving to the place where an empty house is located is a necessary act to place oneself in a position to receive the free gift of occupancy, and there is no apparent benefit to the promisor. However, if the facts were that the owner was in need of a house-sitter and the owner and house-sitter were agreeing to an arrangement for the house-sitting to be accomplished, the promise of rent-free occupancy would be the bargained for exchange for the promise to occupy the house.

Assume that a woman states to her nephew: "If you go to Cornell and refrain from drinking alcoholic beverages during the weeks while classes are in session, I will pay for your tuition." This would appear to be a bargain. A gift of college tuition requires that the nephew enroll in college, but the additional requirement that he refrain from drinking while classes are in session is not a necessary condition to this gift. Assuming the nephew has a legal right to drink, refraining from doing so is a legal detriment, and the facts indicate that the promise was made as a bargained exchange for refraining from drinking. Note again, that although the nephew may have in fact physically and academically benefitted from abstention from alcohol, the fact that he had a legal right to engage in such conduct would make his forbearance from doing so a legal detriment.

§ 2.29 Alternative Promises; Multiple Promises

A contract may permit one party to elect between alternative performances. If X contemplates selling one of his two cars, Y may offer to buy "whichever one you decide not to keep" for a stated price. If X accepts this offer, there is a valid bargain. X has a choice to make, but X is obligated to deliver one car or the other and either performance constitutes consideration for Y's promise to pay.

If a purported bargain gives one party a choice among alternatives, each alternative must be analyzed to determine whether it would constitute consideration for the return promise. Assume that S agrees to sell and B agrees to buy between 400 and 600 tons of fertilizer in installments as ordered by B. There is consideration for S's promise because B must order and pay for at least 400 tons of fertilizer.

However, if one of the alternatives that could be chosen by the promisee is something that would not be consideration if it alone had been bargained for then there would not be consideration given by the promisee. An example of this would be a promise by X to pay $100 to Y in return for Y's promise either to refrain from smoking OR to refrain from spraying graffiti on public buildings. Assuming Y has a legal right to smoke, refraining from doing so would be a detriment to Y. However, Y has a preexisting duty to forbear from defacing public buildings with graffiti. Therefore, because Y's promise includes an alternative performance that would not be consideration, X's promise is unenforceable.

Assume that A owes B an undisputed debt of $5,000 payable in five years. A makes a subsequent promise that he will either pay $4,000 at the end of the first year or pay the debt at maturity; in return B promises to accept the $4,000, if paid at the end of the first year, in full satisfaction of the debt. A's subsequent promise is not consideration for B's return promise since the alternative of performing his existing legal duty is not consideration. (Illustration number 6 in Restatement § 77.) Therefore, when A tenders the payment of $4,000 at the end of the first year, B is free to reject it and insist upon payment of the full $5,000 at the end of five years, the time it was originally due.

Care must be taken in distinguishing promises that are in the alternative as compared to multiple promises that are in the conjunctive. As stated in Restatement section 80(2), "The fact that part of what is bargained for would not have been consideration if that part alone had been bargained for does not prevent the whole from being consideration."

Therefore, if X in the first fact pattern above had promised to refrain from smoking AND had also promised to refrain from defacing the buildings, then because X was bound to do one thing that would constitute consideration, Y's promise would be enforceable. X had no choice of performances.

§ 2.30 Illusory Promises

An illusory promise is just what the term signifies—there appears to be a promise but it is an illusion and no promise exists. A promise which is illusory cannot serve as consideration for the return promise of the other party. Promises that are subject to a condition the occurrence of which is within the control of the promisor must be examined with care to determine whether they are in fact illusory.

X promises to pay Y $20 for cutting X's lawn and Y promises to cut the lawn if he feels like it. At the time the "promises" are exchanged, there is no consideration for X's promise. Y has not made a binding commitment. Y's promise is illusory as he has a "free way out." Y's duty to perform is dependent upon his mood or whim. Therefore, because there is no consideration for X's promise, X is not bound. The consideration issue will arise only if Y seeks to enforce a contract. There will be no consideration issue if the party who made the illusory promise is trying to avoid performance. Y in this fact pattern could choose not to "feel like it" and therefore Y would never be in breach of his "promise." A consideration issue arises if Y seeks to enforce a contract. It will be X who will be asserting lack of consideration as the justification for asserting that X has no duty to Y. Therefore, Y, the person with "the free way out" finds that he is hoisted on his own petard because X will use Y's "free way out" to establish that there was no consideration for X's promise.

The result would probably be the same if Y promised to cut X's lawn unless Y decided to go to the football game. Unless one assumes some additional facts that make attendance at the football game a significant event, it would appear that Y has preserved discretionary control over whether he will become obligated to cut the lawn or not. One could view attendance at the football game as an alternative promise by Y, however, it seems readily apparent that this alternative is not a promise for which X has bargained. Attendance at the football game is not an alternative performance of the contract but rather an event that would prevent Y from having a duty to perform. It is thus a condition to Y's duty that is within Y's control leading to the probable conclusion that Y's promise is illusory.

However, a promise can serve as consideration even though the promisor's duty to perform is subject to an event within the promisor's control. As indicated in Restatement section 2, illustration 3:

> A says to B, "I will employ you for a year at a salary of $5,000 if I go into business." This is a promise, even though it is wholly optional with A to go into business or not.

Examples:

Professor who lives in New York has been offered the position of dean at a school in New

Mexico. B promises to buy Professor's house in New York for a stated price and Professor agrees to sell the house provided she accepts the position in New Mexico. One can find consideration for B's promise to buy. Professor's promise to sell is subject to a condition that is within her discretionary control, however, her promise is not illusory. She does not have a "free way out." The decision to accept or reject the offered position is one that will be made based upon many factors other than the house sale contract. It is going to occur or not occur based upon these other factors. If the position is accepted, the duty to convey the house will arise.

S owns and operates a widget factory. B promises to buy and S promises to sell for a stated price all of S's output of widgets for a period of two years. S has a duty to act in good faith (see U.C.C. section 2–305(1)), but assuming appropriate facts, it is possible for S to terminate production of widgets and avoid any obligation on the promise to B. Despite the fact that S may be free to sell or close the plant or otherwise terminate widget production, there is consideration for B's promise to buy. The obligation is subject to an event that is within S's control, but the owner of a widget factory may not terminate production simply to avoid the contract with B.

The presence of a condition within the control of one party creates a more difficult problem when that condition is related to the contract performance. Assume that A promises to pay B a stated sum for transporting A's goods from New Orleans to Puerto Rico for a period of five years, and B promises to haul A's goods if B decides to buy a certain ship. If the ship would be used primarily or exclusively to haul A's cargo, it would appear that there is no consideration for A's promise. B's decision to purchase or not purchase the ship would not reflect B's evaluation of independent factors but would be primarily determined by whether B wanted to perform or avoid B's agreement with A.

Assume that X promises to deliver gravel to Y and Y agrees to order and pay for a specified quantity of gravel unless Y notifies X in writing within 60 days that Y does not wish to perform. Y's duty to perform is subject to a condition within Y's control which has no significance independent of this contract. Y is free to avoid any obligation by simply giving written notice of intent not to perform. Proper analysis leads to the conclusion that at the time this agreement is made there is no consideration for X's promise to deliver gravel. One might find that there is an open offer from X to Y, but X is free to revoke that offer. However, after the 60 days has expired and the right to cancel is gone, there is a binding contract between the parties because the promises are now no longer subject to conditions within their control.

Some court opinions have analyzed situations such as the gravel hypothetical above in terms of alternative performances. One can indulge in the reasoning that Y has a choice between two performances, ordering and paying for gravel or writing a letter stating none will be ordered. Of course, writing a letter does involve doing something that Y was not previously obligated to do and could thus be seen as a legal detriment. However, it is not a bargained for detriment. The parties were not agreeing to a bargain which involved X promising to deliver gravel in exchange for Y's writing a letter stating that Y would not perform.

Another potential problem can arise when the promisor has made the promise subject to a condition that the promisor at the time of making the promise knows cannot occur. For example, assume that X promised to pay one-half of all royalties that he receives from his invention in return for Y's promise to pay $10,000 to X. X's duty of performance is conditioned upon there being royalties which required that a patent be granted. At the time X made the promise X was aware that the patent office had denied X's application for the patent and that it would never be granted. X's promise to pay is subject to a condition that X knows will never occur and therefore X's promise is illusory. There may be other defenses assertable by Y as well, such as misrepresentation or mistake.

§ 2.30.1 Promises Subject to a Condition That Cannot Occur

If both parties know the condition cannot occur, then the purported promise which is subject to that condition will not even be a promise at all. For example, if X promises that X will sell his 1964 Mustang convertible to Y "when Hell freezes over" the issue is not consideration (whether X's promise is illusory). It is evident to both parties that there is simply no promise. (See Restatement §§ 2 and 76, comment b.)

§ 2.30.2 Voidable and Unenforceable Promises

Certain promises are voidable or legally unenforceable due to factors such as age or mental capacity of the promisor or due to improper inducements used by the promisee or the failure to comply with a requirement for a writing. Despite the fact that a promise may be unenforceable for reasons of this sort, it can still provide sufficient consideration to support a return promise for which it was bargained. A minor may be immune from liability upon his promises, but this fact does not preclude his promise from serving as consideration, thus permitting him to enforce the contract. A person with diminished mental capacity may have the right to avoid his obligations under a contract, but the promise can still serve as consideration. The same result is reached when a promisor has the right to avoid his obligations due to the promisee's misrepresentations, or because of mistake, or because the statute of frauds requires his promise to be in writing. Comment "a" to Restatement Second section 78 provides:

> The fact that no legal remedy is available for a breach of a promise does not prevent it from being a part of a bargain or remove the bargain

from the scope of the general principle that bargains are enforceable.

The policy reasons for this rule reflect our desire to provide a defense to certain persons such as victims of misrepresentation, minors and the like. The intent is to give these persons an option to avoid their contract obligations. The law is not designed to give a right of cancellation to the other party.

Promises made by persons totally lacking in capacity are void and would not serve as consideration to permit enforcement on behalf of the incapacitated person.

§ 2.31 Implied Promise to Use Best Efforts or to Act in Good Faith

In determining the presence or absence of a firm undertaking, a court is not limited to the express terms of the agreement. What appears on the surface to be an illusory promise may be properly characterized as a firm undertaking if one can infer that the parties intended an implied promise.

Assume that L agreed to give to W the exclusive right to place L's endorsements on the designs of others, to market L's own designs, and to license others to market them. W agreed to pay L one-half of all profits and revenues. The agreement was for one year and renewable thereafter unless canceled. W made no express promise to do anything beyond his promise to account to L monthly for monies received and pay one-half of the profits to L, duties which would never arise if he never did anything. The court found that a promise by W to use reasonable efforts in marketing L's name and products was fairly implied, and with this implied promise, the court could find consideration to support L's promises. (*Wood v. Lucy, Lady Duff–Gordon* (N.Y. 1917).) The fact that W possessed a business organization suitable for the purposes of the agreement assisted the court in reaching the decision that the parties had intended an implied promise by W that reasonable efforts would be applied to the task. Possibly more important, however, is the apparent fact that the parties intended to enter an agreement which would have business efficacy and that this manifested intention could be effectuated only by concluding that the parties intended that there be a commitment by W. In addition, because this was an exclusive right granted to W, it is logical to assume that both parties must have intended that W be obligated to use his best efforts to market L's products and endorsements, as L could not license anyone else and therefore W would be the sole source of L's income from her name and products.

U.C.C. section 2–306(2) provides:

A lawful agreement by either the seller or the buyer for exclusive dealing in the kind of goods concerned imposes unless otherwise agreed an obligation by the seller to use best efforts to supply the goods and by the buyer to use best efforts to promote their sale.

U.C.C. section 1–203 imposes an obligation of good faith in every contract arising under the U.C.C. It has been suggested that the provisions of this section may permit a court to find enforceable obligations in circumstances in which the express promises of the parties appeared to be inadequate to find a present contract. For example, at common law an "agreement to agree" was found to be too indefinite to be a contract. The provisions of the U.C.C. may induce courts to find an enforceable duty to meet and negotiate in good faith where such an "agreement to agree" has been made. (See §§ 2.1.3 and 2.43.)

§ 2.32 Requirements Contracts and Output Contracts

A requirements contract is one that measures the contract quantity by the requirements of the buyer. Any amount that the seller produces in excess of the buyer's requirements can be sold to third parties, but the seller must deliver a sufficient amount to satisfy the buyer's requirements. The buyer is not permitted to buy from a third party.

An output contract is one that measures the contract quantity by the output of the seller. Any amount that the buyer may need in excess of the seller's output can be purchased from third parties, but the buyer must buy all of the seller's output. The seller is not permitted to sell any of its output to a third party.

Assume that S agrees to sell and B agrees to buy all of B's requirements of olive oil for $12 per gallon. Requirements contracts such as this appear to give the buyer the opportunity to reduce the contract quantity and thus B's obligation to zero or increase the quantity to a great amount depending upon B's choice of future conduct. Because of the apparent illusory nature of B's promise and the problem of certainty of terms, early common law courts had difficulties enforcing contracts in which quantity was measured solely by the requirements of the buyer or the output of the seller.

With respect to the consideration issue, courts came to the position that if B had an established business with existing requirements, the promise to buy was not illusory. If B had a salad dressing factory or a Greek restaurant, his promise to buy his requirements of olive oil was not illusory because his only choice was to buy oil or go out of business. Some court opinions view this situation as involving two alternative performances both of which involve a legal detriment. However, the seller could not logically be found to have bargained for a promise to sell in exchange for B's detriment of terminating his business. The better explanation of this result is that B's alternative of terminating his business has substantial significance to him independent of the olive oil contract. The availability of this alternative does not make his promise illusory; it does not afford him a free way out (§ 2.30) . The same analysis would be applicable if the contract in question was an output contract.

The interpretation of rights and duties in requirement and output contracts is now controlled in part by U.C.C. section 2–306. Both an output seller and a requirements buyer are subject to good faith obligations.

§ 2.33 To Whom and From Whom Consideration Must Be Given

In determining whether a promise is enforceable, there is no requirement in American law that the return promise or performance which constitutes the bargained exchange need come from the promisee. Likewise, there is no requirement that the promise or performance which constitutes the bargained exchange need be made to or rendered for the promisor. Restatement section 71(4) in reference to what constitutes consideration states that, "The performance or return promise may be given to the promisor or to some other person. It may be given by the promisee or some other person."

Consideration can be found in each of these examples:

X and Y enter an agreement in which X promises to pay Y five dollars and Y promises to cut Z's hair.

S and D enter a contract in which S promises to deliver a book to N in return for D's promise to pay $25 to S. Or, S promises to deliver a book to N in return for D's promise to pay $25 to G.

S and R sign a document in which R promises to paint C's house in return for S's promise to repair C's porch without charge. (It matters not whether S promises to repair R's porch or C's porch.)

In the foregoing examples, the person who will be seeking to enforce the promise is not a party to the contract and enforcement will be dependent upon establishing rights as a third party beneficiary. (See chapter 11.) Cases decided under English common law as well as early American cases denied enforcement by third parties because they were persons "from whom no consideration flowed" or because there was no "mutuality of obligation." However, with the general recognition in the United States of enforceable rights in third party beneficiaries, the notion that the plaintiff had to incur some legal detriment as part of the bargained exchange has been rejected.

§ 2.34 Adequacy of Consideration

The fairness or equivalence in the values exchanged is not a direct factor in determining the presence or absence of consideration. The presence or absence of an equal exchange can have great significance in determining the availability of certain defenses or the availability of certain remedies. For those purposes, it will be appropriate to discuss "adequacy of consideration" referring to amount or value. For purposes of determining whether a bargain exists with the requisite consideration, the appropriate vocabulary is "sufficiency of consideration" referring to legal sufficiency rather than fairness or adequacy (§ 2.25).

While benefit to the promisor is often included as an alternative to detriment to the promisee in the traditional definition of what constitutes sufficient consideration, no actual benefit to the promisor need be found. Undoubtedly, most persons who make promises as part of a bargained exchange do so because they anticipate a benefit for themselves, but the requirement of consideration leaves to the promisor the determination of what constitutes a satisfactory bargain. Thus, P may promise to pay $500 to X if X will quit smoking; or if X will start studying; or go to church; or paint the church. The question of benefit to P is not relevant to the discussion of consideration in any of these examples. While P did get someone to conform their life style to P's desires the enforcement of P's promise is not predicated upon the gratification that P is receiving from the performance of the requested acts. Adoption of the notion of psychological benefit as a basis for promise enforcement would logically extend to gratuitous promises and cause one to conclude that they too are given for bargained consideration. Such is not the case.

§ 2.35 Non-bargained Detriment

The making of a gratuitous promise may stimulate or induce various types of responses in the promisee. If X agrees to let Y use X's ladder to reach the apples on Y's tree, it is not uncommon that Y will say thanks and volunteer a few free apples for X's family. Gratuitous promises may induce all manner and means of action in reliance thereon. Despite the presence of a "detriment" on the part of both parties, there is no bargained exchange present. While detrimental reliance may be available as a basis for asserting some contract rights (§ 2.41), it is important to distinguish that theory from the enforcement of bargained exchanges.

To have consideration, it is not enough that the making of the promise induced some conduct or return promise on the part of the promisee. There must be a concurrence of these two elements to create a bargained exchange. Objective manifestations of inducement and bargain are sufficient. There is no inquiry into the undisclosed intention or "true motive" of either or both parties. (See Restatement § 71, comment b.)

§ 2.36 Nominal Consideration: Sham Bargains

Assume that X desires to make a binding promise to give $10,000 to her son, B. Having been advised that a gratuitous promise is not binding, X agrees to buy from B for $10,000 an old book that is actually worth less than $5. B agrees. The question is whether there is sufficient consideration to support X's promise and make it legally enforceable.

Many basic principles of the law of consideration are involved here.

1) To enforce a promise at common law consideration need only be legally sufficient, it need not be adequate (§ 2.25). When people contract to pay

money for goods or other property, we do not inquire into the value placed upon the property in the exchange. Determination of how much property is worth is left to the parties and their negotiations.

2) However, the promisee must not only incur some legal detriment, that legal detriment must be incurred as a bargained exchange for the promise (§§ 2.25 and 2.28).

3) But, the requirement of a bargain does not mean that the return promise need be the actual inducement or motivation for the promise. One is entitled to the agreed upon salary for teaching Contracts even if the teacher is independently wealthy and admits that the motivation for teaching is nothing but the pure joy of watching people learn.

4) Consideration is a formality designed to provide a basis for enforcement of promises under our legal system.

Application of these principles to the hypothetical problem discloses some tension and perhaps some contradiction. X has offered to pay $10,000 for a book. Principle number 1 above directs us to leave questions of valuation to the parties. If X wishes to pay $10,000 for a book, she is free to do so. In fact, being able to buy and sell what we want for what price we can get is one of our fundamental freedoms.

Skipping principle number 2 for the moment, principle number 3 indicates that we do not require that a person make a promise or perform an act for the purpose of getting the return promise. A citizen who supplies information to the police leading to an arrest and conviction may collect a reward offered for this act. The right will not be defeated because the citizen would have supplied the information in any event. If this is correct, do we conclude that motivation or inducement are not factors to be analyzed in determining whether a promise is enforceable? The offeree must act with the intention of accepting the offer, and there is some case law that indicates that the offer must motivate the act but the law is not consistent on this point ..

Principle number 2 now comes into focus. What is a bargain? Conceptually, we are enforcing a promise because the other party to the transaction incurred a legal detriment and thereby paid a price for this promise. Is it accurate to describe an exchange as a bargained exchange if the price paid by one party did not motivate or induce the promise made by the other?

The Restatement, First of Contracts (1932) provided in section 84:

Consideration is not insufficient because of the fact:

(a) that obtaining it was not the motive or a material cause inducing the promisor to make the promise ...

That Restatement gave the following as an illustration of clause (a):

1. A wishes to make a binding promise to his
    son B to convey to B Blackacre, which is
    worth $5,000. Being advised that a gratu-
    itous promise is not binding, A writes to B
    an offer to sell Blackacre for $1. B accepts.
    B's promise to pay $1 is sufficient consider-
    ation.

The Restatement, Second of Contracts does not
deal directly with the question whether the consideration being paid need be the motive or inducement for the return promise. However, that Restatement provides in Illustration 5 to section 71:

5. A desires to make a binding promise to give
    $1,000 to his son B. Being advised that a
    gratuitous promise is not binding, A offers
    to buy from B for $1,000 a book worth less
    than $1. B accepts the offer *knowing that
    the purchase of the book is a mere pretense.*
    There is no consideration for A's promise to
    pay $1,000. (Emphasis added.)

There is a head-on collision of basic policies here.
That creates an issue as to which good lawyering
might change the result that a court would reach. It
creates an issue as to which a good student can
demonstrate to her professor why she is going to be
a very good lawyer and thus deserves a very good
grade. To assist you to get started on your own
analysis, we offer the following.

Your authors argue that consideration is a formality. The common law is unconcerned with com-
parative values and does not require that the detri-

ment incurred by one party be the motivation for the promise of the other. If the parties comply with the formality by making certain that each is incurring a legal detriment and that these detriments purport to be incurred in exchange for each other, then they have made clear their intent to be bound and have complied with the formality that the law requires. The transaction is in the form of a bargain, and the evident intention of the parties that the agreement be enforceable should be respected.

In the alternative, one could conclude that for consideration to exist, there must be a confluence of a detriment to the promisee which was given as a bargained for exchange. Therefore, although the promisee may be technically incurring a detriment, as for example by promising to pay one dollar or promising to deliver an old book, if the parties know or should know that the transaction was intended to be gratuitous, there is no consideration as the promises were not given as a part of a bargained for exchange. Illustration 5 to Restatement section 71 supports this result.

B did make a promise to sell the book which was something B was not previously obligated to do. However, as B knew, A's intent was gratuitous and A's promise to pay the money was not given in exchange for B's promise to deliver the book. There may have been a detriment to B, but there was no bargain.

One final observation. If this issues is litigated and the judge expresses the opinion that the old

book or the $5 is a "mere pretense," you can be
certain that B just lost his case. If one believes that
$5 can be a bargained exchange for a valuable
parcel of land, then the agreement is not a "pretense" but rather is quite real. If one takes the
position that B's promise must be viewed by his
parent as a true bargain for Blackacre, then "pretense" is an accurate label and the promise will not
be enforced.

§ 2.37 False Recitals of Consideration

Consideration will not be found even though the
parties have reduced their agreement to written
form and the writing contains a recital of consideration that would make the agreement enforceable
but for the fact that it is not true. Illustration 4 to
Restatement section 71 provides:

> A desires to make a binding promise to give
> $1,000 to his son B. Being advised that a gratu-
> itous promise is not binding, A writes out and
> signs a false recital that B has sold him a car for
> $1000 and a promise to pay that amount. There is
> no consideration for A's promise.

Here, the problem is not that the consideration
given by B is only of nominal value. The problem is
that there was nothing done or promised to be done
by B at all. Therefore there was neither detriment
to B nor was there anything for which A was
bargaining.

While consideration is often viewed as a formalistic requirement, most courts have resisted the ar-

gument that a false recital of consideration in a writing should be sufficient to make a promise enforceable. Most jurisdictions permit the promisor to go behind the document to prove that the recital was in fact a sham to create the appearance of a bargain where none was in fact present.

§ 2.38   Option Contracts: Nominal Consideration or False Recitals of Consideration

An option contract is a contract in which a promisor promises not to revoke some offer that the promisor has made. As with other types of promises, a promise not to revoke an offer can be enforced if it is made as part of a bargained exchange for some return consideration.

For example, assume that S offers to sell Blackacre to B for $6 million cash. In exchange for $1,000 paid by B to S, S also promises not to revoke this offer for one week. The option contract consists of B paying S $1,000 in exchange for a promise not to revoke an offer. It is referred to as an "option contract" because it gives to B for a period of time the option to decide whether B wishes to buy the property on the terms stated in the principal offer.

The economic concerns or business concerns of the parties are primarily focused upon the terms of the basic offer (Blackacre for $6 million) and the duration of the option (how long S must hold his property off the market and thus sacrifice other opportunities to sell.) The amount that is paid for the option itself ($1,000 in this case) is ordinarily of no great significance. Many options are given for as little as $1. Since the sum to be paid for the option is often a small sum and is usually not the focus of attention, there are a number of reported cases that involve situations where the parties failed to pay the option money. Frequently there is a writing that recites that the option money has been paid and received, but in fact this was not done.

The differences of opinion as to whether nominal consideration should be sufficient to support any type of return promise is analyzed in section 2.36. With respect to option contracts (enforcement of promises not to revoke offers), there is no dispute. The courts and the Restatement have recognized that the payment or promise to pay nominal consideration (such as $1) is sufficient consideration to make a promise not to revoke an offer enforceable. If the option time is relatively short and the price to be paid if the option is exercised is a fair price, the courts will not inquire as to the relative value of the promise not to revoke in relationship to the price paid for the period of irrevocability.

For example: S offered to sell Greenacre to B for $10,000, its fair market price. B paid S (or promised to pay S) the sum of $1 for S's promise to hold the offer open for ten days. Most courts and the Restatement would find that the nominal consideration was sufficient to enforce the promise of S not to revoke. (See Restatement Second § 87, comment b.)

As to sham recitals of nominal consideration one might conclude for the reasons stated in section 2.37 that such false recitals are of no value. This in fact appears to be the prevailing view accepted by the American courts. However, with regard to the consideration necessary to support an option contract, there is some authority for the proposition that a sham recital of consideration is sufficient to show an intent to create an enforceable obligation that the law should respect. Some courts simply refuse to permit the promisor to introduce evidence to contradict what is stated in the writing. One court indicated that if the promisor had not received the consideration for the option, he could sue for it.

The Restatement section 87, comment c states: "In view of the dangers of permitting a solemn written agreement to be invalidated by oral testimony which is easily fabricated, therefore, the option agreement is not invalidated by proof that the recited consideration was not in fact given." In view of the numerous instances in which the Restatement embraces rules which permit oral evidence to alter or terminate the legal effect of written instruments, solemn or otherwise, it is perhaps more likely that the authors were influenced by the other reason given, which is: "The signed writing has vital significance as a formality, while the ceremonial manual delivery of a dollar or a peppercorn is an inconsequential formality."

The Restatement also takes the position in section 88 that a mere recital of consideration is enough to support a promise to be surety for the performance of a contractual obligation.

It is suggested that there is no doctrinal reason or logic in the common law to relax the requirements of consideration for option contracts or guarantee contracts. Most courts continue to deny enforcement where the recital of consideration is proven to be false.

The Restatement includes option contracts supported by nominal consideration which was in fact given, option contracts in which there is a false recital of consideration, and the recital of consideration in the surety contract under the heading of "Contracts Without Consideration". (See Restatement Chapter 4, Topic 2.)

§ 2.39   Subsequent Promises to Perform Unenforceable Contracts

The following sections deal with the limited circumstances in which courts will enforce a new promise to perform an obligation that was originally not enforceable or that has become unenforceable or been discharged. In order to be bound by the new promise, the promisor must know or have reason to know the essential facts of the previous transaction, but there is no requirement that he have knowledge of the legal effect of these facts. The Restatement also classifies these subsequent promises as "Contracts Without Consideration". (See Restatement Chapter 4, Topic 2.)

In these circumstances there is no bargained consideration and the basis for enforcement of the new promise might be said to be the moral obligation of the promisor. However, use of the concept of moral obligation as a basis for enforcement of a promise is almost always limited to the specific situations described in the following sections.

§ 2.39.1   A New Promise to Pay a Debt Enforceable but for the Statute of Limitations

A new express or implied promise to pay a contractual or quasi-contractual debt barred by the statute of limitations is enforceable without new consideration. Many jurisdictions require the new promise to be in a signed writing. A new promise may be implied from a part payment of the debt or other acknowledgment so long as these acts are not qualified to negate or limit the implication of a promise to pay. The new promise or acknowledgment must be communicated to the creditor. A mere notation by the debtor in his records that he owes the amount is insufficient, as would be a statement to a stranger that the creditor is owed the money. And as discussed below, because the promise being sought to be enforced is the new promise, the claim of the promisee is limited to the terms of the new promise.

It should be noted that the primary purpose of statutes which limit the time within which legal actions may be brought is to avoid stale claims and permit people to discard old records. If a debtor has recently acknowledged an obligation and impliedly promised to pay it, then it is not a stale claim in the sense that it is old and forgotten by the parties. Thus, the purpose of the statute is not defeated by enforcing claims which debtors acknowledge to be unsatisfied and promise to pay.

§ 2.39.2 Debts Discharged in Bankruptcy

Common law permits the enforcement of a new promise to perform an obligation which was discharged in bankruptcy or which is in the process of being discharged in an existing bankruptcy proceeding. Unlike stale claims, the issue here is not one of recollection and available records. Thus, a mere acknowledgment of the validity of the claim and the fact that it has not been satisfied is not sufficient. However, an express and specific promise to perform all or part of a preexisting obligation discharged in bankruptcy is enforceable under contract law despite the absence of any new consideration.

This problem is the subject of specific legislation in the Federal Bankruptcy Reform Act of 1978. The statute requires, among other things, that the agreement to repay the debt contain a conspicuous statement that the debtor may rescind the agreement within a specified time frame and that under certain circumstances the bankruptcy court must approve the agreement as being in the best interests of the debtor and not imposing an undue hardship on the debtor. It will take an unusual set of circumstances to induce a bankruptcy judge to make such findings.

§ 2.39.3 Obligations Unenforceable Due to Statute of Frauds

If an obligation was originally unenforceable because the statute of frauds was not satisfied, and thereafter the obligor signs a memorandum sufficient to satisfy the statutory requirement, the obligation becomes enforceable. The consideration is found in the original oral contract. Some cases discuss the enforcement of the "new" promise contained in the writing and find consideration or a substitute for consideration in the unenforceable oral agreement. (See comment g and illustration 11 to Restatement § 86.)

§ 2.39.4 Promise to Perform Obligations That Were Voidable

If an original obligation was unenforceable because the promisor lacked capacity, a new promise made after the promisor has attained capacity will be enforced although there is no mutual assent or new consideration to support it. This same rule applies to other cases where a promisor had a defense, such as misrepresentation, mistake or undue influence. If after the facts are known or the disability has been removed the promisor promises to perform, this new promise can be enforced although there is no mutual assent or new consideration. A common example is found where a minor enters a voidable contract and then affirms the obligation (or a part of it) after attaining the age of majority. Enforceability again is based on the new promise and will be limited to the extent of the new

promise. In the case of a former infant who has
achieved majority, some jurisdictions may require
the new promise to be in a signed writing.

§ 2.40 Promise to Pay for Benefits Previously Conferred

The law of restitution recognizes an obligation
under certain limited circumstances to pay for benefits conferred where there was no enforceable contract. The basis of the legal right is "restitution"
but is also properly referred to as "unjust enrichment" and in certain cases can be labeled "quasi-
contract." Examples may include benefits conferred
by mistake such as a debtor accidentally paying to a
creditor more than is owing, or benefits conferred
with the expectation of compensation in an emergency such as an emergency room physician treating an unconscious accident victim. (The subject of
Restitution is covered in Chapter 10.)

It follows logically that if one is obligated under
the law of restitution to compensate another for a
benefit conferred, then a promise by the obligor to
pay a specific sum in satisfaction of a restitution
claim needs no additional consideration to be enforced. The promisee is giving up the right to enforce an unliquidated claim in restitution and accepting in lieu thereof a promise to pay a specific
sum in satisfaction of that debt. Nonetheless, Restatement section 86 treats the enforcement of such
promises under the heading of "Contracts Without
Consideration."

B. PROMISSORY ESTOPPEL

§ 2.41 Enforcement of Promises That Induce Reliance

Promises can be enforced based upon a concept commonly called "promissory estoppel". This concept is not based upon the existence of a bargain and therefore neither an agreement nor consideration are necessary. The obligation of the promisor arises because of a foreseeable change of position by the promisee in reliance on the promise and it is possible that the remedy will be measured by the extent of the promisee's reliance rather than the promisee's expectation.

Promissory estoppel had its genesis in promises made between parties where it was unlikely that there would be a bargained for exchange, where the foreseeability of the reliance was high, and that the reasonableness of the promisee's reliance was rather clear. The classic situations were gratuitous promises made to family members or to churches or charities.

One does not customarily bargain with one's grandchildren, or with a church or a charity, and expect some promise or performance from them in return for your promise. Therefore the availability and existence of the mechanism of consideration as the basis for promise enforcement is unlikely to be used.

Also, the relationship is such that the promisor is particularly likely to be able to foresee that the beneficiary will change position in reliance on the promise. The relationship alone makes it reasonable for the promisee to have changed position in reliance. If you can't trust your grandfather or a church member, whom can you trust? And if the promisor is a bailee, my goodness, you have entrusted your goods to the bailee's possession and can assume for example that as such the bailee will obtain the insurance on the goods as the bailee promised.

The principles that must be satisfied to apply promissory estoppel are summarized in Restatement section 90(1) which provides:

A promise which the promisor should reasonably expect to induce action or forbearance on the part of the promisee or a third person and which does induce such action or forbearance is binding if injustice can be avoided only by enforcement of the promise. The remedy granted for breach may be limited as justice requires.

Reliance upon a promise is a distinct basis for creation of contract rights and duties. As stated, it is not dependent upon finding any agreement nor any bargained exchange consideration. Legal historians have found reliance upon a promise to be a historical basis for an action of assumpsit. During the nineteenth century, the bargained exchange became the source of contract rights and duties. However, in the latter part of that century, decisions were reached in the United States in which gratuitous promises were found to be enforceable by one who had substantially changed position (by making significant expenditures or otherwise) as a result of reasonable and foreseeable reliance on the gratuitous promise. Since estoppel was the handiest concept available to explain the enforcement of promises which were not part of a bargained exchange, the phrase "promissory estoppel" was applied to describe the basis for the rights and duties recognized in these cases.

The application of section 90 involves finding that the promisee relied to his detriment. This detrimental reliance must not be confused with the legal detriment element of consideration. To find consideration, the legal detriment need not be harmful, can be of any magnitude, and must be bargained for. The detrimental reliance required to enforce a promise under section 90 must involve significant adverse consequences such that justice cries out for enforcement. The detrimental change of position was not incurred as part of any bargain. (Had it been bargained for, then consideration would be present and there would be no necessity to explore promissory estoppel.)

Providing some measure of recovery to one who has reasonably and foreseeably relied upon the promise of another is an appealing concept. The apparent logic and fairness of this proposition together with its appearance in the First and Second Restatements and in all major works on the subject of contracts would lead one to believe that it enjoys acceptance in all quarters. Such is not the case.

Promissory estoppel is a uniquely American concept. One English case (Central London Property Trust v. High Trees House, KBD (1947)) recognizes the concept, but that case limits its use to providing a defense setting forth the principle that promissory estoppel can be used as a shield but not as a sword. Some jurisdictions have historically limited the application of promissory estoppel to those situations mentioned above: intra-family transactions; philanthropic subscriptions made to educational, charitable or religious organizations; and, promises made by a bailee relating to the bailed goods and on which the bailor relies. These jurisdictions exhibit a reluctance to extend the enforcement of promises on the basis of reliance into other relationships and appear particularly reluctant to extend it into business relationships.

In earlier cases and under the view of the Restatement, First, the courts recognized rights only where there was substantial detriment incurred in reliance upon the promise and it was believed that the only available remedy for detrimental reliance was enforcement of the promise. A further expansion of the application of promissory estoppel was made possible by decisions which recognized an alternative remedy limiting the promisee to reliance damages. Relief can be granted in a greater number of cases if courts have the alternative of limiting the remedy to compensation for the reliance interest, for restitution, or for such other remedy as may be appropriate. The alternative of granting relief other than expectancy damages is recognized in the Restatement, Second, which modified the language of the Restatement, First, by adding this sentence in section 90: "The remedy granted for breach may be limited as justice requires." Also, the Restatement, Second, section 90 deleted the requirement that reliance produce "substantial" detriment.

Promissory estoppel has been used as a basis for enforcement of a charitable subscription where the facts of reliance were questionable at best. It might be concluded from these cases that the policy factors in favor of enforcing charitable subscriptions are sufficiently strong that minimal or tenuous reliance will be sufficient to permit enforcement of the promise. Cases also exist in which the act of getting married is found to be sufficient proof of reliance upon a gratuitous premarital promise. Restatement, Second section 90(2) takes the position that no proof of reliance is necessary in charitable subscription or marriage settlement cases.

Prevention of injustice is the stated underpinning of promissory estoppel cases. In determining whether it might be applicable in a given fact situation, it is necessary to determine whether injustice will result if the remedy is withheld.

§ 2.42   Reliance as a Basis for Holding Offers to be Irrevocable

After an initial period of reluctance to extend the concept of promissory estoppel to commercial transactions (see, for example, *James Baird Co. v. Gimbel Brothers* (2d Cir. 1933)), courts have come to recognize that an offer made in a commercial context may invite reliance by the offeree and lead to considerable injustice if revoked before the offeree can accept. A leading case which enforced a gratuitous promise not to revoke an offer in a commercial setting is *Drennan v. Star Paving Co.* (Cal. 1958). *Drennan* involved a general contractor preparing a bid for a government construction job. Pursuant to industry practice, the general contractor phoned various subcontractors to obtain bids (offers) to do various jobs. These subcontractors were aware that their bids, if low, would be used by the general to calculate its bid for the job. The defendant, a paving subcontractor did not expressly promise not to revoke its bid but such a promise was found to be reasonably implied. The general contractor relied upon this implied promise not to revoke by using the subcontractor's price in computing its own bid to a school district. The court found this detrimental reliance upon the subcontractor's implied promise not to revoke the offer was sufficient to make that implied promise enforceable. Thus, the subcontractor was bound by its implied promise not to revoke its offer until the bids to the school district had been opened and the general contractor had reasonable time and opportunity to accept the subcontractor's offer. Simply stated, reasonable and foreseeable reliance upon a promise not to revoke an offer is sufficient to create an option contract.

The period of irrevocability could be brief. If the general fails to accept the subcontractor's bid promptly after the contract is awarded to the general, the subcontractor is no longer bound. Any further negotiation or counter-offer by the general would permit the subcontractor to revoke. As thus qualified, the *Drennan* position has gained substantial acceptance.

The result of the *Drennan* case was adopted and perhaps expanded upon in Restatement section 87(2) which provides:

An offer which the offeror should reasonably expect to induce action or forbearance of a substantial character on the part of the offeree before acceptance and which does induce such action or forbearance is binding as an option contract to the extent necessary to avoid injustice.

Note that the language of the section presupposes that there is an offer and therefore what is contemplated is a bargained for exchange acceptance and that the degree of foreseeable and actual reliance must be of a "substantial character."

This subsection is not expressly limited to situations in which the offeror expressly or impliedly promises not to revoke the offer. One might reason that the offeror would not "reasonably expect" the offer to "induce action or forbearance of a substantial character" in the absence of at least an implied promise not to revoke.

§ 2.43 Remedies for Reliance in a Commercial Context

The most far-reaching application of promissory estoppel has been recognized in a few cases in which a right of action has been found to arise where a party was reasonably induced to rely on general statements and indefinite promises. This has occurred in a commercial setting in which both parties contemplated entering into a binding bargain. During the course of negotiations, one party made promises which were not sufficiently certain to constitute the basis for an enforceable bargain or which were made without the required manifestation of intent to be presently legally bound. However, the promises were sufficient to induce the other party to change position in reasonable reliance. When this foreseeable reliance occurred, an enforceable right was found to exist.

Commercial cases in which a remedy is granted based upon promissory estoppel fall into at least three identifiable categories.

1) One party to a transaction repeatedly holds out the prospect of a binding contract while encouraging the other party to engage in various activities that will purportedly facilitate entering an agreement. The relying party may be induced to buy property, to relocate, to borrow money or otherwise engage in conduct which will be highly detrimental if the anticipated transaction is not consummated. The hallmark of this transaction is that no definite promises were ever made. Since the promises in question were too uncertain to be the basis of an agreement, the available remedy was of necessity limited to reliance damages rather than the loss of the value of the unfulfilled promise. (See, for example, *Hoffman v. Red Owl Stores* (Wisc. 1965).)

2) One party to a transaction, usually a large corporation, uses a lower ranking employee as a negotiator making clear throughout the negotiations that no agreement shall be binding until approved by a higher ranking officer who is physically located in another city or otherwise unaccessible. The second party to the transaction knows that approval must come from "Mr. Big" but all dealings are with the local negotiator, the man on the scene. These cases usually involve an extended set of facts in which the second party gradually commits itself more and more in reliance upon the transaction being completed. These cases also usually involve a crucial point at which the local negotiator tells the second party that the deal is set. It is all "just a rubber stamp." Or, "don't ask any questions or you will mess up the deal." When the corporation suddenly loses interest in the deal, Mr. Big simply says no. A number of jurisdictions are finding a basis for recovery under the heading of promissory estoppel. (Mahoney v. Delaware McDonald's Corp. (8th Cir. 1985).)

3) The parties execute a formal document, perhaps labeled a "letter of intent," which may contain most or even all of the terms to be included in a proposed transaction, but the document clearly indicates that neither party intends to be legally bound until some further approval process has occurred. Thereafter, one of the parties relies upon the transaction going forward and the other party abandons the negotiations. In *Channel Home Ctrs. v. Gross-*

man (3d Cir.1986), a letter of intent contained clear language that denied any existing obligations and stated that any reliance would be at the relying party's own risk and expense, language that was drafted by the plaintiff. However, the court found that by signing the letter of intent, the parties undertook an obligation to negotiate in good faith to attempt to complete the transaction. Since defendant had simply terminated the negotiations and entered into an agreement with a competitor of plaintiff, plaintiff was allowed to recover reliance damages.

When you have completed your study of this chapter, you may wish to analyze questions 11–17 at the end of this book and compare your analysis with the one given there.

CHAPTER 3

STATUTE OF FRAUDS

A. CONTRACTS WITHIN THE STATUTE

§ 3.1 Statute of Frauds; History

In 1677, the English adopted "An Act for the Prevention of Frauds and Perjuries." This legislation contained provisions on a number of subjects including two sections which imposed the requirement of a writing for certain types of contractual obligations. The subjects covered are presumably those that produced serious litigation in the Seventeenth Century. These two sections provided:

Sec. 4. * * * no action shall be brought (1) whereby to charge any executor or administrator upon any special promise, to answer damages out of his own estate; (2) or whereby to charge the defendant upon any special promise to answer for the debt, default or miscarriages of another person; (3) or to charge any person upon any agreement made upon consideration of marriage; (4) or upon any contract or sale of lands, tenements or hereditaments, or any interest in or concerning them; (5) or upon any agreement that is not to be performed within the space of one year from the making thereof; (6) unless the agreement upon which such action shall be brought, or some memorandum or note thereof, shall be in writing, and signed by the party to be charged therewith, or some other person thereunto by him lawfully authorized.

Sec. 17. * * * no contract for the sale of any goods, wares and merchandises, for the price of ten pounds sterling or upwards, shall be allowed to be good, except the buyer shall accept part of the goods so sold, and actually receive the same, or give something in earnest to bind the bargain, or in part payment, or that some note or memorandum in writing of the said bargain be made and signed by the parties to be charged by such contract, or their agents thereunto lawfully authorized.

Except for Louisiana, all American states have substantially copied section 4 with Maryland and New Mexico adopting it by judicial decision. A comprehensive list of these state statutes can be found in Restatement Chapter Five, Statutory Note.

The provisions of section 17 found their way into the Uniform Sales Act with the sum of $500 being substituted for 10 pounds sterling. With some significant modifications, this law is now embodied in section 2–201 of the U.C.C.

England repealed almost all of its writing requirements in 1954 and this may be an international trend. The 1980 Vienna Convention on the International Sale of Goods (CISG) permits enforcement of oral contracts for the sale of goods in international transactions although individual countries are permitted to opt out of this provision. One of the earlier drafts of the proposed revision to Article 2 had deleted any writing requirement for a contract for the sale of goods. However, the proposed revisions to Article 2 of the U.C.C. retain a writing requirement and the tendency in many states has been to extend the writing requirement to additional types of transaction, many times with the goal of consumer protection. It is not at all clear that American legislators will be able to overcome the impulse to tell people that they "should" put their contracts in writing. Curiously, we are joined in this position by countries who presently have or have recently had communist governments.

A notable exception to the continued vitality of a writing requirement is section 8–113 of the U.C.C. which provides:

> A contract or modification of a contract for the sale or purchase of a security is enforceable whether or not there is a signed writing or record authenticated by a party against whom enforcement is sought, even if the contract or modification is not capable of performance within one year of its making.

The official comment to this section offers this explanation:

> With the increasing use of electronic means of communication, the statute of frauds is unsuited to the realities of the securities business. For securities transactions, whatever benefits a statute of frauds may play in filtering out fraudulent

claims are outweighed by the obstacles it places in the development of modern commercial practices in the securities business.

A requirement of a writing can serve three functions: evidentiary, cautionary, and channeling. The original purpose of the requirement of a writing for the enforcement of certain contracts was undoubtedly evidentiary, to provide evidence of the existence and terms of the contract. Incorporation of the requirement in sections of an act adopted "for the prevention of frauds and perjuries" is a fair indication of such purpose and historians have indicated that there is no evidence of any other purpose. However, courts have permitted enforcement of contracts within the statute based upon oral testimony as to the contents of a lost writing (§ 3.3), and it is apparent from this and other accepted methods for avoiding the application of the statute that it does not always fulfill an evidentiary purpose today. The requirement of a signed writing undoubtedly has a cautionary purpose guarding the promisor to some degree against ill-considered promises. The requirement no doubt also serves what has been characterized as a channeling function by providing a form or format by which people undertake binding obligations for such transactions as the sale of real property. In the process of reducing an oral agreement to writing, people might naturally be expected to cover more details and refine their agreement in more precise terms. By requiring a writing, those agreements intended to be binding are distinguished from those which were intended as tentative or exploratory expressions of intention.

What purpose or function the statute of frauds is designed to serve should be a significant inquiry when an attempt is made to formulate rules permitting its avoidance.

§ 3.2 Contracts Within the Statute of Frauds

While all common law jurisdictions in the United States have adopted writing requirements roughly paralleling the original statutory enactments, the details of the coverage vary from state to state. Most states have also adopted a substantial number of additional writing requirements. These tend to be scattered in many different statutes relating to varied subject matter running from government contracts to consumer protection statutes.

Basic statute of frauds sections might include the following:

(1) An agreement that by its terms in not to be performed within a year from the making thereof.

(2) A special promise to answer for the debt default, or miscarriage of another . . . .

(3) An agreement made upon consideration of marriage.

(4) An agreement for the leasing for a longer period than one year, or for the sale of real property, or of an interest therein, such an agreement, if made by an agent of the party sought to be charged, is invalid, unless the authority of the

agent is in writing, subscribed by the party sought to be charged.

(5) An agreement authorizing or employing an agent, broker, or any other person to purchase or sell real estate, or to lease real estate for a longer period than one year, or to procure, introduce, or find a purchaser or seller of real estate or a lessee or lessor of real estate where the lease is for a longer period than one year, for compensation or a commission.

(6) An agreement that by its terms is not to be performed during the lifetime of the promisor.

(7) An agreement by a purchaser of real property to pay an indebtedness secured by a mortgage or deed of trust upon the property purchased, unless assumption of the indebtedness by the purchaser is specifically provided for in the conveyance of the property.

To this list must be added the writing requirements from the U.C.C. which include:

1. A contract for the sale of goods for the price of $500 or more (§ 2–201);

2. A contract for sale of other personal property to the extent of enforcement by way of action or defense beyond $5,000 (§ 1–206); and

3. A lease of goods in the total amount of $1,000 or more (§ 2A–201).

4. An agreement which creates a security interest in personal property if it is not in posses-

sion of the secured party, and crops growing or to be grown, or timber to be cut (§ 9–203(1)(a)).

In addition, different states have additional classifications of agreements which are the subject of writing requirements which may include:

1. An agreement by which a principal appoints an agent to execute a contract which is itself within a provision of the statute of frauds (a so-called "equal dignities" rule);

2. Promises to pay debts, the enforcement of which was barred by the statute of limitations;

3. Promises to pay debts discharged in bankruptcy;

4. Numerous types of consumer transactions including sales warranties, contracts for vehicle repairs, detailed data relating to loans and other consumer transactions; and

5. Specific writing requirements in some states in particular areas of law relating to everything from contractors' bids on government construction projects to contracts for the purchase of edible nuts. (For penalties imposed upon nut buyers in California who fail to execute written contracts with certain specific terms, see Cal. Food & Ag. Code §§ 62801, et seq.)

The list of contracts for which a writing is required varies from state to state. The subject matter covered varies widely and is not necessarily intuitive. The only proper approach is to raise a warning flag anytime one encounters a fact situation in which a party is attempting to enforce an oral contract. The possibility of a writing requirement should always be considered.

§ 3.2.1 A Contract That, by Its Terms, Cannot Be Performed Within One Year

The one year period referred to in this section is measured from the time of the making of the agreement, not from the date performance is scheduled to begin.

If A enters into an oral contract on June 1 to work for X for one year commencing July 10, the contract is within the statute of frauds and a writing is required. If performance were to begin immediately, the oral contract would be enforceable. An oral contract with Performer to work for one year commencing immediately would be enforceable notwithstanding the absence of a writing, but a contract entered into today booking Performer to work for one week thirteen months from now would be required to be in writing.

In addition to noting the time from which the one year period is measured, one must also be concerned about what is meant by "by its terms" and what is meant by "cannot be performed." Consider a hypothetical situation in which the parties orally contracted for a major construction project which will in fact take several years but with no contract term that precludes performance within one year. There is substantial case authority for the position that this contract is not by its terms incapable of being performed within one year. As for "by its terms" the test is whether the oral contract expressly requires performance to extend beyond the measuring one-year time period. Many courts ask simply whether the terms of the contract preclude performance within one year. Under this interpretation, the statute does not preclude enforcement of an oral contract to build the Empire State Building or the Grand Coulee Dam unless the express terms of the contract preclude completion of performance within one year. Suppose X Co. orally agrees to insure A's house against loss by fire for three years. A court could find that the contract is capable of performance within one year since the house may burn and be totally destroyed tomorrow.

There is a different line of cases that look to the actual intended duration of the contract. Thus a contract by which an apartment house owner agreed to hire a first-year law student to manage the apartments for as long as he remained in law school could be found to be within the one-year provisions of the statute of frauds because the parties contemplated a three-year educational program and thus intended the contract performance to extend for something in excess of two years from the date of its making.

The related problem of what is meant by "performance" is illustrated by the following. An agreement to pay an annuity for life is capable of performance within one year since the promisee may die at any time. However, a contract to support a sixteen-year-old minor until the attainment of age twenty-one is within the statute of frauds since full performance cannot be had unless the minor lives five more years. An early death by the minor would merely constitute a discharge of performance. Tantalizing questions arise if you assume a promise to support the sixteen-year-old for life or until age twenty-one, whichever is shorter. Or consider a contract which is orally agreed to be for 5 years, but gives one of the parties the right to terminate the contract by giving 30 days notice. The contract could be terminated within one year by the giving of notice and therefore its duration could be less than one year. The problem arises as to how a court characterizes the event of giving notice of termination. If it is characterized as exercising a right to determine the length of time required for performance of the contract, the oral contract is enforceable against both parties for the 5–year term (if the right to terminate is not exercised). However, if the event of giving notice of termination is characterized as an event that could terminate the contract rightfully but prematurely prior to the 5–year term, then the contract is not capable of being fully performed within one year and is unenforceable from its inception unless the statute of frauds is satisfied.

Hopper v. Lennen & Mitchell, Inc. (9th Cir.1944) involved an oral five-year employment contract in which the employer had the right to terminate by giving four weeks notice at the end of any twenty-six week period. The court permitted the employee to enforce this contract holding that it was not within the statute of frauds because if it were terminated at the end of the first twenty-six week period, it would be fully performed within one year. Consider what the result would have been had the employer been suing for damages for breach of the entire five-year contract period. One could hardly justify the conclusion that the contract is capable of being performed within one year if enforcement is sought by one party but is not capable of being performed within one year if enforcement is sought by the other. Yet, holding an employee bound to a five-year oral employment contract would appear to be a clear violation of legislative intent. When the original statute of frauds was enacted over three hundred years ago, indentured servants and their long-term contracts were presumably a social issue of some significance.

§ 3.2.2   A Promise to Discharge the Duty of Another; Exceptions Thereto

The statute of frauds writing requirement applies to a promise made by a surety or guarantor to a creditor to pay the debt or perform the obligation of the principal debtor if the creditor has reason to know of the surety relationship. In many jurisdictions a similar statute of frauds requirement protects executors or other personal representatives who promise to pay out of their own funds the obligations of the estate which they represent.

In order for there to exist a "promise to pay the debt of another," there must be a principal debtor who is primarily liable. If R says to E, the owner of a shoe store, "Sell a pair of shoes to X, and I will pay you," there is no writing requirement. The promise of R is the primary promise, not a guarantee of any obligation of another. If R said to E, "Sell X a pair of shoes, and if he does not pay you, I will," the promise of R is collateral to the primary liability of the principal debtor, X. R is a surety or guarantor, and his promise is within the statute of frauds.

The writing requirement does not apply to the promise to pay the debt of another if the promisor's main purpose is to obtain an immediate and direct economic benefit or advantage for himself. Assume that X, a contractor, has a substantial obligation owing to Lumber Co. (L) for prior purchases and that L denies further credit to X. To hasten completion of his home that X is building, Homeowner (HO) phones L requesting that X be given additional credit and promising to guarantee X's obligations. This promise is not within the statute of frauds because HO's main purpose is to obtain a direct economic benefit for himself.

The writing requirement of the statute of frauds does not apply to a promise to pay the debt of another where the promisor is promising to pay with funds which belong to the debtor or funds which the promisor holds for the purpose of paying the debtor's obligations.

If the creditor accepts a promise in satisfaction of the previously existing obligation of a third party, this does not involve a suretyship arrangement and is not within the statute of frauds. Thus, if the new owner of a business promises to pay the rent in exchange for the landlord agreeing to release the former tenant from his remaining obligations, this is not within the statute of frauds. It is a novation and not a suretyship agreement (§ 13.3).

§ 3.2.3 A Contract in Consideration of Marriage

Contractual promises made in consideration of marriage, other than mutual promises to marry, must be in writing. Hence, A's oral promise to marry B in return for B's promise to marry A need not be in writing. However, if in consideration of B's promise to marry A, A promises to marry B and promises to transfer to B one-half of A's stock options in A's company, the contract would have to be in writing. And D's promise to pay $50,000 to A if A marries B is within the statute.

Care must be taken to distinguish between marriage which is promised as part of the consideration and marriage which is just a condition to the performance of a contract. For example, assume A and B are engaged and subsequently A and B orally agree that when they get married, A will sell A's house and give B one half of the proceeds and that the couple will then live in B's house. Marriage is not part of the consideration for either party's promise. Marriage is merely a condition. Therefore the oral agreement would not be subject to the marriage provision of the statute of frauds.

§ 3.2.4 A Contract for the Transfer of an Interest in Realty

The critical element of this section is the analysis of what does and does not constitute an "interest in real property." Promises to sell or transfer legal or equitable interests in real property are within the statute. However, the following are not within the statute: (1) An agreement to share profits from the sale of real property; (2) A partnership agreement to deal in real property; (3) Agreements settling boundary disputes which have been implemented by marking or use of the land; (4) A license, even though irrevocable because of improvements. A determination must be made as to whether an interest is an easement, a profit or a license, because unlike a license, easements and profits are subject to the statute.

The statute will apply not only to a promise to transfer but also to a promise to buy an interest in realty.

§ 3.2.5 An Oral One–Year Lease

Most jurisdictions include within the statute of frauds leases of an interest in land with a duration of more than one year. Assume that L and T enter into an oral contract for a one-year lease to commence on the first day of the following month. This contract does not involve an interest in real property of more than one-year's duration, but it is a contract that is not capable of being performed within one year of the day of making. Some jurisdictions, probably the majority, hold that the dominant nature of the agreement is an interest in land, and since it does not come within the statute of frauds as an interest lasting beyond one year, there is no writing requirement. (See Restatement § 125, comment b.) Other jurisdictions, e.g. California, hold that since the contract cannot be performed within one year, it comes within a section of the statute and a writing is required.

§ 3.2.6 A Contract That Cannot Be Performed During the Lifetime of the Promisor

This provision is included in the statute of frauds in a minority of jurisdictions. It provides the estate of a decedent with some measure of protection against oral claims. For example, assume R orally promises to pay E $5,000 in return for E's promise to attend R's funeral The statute requires a writing since R's duty to perform will not arise until after R's death. Note that in these jurisdictions, a contract to devise real property receives double coverage under the statute, since it is both a contract to transfer an interest in realty as well as a contract which, by its terms, cannot be performed during the lifetime of the promisor.

§ 3.2.7 A Contract for the Sale of Goods for the Price of $500 or More

Section 2–201 of the U.C.C. is the relevant statutory provision. It will apply only if there is a contract for the sale of goods the price of which is $500 or more. Such a contract is "not enforceable by way of action or defense unless there is some writing sufficient to indicate that a contract for sale has been made between the parties and signed by the party against whom enforcement is sought or by his authorized agent or broker."

Section 2A–201 requires a signed writing for any lease of goods to be enforceable in the total amount of $1,000 or more.

B.   SATISFACTION OF THE WRITING REQUIREMENT
§ 3.3   Sufficiency of the Written Memo

Restatement section 131 provides:

Unless additional requirements are prescribed by the particular statute, a contract within the Statute of Frauds is enforceable if it is evidenced by any writing, signed by or on behalf of the party to be charged, which

(a) reasonably identifies the subject matter of the contract,

(b) is sufficient to indicate that a contract with respect thereto has been made between the parties or offered by the signer to the other party, and

(c) states with reasonable certainty the essential terms of the unperformed promises in the contract.

Note that the writing to be sufficient must identify the subject matter, evidence a contract between the parties or an offer by the signer and also contain "the essential terms of the unperformed promises in the contract."

However, if the contract is the for the sale of goods, U.C.C. section 2–201 requires only that the writing be sufficient to indicate that a contract for sale has been made between the parties. However, this section limits enforcement to the quantity shown in the writing and thus a quantity term must be included in the writing or be determinable from the writing.

The writing need not be a single document, but may consist of several writings including unsigned writings that were prepared by the party to be charged (or an agent thereof) and which clearly refer to those which are signed. The writing(s) need not be made for the purpose of memorializing the contract and need never have been delivered to or come into the possession of the party who is seeking to enforce the contract. The writing need not be made at the time the contract is consummated. An intra-company signed memorandum to the production department advising of a contract with X for 100 widgets could serve as a writing sufficient to satisfy the statute.

Courts have permitted the use of oral testimony to establish the existence of a lost writing to satisfy the statute of frauds. This enforcement of contracts where the writing cannot be produced clearly derogates from the evidentiary function of the statute, but is in accord with the cautionary and channeling functions.

Some court opinions have had difficulty with the writing requirement in cases in which the party to be charged has signed only an offer. The theory is that the writing evidences only an offer and not a contract. The better result is to find that the defendant's signature on the offer is sufficient to comply with the purpose and function of the statute of frauds. The latter portion of subsection (b) of Restatement section 131 supports this result.

Since "writing" is defined in U.C.C. section 1-201(39) to include "printing, typewriting or any other intentional reduction to tangible form," it would appear that dictating the terms of a contract onto a tape could constitute a "writing." If self-identification by name and the use of voice print for identification can be found to satisfy the signature requirement, a tape recording can constitute a signed writing.

Storage of data on a computer is "intentional reduction to tangible form" and the person who makes the computer entry in a business organization will ordinarily have some symbol that is adopted to authenticate the entry and identify its source. Assuming such authentication, such entries should be sufficient to constitute a signed written memorandum of the transaction. Given the virtually universal use of computers to record information that formerly was the subject of "file memos," utilizing data stored in computers to establish the authenticity of a contract and satisfy the formality requirement of a "writing" does not appear to be a distortion of the legislative intent nor of the language of the statute. Imaginative lawyering should lead to a discovery of a "signed writing" in many situations which on the surface appear to involve nothing more than an oral contract. Current court decisions indicate that not all of the judiciary is

ready to accept electronic storage as the equal of a
piece of paper.

There is statutory recognition of electronic recor-
dation replacing the traditional "writing" in some
circumstances. For example, U.C.C. section 5–
102(a)(14) applicable to letters of credit provides:

> "Record" means information that is inscribed on
> a tangible medium, or that is stored in an elec-
> tronic or other medium and is retrievable in
> perceivable form.

It is likely that the revisions to Article 2 will
replace "writing" with "record" with a similar definition. See section 3.5

§ 3.4 The Signature

A signature may include any symbol executed or
adopted by a party with present intention to authenticate a writing. This includes initial and im-
printed signatures and under a liberal reading
would also include letterhead stationery or a firm
logo on documents such as purchase orders. Such
logos and letterheads are "symbols" and they are
adopted with the intention of "authenticating" the
source of the document in question.

The writing may be signed by an agent although
some jurisdictions require that the agent's authority to sign must itself be established in a signed
writing.

The writing need only be signed by the party to
be charged, which is the person against whom enforcement is sought. This leads to situations in

which one party can enforce the contract while the other cannot. Courts find no problem concerning the impact of this situation upon the issue of consideration. If the underlying oral contract is a valid contract, then the fact that one party cannot enforce it because of the existence of some defense does not destroy the bargain. However, there is certainly a legitimate concern with the fairness of this result. The careful party promptly sends a written confirmation of an oral contract (or at least signs a memo for the files) while the slovenly soul does not bother with such details. The result is that the careless party can enforce the contract against the party who signed a written confirmation. Even if the writing is merely a signed memo that the defendant placed in its own files, this is sufficient to permit enforcement against that party.

§ 3.4.1 Signed Confirmation Sent by One Merchant to Another Merchant

In a sale of goods between merchants, a writing that is sufficient to make the contract enforceable against the person who created it can be enforced against the other party if that other party receives a copy and fails to object in writing within ten days. Section 2–201(2) produces this result if the following requirements are met:

1.   the contract is for the sale of goods; and

2.   both parties are merchants; and

3.   one merchant has, within a reasonable time of the making of the oral contract, sent a signed

writing which would satisfy the statute as against the sender; and

4. the writing was received by the other merchant; and

5. the receiving merchant failed to send a written notice of objection within ten days of the date of receipt of the confirmation.

The effect of the above is to make the memo which satisfied the statute of frauds as against the sender also effective to satisfy the statute of frauds as against the recipient even though the recipient did not sign it.

§ 3.5 Proposed U.C.C. Revisions: the "Record"

The proposed revision of the U.C.C. has been discussed in section 2.18. As noted therein, it is proposed that the terms "writing" and "written contract" be replaced by the term "record." "Records" will include not only things that are "inscribed on a tangible medium" which corresponds at least generally to our past notions of what is a "writing," but will also include "information * * * that is stored in an electronic or other medium and is retrievable in perceivable form." While Article 2 of the U.C.C. is applicable only to transactions in goods, its provisions can be very influential in other cases. Creation of this new concept and category of "records" will likely induce all courts to recognize that the formality requirements and special rules that historically have been associated with "writings" now must be extended to modern methods of preserving information.

C. AVOIDANCE OF THE WRITING REQUIREMENT
§ 3.6 Basis for Avoidance of Writing Requirement

The statute of frauds requires a signed writing in many circumstances. Many people ignore this requirement making oral contracts upon which they rely. When performance does not occur, the question is whether there is some basis for granting a remedy despite the absence of a writing.

Several statutes that create writing requirements contain specific provisions that permit enforcement in certain circumstances even though the party to be charged has not signed a writing. In succeeding sections we will analyze various subsections of U.C.C. section 2–201 which contains at least four such specific exceptions.

Common law decisions have created rules for the enforcement of contracts or the granting of some remedy based upon factors which courts have found to be sufficiently compelling. Proof that the plaintiff incurred substantial detriment by relying upon the oral contract or perhaps by relying upon a representation of fact such as "the signed contract is in the mail" has been the most commonly utilized exception to the statute of frauds created by the judiciary.

The following sections deal with special situations that have been found to justify enforcement of oral contracts. One should distinguish between statutorily created rules that permit enforcement of oral contracts which will be universally recognized and court-created exceptions. The latter are resisted by some courts because they derogate from the apparently clear intent of the legislature. This can be a particular problem when dealing with statutes such as U.C.C. section 2–201 where in subsection (1) the statute itself states rather clearly that the *only* exceptions to the writing requirement are found in that section.

§ 3.6.1 Effect of Part Performance; Sale of Goods

The statute of frauds does not prevent enforcement of contracts for the sale of goods to the extent that payment has been made and accepted or the goods have been received and accepted. The original statute of frauds (§ 3.1) and most pre-U.C.C. statutes provided that part performance made the entire contract enforceable, but U.C.C. section 2–201(3)(c) makes the contract enforceable only to the extent that performance has been tendered and accepted. Caution is needed here as to what constitutes "acceptance" of the goods by the buyer and one must consult U.C.C. section 2–606.

Assume that B and S enter into an oral contract for the sale of 100 gross of pencils for ten cents each or $1,440. Thereafter S delivers and B accepts one gross of pencils. The contract is enforceable to the extent of one gross and S can enforce B's duty to pay $14.40. The balance of the oral contract remains unenforceable absent some other basis for avoiding the writing requirement.

The U.C.C. also provides that the writing requirement does not preclude enforcement of a contract for specially manufactured goods that are not suitable for sale to others in the ordinary course of the seller's business, once the seller has made a substantial beginning on their manufacture or commitments for their procurement (§ 2–201(3)(a)). The party seeking to enforce the contract must establish circumstances reasonably indicating that the goods were intended for the buyer.

§ 3.6.2 Effect of Part Performance; Real Property

Failure to comply with the statute of frauds will not preclude enforcement of a contract for the sale of land where there has been a change of possession referable to the sale and the buyer has made permanent improvements on the real property. This is referred to as "part performance" despite the fact that the critical element, making improvements, is not really part of the performance called for in the contract. (See Restatement, § 129, comment a.) Some jurisdictions will accept part performance in lieu of the required writing where the buyer has made rather minor improvements or paid a portion of the purchase price in addition to taking possession. Case law in different states varies widely as to what acts of part performance are sufficient to make an oral contract for an interest in real property enforceable.

§ 3.6.3 Full Performance; One–Year Provision

Part performance does not make enforceable an oral contract which cannot by its terms be performed within one year. However, once one party has completed full performance, the one-year provision does not prevent enforcement of the return promise.

If a transaction involves an offer for a unilateral contract to be accepted by performance of an act that will take more than one year, the one-year statute of frauds provision is generally held not to be applicable. If one adopts the theory that the unilateral contract is not formed until performance is completed, then the contract is not incapable of being performed within one year from the time of its making as the promisee has already completed performance as of the time of making. And if it is the promisor's promise that cannot be performed within one year of the date of the making of the contract, the fact that the promisee has already fully performed takes the contract out of the statute of frauds.

§ 3.6.4 Reliance as a Basis for Avoiding the Statute of Frauds

A well established line of cases has permitted enforcement of oral contracts that are within the statute of frauds where the promisor has made a representation pertaining to the writing that would be necessary and the party seeking enforcement has changed position to his detriment in reliance upon that representation. These cases indicate that the party who would assert the statute of frauds as a defense is estopped from doing so because of the representation which he made and upon which the other party reasonably relied. Estoppel has been applied where there was reliance on a representation that a writing will be executed; that a writing has been executed; that the statute of frauds will not be asserted as a defense or that the statute of frauds is not applicable to the transaction in question. The more difficult question is whether an estoppel arises if the other party simply relied upon the making of the oral contract itself.

The Restatement provides:

Sec. 139. Enforcement by Virtue of Action in Reliance

(1) A promise which the promisor should reasonably expect to induce action or forbearance on the part of the promisee or a third person and which does induce the action or forbearance is enforceable notwithstanding the Statute of Frauds if injustice can be avoided only by enforcement of the promise. The remedy granted for breach is to be limited as justice requires.

(2) In determining whether injustice can be avoided only by enforcement of the promise, the following circumstances are significant:

(a) the availability and adequacy of other remedies, particularly cancellation and restitution;

(b) the definite and substantial character of the action or forbearance in relation to the remedy sought;

(c) the extent to which the action or forbearance corroborates evidence of the making and terms of the promise, or the making and terms are otherwise established by clear and convincing evidence;

(d) the reasonableness of the action or forbearance;

(e) the extent to which the action or forbearance was foreseeable by the promisor.

Except for one word which does not appear to be of consequence, subsection (1) restates the elements of Restatement section 90(1), which as you recall is used to make a promise enforceable notwithstanding the absence of consideration (§ 2.41). However, subsection (2) expands upon the plaintiff's burden of proof beyond anything required in section 90. The comment to section 139 states:

Like Section 90 this section states a flexible principle, but the requirement of consideration is more easily displaced than the requirement of the writing. * * *

Referring to subsection (2), the comment states:

Each factor relates either to the extent to which reliance furnishes a compelling substantive basis for relief in addition to the expectations created by the promise or to the extent to which the circumstances satisfy the evidentiary purpose of the Statute and fulfill any cautionary, deterrent and channeling functions it may serve.

Analysis of existing case law indicates that the courts in many jurisdictions are unwilling to find that a party is estopped from asserting the statute of frauds as a defense where the other relied upon nothing more than the existence of the oral contract. The apparent cause of the courts' reluctance to accept this position is that it could result in a virtual judicial repeal of the statute of frauds as a defense. Most estoppel cases purport to be based on reliance upon some additional statement or promise as discussed at the start of this section.

One can make a credible argument that in all of these estoppel cases, the person who changes position in reliance is in fact relying upon the oral contract itself rather than some ancillary promise or representation relating to a writing. The Restatement now provides authority for courts to recognize such reliance on the oral contract as sufficient to preclude a statute of frauds defense, and there is a substantial body of case law that takes this position.

Even assuming that facts exist to establish a basis for estoppel, there have been many cases which have addressed the issue of whether estoppel should be applied to a sale of goods. This is because U.C.C. section 2–201 purports to contain an exclusive list of exceptions to the writing requirement but does not make any reference to the use of estoppel. The majority of cases that have addressed this issue have concluded that estoppel can be applied to prevent a party to a contract for the sale of goods from asserting successfully the statute of frauds. These cases so holding have relied upon section 1–103 of the U.C.C.

§ 3.7 Judicial Approach to Enforcement of the Statute of Frauds

The statute of frauds is a defense. It is raised by a promisor to prevent enforcement of a promise that has not been performed. In a trial involving contract law, the plaintiff must first prove the existence of a contract, the occurrence or excuse of all conditions precedent to the defendant's duty to perform, and the fact that defendant failed to perform thereby causing damages to the plaintiff. If any of these points is not proven, plaintiff has no case. There is no need to discuss defenses.

Assuming that the plaintiff is successful in avoiding a dismissal of the case prior to the commencement of the trial, by the time one arrives at the point in the trial court proceedings where the court addresses the issue of a writing requirement, the evidence will ordinarily have already established the existence of an oral contract under which the defendant had an apparent duty to perform but failed to do so. Now we turn to the defendant's argument that there should be no liability because the contract should not be enforced due to the lack of a writing.

The statute of frauds thus comes up in the context of the defendant trying to avoid its promise because of what many people view as a technicality, that being the absence of a sufficient signed writing. Very few people, judges included, enjoy seeing cases won or lost on the basis of a technicality. The statute of frauds issue often presents itself as the question whether we are going to let this contract breacher "sneak out" of his obligations because of this technicality. Most people believe that one should "keep his word" and that contract duties should be performed, whether oral or written. Therefore, when a judge finds that the parties in fact had an oral contract which the defendant failed to perform, the judge may well be motivated to find a way to enforce it.

Legislators see a writing requirement from a different perspective. The problem is presented in terms of what we think people should do. Our representatives are encouraged to vote to add new writing requirements to contract law with the argument: "People should put contracts for important subjects like this in writing." It is hard to deny that this is what folks "should" do, so the majority votes "yes."

Judges deal with the problems that are created by what people actually do. Courts have the task of dealing with actual cases. These do not involve what people "should" do but rather what certain people in fact did do in the particular case before the court. If the court finds that both parties orally agreed to perform certain promises, it does no good to preach about the virtues of putting contracts in writing. The judge must decide whether the court is going to recognize any contract rights given what the parties did do.

Where there has been partial performance or reliance upon an oral contract, many argue that justice requires a better answer than simply saying: "Case dismissed." Thus, there is a significant body of case law that avoids the writing requirement by finding a basis to give a remedy where the equities of the case seem to require it. However, several jurisdictions have refused to circumvent or "erode" the statute of frauds noting that the legislature has created the requirement of a writing signed by the party to be charged, and it is the task of the legislature to establish exceptions if there are to be any. Some of these decisions take the position that experienced parties know the requirement of a writing and therefore reliance upon an oral contract simply cannot be reasonable.

§ 3.8 Effectiveness of the Unenforceable Oral Agreement

While many state statutes describe the contract that is not embodied in a signed writing as being "void," such contracts have considerable legal force and the lack of a writing may be considered as only rendering the oral contract unenforceable. The oral contract is in fact valid. If a party does not timely assert absence of a writing as a defense in accordance with the jurisdiction's rules of civil procedure, this defense may be deemed to be lost or waived. If the contract were truly "void" then the exceptions should not operate to make a "void" contract enforceable.

The absence of a writing is a personal defense in that only a party to a contract or his successor in interest can assert the statute of frauds to challenge the enforceability of the contract. Thus, an oral contract to buy a house can give the buyer an insurable interest. If the house burns before title passes, the insurance company cannot challenge the buyer's interest in the property on the basis of the statute of frauds. The tort of interference with contractual relationships can be found despite the fact the contract is oral. The existence of an unenforceable oral agreement may be introduced into evidence in any action for purposes other than its enforcement.

§ 3.9 Enforcement of Admitted Oral Contracts Under the U.C.C.

The U.C.C. provides that a party who admits the making of an oral contract cannot rely upon a statute of frauds defense. Section 2–201(3)(b) provides:

(3) A contract which does not satisfy the requirements of subsection (1) but which is valid in other respects is enforceable * * *

    (b) if the party against whom enforcement is sought admits in his pleading, testimony or otherwise in court that a contract for sale was made, but the contract is not enforceable under this provision beyond the quantity of goods admitted; * * *

If the purpose of the statute of frauds is viewed as solely evidentiary, then the thrust of this subsection will be appreciated. However, whatever cautionary or channeling functions the statute of frauds serves are destroyed by this Code provision that makes oral contracts enforceable against all honest people with decent memories.

When you have completed your study of this chapter, you may wish to analyze questions 18–22 at the end of this book and compare your analysis with the one given there.

CHAPTER 4

CONTRACT INTERPRETATION

A. GENERAL INTERPRETATION PROBLEMS

§ 4.1 Basic Considerations: Subjective and Objective Intent

The primary concern of contract law is the protection of the reasonable expectations of persons who have become parties to the contract. Protecting reasonable expectations is easier said than done. It obviously requires that a court determine what expectations are in fact reasonable. For example, if a seller of goods makes a statement which causes the buyer to believe that the goods are of a certain quality, then the buyer has expectations of receiving such goods. If the seller did not in fact intend that its words be understood to communicate the meaning which the buyer inferred from those words, then the expectations of the two parties will be different. If this difference becomes a source of dispute then a court has two choices: It may find that there is simply no agreement and thus no contract, or it must find that the expectations of at least one of the parties will not be met. Some authorities would hold that a court might find that

224

the true meaning of the contract is something different from what either party expected.

In many cases contract disputes that arises between the parties will involve the meaning of the language used by the parties. Interpretation of oral contracts is a matter for the trier of fact, meaning the jury if there is one. Since the terms of oral contracts are usually remembered somewhat hazily, figuring out what was said often becomes more critical than determining what the words mean. Interpretation of written contracts is a question of law and is therefore done by the judge and reviewed *de novo* by appellate court judges. The discussion which follows refers primarily to written contracts or contracts in which the terms at issue were in writing.

Assume that M owns Old Acre, a farm with a barn on it. M recently bought New Acre on which there existed an old dilapidated barn. M sent a letter to X offering $1,000 "if you will tear down my old barn." Not knowing of the purchase of New Acre, X tore down the barn on Old Acre while M was fly fishing in Montana. Litigation follows between M and X, and the court faces the task of interpreting the intention of the parties which in this case will require a focus upon M's communication. The question to be resolved is to which barn did the letter refer?

Finding Subjective Intent

Restatement Section 201(1) requires that the court first determine the subjective intention of both parties. The "subjective" intention is the true intention that people actually had in their heads. It may be unspoken. It may be different from what the person outwardly manifested. Subjective intention refers to what each person had in mind when the contract was made.

We know X's subjective intention because the facts establish that X only knew of one barn that matched the description of "my old barn" in M's letter. The fact that X tore down the Old Acre barn is also strong evidence that this is the barn that X subjectively intended to be the subject of their contract. (One might speculate that X could have intentionally torn down the barn that he knew to be the wrong barn, but this is very unlikely conduct.)

We do not yet know M's subjective intention in this fact situation. If you think you know M's subjective intention without more facts, then you do not yet understand what subjective intention is. Maybe M likes the old dilapidated barn on New Acre. Maybe it has historical significance. We do not know which barn M wanted torn down. Knowing the facts we know, it might appear to us that M was intending to have the New Acre barn torn down but that reasoning involves an analysis of objective intent, and we are still searching for subjective intent.

It is probable that the only way to learn M's subjective intent as to which barn he wanted torn down is to ask him. There may be other facts that bear upon the court's findings as to M's truthfulness (such as a conversation that he had with a third person in which he told them what his plans were). But subjective intention is the intention that M actually had in his head and the most direct way to discover this is to ask him.

If it is established that M intended to have the Old Acre barn torn down, then we have just found that both parties intended their contract to apply to the same barn. Since both subjectively intended the same interpretation of the language used, that is the interpretation that the court must reach. Their understanding might seem a bit strange to the judge under some circumstances. However, contract law is designed to protect the reasonable expectations of the parties, not the reasonable expectations of the court.

Finding Objective Intent

Since the parties are engaged in a dispute, it is most likely that their subjective intentions were different from each other. Each was thinking about—or intending—a different barn. The court is now forced to inquire into what meaning each party should have attached to the communications. Explanations of this process tend to be either overly simplified or convoluted. We will try to find some middle ground.

Contract law attempts to protect the reasonable expectations of the parties. Therefore, we are trying to ascertain what these two parties should have reasonably understood each other to mean. We take these two people and analyze the specific facts of the case to determine what each knew or should have known and what each should have understood the other party to have known. We require them to think and react reasonably but this reasonableness is applied within the framework of these two individuals and what they knew about each other.

We are going to look to the plain meaning of the words that the parties communicated to each other. We are going to consider the parties' course of performance of this contract and any prior course of dealing between them or usage of trade in the community. We are going to apply some common sense to determine what meaning was reasonably communicated.

Restatement Section 201 is entitled "Whose Meaning Prevails." That section provides:

(1) Where the parties have attached the same meaning to a promise or agreement or a term thereof, it is interpreted in accordance with that meaning.

(2) Where the parties have attached different meanings to a promise or agreement or a term thereof, it is interpreted in accordance with the meaning attached by one of them if at the time the agreement was made

(a) that party did not know of any different meaning attached by the other, and the other knew the meaning attached by the first party; or

(b) that party had no reason to know of any different meaning attached by the other, and the other had reason to know the meaning attached by the first party.

(3) Except as stated in this Section, neither party is bound by the meaning attached by the other, even though the result may be a failure of mutual assent.

When one sorts out the meaning of subsections 2(a) and (b), it becomes evident that the authors of the Restatement were of the opinion that one of the parties was justified in his interpretation. In the hypothetical at hand, this analysis is appropriate because there are only two barns from which to choose, so either M or X must be correct. However, in more complex situations, we may find that each party presents in court a self-serving and detailed accounting of his or her subjective intention on a whole range of issues. Courts are not limited to selecting "whose meaning prevails" but may find that the manifested intention of the parties which each should reasonably have understood is something a bit different from the detailed subjective intent of either party.

For example, assume a business arrangement in which X gets royalties from each sale of goods made by Y. The contract contains an elaborate formula concerning promotion efforts to be made by Y. When a dispute arises, each party may have its own interpretation of how this formula is to be interpreted. The court may find that neither of them has it quite right and that the actual terms of the contract are something different from that which each professes to believe.

§ 4.1.1 Subjective and Objective Intent: Philosophical Debate

Much has been written about the views of the two giants of American contract law from the first half of the twentieth century. Prof. Williston of Harvard is credited with advancing the view that the objectively manifested intent controls without any regard to what the parties may have actually intended. Although a great jurist, Judge Learned Hand, wrote an opinion or two that expressly stated that contract terms, strictly speaking, have nothing to do with the actual intention of the parties (*New York Trust Co. v. Island Oil & Transport Corp* (2d Cir. 1929) and *Hotchkiss v. National City Bank* (S.D.N.Y. 1911)), it is not likely that Williston's views on this, or on most other subjects, were as dogmatic or simplistic as a few later day writers sometimes indicate. Professor Williston was the Reporter and dominant voice in the writing of the Restatement, First which tends to reflect his views.

Set off against Williston in the historical analysis of this subject are the views attributed to Professor Arthur L. Corbin of Yale. Professor Corbin's legacy on this issue is a concern for the subjective intention of the parties, and the Restatement, Second reflects much of Corbin's views on this and other subjects. However, both Williston and Corbin were powerful thinkers with complex views. The memory of these scholars is not well served by attempting to attribute their names to simple labels.

A few hours observing trial court judges in action interpreting written contracts cases will likely convince the observer that trial court judges are concerned with:

1) what the contract "says," and

2) what the parties meant.

All judges are painfully aware that these concerns will be antagonistic in some cases. The judge will listen, usually patiently, to the buyer telling what he or she thought the contract provided. If the judge concludes that this understanding is not in accord with what the contract language reasonably states, the judge will consider the factors mentioned in Restatement section 201(2) (quoted above). Finally the judge may rule for the seller telling the buyer that the buyer must read and understand contracts before he signs them, or the judge may rule for the buyer telling the seller that the seller should have understood what the buyer thought the contract stated. The judge will then retire to chambers muttering about what an imperfect world we live in.

As counsel for the parties, your job is to present the best arguments possible supporting the position that your client seeks. The best chance a judge can have to do the right thing is to have good attorneys present the competing arguments in the best possible light. As students your goal is to demonstrate to your professor that you are going to be able to perform that task well.

§ 4.2 Objective Intent: The Search for Some Answers

There is a perceived need for uniformity, consistency and predictability in the interpretation of contracts. Commerce thrives on certainty and uncertainty interferes with the functioning of a healthy economy. Jobs and our standard of living are dependent upon a free flow of commerce to a degree that Americans tend to ignore. Our media fail totally to communicate to us the significance of this factor upon the economic success of countries such as Canada, the U.S., Japan and those in the E.U. In some situations, one can make a strong case for the proposition that certainty and predictability are more highly-valued goals than justice. If rules work unfairly in certain circumstances, parties will learn to contract around those rules.

Attributing a standard meaning to language used in a contract promotes consistency and predictability just as introduction of subjective meaning to alter contract relationships derogates from these goals. Therefore, courts are concerned with the plain meaning of contract language. This is perhaps even more important in international transactions where deviation from the literal meaning of contract terms in the interpretation process may open the door even wider to unexpected results. The following rules are designed in part in response to these concerns.

If the terms of a contract have been reduced to writing, determination of the meaning of that writing is considered to be a matter of law to be decided by the court rather than a question of fact which would be decided by the jury in a jury trial. Treating the interpretation of written contracts as a matter of law also permits appellate courts to review fully the trial court's interpretation thereby permitting the appellate judges to reach their own conclusions as to the meaning of contract terms and the intention of the parties. This greater level of review contributes to consistency and predictability in interpretation.

In attributing specific meaning to contract language, the court is concerned with what each party knew or had reason to know. This includes a concern for what each party should have understood what the other party knew.

In the hypothetical in section 4.1 above, when the owner of the farm properties wrote proposing a contract for the tearing down of "my old barn," the first conclusion that one must reach is that the language of the offer is either vague or ambiguous. In this case it is ambiguous because it is subject to two or more distinctly different meanings as distinguished from being vague which would mean that it is subject to various shades of different meaning (§ 6.6). Since the language is subject to two or more distinct interpretations, there is no plain meaning for the court to find and apply. It becomes necessary to determine what each party should reasonably have expected the terms of the contract to be.

The court is properly concerned with what the offeree knew or had reason to know about the offeror's barn or barns. M had "recently" purchased New Acre on which the second barn was located. It is apparent from the facts that the offeree did not know of this new acquisition and since the purchase was "recent," one might conclude that the offeree had no reason to know of the existence of a second barn. The court is also properly concerned with whether the offeror knew or should have known about what the offeree knew or should have known. For the same reasons noted above, the offeror should have realized that the offeree could be unaware of the newly acquired property. It might also be noted that the offeror referred to "my *old* barn" which might connote the barn that he had owned for a long time rather than the barn he had just acquired.

The proper conclusion is that the objective meaning of the contract terms refers to the barn on Old Acre. This happens to be consistent with the offeree's subjective understanding, but it is the proper result because that is the meaning that reasonable people would attribute to the language used given the circumstances and knowledge of each party.

§ 4.3   Course of Performance; Course of Dealing, and Usage of Trade (Custom)

A primary factor that can be looked to for interpretation of a contractual agreement is course of performance. The U.C.C. provides in section 2–208(1):

Where the contract for sale involves repeated occasions for performance by either party with knowledge of the nature of the performance and opportunity for objection to it by the other, any course of performance accepted or acquiesced in without objection shall be relevant to determine the meaning of the agreement.

Course of performance that is accepted without objection or comment is perhaps the most reliable single indicator of the actual meaning the parties wished to attach to their contract agreement. Thus "course of performance" refers to a pattern of performance of the contract that is the subject of the dispute, as contrasted to "course of dealing" which refers to the pattern of performance in prior contracts between the same parties.

The U.C.C. defines "course of dealing" as "a sequence of previous conduct between the parties to a particular transaction which is fairly to be regarded as establishing a common basis of understanding for interpreting their expressions and other conduct." (U.C.C. § 1–205(1)) It might be appropriate to look upon course of dealing as the parties own private usage of trade that they have developed for themselves in their prior dealings with each other to control their transactions. Since it is thus personalized, an established course of dealing will control a usage of trade where the two are in conflict.

Section 2–208(2) provides:

The express terms of the agreement and any such course of performance, as well as any course of dealing and usage of trade, shall be construed whenever reasonable as consistent with each other; but when such construction is unreasonable, express terms shall control course of performance and course of performance shall control both course of dealing and usage of trade (§ 1–205).

Using such vocabulary as "custom," "custom and usage" or "usage of the trade," common law courts have recognized the necessity of learning how people in a particular trade or business usually talk and what they usually mean by their language before one interprets their contracts. If by trade custom two bundles of shingles of a certain size are referred to as "1,000 shingles," then a contract for 4,000 shingles will be fulfilled by delivering eight bundles of the designated size even though the actual count of shingles in the eight bundles is some other number such as 2,500. Special trade usages which, depart from dictionary definitions are always "strange" when we first learn of them, and "obvious" when we have dealt with them for a long period of time. Anyone who has worked with lumber knows that a finished "2x4" ("two by four") is not two inches by four inches but approximately one and three-fourths inches by three and five-eighths inches. So also, eight foot studs are not 96 inches long but only about 92½ inches long. (There is usually a logical reason behind such usages. "Eight foot studs" are cut to create standard-sized walls eight feet high. Since there will be a "2x4" nailed on each end, the studs are intentionally pre-cut to span eight feet after two 2x4s are tacked on.)

At early common law, "trade customs" were required to exist from "time immemorial" and had to be universally observed. Of course, when there was minimal written history, "time immemorial" no doubt meant "for as long as the witness can remember." U.C.C. section 1–205(2) defines "usage of trade" as "any practice or method of dealing having such regularity of observance in a place, vocation or trade as to justify an expectation that it will be observed with respect to the transaction in question." This definition reflects modern common law decisions.

Usage of trade is thus found not in the terms of the contract nor in prior discussions or dealings of the parties but rather from community practices. One basic problem is describing or defining the appropriate place, vocation or trade. If the place is Remote County in Isolated State, more usages will exist and they will be more readily proven than if the place is the entire United States. A usage of trade must be a specific usage or meaning and must be observed with regularity. The fact that it is "often" done that way is not enough. It must be a usage that is observed in virtually all cases except where it is expressly disavowed or altered.

An additional problem with proving usage involves the situation in which one of the parties is not a member of the trade or vocation or is not a resident of the place where the practice is observed. Where one party is an "outsider" and unaware of local usages, it may not be justified to expect that a usage of trade will be observed in a transaction with that person.

§ 4.4 Interpretation Against Drafter, Adhesion Contracts

It is often stated that in choosing among reasonable meanings, a contract will be interpreted against the interests of the party who drafted it. It is assumed that the party responsible for drafting the contract will provide for his own interests and will have reason to be conscious of uncertainties and obscure provisions. Thus, there is a certain justice in interpreting the contract against the interests of that party in cases of doubt. If the drafter created an ambiguous agreement, it is reasonable to hold that party to the actual subjective meaning that the other party attached to the ambiguous provisions. This rule has no application where the contract terms were the product of the joint efforts of the two parties.

Adhesion contracts are those which are drafted by one party and usually reduced to a form which is presented to the other party under circumstances in which there is no realistic opportunity to negotiate. A typical situation exists where the adhering party is dealing with an agent who possesses no authority to modify the terms of the contract form but can only say "take it or leave it."

Adhesion contracts are not *per se* objectionable. One could not get through the typical day if it were necessary to negotiate every transaction starting with the price of a cup of coffee, particularly where the coffee is purchased from a vending machine. However, adhesion contracts are subjected to greater judicial scrutiny than other types of contracts. Provisions such as interpretation against the interests of the draftsman certainly apply, and if unconscionable terms are present, a court may take appropriate action (§ 6.10).

The Restatement makes the following observations about adhesion contracts in comment b to section 211:

> b. Assent to unknown terms. A party who makes regular use of a standardized form of agreement does not ordinarily expect his customers to understand or even to read the standard terms. One of the purposes of standardization is to eliminate bargaining over details of individual transactions, and that purpose would not be served if a substantial number of customers retained counsel and reviewed the standard terms. Employees regularly using a form often have only a limited understanding of its terms and limited authority to vary them. Customers do not in fact ordinarily understand or even read the standard terms. They trust to the good faith of the party using the form and to the tacit representation that like terms are being accepted regularly by others similarly situated. But they understand that they are assenting to the terms not read or not understood, subject to such limitations as the law may impose.

The text of section 211 provides:

(1) Except as stated in Subsection (3), where a party to an agreement signs or otherwise manifests assent to a writing and has reason to believe that like writings are regularly used to embody terms of agreements of the same type, he adopts the writing as an integrated agreement with respect to the terms included in the writing.

(2) Such a writing is interpreted wherever reasonable as treating alike all those similarly situated, without regard to their knowledge or understanding of the standard terms of the writing.

(3) Where the other party has reason to believe that the party manifesting such assent would not do so if he knew that the writing contained a particular term, the term is not part of the agreement.

The goal is to interpret adhesion contracts so as to enforce only those provisions that the reasonable person signing such a contract would anticipate. Provisions that a reasonable person would not anticipate and to which a reasonable person would not willingly agree are not considered part of the bargain. The fact that a contract is an adhesion contract may also be a relevant factor if one of the parties is asserting that the contract is unconscionable. (See § 6.10.)

B. PAROL EVIDENCE RULE

§ 4.5 When the Parol Evidence Rule Applies

The parol evidence rule is applicable to contracts, wills and deeds. Because of the nature of this work, the following discussion will be limited to the application of this concept to contracts.

The term "parol evidence rule" is a misleading expression. This topic does not involve a single rule nor even a single concept. It involves questions regarding the admissibility and exclusion of written as well as "parol" (oral) evidence. It is a substantive rule of contract law and not a rule of evidence.

Parol evidence rule issues can arise when parties to a contract have reduced at least part of their agreement to a writing or writings and one party seeks to use evidence of prior agreements to add to or modify the terms of the writing. (If any of these elements is not present, there is no parol evidence rule problem.) The party who wishes to exclude this extrinsic evidence will attempt to invoke the parol evidence rule to establish that the prior agreement is not, as a matter of law, part of the legally enforceable contract between the parties. There may be a single writing involved, or the "writing" may in fact include more than one document.

When faced with a question of interpretation of a writing or a question of the applicability of the parol evidence rule, the court must first determine whether the writing of the parties constituted a final expression of the parties' agreement at the time it was adopted. At this stage, the court is simply attempting to determine whether the writing was intended to be merely a tentative draft of their agreement or was a receipt or invoice intended only to serve as evidence of some aspect of a transaction or whether the writing was intended to be an operative expression of assent to a contract.

If the writing is in fact a final expression of at least a portion of the parties' agreement, the court must next determine whether it is a partial integration or a complete integration of the terms to which the parties wished to be bound. As the name implies, a writing is a "complete integration" if the court finds that the parties intended that writing to be a complete statement of the terms of their agreement. The question is, "Did the parties intend the writing to represent the final and complete embodiment of their agreement?" If so the writing may be referred to as a "total integration" or a "complete integration."

If the court finds that the parties have expressed their contract in a completely integrated written agreement, neither party may offer evidence of extrinsic agreements (additional terms) that were communicated prior to or contemporaneously with the signing of the writing for the purpose of adding to or modifying the terms of the writing. This is so because the legal conclusion that the writing was intended to be the final and complete embodiment of the total agreement means that whatever agreements may have been made prior to the writing must have been left out on purpose. These prior extrinsic agreements are no longer intended to be part of the contract (or never were intended to be part of the contract when the contract was made). The parties' intent that the writing represent the entire contract means that the parties intended to discharge or supercede whatever prior agreements existed that did not make their way into the writing.

If the writing is found to be a final expression but contains only a portion of the total agreement, that writing is identified as a partial integration. If the court finds that the parties have expressed their contract in a partially integrated written agreement, the court is saying that part of the contract terms are in the writing and part must be found from other sources. Therefore, a party may offer evidence of extrinsic agreements made prior to or contemporaneously with the signing of the writing. This evidence of the extrinsic agreements will be limited, however, to terms that are consistent with the writing and are such that similarly situated people might naturally have considered it unnecessary to include them in their written contract. Some courts state that these extrinsic terms must either be supported by separate consideration or are such terms as might naturally be omitted from the writing even though the parties intended these terms to be a part of their contractual agreement. In determining what might naturally be omitted from the writing, one considers what might be expected of similarly situated parties entering into an agreement of a similar nature. Terms that are inconsistent with the writing are excluded because by adopting the writing, the parties must have intended to discharge any prior agreements that were inconsistent with the terms of the writing.

Specific observations can be made as to when a parol evidence issue is properly raised.

(1) There can be no application of the parol evidence rule unless there is a written contract. The concept is applicable only where there is a writing that the court concludes to have been intended by the parties as the final expression of their agreement or of some portion thereof.

(2) Despite the misnomer "parol," the rule applies to all evidence of extrinsic agreements, oral or written, made prior to the the writing. The rule also applies to oral statements or agreements made contemporaneously with the writing or writings. It is not difficult to justify the notion that prior agreements which were omitted from the final writing must have been omitted because they did not constitute a part of the bargain at which the parties ultimately arrived. However, statements that are made or agreements which are reached contemporaneously with the creation or signing of the writing present a different issue than those made prior to the signing process. It is more difficult to justify the conclusion that agreements expressed contemporaneously with the signing of the writing were not intended to be part of the "final" agreement. Nonetheless, the courts have taken the position that contemporaneous oral agreements are treated in similar fashion to prior oral agreements.

Contemporaneous writings are handled differently from contemporaneous oral agreements. It is usually possible for the court to construe two or more contemporaneous writings to be part of a single agreement. Thus, contemporaneous writings are usually not barred by the parol evidence rule.

(3) The parol evidence rule only applies to the use of prior or contemporaneous extrinsic agreements that are offered for the purpose of adding to or modifying the terms of the writing. The rule has no application to extrinsic evidence that is offered to prove a defense such as misrepresentation, mistake, duress, lack of capacity or undue influence, nor does it apply to extrinsic evidence offered to establish facts from which unconscionability, violation of public policy or illegality might be found. The majority of court opinions find that the rule has no application when extrinsic evidence is being offered to show that a writing that appears to be a contract was not intended to create contractual obligations or was intended to become effective as a contract only upon the happening of some contingency. The rule does not preclude use of extrinsic evidence offered for the purpose of lending meaning to contract terms (§ 4.8). Nor does the rule bar evidence to show that a recital of a fact as stated in the writing is false.

(4) The parol evidence rule does not preclude a party to a written contract from proving the existence of a separate distinct contract between the same parties. Nothing precludes people from having two contracts with each other, and proof of the existence of a written contract does not, in itself, bar proof of another contract. However, both contracts must be sufficient in and of themselves to

constitute valid enforceable contracts, e.g. the "separate agreement" must be supported by "separate" consideration. While there is case authority for the proposition that the consideration for the promise in the collateral contract could be the promisee agreeing to enter into the written contract, this is not a generally accepted principle.

Attempting to prove a separate contract when an integrated written contract exists between the parties can present other problems. If the separate contract was entered into before the execution of the integrated writing and is inconsistent with its terms, then the execution of the writing will be found to discharge the prior contract. If the subsequent contract is found to be a complete integration, it will logically be found to indicate the parties' intent to discharge all prior agreements involving subject matter within its scope.

(5) The parol evidence rule does not bar evidence that would tend to prove a subsequent modification of the contract. Evidence of agreements made subsequent to the signing of a written contract are not subject to the parol evidence rule. The underlying assumption of the parol evidence rule is that where the parties adopted a completely integrated writing, what was left out of the writing was not intended to be part of their total bargain. However, the parties to a contract remain free to modify it at a later time (Ch. 5) and the writing could not be expected to contain modifications that were agreed upon after the writing was adopted. Terms of the writing that require written modifications create their own is-

sues (Ch. 5) but do not create parol evidence rule issues.

(6) The parol evidence rule does not preclude proof of course of performance, course of dealing or usage of trade when offered to add a consistent additional term to a written agreement. These sources can also be used to interpret or explain the contract language and course of performance can be used to show a modification of the contract or waiver. It is generally stated that course of performance, course of dealing and usage cannot contradict an express term of the written agreement, but in fact they are used to define contract terms and thus give them a meaning that they would not otherwise have. (See U.C.C. § 2–208 and § 1–205.)

Remember the 2x4 example. The evidence was not being introduced to contradict "two inches," but merely to explain that in the trade "two inches" does not mean two inches.

In summary then:

(A) Prior Agreements

1) Extrinsic evidence of prior agreements is not admissible to contradict the terms of a writing intended to be an integration, whether partial or total.

2) Extrinsic evidence of prior agreements is admissible to explain the language contained in the writing if the language in the writing is found to be ambiguous or if the language in the writing

is reasonably susceptible of that interpretation (§ 4.8).

3) Extrinsic evidence of a prior agreement is not admissible to prove an additional or supplemental agreement not contained in the writing if the writing is a total (final and complete) integration.

4) Extrinsic evidence of a prior agreement is admissible to prove a consistent additional agreement if the writing is only a partial (final as to what it contains, but not complete) integration.

(B) Course of performance; course of prior dealings; trade usage:

Extrinsic evidence of a course of performance, course of prior dealings, or trade usage is admissible to explain the language in the writing even if the language is not ambiguous and is also admissible to add to or supplement the writing. But if the express words of the writing are inconsistent with such extrinsic evidence, the express terms will control.

As one can see, it is imperative to identify two things:

1. What is the nature of the extrinsic evidence offered—is it a prior oral or written agreement of the parties, or is it a course of performance, course of prior dealings, or a trade usage or custom?

2. What is it that the party is seeking to do with the extrinsic evidence—explain the words in the writing or prove an additional agreement not

contained in the writing or contradict the writing?

§ 4.6 Determining the Question of Integration

If a party attempts to introduce evidence of a prior oral or written agreement (contending that the prior agreement was in addition to the terms in the writing) and there exists a writing that represents the contract, the question becomes how does the court determine whether that writing was intended to be a total integration (final and complete) or just a partial integration (final as to what it contains but not complete). The focus is still upon the intentions of the parties, specifically as to what effect they intended the writing to have upon any prior agreements not contained in the writing. This question regarding integration is a question of law, not of fact, and is thus to be decided by the judge, not the jury, and is subject to full appellate review.

One item of evidence that the court must consider is the writing itself. The completeness and specificity of the writing may reasonably indicate that it is intended by the parties as a full and complete or "complete and exclusive" statement of terms thus constituting a completely integrated agreement. A court may also consider the nature and terms of the prior extrinsic agreement that one of the parties seeks to prove to assist in determining whether the writing was intended to represent the complete agreement between the parties.

In some jurisdictions courts purport to follow the "face of the document" rule pursuant to which a document which appears "on its face" to be a complete integration will be held to be a complete integration. It is sometimes stated that the document is taken "by its four corners" to determine whether it appears to be a complete integration or a partial integration. The hallmark of this approach is that the court makes the decision as to the extent of the integration or non-integration of the writing by looking only at the writing and without considering the extrinsic evidence that a party is offering to prove there was an additional agreement that was not included in the writing.

In what would appear to be a majority of jurisdictions, questions concerning the admissibility of parol evidence cannot be resolved without going beyond the "face of the document" and considering the nature and scope of the extrinsic evidence that is being offered. The court must consider the extrinsic evidence that a party is attempting to prove as well as the contents of the writing to determine whether the writing should be found to be a complete or only a partial integration. There are differing views concerning how this decision is to be reached or how the test is to be articulated.

The Restatement, First, section 240(1)(b) provides:

An oral agreement is not superseded or invalidated by a subsequent or contemporaneous integration, nor a written agreement by a subsequent integration relating to the same subject matter, if the agreement is not inconsistent with the integrated contract, and * * *

(b) is such an agreement as might naturally be made as a separate agreement by parties situated as were the parties to the written contract.

Restatement, Second, section 216 provides:

(1) Evidence of a consistent additional term is admissible to supplement an integrated agreement unless the court finds that the agreement was completely integrated.

(2) An agreement is not completely integrated if the writing omits a consistent additional agreed term which is

(a) agreed to for separate consideration, or

(b) such a term as in the circumstances might naturally be omitted from the writing.

This approach is stated somewhat differently in comment 3 to U.C.C. section 2–202 which provides:

If the additional terms are such that, if agreed upon, they would certainly have been included in the document in the view of the court, then evidence of their alleged making must be kept from the trier of fact.

Application of these standards requires taking into account the nature of the written contract and of its terms along with the proposed terms which are being offered. One must also consider the parties, the circumstances under which the writing was prepared, and such matters as whether the writing was a standard form or a hand-tailored writing.

Because the issue of integration is a matter of law for the court, the judge must place himself or herself in the position of the parties and ask, considering the totality of the circumstances, whether it was natural for the parties to have left the alleged agreement out of the writing. If the answer is "No", then as to that extrinsic evidence the court has determined as a matter of law that the writing is the complete and final embodiment of the parties' agreement, as they must have intended to discharge the prior agreement. Because if the prior agreement had been intended to be part of the final deal, it would not have been natural to leave it out of the writing. If it would have been natural for the parties to have left such an agreement out of the writing, then the writing is only a partial integration and the jury is permitted to consider the evidence and determine whether the agreement was in fact made. Using the U.C.C. standard, the question for the court would be, if the prior agreement had been made, whether it would certainly have been put into the writing.

§ 4.7 Merger Clauses

A writing may contain language to the effect that the writing is intended to be the complete expression of the agreement between the parties or that there are no understandings or agreements between the parties other than those contained in this writing. Such provisions in the writing manifest the parties' intent that all prior communications are "merged" into the written agreement. Many cases take the position that such a clause is conclusive as to the issue of integration and must be enforced in the absence of a showing of fraud, mistake or other personal defense that would establish that the clause did not express the parties' intent.

Some cases distinguish between merger clauses contained in writings negotiated by the parties which are ordinarily given full effect, and merger clauses contained in standard form or adhesion contracts where the clause is less likely to be given literal meaning. Parol evidence issues arise with some frequency in cases where the parties used standard form contracts. These contracts usually do not lend themselves to convenient alteration to include special terms to which the parties agreed, and for this reason, a court is less likely to hold a form contract to be a complete integration.

§ 4.8 Use of Extrinsic Evidence to Aid in the Interpretation of the Contract Language

Evidence is admissible to show the background and circumstances in which a contract was negotiated as well as such matters as the identity of the parties. Assume that a farmer handed a letter to a contractor offering to pay $1,000 "if you will tear down my old barn." Assume further that there is now a dispute between these parties as to which barn was intended as the subject of the offer and that one of them is attempting to prove that at the time the letter was handed to the contractor, the two parties were standing in front of one particular old barn that belonged to the farmer. This evidence should be admitted. It has probative value to assist in determining to which barn the letter refers.

Where a court is unable by the usual methods of judicial interpretation to establish the meaning of contract language, then the contract is ambiguous. In this situation, in addition to the general evidence relating to background facts and circumstances, parties may introduce evidence of specific statements and agreements to show intended meaning of contract terms. The general application of this principle is rather narrow, however, because it is usually found to be applicable only where the court is unable to interpret the contract. Where the court is able to decide which of two available meanings is the "proper" one, the contract becomes plain and unambiguous, and evidence will not be admitted to assist in its interpretation.

In *Pacific Gas & Electric Co. v. G.W. Thomas Drayage & Rigging Co.* (Cal. 1968) the California Supreme Court established the principle that evidence of an extrinsic agreement or understanding as to the meaning of contract language can be admitted to assist in the interpretation of a written contract so long as the evidence is being offered to prove a meaning to which the language of the writing is reasonably susceptible. This represents a significant expansion of the use of extrinsic evidence to prove the intended meaning of contract terms because it is not dependent upon finding that the contract language is ambiguous. Use of extrinsic evidence to show the parties' intended meaning is consistent with the Restatement, Second, approach to contract interpretation (§ 4.6). If the actual meaning that the parties themselves attached to contract language is a primary concern, then one must logically admit evidence of communications between the parties as to the meaning of contract language.

C. IMPLIED TERMS AND TERMS IMPOSED BY LAW

§ 4.9   Terms Found by Implication or Construction

Some contract terms are properly labeled "express" terms because the parties set forth these terms in specific language. There are other contract terms that are not expressed in their agreement. Contract terms can be found because the court concludes that from the express language used and the other circumstances in the case it is apparent that the parties impliedly intended that these additional terms be part of their agreement. Contract terms can also be imposed by the court as a matter of law without regard to the intention of the parties. In many situations, it is not totally clear which of these processes is at work.

When terms are found based upon the apparent intention of the parties, they are described as "implied" terms or "implied-in-fact" terms meaning that they were implied by the parties. When terms are imposed by the court without regard to the intention of the parties, these are variously described as "constructive" terms (because their source is judicial construction) or implied-in-law terms. Use of the phrases "implied-in-fact" and "implied-in-law" is a sure formula for confusion. Both phrases will eventually be shortened to "implied" and we will end up using the term "implied" to describe two quite different subjects. Therefore, the favored vocabulary is "constructive" and "implied" with "implied" being used only to refer to implied-in-fact.

Assume that S and B agree to the sale and purchase of six computers of a certain type and model for a price of $9,000 with no time or place stated for delivery and no other express terms. One might contend that this agreement is not a contract because it has inadequate terms, but modern common law would not reach such a result and the U.C.C. clearly mandates (§ 2–204) that the court should not fail to enforce this agreement simply because terms such as delivery time and place were not specified. The law is going to enforce this agreement and the question becomes where one looks to supply the missing terms. (There are more terms missing than might appear at first glance.)

Time of performance: Since no time was specified, delivery is going to be required within a reasonable time (U.C.C. § 2–309(1)). The question is whether the court arrived at this result by examining the apparent unspoken intention of the parties or whether this term was imposed by the law as a matter of judicial construction. It would appear that time of delivery is a matter about which the law has no policy to impose and that delivery should be whenever the parties intended. Thus, one might conclude that by failing to specify a particular date, the parties impliedly manifested the intent that performance would be within a time period that was reasonable under all of the circumstances. While the law (in this case the U.C.C.) does dictate this result, section 2–309(1) is only a codification of the standard common law interpretation which is probably based upon party intent.

Place of performance: U.C.C. section 2–308 provides rather detailed rules regarding place of delivery. Depending upon the particular facts of the case, the place of the delivery could be at S's place of business, at S's residence, or at the place where the six computers are actually located. Of course, the parties may specify place of delivery in the contract, but having failed to do so, the law appears to impose a specific place of delivery as a constructive term; one imposed by the law without regard to party intent.

Assume one further fact: In three prior transactions involving other types of electronic equipment, S has always delivered the goods to B's place of business and S's employees have handled installation. If S refuses to deliver the six computers to B's place of business, B's argument will be that the prior course of dealing establishes the parties' implied intention that delivery and installation are part of the contract terms.

Section 2–308 specifically provides that the rules stated therein regarding place of delivery only apply "(u)nless otherwise agreed." One might reasonably conclude that course of dealing, like course of performance and usage of trade, are in fact sources from which we find the terms that the parties impliedly understood to be included in their agreement. If prior course of dealing is properly characterized as an implied term, then delivery to B's location and installation by S are part of the agreement between the parties and therefore the delivery rules contained in section 2–308 do not apply. In resolving this issue, the interplay is between finding the intention of these particular parties (which is always required to find implied terms) as distinguished from imposing upon the parties standard terms found in the law or construed by the courts.

Matters such as time of payment will be handled in a fashion similar to place of delivery. U.C.C. section 2–310 specifies time of payment where the contracting parties do not "otherwise agree." As with place of delivery, the U.C.C. provisions do not represent a strong policy position of the law and can thus be overcome by any implied understanding as to time and manner of payment.

Quality of goods: Assume that there is a dispute concerning the performance of the six computers that B purchased from S. There are no express terms in the contract that resolve this issue. If S is a merchant, the law will impose terms relating to quality of goods and even matters such as packaging (U.C.C. § 2–314). Section 2–314 has many details, but basically the computers must be of fair average quality that will pass without objection by the average buyer and seller in the computer trade.

The policy considerations that cause us to impose on merchants a duty to comply with an implied warranty of merchantability are strong. They are so strong that these constructive terms of the contract will prevail over implied terms including such things as prior course of dealing. To defeat these terms, S must use express language and must comply with requirements relating to language and conspicuousness (U.C.C. § 2–316).

Duty of Good Faith: Assume that S and B agree upon a time and place of delivery at which time S tenders only five computers instead of six and B wishes to reject all of the computers because of this breach. The controlling law of the U.C.C. is found in section 2–601 which states that B may "reject the whole" or may "accept any commercial unit or units and reject the rest." Literally, the section states that B may accept one computer, or three, or five, or none.

The law imposes a contract term requiring that parties act in good faith. This is found in the U.C.C. in section 1–203 which provides: "Every contract or duty within this Act imposes an obligation of good faith in its performance or enforcement." The details relating to B's right to reject goods will be explored in the chapter dealing with performance, and the concept of good faith will be analyzed in sections 4.11 through 4.13.1. At this point what should be understood is that in exercising the power to reject all or part of the computers, B must act in good faith. This is a duty imposed by the law without regard to any other terms of the contract. Therefore, the parties may not disclaim this term. It is there whether they wanted it or not.

§ 4.10 Mandatory Terms, Permissive Terms, and Default Rules

There are contract terms in every legal system that are mandatory. These terms represent fundamental public policy and therefore the parties may not change them even by express agreement. One example of a mandatory term is the requirement of good faith or good faith and fair dealing which is discussed in the previous section. Another example of a mandatory term is found in minimum wage laws. Where these laws apply, the minimum wage is a mandatory term in employment contracts. The parties may not contract for a lower wage by use of any express or implied agreement between them. Other examples are found in legislation such as consumer protection statutes which mandate certain contract terms that the parties are not free to modify.

Mandatory terms obviously limit freedom of contract. To the extent that society imposes contract terms, the freedom of parties to negotiate their own terms is denied. Thus, the decision as to what terms should be treated as mandatory is a basic political decision that each society must make. Mandatory terms are usually adopted to protect groups that are felt to have inadequate bargaining power or are otherwise unable to negotiate effectively for themselves. For that reason, mandatory terms are most common in areas of the law dealing with such categories as consumer contracts, non-commercial rental agreements, employment contracts, and the like.

There are contract terms imposed by law which the parties are permitted to change. In some cases, special formality, such as a writing or specific contract language, is required to change them but they can be changed by agreement of the parties. An example of this type of term is the implied warranty of merchantability which was discussed in the previous section. Parties may change this rule but there are procedural safeguards designed to limit the manner in which this can be accomplished.

Finally there are contract terms that the law imposes only because the parties failed to provide for this particular term. These are called "default rules" (applied only by default where the parties intention cannot be found from their agreement) or "gap fillers." Examples are found in the previous section and include place of delivery, time of delivery, time of payment, method of payment and the like.

With respect to gap fillers, the law is not expressing any strong policy considerations. It is not critical to our society whether buyers pay in cash or pay by credit card, check or money order. Gap fillers exist only because parties frequently omit such terms and we do not want to deny enforcement of these contracts simply because such terms were not agreed upon. Default rules or gap fillers are designed to provide reasonable workable rules where the parties did not provide otherwise. Because they do not represent major policy objectives, these standard terms can be displaced by terms reasonably implied from any source.

§ 4.11 Duty of Good Faith and Fair Dealing

Most states now recognize an implied obligation of "good faith" or of "good faith and fair dealing" in the performance and enforcement of contracts. See Restatement Second section 205 and U.C.C. section 1–205. It is generally accepted that the formation of the contract gives rise to this implied duty. Because the duty is created by the contract, it does not yet exist during the negotiation stage unless the parties already have an existing contract relationship.

The concept of implying an obligation of "good faith" was not recognized until the second half of the twentieth century. Specifics concerning definitions and applications are still evolving, and this is an area in which one must proceed with caution. One should not attempt to substitute a general notion of "doing right by the other person" for more specific contract terms and principles. For example, a general obligation of good faith and fair dealing is not an appropriate substitute for an analysis of specific contract defenses. Likewise, a judge or jury should make an honest effort to determine the intention of the parties before substituting the judge's or jury's notion of what is appropriate contract performance.

§ 4.11.1 Bad Faith Torts Distinguished

The distinction between contract and tort is well grounded in common law because these two subjects have divergent objectives. Tort law is predicated upon societal standards and its primary objective is to further that social policy. The controlling law in a tort case is found in rules of law, not what the parties agreed upon. In limited situations, the parties may affect their tort rights and liabilities, such as by expressly assuming a risk, but generally tort law affects people without regard to any consensual agreement.

Contract law is concerned primarily with the intention of the parties. The goal is to enforce the agreement that is understood to exist between them. There are some limitations designed to balance the playing field, such as denying enforcement to terms that are found to be unconscionable. Except for these limited situations, the outcome of contract cases is determined by the agreement of the parties and not by notions of what agreement the trier of fact thinks that they should have made.

Bad faith as a tort invokes the social policy of tort law and produces tort remedies. This law emerged in California in the 1950s with cases involving insurance carriers acting wrongfully in the settlement of claims involving their insureds. Of those jurisdictions that recognize this tort action, most confine it to acts committed in the performance of contracts that are affected by a public interest, such as insurance contracts. These are sometimes described as contracts in which there is a special relationship between the parties.

One view of the obligation of good faith in contract law is that it is implied in order to protect the express covenants or promises of the contract, not to protect some general public policy interest which is not directly tied to the contract's purposes. This is a fundamental distinction between tort and contract. The notion is that contracting parties should be permitted to control their obligations and their destinies by the intentions that they manifest. Thus, any duty of good faith and fair dealing must be consistent with the express terms of the contract and any other manifested intentions of the contracts. This use of the implied duty of good faith and fair dealing to implement the intention of the parties is consistent with our basic notions of freedom of contract.

An alternative view of the obligation of good faith and fair dealing is that the rights and duties of contracting parties are to be determined by an abstract general obligation of good faith without regard to, or despite, their expressed or apparent intentions. With respect to matters falling within the scope of the implied covenant, rights and obligations are controlled or governed by community standards as those standards are determined by a jury or judge.

It is clear that parties to a contract may agree to terms that jurors might find to be unfair. The fundamental contract law question presented is: "Which prevails, the parties' stated intentions or the jurors' notions of what is right or proper?" The answer to this question may still be evolving. The question is not avoided by applying tort law to a purported act of "bad faith." If a party is asserting rights apparently granted by to it by the terms of the contract, labeling that conduct "bad faith" raises the same serious policy questions about the intersection of freedom of contract and competing social policies, whether we label the problem as "tort" or "contract.".

§ 4.12   Defining Good Faith and Fair Dealing

It is difficult to develop definitions of "good faith" or "fair dealing" and many courts frankly state that they will not attempt it. On the assumption that a rudimentary definition may be better than nothing, we offer the following general thoughts.

The basic definition of good faith that appears in U.C.C. section 1–201(19) is "honesty in fact in the conduct or transaction." This is a very minimal standard. It is subjective standard of conduct in that one presumably will not be found to be acting in bad faith if one bases his actions upon an inaccurate understanding of the facts, no matter how implausible. It is a very minimal approach to the concept of good faith in that it does not require that one's conduct be reasonable or consistent with any external standards.

There is a second definition of good faith in the U.C.C. section 2–103(1)(b) that requires of merchants "observance of reasonable commercial standards of fair dealing in the trade" in addition to being "honest in fact." This definition, which is also incorporated into U.C.C. article 2A dealing with the leasing of goods, requires that the court look to actual practices in an industry or trade but permits the court to reject practices that are not reasonable or fair and presumably substitute practices that do meet reasonable standards of fair dealing in the trade. Non-merchants are not subject to these standards.

The various articles of the U.C.C. do not adopt a uniform definition of good faith. Articles 3, 4, 4A and 8 all adopt a definition that involves both honesty and "observance of reasonable commercial standards of fair dealing" but delete the language "in the trade" which is found in articles 2 and 2A. Articles 5 and 7 adopt only the "honesty in fact" standard found in section 1–201(19) of article 1. Legislative history establishes that these differences are not accidental.

Some common law jurisdictions require only "good faith" whereas others define the implied term as "good faith and fair dealing" yet this difference does not appear to affect the results of the cases decided in these different states. California uses the expanded version and its Supreme Court has quoted the following language from a law review article: " ...the covenant has both a subjective and objective aspect—subjective good faith and objective fair dealing. A party violates the covenant if it subjectively lacks belief in the validity of its act or if its conduct is objectively unreasonable." Carma Developers, Inc. v. Marathon Developers, (Cal. 1992). This is apparently consistent with the U.C.C. formula of good faith for a merchant that requires both honesty and reasonableness. However, unlike the U.C.C., California would not give a free ride to non-merchants when it comes to reasonableness.

While judges and professors may experience difficulty attaching a specific definition to the term "good faith," that does not prevent either from asking the attorney or the student to provide such a definition. As with all newer legal concepts that appear to have the potential of being open-ended, one will present a stronger case if one can articulate a definition that accomplishes your immediate purpose yet has definable limits. As is the case with the defense of unconscionability, a court will be quicker to apply good faith to a situation if the parameters of the concept can be stated.

§ 4.13 Impact of the Good Faith and Fair Dealing Obligations

Good faith can be used in various ways in the analysis of a legal problem. We present some distinctions which we describe in terms of four "levels." This vocabulary should not be treated as

words of art but is offered only to facilitate understanding.

First level. Good faith (or good faith and fair
dealing) can be used in quite different ways in the
interpretation of contracts. At the most basic level,
one can note that everyone has a duty to act in good
faith and not breach the contract. When one
breaches the contract, this is not good faith performance and the breaching party may be liable for
resulting damages. As used in this context, "good
faith" means virtually nothing. The phrase could be
removed from the analysis and the result would not
be changed. The promisor had a duty to perform
and he didn't perform and therefore he has breached the contract. Discussion of good faith simply fills
space. Worse, it may carry with it the connotation
that people are liable for breach of contract only
when they act (or fail to act) with improper motives.
This is incorrect. Contract liability is strict liability
in which promise breachers are not exonerated because they tried or did their best.

Second level. Good faith (or good faith and fair
dealing) can be used simply to define contract rights
and duties. When a contract permits one party to
exercise discretion that will have a serious impact
upon the other, that discretion must be exercised
fairly and reasonably. For example, U.C.C. section
2–601 gives a buyer of goods that are to be delivered
in a single lot the right to reject all or certain parts
of the goods "for any defect in tender." On its face,
this gives the buyer the right to reject a new car
because it is delivered ten minutes late. However,
most commentators assume that such a right to

reject is properly qualified by the buyer's obligation to act in good faith under section 1–203. If the buyer is a non-merchant, the U.C.C. purports to require only that the buyer be honest. But it has been suggested that honesty involves honest dissatisfaction with the tender because it is ten minutes late and not utilizing the small discrepancy in delivery times as an excuse to get out of a bargain with which the buyer is no longer happy.

Suppose that the buyer honestly states that he is delighted by the fact that the seller is ten minutes late because he has changed his mind and no longer wants the car and therefore intends to use the ten minute delay as an excuse for rejecting. Call him what you will, this buyer is "honest." This example underscores the weakness of the U.C.C. definitions of good faith and demonstrates why many courts choose to use fluid definitions of this term.

Third level. Good faith (or good faith and fair dealing) can be used to create or expand contract rights and duties. Before the term "good faith" came into usage in contract law around the mid-twentieth century, court opinions could be found describing implied promises or implied conditions to effectuate the expressed terms of the contract. Thus one who would have the exclusive right to utilize the name of a famous person for a marketing activity would be found to have impliedly promised to use reasonable efforts or best efforts to promote those sales (Wood v. Lucy, Lady Duff Gordon, (N.Y. 1917)). Today the same result might be reached by application of the obligation of good faith and fair dealing. Thus, failure to use reasonable efforts or best efforts to market the product could be characterized as bad faith. Judges have noted this modern day substitution of good faith for implied terms (*Tymshare, Inc. v. Covell* (D.C.Cir.1984)).

This usage of good faith which we have described as third level may extend beyond those cases in which a court would have been able easily to imply a term. If a contract requires notice to one party to be sent to an address on 10th Street, sending notice to 10th Street may be an act of bad faith if one knows that the other party has relocated her office to 5th Avenue.

Fourth level. The ultimate expansion of the usage of good faith is to create contract rights that go beyond those expressed or implied by the parties or that are antagonistic to or contradict the express terms of the contract. The notion here is that a defendant who was found not to have breached any promise made in the contract can still be liable for breaching the implied obligation of good faith and fair dealing. In a noteworthy case, one corporation terminated its long-term contract with another corporation and the latter sued for breach of contract and breach of the covenant good faith and fair dealing. The jury found that the termination was not a breach of contract. However, the jury assessed full contract damages after finding that there was a breach of an obligation of good faith, and the judgment based upon this verdict was affirmed (*Sons of Thunder v. Borden* (N.J. 1997)).

To the extent that interpretation of the obligations of good faith are left to the jury as was done in *Sons of Thunder,* acceptance of the concept of normative good faith would appear to invite a jury to substitute its impressions of what the terms of the contract should have been for those agreed to by the parties. Even if discretion is reserved to the judge, concepts of freedom of contract appear to suffer in this process. Use of the concept of good faith to create contract rights and impose duties different from those intended by the parties brings about the socialization of contract law. It involves normative standards of good faith as distinguished from contextual standards. Some critics express the concern that it is the task of the legislature and not the judiciary to engage in socialization of contract law. Some who believe that courts should develop further contract norms view the doctrine of good faith as ill-suited for this purpose. It can be anticipated that this will continue to be a contentious area of contract law.

§ 4.13.1 Carrying Out the Parties' Intentions or Imposing Obligations

As suggested in the preceding section, many courts have concluded that good faith is read into contracts in order to protect the express covenants or promises of the contract, not to protect some general public policy interest not directly tied to the contract's purpose (*Foley v. Interactive Data Corp.,* (Cal. 1988)). The question then is one of deciding whether such conduct, though not prohibited, is nevertheless contrary to the contract's purposes and the parties legitimate expectations (Carma Developers, Inc. v. Marathon Development, *supra*). As thus presented, good faith involves finding and implementing the parties' intentions, or perhaps the parties' proper intentions. However, something more is at work in this area.

If good faith had to do with nothing more than carrying out the parties' manifested intentions, one might logically conclude that the parties could agree that it would not apply in their contract. However, it is consistently held that a contract clause that removes the implied covenant of good faith is void. Thus, it is evident that good faith involves more than merely implementing the parties' intentions. It also involves requiring that parties exercise the rights given to them under the contract and fulfill the duties imposed upon them in a manner that meets some basic societal standards. At the same time, implied terms should never be read to vary express terms and no covenant of good faith or good faith and fair dealing can be implied which forbids acts and conduct authorized by the express provisions of the contract.

When you have completed your study of this chapter, you may wish to analyze question 23 at the end of this book and compare your analysis with the one given there.

CHAPTER 5

DEFENSES

A. DEFENSES AFFECTING ASSENT

§ 5.1 Defenses Affecting Assent to Be Bound

The sections that follow deal with the subjects of capacity, duress, undue influence, mistake, and misrepresentation. Each of these matters, when present, has a direct bearing upon whether one party, or in some cases both parties, in fact assented to any agreement or to what agreement they consented.

An analysis of these defenses could appropriately be included in the chapter dealing with contract formation because they impact directly upon the agreement process. However, the approach most used to determine the presence or absence of an enforceable contract is to consider first whether there are sufficient manifestations and conduct by the parties from which one can find apparent assent to a bargained exchange. Only when it is established that there is a plausible case for finding a contract do we turn to the matter of searching for facts that might support a defense to the formation or enforcement of this contract or a basis for altering its interpretation and meaning.

The sections relating to the agreement process dealt in substantial measure with objective intent.

The subject of defenses affecting that assent frequently requires analysis of the subjective intent of one or both parties. We are dealing here with the qualifications upon the law of contracts that permit subjective intentions to be considered in appropriate circumstances to avoid the injustice that might otherwise result from an approach that considers nothing but what was objectively manifested. These defenses were originally recognized in courts of equity They have the general effect of introducing elements of basic fairness and justice that might otherwise be lacking in the law of contract formation.

Some authors have chosen to group these and other defenses under headings such as "policing the bargain," and in a sense, they do serve such functions. Others have attempted to restate contract defenses under a single heading or concept such as "fairness." We feel that a student will pass more exams and attorneys will win more cases if they have a specific understanding of each of the different defenses and can appreciate and articulate the circumstances in which courts will grant relief for each. This requires that one avoid generalized combined treatment of contract defenses.

§ 5.2 Capacity to Contract

Adults are generally assumed to have capacity which is the legal power to form contracts. If evidence is offered to refute this assumption, it may establish a total incapacity in which case any manifestation of intent to enter a bargain is a nullity and the purported agreement is void. A person whose property is under legal guardianship by reason of an adjudication of a mental defect is deemed to be totally lacking in capacity to contract and any attempted contract by or with that person is void.

If the incapacity is only partial, the result can be a contract that is voidable at the option of the impaired party.

§ 5.2.1   Infants (Minors)

The age of majority at which a person has full capacity to contract varies based upon state law. Persons below the established age of majority are termed "infants," and their contracts are generally held to be voidable or, in the case of the very young, void. At early common law the age of majority was twenty-one, but most states have lowered it to eighteen and in some cases nineteen. There are states which provide for the enforcement of certain types of infant's contracts, in some cases with the requirement of court approval. Considerations of public policy also dictate the enforcement against infants of some types of agreements such as the promise of an infant parent to support the infant's own child.

Although it is said that minors are under a legal disability in regard to forming a contract, that is not technically accurate because a minor does have the power to form a contract and the contract will be enforceable by the minor against the other party.

However, the contract may be avoided at the option of the minor. The minor therefore is in a favored position. The minor has protection against improvident commitments but has the right to enforce the contract if the minor so desires.

A contract entered into by an infant may be avoided by his guardian or by the infant. Upon attaining the age of majority, contracts made during infancy can still be avoided for a reasonable time. Disaffirmance may be made by act or declaration disclosing an unequivocal intent to repudiate. An infant is not precluded from disaffirming a contract because he misrepresented his age. Misrepresentation may impact the court's decision concerning the obligation to make restitution, and it can be treated as a tort in some jurisdictions. Failure to disaffirm within the appropriate time period constitutes an affirmance by default and thereafter the contract is binding.

If the property which was transferred to or by the minor has been resold to a good faith purchaser for value, that good faith purchaser takes good title which cannot now be defeated. Absent such a sale, disaffirmance by the minor revests title to any property received in the party from whom it was obtained. The minor may disaffirm and will be under no contractual obligations even if the property the minor had received has been consumed or destroyed. However, some jurisdictions have held minors liable in restitution to the other party for the fair value of property that cannot be returned as well as for services or other benefits received.

Infants can be held liable in restitution for the reasonable value of necessities furnished to them or their spouses or children. One purpose for recognizing this liability is to permit infants to obtain necessities of life that would be more difficult to obtain if infants could not be made to pay. Liability is limited to reasonable value rather than contract price as the contract has been avoided. The question of what constitutes necessities may depend upon the infant's background and standard of living and upon whether the infant is still being supported by the parents or has been emancipated.

The law distinguishes between a contract entered into by a minor which may be voidable by the minor and a conveyance or other transfer of property (which does not involve a promise and thus is not a contract). If a conveyance or other completed transfer occurs, it is possible that the transferee will take free of any claim of the minor to rescind the transfer, and even if the transfer was voidable at the option of the minor, a bona fide purchaser from the transferee may take free of the minor's claim provided the bona fide purchaser took without notice of the minor's claim.

Comment c to Restatement, section 14 provides:

The problems arising when an infant seeks to disaffirm a conveyance or executed contract are beyond the scope of the Restatement of this Subject, whether the disaffirmance is attempted before or after he comes of age.

In other words, the validity of a completed conveyance of property is not a matter that relates to contract law.

Contract rules also may not be applicable to issues relating to negotiable instruments which include certain types of notes and checks. Regarding the liability of minors on a negotiable instrument, U.C.C. section 3–202 provides in part as follows:

(a) Negotiation is effective even if obtained (i) from an infant * * * .

(b) To the extent permitted by other law, negotiation may be rescinded or may be subject to other remedies, but those remedies may not be asserted against a subsequent holder in due course or a person paying the instrument in good faith and without knowledge of facts that are a basis for rescission or other remedy.

§ 5.2.2 Parties With Mental Defects or Illness

Mental defects which partially impair a person's thought processes may be a basis for contract avoidance. The law must balance the interest in protecting the mentally ill with the interest in permitting them to pursue their right and freedom to contract. It is a simple fact that if you know you cannot enforce a contract against me, you will not be eager to enter into a bilateral contract with me. The law must also consider the question of protecting the rights of the other party to the bargain.

Many cases distinguish between mental conditions that impair a person's cognitive ability (the ability to understand the nature and consequences of the transaction), and mental conditions that impair a person's motivation or ability to act reasonably. Where a party to a contract lacks cognitive ability or understanding, the contract may be voidable without regard to whether the other party knew or had reason to know of the mental impairment. Where a party has impaired motivational control, the contract is usually held to be voidable only if the other party knew or had reason to know of the mental impairment. There is a significant minority position (known as the Faber rule) which also permits avoidance of the contract if the status quo can be restored (even if the other party had no reason to know of the mental disability).

A person seeking to avoid a contract has the burden of proof of the requisite facts. If the contract is still executory, the appropriate remedy is rescission. If the other party to the contract was not taking advantage of an apparent mental weakness and if the contract is not otherwise unfair, the right of avoidance may be lost to the extent that the contract has already been performed. If an unfair contract that resulted from mental impairment has been partially performed, the court may reform the contract or limit the non-impaired party to restitutionary recovery limited to the value of benefits conferred.

The defense of incompetency or lack of contract capacity is often raised in conjunction with other contract defenses. To the extent that there is evidence that tends to establish some degree of impairment of the cognitive or motivational type, this may properly be considered as a factor in determining whether relief should be granted on the grounds of mistake, misrepresentation or duress. The presence of mental impairment is of particular significance in cases involving undue influence.

§ 5.2.3 Persons Under the Influence of Drugs or Intoxicants

As previously noted, the law attempts to accommodate two conflicting goals: (1) protecting reasonable expectations and provide stability in commercial transactions, and (2) protecting those who have mental impairment. When one considers these policy factors, it becomes apparent why the cases distinguish sharply between those who are voluntarily intoxicated or under the influence of "recreational" drugs and those who are under medical care or are somehow involuntarily drugged or intoxicated.

Persons who voluntarily drink or take drugs to the point that they lose cognitive ability or motivational control will be permitted to avoid their contracts only where the other party knew or had reason to know of the degree of impairment. In practice, courts exhibit little sympathy for the party who claims intoxication as a defense, and contract avoidance is permitted only where it is apparent that the other party either created the situation or was knowingly taking advantage of an apparent incompetent.

Persons who are under medication or who are involuntarily drugged or intoxicated are treated in the same manner as persons with mental defects or illnesses.

§ 5.3   Duress; What Must Be Threatened

An apparent manifestation of assent may be defeated and the resulting contract avoided if assent was obtained by coercion which constitutes duress. A finding of duress requires an improper threat of sufficient gravity to induce the other party to manifest assent to an agreement and assent must have in fact been induced by this threat.

The threat may be express or implied from words or conduct and must communicate an intention to cause harm or loss to the other party. Many threats are quite proper. An auctioneer spends the entire auction threatening everyone in attendance that if they do not bid quickly, he will sell the goods to someone else. This is not an improper threat.

Historically court opinions have stated that to constitute a basis for the defense of duress, there must be a threat to do something unlawful or tortious. Many current writers express the opinion that this is too narrow a test because the circumstances in which the courts find duress today have been expanded. However, most of the expansion has resulted not from a change in the law of duress but rather the law has expanded its notions as to what conduct is wrongful or unlawful in the sense of being criminal or tortious. There follows a list of some types of threats which have been held to provide a basis for a finding of duress justifying rescission of a contract. As will be noted, each item can be classified as constituting a threat to engage in wrongful or unlawful conduct.

(1) A threat to commit a criminal or tortious act that will injure the person, family or property of the victim.

(2) A threat to institute criminal action to compel conduct. (Such conduct would be viewed as using the criminal justice process for private gain and itself constitutes criminal activity in virtually all jurisdictions—sometimes called extortion.)

(3) A threat to commence a civil action in circumstances where the use of the civil process of the courts would be characterized as an abuse of process (which is a tort).

(4) Threats not to engage in business dealings with the victim either by refusing to sell goods or refusing to purchase output in particular circumstances. Where this type of threat would provide the foundation for a defense of duress, it will also constitute a violation of state or federal antitrust or trade laws and is thus both criminal and tortious.

(5) A threat to disclose embarrassing facts to other parties or to the community which can constitute the crime commonly called blackmail.

There are a few examples of threats that have been found to be a proper basis for duress where no tort or criminal activity is involved. The following are examples.

(1) A bad faith threat not to perform a contract that is intended to extract an economically unjustified modification or collateral contract from the victim will provide a defense against enforcement of a resulting contract modification. This may be classified as duress. Comment 2 to U.C.C. section 2–209 states "the extortion of a 'modification' without legitimate commercial reason is ineffective as a violation of the duty of good faith."

(2) A threat to terminate the terminable-at-will employment contract of the victim or some relative or close acquaintance of the victim unless the victim consents to some agreement not connected with the employment contract has been found to provide a basis for a defense of duress. It is recognized in many cases today that an employer may not terminate a terminable-at-will employee for improper reasons (e.g., *Sheets v. Teddy's Frosted Foods, Inc.* (Conn. 1980)). Thus, a threat to discharge for refusal to manifest assent to an unrelated transaction is very possibly a threat of a wrongful breach of contract and in some circumstances could be a tort.

Subtle variations of this fact situation can produce difficult cases. Assume an employer is invited to the home of his employee's mother. While there, the employer admires an antique mantle clock and offers $500 for it. After mother rejects the proposal, the employer notes what a healthy impact upon her son's employment relationship could be effected if she would only reconsider. When mother digests this message, she agrees to sell for $500. The resulting contract may be voidable on grounds of duress. The results often will be dependent upon the particular facts of each case with the court focusing upon the degree of wrongfulness of the offending party's conduct and the state of mind or mental strength of the party who claims to have been the victim of the duress.

When dealing with problems of this nature, it may be helpful to remember an old axiom: Contract law is designed to protect the reasonable expectations of the parties. Sometimes answers become clearer if one asks the rhetorical question: What are the reasonable expectations of an employer who obtained an elderly lady's assent to the sale of her clock by threatening her son's job?

The Restatement utilizes the term "improper" to characterize threats which can provide a basis for the defense of duress, and it provides in section 176:

(2) A threat is improper if the resulting exchange is not on fair terms, and

(a) the threatened act would harm the recipient and would not significantly benefit the party making the threat,

(b) the effectiveness of the threat in inducing the manifestation of assent is significantly increased by prior unfair dealing by the party making the threat, or

(c) what is threatened is otherwise a use of power for illegitimate ends.

Some court decisions find duress based upon threats that are shockingly immoral or wrongful and result in purported bargains that are unconscionable. While this type of activity is sometimes labeled "duress", it is properly a matter of unconscionability and is treated in section 6.10.

§ 5.3.1 Duress; Sufficient Gravity to Induce a Manifestation of Assent

"If a party's manifestation of assent is induced by an improper threat by the other party that leaves the victim no reasonable alternative, the contract is voidable by the victim." (Restatement § 175(1).)

The degree of compulsion which must be established is highest in cases in which the threatened conduct is in the category sometimes referred to as "economic duress," such as threatened refusals to deal. Even where the threatened activity involves an obvious criminal act, it will not provide a basis for duress unless it threatens sufficient harm or damage to the victim as to justify finding that it would induce and did in fact induce a manifestation of consent which he would not otherwise have given.

In determining whether a given threat was sufficient to deprive the victim of his free will, the experience, sophistication and other personal characteristics of the aggrieved party are proper considerations.

§ 5.4 Undue Influence

Undue influence may be available as a defense where a person entered into an unfair transaction induced by improper persuasion. There are two distinct examples in which a defense of undue influence may properly be asserted. The first type involves finding that the victim was prevented from exercising free choice in the transaction due to the other party taking conscious advantage of a weakened mental state. The other involves breach of a fiduciary relationship which can exist despite the absence of any conscious wrongdoing.

Undue influence can be viewed as filling the niche between incapacity and duress. The victim may not be so lacking in capacity as to be able to assert a defense on that ground and the misconduct of the other party may not be sufficient to establish duress, but the combination of the victim's weakness and the other party's conscious taking advantage of that condition is sufficient to provide a defense to the enforcement of an unfair bargain. The weakened state of mind can result from illness, advanced age, immaturity, recent death of a spouse, excessive use of alcohol or drugs, or any other circumstances that tend to deprive a person of the ability to make sound decisions. One who is aware of these circumstances and takes advantage of them can be denied the fruits of this wrongdoing.

The other basis for asserting an undue influence defense involves breach of a fiduciary relationship. A fiduciary relationship exists where one party occupies a position of trust and confidence with respect to the other. These are commonly found in intra-family relationships such as the aunt who has often provided financial advice to her nephew. A fiduciary relationship exists in a professional-client relationship such as exists between an attorney and her client. Fiduciary status may also be found in any circumstances in which one party has imposed trust and confidence in another and come to rely upon the judgment of that other person.

If a contract between fiduciaries is found to produce an unfair result for the dependent person, it will be set aside on the grounds of undue influence. No additional wrongdoing such as a conscious taking advantage of the dependent person need be shown. Entering an unfair bargain with the dependent person is the only misconduct required. As a future attorney, one must realize that if one buys a farm from an estate you represent, one of two things can happen. If it goes down in value, you lose and no one feels sorry for you. If it goes up in value, the transaction can probably be set aside on the grounds of undue influence. From the attorney's perspective, it is a "heads you win tails I lose transaction." Good motives are no defense.

§ 5.5 Mistake Defined

Mistake is generally used as a contract defense whereby a person can avoid an otherwise valid contract. It can also be the basis for revising or reforming a contract with the result that the court will alter the rights and obligations of the parties. As used in the law of contracts, the term "mistake" refers to a belief that is not in accord with the facts. It must relate to a present factual matter existing at the time the contract is made. Proof of the existence of a mistake does not, in itself, afford a basis for relief from a contract or revision of the contract. It is simply the first step in establishing a right to avoid or reform a contract.

If a party contracts on Tuesday to purchase a commodity whose price declines sharply on Thursday, one might be inclined to state that the buyer made a mistake, but this is actually an error in judgment or an error in prediction. There were no facts existing on Tuesday, when the contract was made, about which either party was mistaken, and thus there can be no mistake of fact. Mistake requires a belief that is not in accord with existing facts.

Factual mistakes must be distinguished from errors in judgment. Assume that a party contracts to move a pile of dirt for a certain price thinking that the pile contains 800 yards of dirt. If the pile in fact contains 1,000 yards of dirt, there was a mistake of fact. (This may not be sufficient to excuse performance, but there is a mistake of fact.) If there is in fact only 800 yards of dirt but the actual cost of moving the dirt exceeds the contract price, there is no mistake of fact but rather an error in judgment.

Assume that two people contract for the sale of a horse for $4,000 thinking the horse is sound and can win races. If the horse in fact has a broken bone in its leg, there is a mistake of fact. If the horse has no broken bones but has run its last good race and never wins again, there is no mistake of fact. The mistake is one of judgment or prediction as to what the horse will do in the future.

Early common law cases assumed that everyone should know the law. These cases usually took the position that relief could not be granted even though one or both parties were operating under a mistake as to some law relevant to the transaction. An example might be a mistake as to the permitted uses of a parcel of land. The notion that everyone is presumed to know the law may have been an appropriate assumption in days when laws were less complex than they are today. Modern cases treat a mistaken understanding of the law as analogous to a mistake of fact and thus such an error can provide the basis for relief if the other requirements are met.

The law of mistake arose in courts of equity at a time when common law courts were disposed to enforce all bargains without regard to the "equities" of the situation. Today the law of mistake is part of the general law of contracts, but it is still applied and interpreted as a matter of equity. Concepts of fault, good faith, unconscionability and general fairness can be quite relevant in determining the proper disposition of a mistake issue, and all of the general rules that have come to be accepted in this area are subject to overriding considerations of what is fair under the circumstances. In applying the law of mistake, one must keep in mind that contracts are made to be performed and that relief from contracts on grounds such as mistake is the exception.

§ 5.5.1 Mutual Mistake

Restatement section 152 provides in part:

Where a mistake of both parties at the time a contract was made as to a basic assumption on which the contract was made has a material effect on the agreed exchange of performances, the contract is voidable by the adversely affected party unless he bears the risk of the mistake * * * .

Four elements are involved in this statement and each is important.

1) A mistake must relate to facts that exist at the time the contract is made. Events which occur later may provide a basis for avoiding the contract on grounds of impossibility, impracticability or frustration of purpose (Chapter 6), but subsequent events are not properly treated under the law of mistake.

2) The mistake must relate to a basic assumption upon which the contract was made. Court opinions in the earlier part of the twentieth century stated the requirement that the mistake must relate to the subject matter of the contract. When a supposedly barren cow named Rose was found to be pregnant immediately before delivery to a buyer, this focus upon mistake as to subject matter lead to a debate as to the actual subject matter of the contract. Was it a contract for a certain cow named Rose or a contract for a barren cow. If the subject matter was Rose, there was no mistake as to subject matter. If the subject matter was a barren cow, then there was a mutual mistake as Rose was in fact pregnant (*Sherwood v. Walker* (Mich.1887)).

The analysis used to decide the fate of Rose has been rejected in later cases (*Lenawee County Bd. of Health v. Messerly*, (Mich.1982)). Most modern cases focus upon whether the mistake goes to a basic assumption which is a more inclusive term and a more relevant inquiry. If both parties assumed that the cow being sold was barren and this fact had a major impact upon her potential use and value, then there was a mutual mistake as to a basic assumption upon which the contract was made. This modern result is not dependent upon defining the "subject matter of the contract."

Assume that in April a farmer contracts to sell for a fixed price wheat for delivery the following June after it is harvested. An error relating to the then existing market price of wheat on a national exchange would likely be a mistake as to a basic assumption upon which a contract for the sale of wheat was made. An error as to the general market and harvest prospects and conditions for wheat would not be a basic assumption upon which the contract was made. (One might also contend that this is not an existing fact but a future projection. An additional reason for denying relief is that future price changes is a risk that has been allocated by the contract as discussed in § 5.5.3.)

3) To provide a basis for relief, the mistake must have a material effect upon the agreed exchange. Mistakes as to facts that have a relatively minor impact on the transaction cannot serve as a defense or a basis for contract reformation. Merely showing

that this particular party would not have entered the contract if the true facts had been known most likely does not, in itself, establish materiality. It must be demonstrated that the contract as made is severely imbalanced and enforcement would therefore be unfair.

"Material effect" is a general concept not capable of precise definition. In determining whether a mistake produces an effect that is sufficiently material, a court can take into account the existing circumstances at the time the issue is raised and the nature of the relief that is sought or available. A mistake that might not be sufficiently material to avoid a contract might be sufficient to provide a basis for reforming a contract if there is a fair and equitable method to do so. If B and S negotiate for the purchase of a commercial lot on the basis of $2 per square foot and enter into a contract for $200,-000 on the mistaken belief that the property contains 100,000 square feet, the fact that the property only contains 97,000 square feet might be an appropriate basis for reforming the contract by reducing the price by $6,000 (sometimes called an abatement) even though the mistake was not sufficiently material to justify rescission of the contract.

4) The party seeking relief must not have assumed the risk of this mistake.

This final element for a mutual mistake defense relates to allocation of the risk of mistake which is covered in section 5.5.3.

§ 5.5.2   Unilateral Mistake

This subject deals with a situation in which only one of the parties was mistaken. The first question one might pursue is whether the other party induced the mistake. If the non-mistaken party induced the mistake, one should explore the possibility that there is a defense of misrepresentation (§§ 5.7.1 and 5.7.3). If the defense of misrepresentation is not available, then the party seeking relief is limited to proving unilateral mistake.

In order to obtain relief for unilateral mistake, a party must first prove each of the four elements required for mutual mistake as set forth in section 5.5.1 above. This includes proof that

(1) the mistake relates to a fact existing when the contract is made;

(2) the mistake involves a basic assumption upon which the contract was made;

(3) the mistake produces a material effect upon the agreed exchange; and,

(4) the mistaken party did not assume or legally bear the risk as to the mistaken fact.

In addition, to obtain relief on the basis of unilateral mistake, one must also prove either:

a) that the other party knew or had reason to know of the mistake, or

b) that the resulting contract is unconscionable.

One of these added elements must be proven to obtain relief for unilateral mistake as distinguished from mutual mistake.

Unilateral mistake can arise in numerous situations, but a typical example is the case in which one party makes a mathematical miscalculation. An offer may be made to perform a task for a given price which the offeree accepts. Thereafter, the offeror discovers that there was an error in the calculation of the price and seeks to avoid the contract or have it reformed. To resolve this question, one must analyze each of the elements required for relief.

There was an error as to an existing fact at the time the contract was made. The error relates to price which would be a basic assumption upon which the contract was made. Whether the error is sufficiently material in terms of its effect upon the contract performance will depend upon the magnitude of the error in relationship to the total contract. Whether the offeror will be held to bear the risk of this error is a difficult question which is analyzed in section 5.5.3. Finally, because the mistake is unilateral rather than mutual, the party seeking relief must prove either that the other party knew or had reason to know of the error or that the enforcement of the resulting contract would be unconscionable.

One must examine the specific facts of the case to determine whether the other party knew or had reason to know of the error. If the offeree had shopped prices to the point that he had knowledge of the amount that one would ordinarily expect to pay for the job in question, then he might be held to have had reason to know the fact that the offer for a distinctly lower price must be the product of a mistake. If he reviewed the offeror's figures and noted an error in addition, or noted that one item was omitted from the calculations, then he knew of the mistake.

It is sometimes stated that one cannot snap up an offer that he knows to be the product of a mistake. While this may be qualified by limiting it to material mistakes, it is a reasonably accurate generalization. If the offeree actually knew of the mistake, a court can be expected to be rather generous toward the mistaken party in finding the other necessary elements for a mistake defense. This whole subject is one in which the results are dictated by fairness and equity, and there is little fairness or equity in permitting the enforcement of a contract by one who knew that the offer was the product of a mistake. The basic objective of contract law, protecting the reasonable expectations of the parties, does not suffer if we deny a party the benefits of a bargain that he knew to be the product of a mistake.

If the party seeking relief for a unilateral mistake cannot prove that the other party knew or should have known of the mistake, relief will be granted only if enforcement of the contract would be unconscionable. Unconscionability is a difficult concept to define with any precision. In extreme cases, unconscionability is a defense in and of itself without proof of any mistake (§ 5.10). If one is seeking relief for unilateral mistake and has established the other necessary elements, a lesser level of unconscionability is ordinarily sufficient for relief. In the case of an offer that is the product of mathematical miscalculation as discussed above, courts will frequently inquire into whether performance of the contract as made will produce a net loss to the mistaken party. If the error results only in lower profit, the enforcement of the contract might be found not to be unconscionable. If the party would lose money from performance of the contract, that is usually sufficient to find that the requirement of unconscionability is fulfilled. In the context of a mistake defense, proof of "unconscionability" requires far less egregious facts than those required for a pure unconscionability defense where no mistake can be proven.

Cases dealing with mistake often inquire into additional factors. It is stated that relief will be more readily granted if the mistaken party discovers the error and seeks relief promptly. Court opinions sometimes inquire into the effect upon the non-mistaken party of granting relief. What additional burdens will the non-mistaken party now be required to bear if relief is granted? If performance has already begun so that simple rescission of the contract is no longer an available alternative, courts may be more reluctant to grant relief. Relief for mistake may also be denied because a third party has relied upon the transaction and would now be adversely affected by a rescission. The law of mistake is administered by courts of equity and all considerations of fairness and justice are properly weighed.

§ 5.5.3 Allocation of Risk of Mistake

When a party has assumed the risk of mistake
with respect to the accuracy of certain facts existing
at the time a contract is made, that party cannot
obtain relief if those facts are incorrect. This allocation of risk is an overall control on the availability
of mistake as a basis for contract relief.

A party may bear the risk of mistake as to certain
factual matters because the contract allocated that
risk to that party. In a sale of land, the contract
may provide that the buyer has obtained information about the lawful use of the property and is
relying completely upon his own investigation of
this matter. If the buyer later seeks to avoid this
contract on the grounds that the buyer was mistak-
en (or that both parties were mistaken) as to the
zoning or the availability of a use permit for a given
activity, the court might well conclude that the risk
of such factual errors was allocated to the buyer in
the contract.

Assume that a contract provides: "Purchaser has
examined the property and agrees to accept same in
its present condition." One might expect a court to
conclude that mistakes as to compliance with local
health codes are not available to the purchaser by
way of defense because the purchaser assumed that
risk (*Lenawee County Bd. Of Health v. Messerly*,
(Mich.1982)).

In some construction contracts subsurface soil
conditions are quite important. These contracts frequently contain provisions regarding which party

has investigated these conditions. If responsibility for these matters was placed on the contractor, a court will deny relief for a later discovered mistake on the grounds that the contractor assumed this risk.

Parties cannot obtain relief based upon mistake if they enter into contracts knowing that their knowledge of relevant facts is limited. If these parties knowingly treat their limited knowledge as sufficient and proceed to enter into a contract, the risk of factual error will be allocated to them. One cannot claim to be mistaken if you knew you were ignorant as to the facts.

Assume that Lumber Co. contracts to pay a stated sum to Landowner for the right to cut certain size logs on Blackacre. Prior to entering the contract, a representative of Lumber Co. walked across Blackacre and the parties discussed waiting until a detailed timber cruise could be performed to make a precise estimate of the quantity of timber available for cutting. However, Lumber Co. proceeded to enter into the contract without bothering to make a formal inventory of the trees. If Lumber Co. later learns that there is less timber than it believed, no mistake defense is available. The risk that there is less (or perhaps more) timber than the parties assumed will properly be allocated to the adversely affected party.

The risk of mistake may also be allocated to a party on the grounds that it is reasonable to do so. In a construction contract the risk as to unexpected subsoil conditions may be allocated to the contractor as a matter of law even though the contract does not mention this matter. In a land sales contract, the risk that oil might be discovered under land after the contract is made is a risk that is allocated to the seller and no relief will be granted on the grounds of mistake.

Assume that two violinists, S and B, contract for the sale of a violin. Each knows that the instrument is old and is exceptionally good. Before concluding the contract, they discuss the fact that it could even be a Stradivarius. In fact, it is a Stradivarius. The contract should not be subject to avoidance as the seller was aware that he had limited knowledge as to the identity of the instrument but chose to treat his limited knowledge as sufficient.

Allocation of risks involves policy determinations. Assume that an injured party signs a release for all injuries, known and unknown, in exchange for a settlement of a tort claim. The contract language expressly allocates to the injured party the risk that the injuries might be more serious than presently assumed, and the injured party was aware that he had limited knowledge at the time he signed the release. If it later develops that the injuries are far more extensive than was assumed, a court may review the facts carefully to determine as a matter of policy whether the risk of this mistake should be allocated to the victim.

§ 5.5.4 Fault in the Mistake Context

A party may be precluded from obtaining relief for mistake where the mistake occurred due to that party's fault. This issue arises with some frequency in the context of an erroneous calculation of prices or costs. The mere fact that a party could have avoided the mistake had he been more careful is not sufficient "fault" to deny relief.

It is generally stated that "simple negligence" will not bar a person from relief, whereas "gross negligence" or the violation of a "positive legal duty" will bar relief. The problem with such vocabulary is that there is no workable definition of "gross" as distinguished from "simple" negligence, and such characterizations tend to patch over the uncertainty rather than providing definitive answers.

The Restatement takes the position in section 157 that fault will bar relief only where it amounts to a failure to act in good faith and in accordance with reasonable standards of fair dealing. Comment (a) contains the following:

> * * * The general duty of good faith and fair dealing, imposed under the rule stated in § 205, extends only to the performance and enforcement of a contract and does not apply to the negotiation stage prior to the formation of the contract. See Comment c to § 205. Therefore, a failure to act in good faith and in accordance with reasonable standards of fair dealing during pre-contractual negotiations does not amount to a breach. Nevertheless, under the rule stated in this Section, the failure bars a mistaken party from relief based on a mistake that otherwise would not have

been made. During the negotiation stage each party is held to a degree of responsibility appropriate to the justifiable expectations of the other. The terms "good faith" and "fair dealing" are used, in this context, in much the same sense as in § 205 and Uniform Commercial Code § 1–203.

So long as obvious illustrations are utilized, the "good faith" and "reasonable standards of fair dealing" tests can be applied, but they are of little help in the situation in which a party seeks relief from a "dumb, inexcusable" mistake such as leaving out the cost of the roof in preparing an estimate for a construction contract. While imprecise, the "simple negligence"-"gross negligence" analysis may be as close as one can come to stating the question that the courts are attempting to resolve here.

Mutual mistake cases can involve situations in which both parties share blame or fault for having failed to discover a mistake. Resolution of the issue may involve an overt effort to compare negligence or fault in this mistake case as many jurisdictions now do in negligence cases in tort.

§ 5.5.5 Mistake Resulting From Failure to Read

The basic rule is that one who manifests assent to the terms of a writing is presumed to know its contents and is bound to what he would have discovered and known had he read it. With some exceptions in the area of adhesion contracts (§ 4.4), this is the rule that is applied where the writing in question represents the product of the offer and acceptance process and is the only manifestation of the assent of the parties.

A different problem is presented where parties have previously concluded an agreement and thereafter reduce it to written form or to a more formal writing. In this situation, a contract exists; the parties presumably know and understand its terms, and the purpose of the writing is to memorialize the agreement or reproduce it in a "cleaner" document. If the new writing does not accurately reflect the existing agreement between the parties, either party can seek relief by way of reformation of the writing on the grounds of excusable mistake, and the failure to read or to read carefully does not necessarily bar relief.

§ 5.6 Mistakes or Misunderstandings That Prevent Formation of a Contract (As Distinguished from Merely Providing Grounds to Rescind or Reform a Contract)

The existence of a mistake of fact may prevent the formation of a contract. This can occur if there is a mistake as to parties or other fundamental error by one party which is known to the other. It can also occur where there is a misunderstanding as to essential terms that the court cannot resolve.

If an offeror intends to make an offer to X but mistakenly makes that offer to Y who is aware of the error, Y cannot accept the offer. Assume that S intended to make an offer to the State Machinery Company in Connecticut. By inadvertence, S's employee addressed the offer to the Nutmeg State

Machinery Corporation, an error that is perhaps understandable because Connecticut is the Nutmeg State. The communications from S referred to specific prior transactions between the parties. Nutmeg had no prior transactions with S and thus had reason to know that S was operating under a mistake of identity. There is no valid offer, and Nutmeg's purported acceptance will not produce a contract. If Nutmeg had no reason to know of the error, S would be bound to a contract on the terms of the objective manifestations made to Nutmeg.

If an offeree knows that an offer is the product of a mistake, there is no offer and there can be no acceptance. Assume that there is an established market for oranges with the price ranging from $2.60 to $2.65 per box. S sends what appears to be an offer to B by wire which states that S will sell a stated quantity of oranges for $2.00 per box. In the absence of unusual facts, B would have reason to know that the purported offer contained a mistake. There is no offer, and B cannot form a contract by attempting to accept.

No contract results from an exchange of communications if the parties attach a materially different meaning to their communications and neither knows nor has reason to know the meaning attached by the other. This situation can arise if the language used by the parties is ambiguous or otherwise subject to more than one meaning, and the court cannot find that either party should have known of the meaning intended by the other. Assume that A offers to sell and B agrees to buy for a

stated price the ship "Peerless." Unknown to either
party, there are two ships named "Peerless" and
each intended a different ship. Assuming that there
is no basis for finding that one party should have
known that the other intended a different ship,
there is no contract. In the unlikely event that both
parties knew or had reason to know of the ambiguity yet did not resolve the question of which ship
was intended, there would likewise be no contract.
(Students of contract law will encounter a "Peerless" case with facts different from this hypothetical. It is suggested that in the actual case, the court
overlooked various possibilities for finding an enforceable contract.)

§ 5.6.1 Vagueness and Ambiguity Distin-
guished

A contract for the sale of a quantity of eviscerated
"chicken" may be unenforceable due to ambiguity if
the buyer subjectively intends to buy fryers and the
seller subjectively intends to sell stewing hens. (See
Illustration 4 to Restatement § 201.) The term
chicken is ambiguous because it could mean fryers
or stewing chickens or perhaps some other category
of chicken. A term is ambiguous when it is subject
to two distinct meanings and there is no satisfactory way to resolve to which meaning it refers. The
Restatement indicates that the proper result in the
chicken hypothetical is that there is no contract due
to the inability to resolve this ambiguity.

The term chicken may also be vague in this
context because it is not clear how large the chick-

ens are to be. An interesting hypothetical helps distinguish between vagueness and ambiguity. Assume that B contracts to purchase one gross of red ball point pens. The subject matter is ambiguous because it is unclear whether the pens are to have red ink or whether the exterior of the pens themselves is to be red. Assume a different transaction in which buyer purchases one gross of red T-shirts. In this context the term red is vague because there are a number of different shades of red and it is not clear exactly what shade the seller may provide. This topic is well developed in Drafting Contracts (2d Ed. Burnham, Scott J. Mitchie Co., 1993).

§ 5.7 Avoidance of Contract on Basis of Misrepresentation; Misrepresentation Defined

A misrepresentation is an assertion which is not in accord with the facts. A misrepresentation can exist regardless of the guilt or innocence of the person who makes the misstatement. Misrepresentations may be intentional. Misrepresentations can result from negligent failure to check facts. Misrepresentations can be totally innocent. Compare the term fraud which is defined to include intentional wrongdoing and usually also includes scienter, an intention to deceive and induce reliance by the other party. The terms "misrepresentation" and "fraud" are not synonymous.

The law requires honesty but does not necessarily require candor. Nondisclosure does not constitute a misrepresentation unless there is some legal basis for imposing upon the party a duty to disclose the fact in question. Such a duty to disclose is recognized where there is a relationship of trust and confidence between the parties. The duty also exists where disclosure is necessary to correct a previous assertion that may not have been misleading when made but has become inaccurate due to a change in circumstances. A growing number of statutes create a duty to disclose pertinent information in various types of transactions. Frequently these pertain to consumer transactions and to contracts relating to specific subjects such as sale of real property. These statutes may provide their own specific relief or remedies, but if such a statute exists, nondisclosure would constitute a misrepresentation.

Conduct that is designed to prevent, or likely to prevent another from learning a fact is equivalent to an assertion that the fact does not exist. An example would be a seller painting over the water stains to hide the fact that the roof leaks. This is referred to as a concealment. Mere silence is not a misrepresentation unless there is an affirmative basis for finding a duty to disclose, in which case the misrepresentation would be found in the nondisclosure.

A misrepresentation defense can be based upon a half-truth. A half-truth is a statement that is literally true with respect to the fact stated but which produces an implication which is false with respect to other facts. A statement by a dog seller that the dog ate well last night is a half-truth and thus a misrepresentation if the dog later became so sick that the veterinarian pumped its stomach. If the statement about the dog eating well was made before the dog became ill, this would create a duty to disclose as discussed above.

§ 5.7.1 Fraudulent Misrepresentation and Material Misrepresentations

One who seeks to utilize the defense of misrepresentation to avoid a contract must show that the misrepresentation was either material or fraudulent. Material misrepresentations can be divided into two categories. A misrepresentation is material if it would be likely to induce a reasonable person to manifest his assent to a bargain. A misrepresentation is material in a particular situation if the person who made it knew or should have known that it was likely to induce the particular person to whom it was made to manifest assent to a bargain. If a misrepresentation is material, it can provide grounds for avoiding contract even if it was only a negligent or even an innocent misrepresentation.

In order to establish that a party's misrepresentation was fraudulent, one must prove that the misrepresentation was made with the intention of inducing the other party to rely on it and that it was made with knowledge of its falsity, or with knowledge that the party did not have the factual basis that he asserted or implied to support the assertion. In other words, the maker of the misrepresentation must know that it is false or must know that he doesn't know whether it is false or not. In matters of opinion, which are discussed in the next section, it is also sufficient if the maker of the misrepresentation believes that his assertion is false. This requirement of knowledge or belief in the inaccuracy, or inadequate foundation of one's assertions, is often labeled scienter. It is a required element in the tort of fraud in most jurisdictions. It is only an alternative element in the contract defense of misrepresentation and only need be established if there is inadequate evidence that the misrepresentation was material to the transaction. Since almost all decided contract cases do involve misrepresentations that are material, the question whether they were made fraudulently may not appear to be critical. However, it may have great practical significance in determining whether the finder of fact will find the victim's reliance to have been reasonable or justified.

In contract cases involving the subject of misrepresentation, the terms "fraud" and "fraudulent" are often used rather loosely. So long as the misrepresentation was material, this imprecise usage of the term is of no great consequence. However, if materiality is not established, the requirement of scienter becomes critical if the misrepresentation is to serve as a basis for avoidance of the contract.

§ 5.7.2 Reasonableness of Reliance; Misrepresentations of Fact, Opinion, Law and Intention

A party cannot seek to avoid a contract on the basis of misrepresentation unless he relied upon it to the extent that it contributed significantly to his decision to enter into the contract on the agreed terms. This reliance must have been to the party's detriment either in a pecuniary sense or in the sense that he has not received the bargain which he thought he was getting.

Reliance on the misrepresentation must be reasonable. All surrounding factors and circumstances in each case can be relevant including the party's age, education, experience and other qualities. It would include the subject matter and nature of the transaction and the circumstances under which it is being made.

One critical factor in determining the reasonableness of the reliance is the source of the misrepresentation. One who concocts an elaborate scheme to defraud which is so bizarre that it should be obvious to any person with an ounce of common sense, will not be heard to complain that his victims should have known better than to fall into the trap that was laid. Conversely, a misrepresentation that is the product of an innocent or negligent mistake is not likely to justify rescission of a contract if the party who relied is more at fault than the party who unintentionally misrepresented existing facts.

Reliance upon an expression of opinion presents additional considerations. Some opinions are nonfactual and provide no basis for reliance; e.g., "Where we are standing on the porch of this cabin is the best view on the entire lake." This opinion is sufficiently devoid of factual basis that any reliance upon it would presumably be unreasonable. However, if the person to whom this statement is made is blind, it might be reasonable for the blind party to rely upon the opinion as at least representing the speaker's honest opinion. The statement of opinion is an expression of fact as to what the speaker believes it to be true. Thus, a dishonest statement as to one's opinion is a misstatement of fact, and if the blind person is found to have reasonably relied, rescission for misrepresentation should be available.

Many expressions of opinion clearly infer that the speaker knows facts upon which the opinion is based or at least that he does not know facts that are incompatible with that opinion. The statement, "You should be able to grow good tomatoes on this ground," infers that the speaker knows that the soil is compatible with tomatoes or at least that he does not know that the ground will not grow tomatoes. As in the case of other misrepresentations, surrounding facts and circumstances will determine whether reliance upon this representation was reasonable.

An expression of opinion by one who possesses or appears to possess superior knowledge may justify reliance. This is particularly true if the parties have some relationship of trust and confidence or if other facts exist from which one might justify reliance upon such an expression. The seller who makes his living as a mechanic and who tells his sister-in-law that the car that he is selling her has a "good engine" expresses an opinion that can become the basis of justified reliance and provide grounds to rescind a contract if erroneous.

It is sometimes stated that one cannot rely on a misrepresentation as to domestic law because all persons are presumed to have equal access to the law. There are still cases that appear to take the position that reliance upon a representation as to the law is not justified. The better approach is to subject the assertion to the same inquiries as are applied to representations of fact. The representation may be one of fact, e.g., "I just read the new law and it states that it does not go into effect until next January." The representation may be a completely nonfactual opinion, e.g., "Now that the composition of the Supreme Court has changed, that statute will be held to be unenforceable." Reliance may be justified because the person who expressed the opinion has or appears to have superior knowledge. Misrepresentations as to matters of law are not fundamentally different from misrepresentations of fact and should be resolved in similar fashion.

Statements of future intentions do not ordinarily provide a basis for reasonable reliance by the other party to a contract. It is apparent that intentions may change and the future intentions of one party are not ordinarily deemed to be of significant concern to the other, thus they are not the proper basis for reliance. The classic example of this principle and of the exception to the rule involves the buyer who misstates his intended use of the property that is the subject of the sale. Stating that he wants the property for a pasture when he plans to build an oil refinery is ordinarily not the proper basis for a misrepresentation action. However, if the seller is selling only a portion of his property and would be harmed or offended by the construction of the refinery next to his remaining holdings, then the misrepresentation by the buyer of his present intention may justify such reliance as to provide a basis for rescission of the contract.

§ 5.7.3 Misrepresentation and Mistake Compared

A party who seeks to avoid a contract or reform a contract on the grounds of misrepresentation is, of necessity, telling the court that he was mistaken as to the true facts. If the victim relied upon a misstatement of fact, then the victim must have been mistaken as to an existing fact at the time the contract was made. Conversely, in a mistake case, if one states that the mistake was induced by the other party, then it is apparent that the other party must have misrepresented the true facts. Thus, one should not be surprised to see arguments relating to mistake and misrepresentation existing in the same fact situation.

The defense of mistake and the defense of misrepresentation may coexist in the same fact situation. One does not need two defenses, however, when two defenses are available, one may do the job when some failure in the evidence prevents the use of the other. For example, if the issue is mistake, one may find that the evidence does not really support a finding that the fact in question was a basic assumption on which the contract was made. If the mistake resulted from a misrepresentation by the other party, then the issue may be cast in the alternative as one of misrepresentation and this failure of proof (regarding basic assumption) might not preclude a successful defense.

A question regarding the duty to disclose is presented where one party knows that the other is mistaken as to a basic assumption on which that party is making the contract. For example, the first party knows about a certain fact that is material to the contract. The second party is unaware of this fact. Whether and to what extent there is a duty to disclose the true situation is a major policy question as to which courts are divided. Some require the seller to advise the buyer about such matters as the fact that there are termites in the house. Others assume that the buyer should ascertain such facts so long as the seller has not acted to conceal the defect. Where disclosure is required, it is usually a case in which one party has special knowledge or a special means of obtaining knowledge as to the facts in question. Some states have adopted statutes that impose higher duties to disclose than those recognized at common law.

If one party knows that the other party is operating under a mistake of fact, such as an error in arithmetic or an error as to the contents of a writing, this may give rise to a duty to disclose. To avoid the contract on the basis of a defense of mistake ordinarily requires a showing of materiality of the error and that the risk has not been allocated to the party claiming mistake. If basic standards of fair dealing require that the party who knew of the mistake should have disclosed it, then failure to disclose is a misrepresentation, and the defense of misrepresentation may be available to avoid the contract even though the error did not relate to a material matter.

For example, a contractor who makes a minor error in calculating the price might be precluded from getting relief under the law of mistake. However, if the owner knew of the error, he would presumably be found to have a duty to disclose the mistake to the contractor. Given that duty, failure to disclose may constitute a fraudulent misrepresentation which can then provide a basis for avoiding or reforming the contract.

§ 5.8 Misrepresentation, Duress or Undue Influence by a Third Party

If a party to a contract knows or has reason to know that the other was induced to enter the contract as the result of misrepresentation, duress or undue influence committed by a third person, then the victim may avoid the contract. There is also authority for the proposition that even if the other party has no reason to know of the improper conduct, the victim may still avoid the transaction unless the other party has materially relied upon the transaction or given value.

For example, assume that E, while driving a truck owned by his employer, Acme, was injured in an accident caused by the negligence of T. Acme, in order to obtain a prompt settlement of the property damage to its truck, threatens to fire E unless E settles his personal injury claim with T's insurance carrier for a sum less than that to which E may be entitled. The wrongful conduct of Acme may permit E to obtain rescission of the settlement agreement and pursue his tort claim against T. This result would be easier to reach if the facts indicated that T or T's insurance carrier was aware of the improper threat made by Acme.

§ 5.9 Misrepresentation That Prevents Formation of a Contract

Misrepresentation ordinarily is simply a contract defense that allows one party to avoid the contract. However, under certain circumstances misrepresentation can prevent even a voidable contract from being formed. No contract results when a person's purported consent is obtained by a misrepresentation that prevents the person from being aware of what he is doing. For example, assume that a baseball player is signing autographs. A crowd of people is handing him programs and scraps of paper to sign. Someone hands the player a promissory note which he signs without any awareness of its contents. The misrepresentation can be labeled "fraud in the factum," and no legal obligation results.

These are relatively rare fact situations that are in some ways comparable to the mistake cases where no contract is formed (§ 5.6). The party seeking to avoid the apparent obligation must establish that he neither knew nor had reasonable opportunity to know the nature of the document that he was signing. The apparent manifestation of consent does not result in a contract that can be avoided. It simply does not result in any contract at all.

The significance of a transaction being void rather than merely an avoidable contract involves the rights that third parties may acquire. If one signs a voidable promissory note, the right to avoid it will be lost if the note is negotiable and is transferred to a holder in due course. If the note is void because of fraud in the factum, no one can acquire rights under it.

If Y acquires X's goods such as a bike pursuant to a voidable contract, Y may only have voidable title but if Y transfers the bike to a good faith purchaser for value, that purchaser takes good title and X's right to recover the bike is lost (U.C.C. § 2–403(1)). In some situations, however, X could lose his bike even if there was no contract and Y took no title. This could occur if Y was a merchant who dealt in goods of that kind who was entrusted with possession of the goods by X and Y sold them to a person who qualifies as a buyer in the ordinary course of business. (U.C.C. § 2–403(2).) These matters relating to title are properly categorized as issues of property law rather than contract law as they involve questions of title rather than enforcement of promises.

B. DEFENSES BASED UPON POLICY
§ 5.10 Unconscionability as a Defense; Procedural and Substantive

While all defenses reflect policy choices, those discussed in the first part of this chapter relate to the question whether there was freely manifested assent to the bargain. The question of fairness of the bargain is frequently a relevant issue when a party asserts a defense based upon lack of capacity, undue influence, duress, mistake or misrepresentation. (See §§ 5.1–5.9 above.) When one or more of these defenses is asserted, a finding that the purported bargain is unfair to one party may be necessary to establish the right to relief. Even if unfairness is not expressly required as an element of the defense, the presence of unfairness is certainly helpful when one seeks to induce a court of equity to grant relief. "Fairness" is thus an important factor in contract defenses, but unfairness alone generally does not provide grounds for relief.

In the absence of one or more of the above mentioned defenses, courts have demonstrated a marked reluctance to deny enforcement to contracts for the sole reason that they are "unfair." It is generally deemed appropriate to leave the determination of what is and is not an appropriate bargain to the parties themselves. This reflects the notion that freedom of contract is important, and that courts should enforce agreements as the parties made them and intended them without passing judgment upon their substance.

In contrast to common law rules, courts of Equity historically withheld equitable relief (such as specific performance) in the absence of an affirmative showing that the bargain was fair. Courts of Equity would deny any remedy if that required enforcing a contract that was deemed to be unconscionable. Today, courts exercising equity jurisdiction continue to require proof that the transaction was fair when made before granting equity relief such as specifically enforcing the obligation or enjoining its breach.

Legal remedies, as distinguished from equitable remedies, are ordinarily granted without any inquiry into fairness. However, starting in the later half of the twentieth century, common law courts in some jurisdictions began to transport the equitable concept of unconscionability into the common law and recognize it as a defense. If the facts of a particular case are sufficiently egregious, enforcement of all or part of a contract can be denied on the grounds of unconscionability. This borrowing of an equitable defense and transporting it into the common law is nothing new. As previously noted, all of the defenses discussed above with the exception of some aspects of the law relating to lack of capacity were originally developed in courts of equity and then came to be adopted over a period of time by common law courts.

Prior to the adoption of the U.C.C. (generally in the mid–1960's), there were only a small handful of common law cases that denied enforcement of a contract or a particular provision in a contract because it was unconscionable. These opinions do not articulate any specific standards or rule beyond the vague notion that the contract would not be enforced because it shocked the conscience of the court. This rather vague standard was incorporated into U.C.C. section 2–302 which provides:

Section 2–302. Unconscionable Contract or Clause

(1) If the court as a matter of law finds the contract or any clause of the contract to have been unconscionable at the time it was made the court may refuse to enforce the contract, or it may enforce the remainder of the contract without the unconscionable clause, or it may so limit the application of any unconscionable clause as to avoid any unconscionable result.

(2) When it is claimed or appears to the court that the contract or any clause thereof may be unconscionable the parties shall be afforded a reasonable opportunity to present evidence as to its commercial setting, purpose and effect to aid the court in making the determination.

All jurisdictions except Louisiana (which did not adopt Article 2) and California adopted this section. In 1979 California adopted a general law applicable to all contracts that contains identical language (Cal. Civ. Code § 1670.5). The Restatement has now adopted a provision (§ 208) that parallels U.C.C. section 2–302 and is applicable to all contracts, not just transactions in goods. These developments together with court decisions in a number of jurisdictions have brought the defense of unconscionability into the mainstream.

Unconscionability focuses upon the fairness and effect of the terms as circumstances existed at the time the contract was formed and not as of the time of performance of the contract. The doctrine of unconscionability was intended to prevent oppression and unfair surprise and not to relieve a party from the effect of a bad bargain. Case law has provided some definitional parameters to identify what is unconscionable, usually utilizing the concepts of procedural unconscionability and substantive unconscionability.

Procedural unconscionability has to do with how a term becomes part of a contract. It can relate to matters bearing upon a party's lack of knowledge or understanding of the contract terms due to factors such as inconspicuous print, unintelligible legalistic language and a party's lack of opportunity to read a contract or ask questions concerning its terms and meanings. Illiteracy or lack of sophistication may be relevant here. Procedural unconscionability can also relate to a lack of voluntariness arising from great disparity of bargaining power that makes the stronger party's terms non-negotiable. These situations frequently involve an adhesion contract, which is simply a contract drafted by the dominant party and then presented to the other, the "adhering" party, on a take-it-or-leave-it basis. (See § 4.4.) Adhesion contracts are not *per se* objectionable, but the presence of an adhesion contract, with the attendant lack of any ability to negotiate, may bear upon contract interpretation and defenses and may provide a basis for finding procedural unconscionability.

Substantive unconscionability is the term used to describe contracts or portions of contracts that are oppressive or overly harsh. In determining whether substantive unconscionability is present, courts have focused upon

(a) provisions that deprive one party of the benefits of the agreement or leave that party without a remedy for the nonperformance of the other;

(b) provisions that bear no reasonable relation to the business risk involved;

(c) provisions that are to the substantial disadvantage of one party without producing a commensurate benefit to the other or,

(d) an excessively large disparity between the cost and the selling price of the subject matter of the contract with no objective justification.

Some courts refer to contract provisions such as exculpatory clauses in terms of unconscionability, but such items are usually treated as matters of public policy or illegality which are discussed in the next section.

It is unlikely that relief will be granted on the grounds of unconscionability unless elements of procedural and substantive unconscionability are both present. So long as the contract was fair when made, disparity of bargaining power, illiteracy, or other factors relating to voluntariness of the agreement will probably not provide a basis for avoiding the contract terms. Conversely, almost every case that has granted relief in a substantively unconscionable transaction has contained elements of procedural unconscionability. Given our respect for principles of freedom of contract, it is difficult to justify relieving a party from a contract on the grounds of fairness if none of the factors relating to procedural unconscionability are present.

It should not be assumed that this defense is available only to those who are unsophisticated and economically deprived. In fact, many of the cases appearing in the appellate reports involve contracts between business entities or other relatively sophisticated parties.

The defense of unconscionability should not be confused with the duty of good faith that arises as a result of the making of the contract (U.C.C. § 1–203 and Restatement § 205). Good faith controls the conduct of the parties in the performance and enforcement of the contract after it is made. It is not generally applicable to the formation of the contract (*see* §§ 4.11 and 4.12). However, some courts have discussed the concept of bad faith in negotiations, indicating that its presence might fulfill the procedural element for a finding of unconscionability.

§ 5.11 Public Policy or Illegality as a Defense (*in pari delicto*)

All of the defenses discussed above in sections 5.1–5.10 relate to concerns for the protection of a party to the contract. Illegality or violation of public policy is a defense which involves the public welfare and the courts' reluctance to allow the judicial process to become involved with the enforcement of certain transactions. Since justice for the parties is not the reason for this defense, one will get quite confused attempting to apply it if one does not realize at the outset that fairness to the parties is not the name of the game here. In some cases there may be a motive to punish a party for making a bargain that is deemed anti-social, even if the corollary is that the other party receives the totally unjustified windfall of escaping from his contract obligation and retaining any benefits already received.

The defense of illegality apparently traces its existence to the Highwayman's Case, an unreported English decision from 1725. After a successful season robbing travelers, one highway robber sued his fellow robber for failure to account for "partnership profits." The court dismissed the action and fined plaintiff's counsel for the scandalous impertinence of even bringing the matter into court. Denial of recovery was not predicated upon any notion of fairness or justice as between the parties. The concern in these cases is not with protecting the defendant from an unfair bargain but with preventing the use of the courts to enforce anti-social contracts. The judge apparently was willing to abide the presence of robbers in the courtroom for criminal proceedings, but the judge was not going to have his courtroom used to settle civil disputes between these miscreants.

There is a general policy that freely-made bargains should be recognized as valid contracts. This goal will be overridden when a court finds compelling public policy reasons to deny enforcement. This is not a defense that need be raised by a party. The judge will raise this point *sua sponte* (on its own motion). The source of this public policy may be derived from case law or statutes, but not every violation of statute, even a criminal statute, will create a policy concern strong enough to deny enforcement of an otherwise valid contract.

Examples of terms that have been found by judicial decision to raise questions concerning enforceability include:

(1) contracts requiring a performance that violates criminal laws;

(2) contracts requiring a performance that is a tort;

(3) contracts that involve a performance that will constitute a restraint of trade or interference with contractual relationships of another (which are also torts);

(4) contracts to engage in conduct which, though not illegal, contravenes public morals;

(5) contracts that impair family relationships;

(6) contracts that interfere with the administration of justice; and,

(7) contracts that purport to affect legal relationships in ways objectionable to the court, such as:

a) agreements to be bound by the law of another jurisdiction where the apparent purpose is to avoid rules of law viewed as fundamental in the local jurisdiction;

(b) agreements not to be bound by laws relating to such matters as usury or statutes of limitations or consumer protection legislation;

(c) agreements not to hold a party responsible for misrepresentation of fact;

(d) exculpatory clauses that would relieve a party from liability for harm caused by intentional or reckless conduct (§ 5.11.2); and,

(e) contracts that are otherwise violative of a public duty.

Some statutes prohibit certain conduct and expressly provide that contracts made in violation of the statute are not enforceable. For example, many jurisdictions have statutes that prohibit contingency contracts for lobbyists. A more complicated question arises where legislation has proscribed certain conduct with no clear indication whether violation of this legislation should preclude the enforcement of a contract. In this situation where the legislative intent is not ascertainable, the court must resolve the question by analyzing whether the statute establishes a fundamental policy, violation of which should provide a basis to deny enforcement of a contract.

In determining when a violation of public policy will prevent enforcement of a contract, the courts must consider not just the gravity of the misconduct but also the closeness of the connection between the misconduct and the contract performances. There may be a direct connection if the contract performance itself is violative of public policy. In another case the contract may involve no objectionable performance but the agreement may have been obtained by improper methods such as by bribing an agent. A more remote connection exists if one party in fact performs an illegal act in the course of performing the contract.

The contract performance may be perfectly proper in itself but be designed to further an improper purpose. Ordinarily only one party is directly involved with the intended improper purpose. For example, a contract for the sale of a chemical may be legal, but the issue of violation of public policy may arise if it is established that the person buying the chemical intends to use it to manufacture illegal drugs. In these cases, the courts are concerned with the gravity of the threatened misconduct and the level of involvement of the "innocent" party as well as the closeness of the connection between the contract performance and the intended anti-social activity. It can be anticipated that the party with the improper intent may not enforce the contract. The problems thus relate primarily to the question whether the other party may enforce it. If the other party has substantially performed, a court will be motivated to permit him to enforce the contract unless he became actively involved in furthering the improper purpose or he knew of the intended use and that use involves grave social harm. (See Restatement § 182.)

The seriousness of the violation of public policy is a factor that a court can be expected to weigh, along with the relative guilt or innocence of the parties. Minor violations and violations which resulted from ignorance or other relatively innocent conduct will ordinarily not preclude enforcement.

§ 5.11.1 Enforcement When Parties Are Not in Equal Fault; Laws Designed to Protect One of the Parties

If a law or policy has been created to protect a class of persons of which the party seeking to enforce the promise is a member, then violation of that law or policy will not preclude enforcement. Thus wage earners can enforce contracts that were made in violation of minimum wage laws. These laws were designed to protect workers and the purpose would be frustrated if these laws were used to deny a remedy. However, one must exercise care in applying this principle. Laws prohibiting the employment of certain immigrants are not designed to protect those immigrants but rather to protect other American workers. Therefore, illegal immigrants or immigrants whose status does not permit employment have been denied the right to recover wages under employment contracts made in violation of these laws.

The minimum wage cases are examples of situations in which the parties are not *in pari delicto*, or not equally at fault. The employer, being more at

fault, could not enforce a below minimum wage
contract whereas the employee could enforce it and
also recover the additional wages due under the
law.

§ 5.11.2 Exculpatory Clauses

Exculpatory clauses are contract terms by which
one party agrees not to hold the other party liable
for future harm. They are designed to shift the risk
of harm for personal injury or property damage.
Since these terms would have the effect of absolving
a tortfeasor from liability for the tort and leaving
tort victims with no source of compensation, they
are often found to violate public policy and are thus
unenforceable.

There is general agreement that a party may not
enforce a contract term that would relieve that
party from liability for harm caused intentionally or
recklessly. Exculpatory clauses that relieve a party
from liability for harm caused by simple negligence
are also held to be unenforceable in certain relationships. Cases have denied enforcement of such a
clause asserted by an employer against an employee. Public utilities and other public service businesses are held to be unable to assert exculpatory
clauses if the harm was caused in the course of
fulfilling the public utility or public service function. Thus, a railroad could not use an exculpatory
clause to avoid liability for negligent maintenance of
its trains, but it might be able to enforce an exculpatory clause in a commercial lease of a warehouse
owned by the railroad.

Exculpatory clauses have enjoyed a mixed response from the courts when used by landlords to exculpate themselves from liability to their tenants for defective premises; by amusement parks and other places of entertainment such as horse rental concessions and golf cart concessions to avoid liability to patrons. The factors that a court might consider in this type of case were well articulated in a decision involving a contract between a patient and a university research hospital whereby the hospital asserted that it was relieved from vicarious liability for torts of its employees. The California Supreme Court held this contract term to be invalid, stating:

In placing particular contracts within or without the category of those affected with a public interest, the courts have revealed a rough outline of that type of transaction in which exculpatory provisions will be held invalid. Thus the attempted but invalid exemption involves a transaction which exhibits some or all of the following characteristics. It concerns a business of a type generally thought suitable for public regulation. The party seeking exculpation is engaged in performing a service of great importance to the public, which is often a matter of practical necessity for some members of the public. The party holds himself out as willing to perform this service for any member of the public who seeks it, or at least for any member coming within certain established standards. As a result of the essential nature of the service, in the economic setting of the transaction, the party invoking exculpation

330 CONTRACTS § 5.11.2

possesses a decisive advantage of bargaining strength against any member of the public who seeks his services. In exercising a superior bargaining power, the party confronts the public with a standardized adhesion contract of exculpation, and makes no provision whereby a purchaser may pay additional reasonable fees and obtain protection against negligence. Finally, as a result of the transaction, the person or property of the purchaser is placed under the control of the seller, subject to the risk of carelessness by the seller or his agents. (*Tunkl v. Regents of University of California* (Cal. 1963).)

§ 5.11.3 Violation of Licensing Requirements

All states have numerous laws requiring that certain activities be conducted only by persons who possess the required license. The contract enforcement issue arises when an unlicensed person enters a contract in violation of these laws. Some statutes and ordinances which impose licensing requirements expressly provide that contracts made in violation of the terms of these laws are unenforceable by the party who was supposed to be licensed. Courts are bound to comply with such mandates, but cases exist that demonstrate imaginative methods of providing some relief, such as permitting an unlicensed contractor to collect for the value of the materials consumed in a job despite the fact that the law denies a contract recovery.

Most statutes that create licensing requirements are silent as to the enforceability of contracts made by unlicensed people. Such contracts can be divided into two categories. If the license is required primarily to raise revenue, then failure to obtain the license is not a basis for denying enforcement of a contract. For example, a medical doctor who fails to obtain a city business license may still enforce a contract for professional services. Licenses that are designed primarily to protect the public by regulating access to a trade or profession are treated differently. Unlicensed persons are generally held not to be able to enforce contracts made in violation of such a licensing statute. A person who is not admitted to practice law in a jurisdiction will not be able to enforce a contract for the rendition of legal services.

§ 5.11.4   Severability of Offending Provisions

If contract performances are severable and severance of a portion will cure the offense against public policy, the remaining portion of the contract may be enforced. If a contract is capable of being apportioned into corresponding pairs of performances that the parties apparently treated as equivalent exchanges and that are not interdependent for their value, then the contract may be treated as severable if this is consistent with the apparent intention of the parties.

A court may rewrite a contract to remove terms that violate public policy and enforce the rest. This is clearly a desirable result in cases where the party seeking to enforce the contract is not the source of the offending terms. Assume that an employment contract contains a covenant not to compete that involves an excessively large geographical area or is to endure for an excessively long time and thus constitutes an unreasonable restraint of trade and is unenforceable. A court should permit the employee to enforce the balance of the employment contract assuming that the employee is not guilty of wrongdoing. A more difficult question is presented if the employer seeks to enforce that part of the covenant which, standing alone, does not contravene public policy. For example, if a covenant not to compete extends to an area beyond that permitted by statute, may the employer enforce this contract term with respect to the maximum area that the law will allow? Some cases have permitted this result despite the fact that it would appear to encourage people to draft illegal contracts, safe in the knowledge that if challenged, the court will still give you all that the law allows.

§ 5.11.5 Restitution Where Public Policy Precludes Enforcement

A party who has not engaged in serious misconduct may withdraw from a transaction before the improper conduct has occurred and become entitled to restitution. For example, one who advances money on account of a contract that is unenforceable, but not extremely shocking to the court's fundamental notions of policy and morality, may rescind the transaction before the improper purpose has been accomplished and obtain restitution of the monies paid.

Restitution is also granted in cases in which the court apparently views the question of non-enforceability as borderline. Thus relief may be granted if the party seeking restitution was unaware of the law, or if the denial of relief would result in a forfeiture disproportionate to the wrong, or if the misconduct of the plaintiff is minor compared to that of the party against whom restitution is sought.

When you have completed your study of this chapter, you may wish to analyze questions 24 and 25 at the end of this book and compare your analysis with the one given there.

CHAPTER 6

EVENTS THAT EXCUSE PERFORMANCE

A. IMPOSSIBILITY OR IMPRACTICABILITY

§ 6.1 Impracticability ("Impossibility") of Performance

Restatement Chapter 11 deals with events that excuse contract performance. The Introductory Note raises a caution flag for this entire subject. It provides in part:

> Contract liability is strict liability. It is an accepted maxim that *pacta sunt servanda,* contracts are to be kept. The obligor is therefore liable in damages for breach of contract even if he is without fault and even if circumstances have made the contract more burdensome or less desirable than he had anticipated.

Contract duties can be excused by the occurrence of an event if the contract was made on the basic assumption that this event would not occur. Events that excuse include those that make performance of the contract literally impossible or that make performance commercially impracticable. Examples of events that can excuse performance include:

(a) death or disability of one whose existence is necessary for the performance of the contract duty;

(b) destruction without the fault of the promisor of the subject matter of the contract or a thing necessary for the performance of the contract; or,

(c) supervening governmental action that prohibits or purports to prohibit the performance of the contract.

If a singer contracts to perform in a nightclub, the death or disability of the singer will excuse the duty to perform.

In a contract for the sale of a specific cow, the death of the cow without fault on the part of the seller will excuse the duty to deliver.

If a contract provides for the sale of shoes to be manufactured in S's factory, destruction of that factory without fault of S will excuse performance.

If a scrap dealer contracts to sell copper to a company in a foreign country, a government regulation that prohibits the export of copper will excuse performance.

A party will not be excused if it can be shown that he assumed the risk that the intervening event would occur. In that situation, the party could be held liable for damages even if actual performance of the promise was literally impossible. Students of contract law sometimes jump to the conclusion that since performance is impossible, any discussion of

the question whether performance is excused or not
is irrelevant. Since damages are the most common
remedy for contract breach, the fact that performance is impossible does not preclude giving a
remedy to the injured party.

§ 6.1.1 Impracticability as a Basis for Excuse

The more difficult questions regarding excuse of
performance often involve events that do not make
performance literally impossible. An event may preclude performance in the contemplated fashion but
leave open alternative methods of performance. An
event may not preclude performance in the contemplated fashion but may make performance more
difficult or expensive to the point that the performing party faces substantial losses on the contract.

Finding acceptable vocabulary in this area is a
difficult task. Since early law would not excuse
performance unless it had become "impossible,"
many court opinions continue to use the term "impossibility" despite the fact that they are finding
performance to be excused based upon events that
simply made performance impracticable in an economic sense or because of events that precluded
performance in the contemplated fashion but left
open some other, and more expensive, method of
performance. In many cases one must "read
through" the vocabulary to find the true nature of
the basis for granting or denying an excuse.

When a party seeks to be excused despite the fact
that performance is still literally possible, the underlying point is that circumstances now make per-

formance by this party more expensive or make the returns that this party will receive from the contract less valuable. The issue is focused upon the question of whether we are going to permit someone to walk away from contract obligations or require that person to proceed with a losing contract.

It is critical to understand that people often enter into contracts for the purpose of shifting the risk of future events. A contract to sell goods for future delivery is made for one of two purposes:

1) to assure a source of supply (for the buyer) or market for goods (for the seller); or,

2) to lock in a price thereby protecting the seller against price decreases and protecting the buyer from future price increases.

If a farmer is growing wheat to be harvested next June, the farmer has a risk that the price may go down before June but the farmer will profit if the price goes up before June. The farmer can choose not to contract for the sale of the wheat until it is harvested thereby bearing the risk that the price may go down before June. Assume that in April the farmer sells his wheat for June delivery for a fixed price. Now the buyer rather than the farmer bears the risk of a price decline between April and June. If the price of grain declines by twenty percent between April and June, this may prove to be an economic disaster for the buyer, but this fact alone cannot excuse performance. Placing this risk on the buyer was the purpose for making the contract. Conversely, if the price increases sharply between

April and June, the farmer is sorry and the buyer makes a large profit, but this is the exact result that the parties contemplated when they made the contract for future sale. A different result might be reached if the sharp price fluctuations were caused by some specific event not contemplated by the parties. The next section will explore what events might provide an excuse.

§ 6.2 Factors Necessary to Support Impracticability as a Defense

Four elements are required to establish the defense of impracticability. The first requirement is the occurrence of an event that has made performance, or performance in the contemplated fashion impossible or impracticable. Death, fire, illness, crop failures, canal closures, government regulations and similar events are the stuff from which these defenses commonly arise. These events are usually acts of God, of third persons, or of governments that are beyond the control of the parties to the contract. Some events make performance literally impossible which definitely satisfies this first element. The event may make performance in the contemplated fashion impossible but leave an alternative method of performance open. In this case, the degree of impracticability is the issue. Increased cost alone is not generally enough, but cost that involves economic waste through unreasonable allocation of labor and resources could make an alternative method of performance legally impracticable.

Where no event has occurred but the parties simply discover facts that existed at the time the contract was formed that make performance impracticable, the appropriate defense to analyze should be mistake. Some cases and the Restatement take the position that the party seeking excuse has a choice of defenses and may assert either mistake or impracticability. The elements required to establish the defense of mistake and the excuse of impossibility are sufficiently similar that the same result should be reached whichever analysis is used. The overriding economic issues and questions of fairness should not change.

A party seeking to utilize the defense of impracticability must establish that it is objectively impracticable (i.e., the thing cannot be done or at least cannot be done in the contemplated fashion) rather than subjectively impossible or impracticable (e.g., I cannot do it, or I do not have the right equipment to do it efficiently). The promise to do the act carries with it the representation that the party has the usual skills and resources to accomplish the task, and thus he assumes the risk of his own shortcomings.

The second element that must be established is that the event must have occurred without the fault of the party who seeks relief due to the occurrence of the event. Misconduct or negligence of the party may be sufficient to deny him the relief which he seeks.

The third factor, expressed in the U.C.C. and the Restatement, is that the nonoccurrence of the event must have been a basic assumption upon which the contract was made. Certain risks are allocated to one party by operation of law. The most common example is the risk that prices will change. As discussed in the previous section, the basic reason for entering a contract for future purchase and sale of goods, other than tying down a source which is necessary in some situations, is to protect oneself against price fluctuations. Both parties are quite aware of the fact that prices will change. That is why they made the contract. Thus, even a substantial change in prices does not excuse performance.

While the fact of change in market price does not excuse performance, market changes that result from events that the parties assumed would not occur may provide grounds for discharge. Comment 4 of U.C.C. section 2–615 states in part:

> ... a severe shortage of raw materials or of supplies due to a contingency such as war, embargo, local crop failure, unforeseen shutdown of major sources of supply or the like, which either causes a marked increase in cost or altogether prevents the seller from securing supplies necessary to his performance, is within the contemplation of this Section.

The fourth factor to be considered in determining whether relief should be granted on grounds of impracticability is whether the party seeking the relief has agreed to assume the risk of the event that is now asserted as a basis for discharge. The third factor may be characterized as an allocation of risk for certain events that is imposed on a party by operation of law. This fourth factor is one which is imposed upon the party because the party assumed a greater risk than what the law would otherwise have imposed. This might result from express language assuming such risk or by negative implication from such things as recital of events that would excuse performance but which omits the event in issue. The fact that the event which occurred was foreseeable does not automatically lead to the result that the party assumed the risk of its happening by failing to provide for it in the contract, nor in the application of the third factor does foreseeability "compel the conclusion that its non-occurrence was not such a basic assumption."

The language of the U.C.C. and the Restatement provides the basis for a substantial expansion of the types of cases for which relief can be granted. Certainly the law has progressed beyond the old common law rules that purported to require actual impossibility before contracts would be discharged. However, events that occurred after the adoption of the U.C.C. and the Restatement, Second, including oil embargoes by exporting nations, closures of canals and a worldwide shortage of raw materials such as yellowcake to supply atomic fuel for reactors, produced litigation that gave the courts opportunities to move into new areas in the subject of impracticability if they chose to do so. The resulting case law has not been as liberal in excusing performance as might have been anticipated.

In predicting results in this area it is wise to remember that there is still a significant judicial tendency to hold parties to their bargains, finding that they assumed the risk of the events that now make their performance difficult.

B. FRUSTRATION OF PURPOSE
§ 6.3 Frustration of Purpose; "Economic Frustration"

After formation of a contract, events may occur that make the performance of the contract useless to one of the parties. While the promised performance is not impossible or impracticable, it will be of no value to the promisee. Restatement section 265 provides:

> Where, after a contract is made, a party's principal purpose is substantially frustrated without his fault by the occurrence of an event the nonoccurrence of which was a basic assumption on which the contract was made, his remaining duties to render performance are discharged, unless the language or the circumstances indicate the contrary.

This doctrine was apparently first recognized in reported cases in the early twentieth century in *Krell v. Henry* (Eng.1904). Plaintiff had contracted to permit defendant to occupy plaintiff's flat on the Pall Mall for two days during which the coronation parades would be passing. The illness of King Edward VII led to the cancellation of the pageantry. The contract made no express reference to the coronation but the apartment had been advertised as one providing a good view of the festivities, the price charged was suitably enhanced, and the time the defendant was permitted the use of the flat was restricted to the daytime. While there was nothing impossible nor impracticable about the defendant using plaintiff's flat and paying money therefor, the contract performance had become totally useless to the defendant, and the court found that defendant's duties were excused.

To excuse performance, it is essential that both parties understand the purpose for which the contract is being made and that the failure of that purpose makes the contract performance totally valueless or almost totally valueless to the party seeking relief. Parties have attempted to apply this concept to a situation in which an event occurred that frustrated plans to make money from the contract performance. For example, parties have sought relief from long term leases of service stations when the highway was moved or gas and tire rationing was imposed. These efforts to obtain relief from unprofitable contracts almost invariably fail. The purpose of the contract is not frustrated; the only frustration is with the profitability of the performance. Courts sometimes refer to this type of situation as being one of "economic frustration," or "commercial frustration" and these are labels that a party wishes to avoid when seeking relief from a contract.

§ 6.4 Relief Afforded in Cases of Impracticability or Frustration

If a party is granted an excuse from performing a contract after the other party has changed position in reliance thereon, the court may award damages for the reasonable money value of the reliance.

A party who is granted an excuse from performing a contract after receiving benefits for which no compensation has been given will be required to disgorge this unjust enrichment. The other party will be entitled to recover in restitution for the value of benefits conferred.

A somewhat different question is presented where the party seeking relief has already partially performed and has thereby conferred benefits upon the other party for which no compensation has been given. In the "Coronation Cases" litigation, some parties had already paid all or part of the agreed rental for flats that would provide them with a view of the parade. While the court granted relief to the renters excusing them from prospective performance of their contracts, it refused to give restitution for the refund of the deposits and other sums that had been paid. Subsequent case law has changed this result permitting the party who seeks to be excused from contract performance to also recover in restitution for benefits conferred for which the return consideration has not been received.

When you have completed your study of this chapter, you may wish to analyze question 35 at the end of this book and compare your analysis with the one given there.

CHAPTER 7

CONTRACT MODIFICATION

§ 7.1 Requirements for Modifying a Contract

The issues that might arise as to the existence and enforceability of a modification of an existing contract are very similar to those that could arise in regard to the existence and enforceability of the original contract itself. However, because there is already an existing contract relationship between the parties, the attempted modification must be measured against the express terms and other duties imposed by the existing contract. Therefore, the modification issues will potentially have some unique aspects that do not exist at the time of formation of the original contract. You should keep in mind when addressing modification issues not only the general principles of contract formation but also the special issues that could arise because of the already existing relationship between the parties. Listed below are the potential issues that could arise in a modification scenario.

a) Was there mutual assent to the modification, not induced by any facts or conduct that would vitiate consent such as mistake, misrepresentation, duress, etc.? And, because there is already a contract relationship in existence which imposes a duty of good faith upon the parties, there could be an issue of whether a party was acting in bad faith in extracting the consent to the modification.

b) Was consideration necessary for the modification, and if so did it exist?

c) If consideration was necessary and it did not exist, could promissory estoppel be utilized to make the modification enforceable notwithstanding the absence of consideration?

d) Is there a statute requiring that the modification be evidenced by a signed writing? And, if there is already a written contract in existence does the existing contract by its terms require that any modification be evidenced by a signed writing?

e) If a signed writing is required because of either or both of the circumstances as stated in d), does a writing exist which satisfies the applicable requirements?

f) If the modification is required to be in writing but it is not, can promissory estoppel be utilized to make the modification enforceable notwithstanding the absence of a writing?

g) If the attempted modification is unenforceable as a modification, could it have resulted in a waiver of a right under the contract?

h) If a party has waived a right provided by the contract, was the waiver timely retracted or will the retraction be too late because of the other party's detrimental reliance upon the waiver?

It is obvious that the last two subsections, g) and h), are unique to modifications and would not arise in a fact pattern involving formation of the original contract. Compare the other subsections to determine the interrelationship between formation and modification issues.

Note that evidence offered to prove a contract modification does not give rise to a parol evidence rule problem because the attempted modification is subsequent to the written contract.

§ 7.2 Consent Required for Modification

Contract modification, like formation, needs mutual assent. A party who has manifested assent to the modification may be able to show that the assent was induced as a result of mistake, misrepresentation, undue influence or duress. All of these defenses to formation of a contract are applicable to modifications and subject to the same rules as discussed in Chapter 5.

The most common and troublesome problems involve threats by a party that do not rise (or sink) to the level necessary for common law or statutory duress, but involve threats of non-performance of the contract. However, because there is an existing contract relationship, the parties will be found to have implied obligations of good faith and fair dealing in regard to their duties of performance, and a threat to breach may be a violation of this contractual obligation.

A court should review carefully whether the purported modification was the result of an improper threat or violation of the obligation of good faith and fair dealing. Care must be exercised in determining what is an improper threat. A threat to breach a contract is likely to be found to be improper and in bad faith if it is made for no reason other than a desire to force the other party to pay more money for the performance to which he is already entitled. This is sometimes referred to as the "hold-up game" or "economic duress" or even "extortion of a modification." The same threat not to perform may be found not to be improper if it is made by a party who has sustained or will sustain increased costs due to encountering unforeseen difficulties and seeks additional compensation to avoid serious out of pocket losses or possible insolvency. While the facts may be insufficient to excuse performance (Chapter 6), these additional costs may be sufficient to justify a demand for additional compensation thereby providing a basis for finding that the "request" and perhaps "demand" for additional compensation was not made in bad faith. Article 2 of the U.C.C. which would apply if the contract involved a transaction in goods recognizes this in Comment 2 to U.C.C. section 2–209 which states in part:

 * * * Modifications * * * must meet the test of good faith imposed by this Act. The effective use of bad faith to escape performance of the original contract terms is barred, and the extortion of a "modification" without legitimate commercial

reason is ineffective as a violation of the duty of good faith. Nor can a mere technical consideration support a modification made in bad faith. The test of "good faith" * * * may in some situations require an objectively demonstrable reason for seeking modification. But such matters as a market shift which makes performance come to involve a loss may provide such a reason even though there is no unforeseen difficulty as would make out a legal excuse from performance.

§ 7.3 The Consideration Requirement

The general common law rule is that a promise which has the effect of modifying a contract is required to be supported by consideration. However, if the contract being modified is for the sale of goods, Article 2 of the U.C.C. would control and it dispenses entirely with any need for consideration for a modification. U.C.C. Section 2–209(1) provides that "An agreement modifying a contract within this Article needs no consideration to be binding." The important limitation recognized by Article 2 however, is that the modification be made in good faith as discussed above.

Assuming that the contract is not within Article 2 of the U.C.C. and that there is no other statute deleting the requirement of consideration, the common law would apply and would require consideration for the modification. When both parties incur a new legal detriment as a bargained for exchange this satisfies the consideration requirement. However, in many instances, a modification is agreed upon in order to accommodate the needs of only of the parties, and it is quite possible that there will be no consideration for the other party's promise to render a new or different performance. Said another way, attempted modifications frequently run afoul of the pre-existing duty rule.

For example, Office Owner (O) and Painter (P) have a contract by which O is to pay P $2,000 for painting an office in O's building with painting to be completed by Friday, June 12. On June 1, O learned that the new tenants desired to take possession on June 10, sooner than expected. O then obtained the agreement of P to complete the work no later than June 9. P's promise to finish earlier would be without consideration because there was no new detriment to O given in return for P's promise to finish early. Had O promised to pay an additional sum of money, or pay earlier, or anything else that O was not already obligated to do, and provided that O's additional promise was a bargained exchange for P's promise to finish earlier, then one could find consideration. If so, the contract modification to include the new performance date of June 9 would be enforceable.

If under similar facts, the parties were O and S, a furniture seller, with a contract by which S was to deliver furniture for the office on a specified date, and S subsequently agreed to deliver the furniture earlier than originally required, S's promise to deliver earlier would be enforceable even though there was no new consideration for S's promise. This would be because the contract was for the sale of goods and U.C.C. section 2–209(1) would allow the modification to be enforced without consideration. If there is no bad faith on the part of O in extracting the promise, S would be obligated to deliver on the new date (assuming of course that any writing requirement is satisfied.)

To change the facts somewhat, assume that after the O and P painting contract had been formed with a completion date of June 12, P learned that O's tenants were planning on moving in on June 13. P approached O and without justification stated that the work would not be done on time unless O paid an additional $500. P had already commenced painting and O, faced with liability to his tenants and unable to find another painter to finish the work within the time required, agreed to pay the additional sum.

Under these facts, O would have two theories for asserting that O's promise to pay the additional $500 was not enforceable. First, P in completing or promising to complete the work by the originally agreed upon date was not doing anything more than he was previously obligated to do, and therefore there was no consideration for O's promise to pay additional money. Second, P's threat of non-performance was in bad faith and the promise to pay more money was "extorted" from O.

Change the facts again. Assume that P, after commencing work, discovered significantly more work was required than had been anticipated. The original contract required P to scrape and sand the old paint, but much to the surprise of both O and P, the old paint was lead-based and the time and costs associated with its scraping and sanding would cause P to lose at least $1,000 on the contract. When P explained this to O, O and P agreed that P would complete the work on time and O would pay an additional $1,200 over the original price of $2,000 for a total price of $3,200. P completed the work on time but O refused to pay more than the original price of $2,000.

O's first possible argument is that there was no consideration for O's promise to pay the additional $1,200 because P was under a pre-existing duty to scrape and sand the old paint.

The following theories might be available to P to avoid the pre-existing duty rule.

a) P was entitled to cease performance of the contract and seek rescission due to mistake of fact. If P in fact was entitled to cease performance because the contract is voidable due to mistake, then P's continued performance was something P was not obligated to do and therefore was consideration for O's promise to pay more money.

b) Even if P was not entitled to cease performance because under the facts and law P's claim of mistake was not meritorious, P had a good faith belief that P was not obligated to continue. Therefore, P's forbearance of asserting his good faith claim of a right to rescission was consideration for O's promise to pay the additional sum.

c) There is what is sometimes called "the unforeseen difficulties exception" to the requirement of consideration for a contract modification. The Restatement in "Topic 2" which is captioned "Contracts Without Consideration" has many sections, one of which is section 89, which provides in part:

A promise modifying a duty under a contract not fully performed on either side is binding

(a) if the modification is fair and equitable in view of circumstances not anticipated by the parties when the contract was made; * * *

This rule is justified because of the ongoing relationship between the parties and the utility that such a rule provides. By doing away with a technical formality such as consideration, freely made modifications of contracts within an existing relationship can be enforced.

Illustration 1 to Restatement section 89 provides the following:

1. By written contract A agrees to excavate a cellar for B for a stated price. Solid rock is unexpectedly encountered and A so notifies B. A and B then orally agree that A will remove the rock at a unit price which is reasonable but nine times that used in computing the original price, and A completes the job. B is bound to pay the increased amount.

Note that the so-called "unforeseen difficulty exception" utilizes the same facts as the two theories set forth in (a) and (b) above that could be advocated by P to find consideration but reaches the result in a more direct manner and without the complexities or perhaps somewhat fictionalized basis for finding consideration.

d) If the facts exist, P might be able to establish that P and O agreed that the original contract was to be mutually rescinded and that a new contract would be substituted at an increased price. If this were found to be true, then upon the rescission of the old contract, neither party is under any duty to the other. There are no preexisting duties and the "new" promises are consideration for each other.

§ 7.4   Promissory Estoppel as a Basis for Enforcement Despite Absence of Consideration

Just as promissory estoppel as set forth in Restatement section 90 can be used to make a promise enforceable between parties who prior to the change of position had no obligations owed or owing, so can promissory estoppel be used to make a promise binding which has the effect of modifying an existing contract. This concept is recognized by Restatement section 89 which provides in part:

> A promise modifying a duty under a contract not fully performed on either side is binding
>
>   * * *
>
> (c) to the extent that justice requires enforcement in view of material change of position in reliance on the promise.

One must carefully analyze the facts to determine if the principle could be applied. There must be foreseeable and reasonable "material" change of position by the promisee in reliance upon the promise sought to be enforced and the remedy to the promisee may be limited to the amount necessary to prevent injustice. In addition, if the promisor retracts the promise in a timely manner, the original terms of the contract could be reinstated unless to do so would be unjust to the promisee because of the material change of position. (See Restatement § 89, comment d.)

§ 7.5 Writing Requirements: Imposed by Statute or by Agreement of the Parties

The requirement of a writing for the modification may be treated differently depending upon whether it is imposed by statute or by the terms of the existing contract. Where the writing requirement is "party-created" that is imposed by the terms of the contract, it is possible to find that the parties agreed to waive this self-imposed writing requirement. Such a waiver will not be subject to retraction if there is material change of position by the other party in reliance upon the waiver. If the requirement for a written modification is imposed by a statute, it is generally held that the parties are not free to waive a legislatively imposed requirement.

Statutes requiring modifications to be in writing

Some jurisdictions have statutes which provide that all written contracts can be modified only by signed writings. If the subject matter of the contract is goods, Article 2 of the U.C.C. in section 2–209(3) provides that: "The requirements of the statute of frauds of this Article (Section 2–201) must be satisfied if the contract as modified is within its provisions."

Whatever statute is applicable must be carefully read to determine its requirements and possible exceptions. Some statutes would exempt from their scope a modification which has been fully performed by the promisee (referred to in the statutes sometimes as an "executed oral agreement") thus permitting the enforcement the other's oral promise.

If the contract is subject to Article 2 of the U.C.C., one must be concerned about the scope of section 2–209(3) quoted above. Does it apply to any modification of any sale of goods contract the price of which is $500 or more? Or does it apply as stated only "if the contract as modified" is of a price of $500 or more? If the latter, then it would appear that a contract for 10,000 widgets for a total price of $10,000 could be orally modified down to 400 widgets for a total price of $400 but changing the delivery date of the original written contract from June 1 to June 2 would have to be evidenced by a signed writing (or come within some exception under section 2–201). The difficulty in the application of the statutory language becomes obvious when one recognizes that the delivery date was not a term that would have been required to be in writing under section 2–201 in the original contract. There-

fore even though the orally agreed upon delivery
date was omitted from the original writing, the
agreement to modify the orally agreed upon original
delivery date must satisfy section 2–201.

Written contracts which require modifications to be in writing

It is not uncommon for a written contract to have
a provision requiring any modification to be by way
of a signed writing. Such provisions are sometimes
for shorthand purposes referred to as "NOM" ("no
oral modification") clauses. Such a mnemonic is
potentially misleading and inaccurate. There is a
difference between a clause which states there shall
be "no oral modifications" of this contract and a
clause which states that "no modification shall be
effective unless in a writing signed by both parties."
As used hereafter, NOM will refer to the latter
clause.

The judicial application of the common law to
NOM clauses has been inconsistent. Some jurisdictions will enforce them and others take the position
that the parties who wrote the contract are always
free to amend it even orally if the oral modification
is adequately proven. This latter view is premised
upon the belief that it is the parties' most recent
manifestation of intent that should govern and if
they orally agreed to modify the written contract
notwithstanding the earlier NOM clause, then they
have agreed to waive their self-imposed writing
requirement and their intent should be recognized.

However, if the contract is for the sale of goods, courts are required to give effect to a NOM clause. This is because of the language in U.C.C. section 2–209(2) which provides in part as follows:

A signed agreement which excludes modification or rescission except by a signed writing cannot be otherwise modified or rescinded * * * .

Note that the subsection specifically includes rescissions. Therefore, an attempted oral rescission would be ineffective if the written contract contained a "no rescission except in writing" clause.

The utility of NOM clauses can be justified if one pictures the possible scenarios in a construction project: changes are requested and perhaps agreed to in part; the work progresses and relationships deteriorate; personnel change; memories become less reliable as to who orally agreed to what. Having the modification in a signed writing protects against false claims and poor or selective memory and satisfies the evidentiary, cautionary and channeling functions which serve as the justification for requiring signed writings.

On the other hand, when party A makes an oral promise which would constitute a modification and party B does the additional or different work or otherwise changes position in reliance on the oral modification, barring enforcement of the modification may be unjust.

This concern will be addressed below.

§ 7.6   If the Modification Is Required to Be in Writing, Does a Sufficient Writing Exist or Is There an Exception?

As to the meaning of the terms "signed" and "writing," see sections 3.3 through 3.5 and U.C.C. section 1–201(39) and (46).

As to what the writing must contain, it would at least have to evidence the modification and the terms allegedly added, deleted or modified as compared to the original contract.

As to exceptions recognized that would allow enforceability of the modification notwithstanding the absence of a writing, one would have to look to the local jurisdiction and the recognized exceptions that exist under the applicable statute of frauds.

If the contract is for the sale of goods, U.C.C. section 2–209(3) would appear to allow any of the exceptions recognized under section 2–201 to be used to enforce the oral modification. For example, if the promisor admits the oral modification under circumstances satisfying section 2–201(3)(b), then the oral modification can be enforced notwithstanding the absence of a signed writing evidencing the modification. Or if both parties were merchants and one sent a signed memo confirming the modification, section 2–201(2) could be applicable.

§ 7.7   Promissory Estoppel As a Basis For Enforcing Oral Modifications

This is very similar to the discussion in section 5.4 and is addressed in a limited fashion in Restatement section 150 which provides as follows:

§ 150 Reliance on Oral Modification

Where the parties to an enforceable contract subsequently agree that all or part of a duty need not be performed or of a condition need not occur, the Statute of Frauds does not prevent enforcement of the subsequent agreement if reinstatement of the original terms would be unjust in view of a material change of position in reliance on the subsequent agreement.

The comments to this section point out that it is complementary to Restatement sections 84 and 89 which dispense with the requirement of consideration in similar circumstances but that it applies as well to promises supported by consideration. It would also be appropriate to review the discussion in section 3.6.4 with regard to the application of promissory estoppel to the Statute of Frauds.

§ 7.8 Ineffective Attempt to Modify; Operation as a Waiver

The fundamental questions are: What Is A Waiver? What Can Be Waived?

An attempted modification that is unenforceable because of failure to comply with a writing requirement or a requirement of consideration may be effective as a waiver. This result can be reached under the common law. In transactions in goods, U.C.C. section 2–209(4) permits the concept of waiver to apply to an attempted modification that does not satisfy the writing requirement.

Waivers do not require mutual assent or consideration and are not subject to any statutory requirement of a writing. However, one must appreciate the limitations that the law places upon the concept of waiver.

A common definition of a waiver is: "a voluntary relinquishment of a known right." One can waive most conditions in a contract. One cannot waive an essential part of the bargain, such as the return performance due. Thus, generally speaking, one cannot waive the right to receive a promised performance nor can one waive a condition that is a fundamental part of the bargain. In a fire insurance contract, destruction of the property by fire is a condition to the insurer's liability. Such a fundamental condition cannot be waived. In that same insurance contract, filing a proof of loss within thirty days of the occurrence of a casualty was perhaps also an express condition to the insurer's liability. This condition can be waived as it is not related to the risk assumed and is not an essential part of the bargain.

Assume that X is to deliver to Y 100 tons of hay on December 1, for which Y has already paid $90 per ton. X advises Y that X can deliver only 80 tons to which Y responds, "That's OK. I'll take 80 tons." Tender of the goods in conformity with the contract was a condition precedent to Y's duty to accept the tender. Y has waived this right to have a complete tender of the entire 100 tons and will be obligated to accept 80 tons. However, Y has not waived the *promise* to deliver 100 tons, and therefore, unless the contract was effectively modified to reduce the quantity, X will be liable for breach for failure to deliver the full amount.

Assume the same facts except that X advised Y that X could not deliver until December 15 and Y stated that this was OK. Y has waived the condition of prompt delivery and must accept the hay if it is tendered on December 15. Y may still recover any damages resulting from the delay absent proof of a legally enforceable contract modification.

Waivers cannot be used to impose new obligations that did not previously exist. Remember the definition of a waiver—"a voluntary relinquishment of a known right." By its definition, it is limited to giving up an existing right, not the creation of a new right. Assume the same facts except that Y advised X that Y needed the hay by November 20 instead of December 1 as provided in the contract, and X stated he would deliver it by November 20. If this is not an enforceable contract modification, then it is not effective to change the contract terms. Y cannot impose upon X a new duty to deliver by November 20 by utilizing the concept of waiver. Again, waivers involve only the giving up of a right by the person entitled to that right.

Finding That a Waiver Has Occurred

Waivers can occur by either words or conduct manifesting intent to surrender a right. The usual vocabulary would be that a waiver manifested by words would be an express waiver and one by conduct would be an implied waiver. Implied waivers can be evidenced by a party's course of performance of the contract. For example, if an express condition in an insurance policy requires filing of a proof of loss within thirty days and this is not done by the insured, conduct by agents of the insurance company after the thirty day period has expired which evidences a continuing intent to pay the claim may be viewed as a waiver of this particular condition.

In cases involving the sale of goods and therefore subject to U.C.C. section 2–209, there is some authority for the proposition that a waiver cannot be established solely by virtue of evidence that a party orally agreed to give up a right if the oral agreement is in derogation of a NOM clause. This view is premised upon the fact that proving the oral agreement that is the basis for the alleged waiver only by oral testimony is what the NOM clause was intended to prevent. Under this view, the court will require that the party who is seeking to assert a waiver would have to prove either conduct by the waiving party which evidences the fact of waiver or else a change of position in reliance upon the oral waiver (*Wisconsin Knife Works v. National Metal Crafters*, Seventh Circuit 1986). Note that under the majority opinion of *Wisconsin Knife,* this evidence of change of position is required merely to establish the existence of the waiver. (Compare the next subsection relating to retraction of the waiver.) The dissenting position in *Wisconsin Knife* notes that the common law consistently defines waiver as a voluntary relinquishment of a known right and there is nothing in the U.C.C. to indicate that some different meaning of the term is intended. Had the majority opinion accepted this definition, it would have recognized that section 2–209(4) does not undo the policy that section 2–209(2) seeks to advance because waiver has a more limited range of application than contract modification. One can release or agree to forbear enforcement of some rights under the concept of waiver, but one cannot substitute new terms, such as an earlier delivery date or a higher price or different quality goods, utilizing the concept of waiver. The failure of the majority opinion to recognize this basic definition of the term probably explains why that opinion goes to such lengths to rewrite the provisions of 2–209(4) by adding a reliance requirement. In effect, the majority opinion seems to conclude that any oral modification of a contract for the sale of goods can be enforced if one relies upon it. While section 2–209(3) is mentioned in the majority opinion, its impact seems to have been completely overlooked.

§ 7.9   Retraction of a Waiver

A further distinction between a modification of a contract and the waiver of a contract right is that a waiver may be retracted and if it is retracted, then the right that had been waived will be reinstated notwithstanding any objection by the other party. Most case authority holds that waivers can be retracted unless the other party has changed position in reliance. Retraction of a waiver must be accomplished in sufficient time to give the other party a reasonable opportunity to comply with the term or condition that is being reinstated. To the extent that a party has materially changed position in reliance upon the other party's waiver, courts will find the waiver to be irrevocable or state that the waiving party is estopped from retracting the waiver.

For goods transactions, U.C.C. section 2–209(5) recognizes the concept of retraction of waivers:

> (5) A party who has made a waiver affecting an executory portion of the contract may retract the waiver by reasonable notification received by the other party that strict performance will be required of any term waived, unless the retraction would be unjust in view of a material change of position in reliance on the waiver.

Some decisions permit waiver of a condition after it has already failed to occur and there is no additional time for its occurrence. These cases usually involve contracts of insurance. An insurance policy may require as a condition precedent to the insurance carrier's liability on the policy that the insured file a form call a proof of loss within a specified time period after the occurrence of an insured-against event. The insurance company that continues to negotiate a settlement of a claim after the insured has failed to make a timely filing of the proof of loss will likely be found have waived that condition even though at the time of the waiver it was no longer possible for the condition to occur and the insured could not have detrimentally relied upon the waiver by forbearing from filing the proof of loss within the required time. Ordinarily it is not possible to find a change of position in reliance upon a waiver that occurs after the condition has already failed. If the court finds a waiver in this circumstance, it is held to be irrevocable even without a change of position by the insured. Perhaps in the interest of symmetry and to avoid doing violence to the concept of waivers and retraction, a better characterization of this situation is to find that the insurance company has elected not to assert the condition precedent to its liability and that such an election is irrevocable. These concepts are developed in the next chapter.

CHAPTER 8

PERFORMANCE

A. PROMISES AND CONDITIONS

§ 8.1 Introduction; Promises and Conditions

The subject of performance involves an analysis of the legal duties that may become due under a contract with special concern for when a given duty to perform will arise and what the effect will be if a duty of immediate performance is breached. Contract duties are created by the promises manifested by the parties. This includes express promises by words, spoken or written, and promises which arise by implication based upon the parties' conduct or other circumstances. When there is a duty of immediate performance of a promise, failure to perform in full is a breach.

A promise is an undertaking or commitment that a certain event will or will not occur in the future. In the most basic form, a contract may contain one unconditional promise. X says to Y: "If you will climb that pole, I will pay you $10," whereupon Y climbs the pole. This unilateral contract has but one promise, the promise to pay the $10. If Y accepted by climbing the pole, then the duty to perform that promise arises immediately upon the making of the contract.

368

Assume a slight change in the facts: Y states that if X will climb the pole, Y will pay $10 to X next Tuesday. When X climbs the pole the contract is formed and there is again but one promise. Even though performance is not due until next Tuesday, the duty to perform it is still unconditional. It is not a duty that is immediately due and owing, but it is an unconditional promise because we know that Tuesday will come. No contingent event need occur before the duty will arise.

In addition to promises, contracts often contain conditions. A condition can be defined as an event, the occurrence or non-occurrence of which gives rise to or extinguishes a duty. Section 224 of the Restatement defines the term more narrowly as "an event, not certain to occur, which must occur, unless its non-occurrence is excused, before performance under a contract becomes due." Note the difference between these two definitions. Under the traditional definition, the occurrence of a condition can terminate an existing duty (a condition subsequent) whereas under the Restatement definition, only those events the occurrence of which give rise to a duty (conditions precedent) are labeled conditions. (See comment e to § 224.) Under the Restatement structure, events that terminate duties are separately treated in section 230.

It might be helpful to think of promises and conditions in the sense that promises are the basis of actions for breach of contract. The breach of a promise can provide a right to recover damages or obtain some other remedy. The occurrence or non-

occurrence of a condition affects whether there
could be breach of a promise at all. For if the
promise is subject to a condition, the plaintiff must
prove as part of the prima facie case that the
condition has occurred or been excused. If it has,
the promised performance was owing. If the condition has not occurred or been excused, then the
duty created by the promise was not owing and
therefore could not have been breached.

§ 8.1.1   Sources of Conditions

An event can become a condition because the
parties manifested the intention that it act as such.
An event can become a condition because the court
concludes as a matter of law that justice will be
better served if a condition is imposed. While the
judge ultimately determines whether a condition
does or does not exist in a given contract, these two
processes for finding conditions are quite different.
In the first, the court is looking to the words and
conduct of the parties in the given circumstances
together with matters such as course of performance or dealing or usage of trade to determine
whether these parties intended that an event should
occur before a duty would arise. When the judge is
involved with construing a condition as a matter of
law to do justice, the judge is concerned not with
finding the manifested or implied intention of the
parties but rather with the demands of justice.
Court imposed conditions do not find their source in
the intention of the parties.

§ 8.1.2   Enforcement of Conditions

The presence of a condition in a contract can result in a forfeiture. If construction of a building precisely in a certain manner is a condition to the owner's duty to pay, then there will be cases in which builders spend a lot of money and effort but fail to fulfill the condition and thus may not get paid. One who builds a structure and does not get paid for the work suffers a forfeiture.

A forfeiture involves a loss in the nature of a punishment. Punishment is appropriate in criminal law and in some issues involving tort law, but the purpose of contract law is to protect reasonable expectations, not to punish. Since punishment is an inappropriate outcome in a contract case, forfeitures are to be avoided where possible.

If a court has imposed a condition in a contract to do justice, that purpose will be defeated if the result of enforcing the condition is to produce a forfeiture. It is a standard rule that the court will impose a condition that the builder build first before the owner is required to pay. But the purpose for imposing this rule is fulfilled if the builder substantially completes the construction. Court imposed conditions need only substantially occur. Where such conditions involve performance by one party, substantial performance is sufficient to fulfill that condition thereby causing the other party's duty to arise.

If the parties themselves negotiated a condition as part of their agreement by including contract

language that expressly requires that a certain
event occur before a duty shall arise, the court will
require more full and literal compliance with that
condition. As stated in comment c to Restatement
section 226: " * * * to the extent that the parties
have, by a term in their agreement, clearly made an
event a condition, they can be confident that a court
will ordinarily feel constrained strictly to apply that
term, while the same court may regard itself as
having considerable latitude in tailoring a similar
term that it has itself supplied."

§ 8.1.3 Labeling of Conditions

Court opinions from different jurisdictions in the
United States do not reflect a consistent use of
terminology to describe different types of conditions. There are even examples of contradictory
vocabulary used within a single jurisdiction. The
goal for students in contract law is to develop a
workable vocabulary so that one can explain this
subject to yourself and others while at the same
time having a tolerance for and understanding of
different labels used by others.

All jurisdictions recognize the existence of conditions created by the parties. It is the general practice to divide such conditions into two categories,
express and implied.

EXPRESS CONDITIONS

Conditions can exist because they are expressly
stated in the terms of the contract. Assume that a
contract for casualty insurance provides that Owner

promises to pay a premium of $750 and Insurance Co. promises to pay for all losses to Owner's house up to some maximum dollar amount if the house is damaged or destroyed by certain casualties including fire. This bilateral contract contains two promises. The promise by Owner to pay the premium is not subject to any conditions and is thus an unconditional promise. The promise by Insurance Co. to pay for losses will be subject to several conditions stated in the policy one of which will be that there is damage to the property resulting from some covered casualty. Fire loss is thus an event the occurrence of which will give rise to Insurance Co.'s duty to pay. If the event does not occur, the duty to pay will never arise. This condition is an "express" condition because the terms of the contract expressly stated that the duty to pay will arise *only if* a casualty loss occurred.

Express conditions are created by the parties by the language used in reaching their bargain. No particular language is required to create an express condition, however, terms such as "if," "provided that," "on the condition that," or "subject to" are commonly used to denote the parties' intentions that an event will function as a condition. If the parties have manifested by their language that they intend an express condition, the courts generally require that this condition be fully and literally fulfilled before the duty subject to that condition will be found to have arisen. The courts attempt to recognize and enforce the parties' objectively manifested intentions.

Assume that NFL Team hires Quarterback on a one-year contract that provides for a salary of $1,000,000 plus an additional $400,000 if Quarterback passes for more than 3,000 yards during the regular season. Passing for 3,000 yards is an express condition to the duty of Team to pay the extra $400,000. Since it is a party imposed condition and is expressly stated in the contract, the court can be expected to respect the parties' manifested intention and enforce the contract as written.

If Quarterback passes for 2,900 yards or even 2,990 yards during the season, the condition has failed and no additional payment is due. There is no forfeiture involved here so there is no reason for the court to intervene by disturbing the bargain that the parties made for themselves .. However, if Team removed Quarterback half way thorough the final game when he had reached 2,990 yards passing, this would raise an issue regarding implied duties of cooperation or perhaps the duty of good faith and fair dealing, but absent such circumstances, the terms of this particular express condition would be respected by the courts.

Courts are prone to hold that an express condition must fully and literally occur before the duty that is subject to this condition will arise. This can cause one party to incur a forfeiture if the condition is substantially fulfilled but has failed in some minor detail. To avoid this result, the court may refuse to find that an event is an express condition. Instead, the court can find it to be a constructive condition in which case substantial fulfillment is sufficient and minor discrepancies will not result in a forfeiture or loss of contract benefits. It is a fair conclusion that courts are not ordinarily motivated to find that a condition is expressed in the contract. Justice can often be achieved simply by labeling the condition "constructive." This point must be kept in mind when drafting a contract. If you want some event to act as an express condition to your client's duty, you must exercise great care to use language that can only be read as language of express condition. If there is a way to read it as simply a promise, that is what a court may do.

Assume that a fire insurance contract states: "The insured agrees to maintain an automatic water sprinkler system in good working condition." If the insured fails to maintain the sprinkler system in working condition and sustains a fire loss, the rights of the parties will depend upon the interpretation placed on the quoted language. If maintenance of the system is an express condition to the insurer's duty to pay, then failure of that condition will prevent that duty from arising. The insured will receive no payment. If maintenance of the system is a promised performance, then the insured is liable for any damages caused by breach of that promise. The burden of proof would then be on the insurance company to show what part of the loss, if any, would have been avoided if the sprinkler system had been operating at the time of the fire. Whatever actual damages the insurance company could prove resulted from breach of the promise would be deducted from the insured's fire loss claim.

Maintenance of the sprinkler system in this hypothetical would undoubtedly be held to be only a promised performance since the agreement used words of promise ("The insured agrees * * * ") rather than words that expressly stated that an operating sprinkler system was a condition to the company's duty to pay. The result would also be influenced by the fact that interpreting the words as words of condition could result in a forfeiture of the insured's right to payment under the contract. Further, if the language is ambiguous, any ambiguity will be resolved against the party who drafted the contract which in this case is the insurance company.

IMPLIED (IN FACT) CONDITIONS

Conditions are also found in contracts where there is no express language of condition but the terms of the contract clearly indicate that the parties intended that some event must occur before a duty would arise. One example is the situation in which one party must do something to permit or facilitate the performance by the other. X agrees to paint Y's house with the color of paint to correspond to a sample to be furnished by Y. Y's furnishing of the sample is a condition to X's duty of performance. While this condition was not expressed in the contract language, its occurrence is indispensable to X's performance and thus the duty to perform cannot arise until the event occurs.

Implied conditions may also be found where the intention of the parties is clear despite the absence of language of express condition. For example, prior course of performance or dealing or usage of trade may make it clear that the parties intended that X, the buyer of goods, would make a cash deposit of 25% of the purchase price before the seller, Y, would commence manufacture of the goods. A court will find that payment of the deposit is a condition to the seller's duty to perform. It is not an express condition because the parties used no express language of condition. It is not a condition construed by the court to do justice because justice is served by following the usual default rules in contracts for sale of goods which provide that payment is due on delivery. Thus, if a condition is found here, it can only be an implied condition.

CONSTRUCTIVE CONDITIONS

Any term supplied by the court and not based upon the apparent intention of the parties is called a "constructive" condition. Comment c to Restatement section 226 states as follows:

c. By a term supplied by court. When the parties have omitted a term that is essential to a determination of their rights and duties, the court may supply a term which is reasonable in the circumstances (sec. 204). Where that term makes an event a condition, it is often described as a "constructive" (or "implied in law") condition. This serves to distinguish it from events which are made conditions by the agreement of the parties, either by their words or by other conduct, and which are described as "express" and as "implied in fact" (inferred from fact) conditions. See Comments a and b to sec. 4. It is useful to distinguish "constructive" conditions, even though the distinction is necessarily somewhat arbitrary. For one thing, it is helpful in analysis and description to have terminology that reflects the two distinctive processes, sometimes called "interpretation" and "construction," that give rise to conditions. (See Uniform Commercial Code §§ 2–313 to 2–315, in which an analogous distinction is made between express and implied warranties.) For another, to the extent that the parties have, by a term of their agreement, clearly made an event a condition, they can be confident that a court will ordinarily feel constrained to apply that term strictly, while the same court may regard itself as having considerable latitude in tailoring a condition that it has itself supplied.

The Reporter's Note to comment c states in part as follows:

* * * Whether a court is inferring a condition from the parties' unclear expression of intention or constructing one as a matter of lawmaking is often unclear, because the processes overlap: the values that encourage a court to construct a condition were usually present when the parties were negotiating and thus support inferences about their actual intentions. * * *

Two centuries have passed since Lord Mansfield set forth the scheme for constructive conditions in *Kingston v. Preston* (K.B. 1773), wherein it is stated:

There are three kinds of covenants: 1. Such as are called mutual and independent, where either party may recover damages from the other, for the injury he may have received by a breach of the covenants in his favour, and where it is no excuse for the defendant to allege a breach of the covenants on the part of the plaintiff. 2. There are covenants which are conditions and dependent, in which the performance of one depends on the prior performance of another, and, therefore, till this prior condition is performed, the other party is not liable to an action on his covenant. 3. There is also a third sort of covenants, which are mutual conditions to be performed at the same time; and in these, if one party was ready, and offered, to perform his part, and the other neglected, or refused to perform his, he who was ready, and offered, has fulfilled his engagement, and may maintain an action for the default of the other; though it is not certain that either is obliged to do the first act. His Lordship then proceeded to say, that the dependence or independence of covenants was to be collected from the evident sense and meaning of the parties, and, that, however transposed they might be in the deed, their precedency must depend on the order of time in which the intent of the transaction requires their performance.

Promises which, by the terms of the contract, are to be performed prior in time are ordinarily construed to be conditions precedent to those promises that are to be performed later in time. A promised performance that requires a period of time, such as painting a house or cutting a lawn, is ordinarily construed as a condition precedent to the promised performance that consists of a single act such as payment of money. (These fall into Lord Mansfield's category #2.)

If both promises are capable of being performed simultaneously and the contract does not require that one occur first, the promises are treated as mutually dependent or concurrently conditioned upon each other. In this case neither party has a duty to perform until the other has performed or tendered performance. Both could wait for the other forever. Neither would ever have a duty to perform, and there would never be a breach. As a practical matter, the party who wishes to conclude the transaction must take the step of performing or tendering his performance so as to give rise to a duty of performance in the other party. In these situations, the duty of each party to perform is conditional. It will not arise as an absolute duty until the other party has performed or tendered. The shorthand language for describing this situation is to say that the performances are concurrently conditioned upon each other. "Concurrent conditions" are not a different type of condition. This term simply describes the situation where neither party has an independent duty to perform because the duty of each is dependent upon the other acting first. This is the "third sort of covenants" to which Lord Mansfield referred. The effect of the conditions being concurrent is that neither party will be obliged to perform until the other tenders performance (or performs). Therefore, it is frequently said that when the performances of each party are concurrently conditioned upon each other, the tender by one party is a constructive condition precedent to the other party's duty of performance.

After one becomes familiar with spotting constructive conditions in a contract, their presence becomes obvious. X promises to pick up Y at the airport at 12:00 noon for which Y promises to pay X $20. It is self-evident that X's act of meeting Y at the airport is a condition precedent to Y's duty to pay. Because it is so obvious, one may be inclined to state that it is an express condition. It is not. It is an express promise. The time and location are expressly stated. But there is no language that expressly states that X's performance of the promise is a condition precedent to Y's duty to pay. Very clearly intended? Yes. Expressed in words? No.

To summarize, constructive conditions are imposed by the court to do justice for the parties. Justice is accomplished if the conditions substantially occur or are substantially fulfilled. Justice does not require that a court-construed condition be literally and fully fulfilled before the other party's duty will arise. If the constructive condition is an event that is also the promised performance, the condition is fulfilled if the promise is substantially performed. It can also be stated that the condition is fulfilled unless there was a material breach of the promise (§ 8.1.2).

§ 8.2 Substantial Performance; Effect of Breach

If one party's promised performance is a constructive condition to the other party's duty to perform, breach by the first party may prevent the other's duty of performance from arising. Thus, if X promises to paint Y's house for $9,000, failure of X to paint will prevent Y from ever having a duty to pay. The first duty is both a promise and a condition (a promissory condition), and these two legalities must each be analyzed.

The first party's failure to perform is a breach of promise for which any resulting damages may be recovered. Performance by the first party was also a constructive condition to the other party's duty. If this constructive condition is not substantially fulfilled, the other party's duty to perform will not arise.

From the perspective of the second party, there are two distinct questions.

1) Did the first party breach? If so, the second party has a right to recover damages caused by that breach. It matters not whether it was a major breach or a minor breach. When suing for damages, a breach is a breach.

2) Was the constructive condition to the second party's duty to perform substantially fulfilled? If so,

the second party has a duty of immediate performance failing which, he will be in breach and can be held liable for resulting damages. Thus, if the breach by the first party was only minor, the second party must proceed to perform because the condition to his duty was substantially fulfilled. If the first party committed a material breach, then the condition was not substantially fulfilled and the second party's duty has not arisen. When defending against an action for breach, the question whether the other party committed a material breach may be very relevant.

Assume that X contracts to build a house for Y for $250,000 payable on completion. X's obligation to build is a promissory condition. It is both a promised performance and a constructive condition to Y's duty to pay. Assume further that X stops performance when the house is completed except for the gutters and down-spouts that were included in the plans. X has breached the promise to build in accordance with plans, and Y can recover damages for this breach. However, it is apparent that X has substantially performed his obligation and thus the constructive condition to Y's duty to pay has been fulfilled. Y has a duty to pay the contract price minus his damages. (Note that when discussing a party's right to damages, any breach that causes foreseeable harm will give rise to a cause of action for damages. Whether the defendant has substantially performed or whether the breach is material is not a relevant question. Damages are available for minor breaches if the minor breach caused harm.)

It can be stated that X has substantially performed thus giving rise to Y's duty to pay. It can also be stated that X's breach is a minor breach as distinguished from a material breach and thus Y has a duty to pay. If there has been substantial performance or substantial fulfillment of the constructive condition, then the breach by X is by definition a minor breach. If X has not substantially performed, then his breach is a material breach and Y's duty to pay will not arise unless the condition is excused for some reason.

§ 8.2.1 Finding Occurrence of Substantial Performance

The term substantial performance is most frequently used in service contracts such as construction contracts. The term material breach is commonly used in contracts involving the sale of land and was used in common law cases dealing with the sale of goods. However, substantial performance and minor breach are often used interchangeably, and the following analysis of substantial performance is also relevant for determining whether a breach is material or minor.

In determining whether a condition has been substantially performed, most court opinions discuss some or all of the factors listed in Restatement section 241, which provides:

In determining whether a failure to render or to offer performance is material, the following circumstances are significant:

(a) The extent to which the injured party will be deprived of the benefit he reasonably expected;

(b) The extent to which the injured party can be adequately compensated for the part of that benefit of which he will be deprived;

(c) The extent to which the party failing to perform or to offer to perform will suffer forfeiture;

(d) The likelihood that the party failing to perform or to offer to perform will cure his failure, taking account of all the circumstances including any reasonable assurances;

(e) The extent to which the behavior of the party failing to perform or to offer to perform comports with standards of good faith and fair dealing.

Assume that Ann, an accomplished attorney, has just obtained a large verdict in a personal injury case. The defendant appeals and Ann, with her client's consent, contracts with Bert, an appellate practice specialist. Bert agrees to write all necessary briefs for the appeal and Ann promises to pay Bert the sum of $30,000 "when the brief is in final form and ready to file with the court."

Bert reviews the transcripts and does the necessary research. Bert prepares drafts of the brief. Bert has a "final draft," but both Bert and Ann agree that there is one further point that Bert should research which may affect one portion of the brief. Before this last work is accomplished, Bert is appointed to a high government position, and he advises Ann that he cannot finish the brief. Ann refuses to pay Bert and Bert sues on the contract.

The first issue which must be resolved is whether Ann's duty to pay is dependent upon the occurrence of an express condition, the completion of the brief. The express language of the contract indicates the time when Ann is to pay: "When the brief is in final form and ready to file with the court." It does not expressly state that failure to get the brief in final form will preclude the duty to pay from arising. No common language of condition such as "unless" or "on the condition that" is used. It can plausibly be argued that since the language used expressly provides that payment will only occur when a the brief is completed, completion of the brief is thus an express condition to Ann's promise to pay. However, such an interpretation would lead to the result that Bert cannot sue on the contract unless he has fully and completely performed (§ 8.1.3). Because of the harshness of this result, the courts would not be disposed to find an express condition, and since the language used in the contract does not appear to compel that result, the completion of Bert's performance would most likely be found to be a constructive condition to Ann's duty to pay.

Assuming that the court finds a constructive condition, the issue that must now be analyzed is whether Bert has substantially performed or, stated another way, whether the condition to Ann's duty has substantially occurred. Whichever way the question is stated or framed, the answer requires the same analysis. Thus, applying the factors quoted above from Restatement section 241, a court has five points to consider.

(a) Ann did receive the substantial benefit of her bargain. The necessary organization and analysis has been accomplished. The missing work can presumably be performed by Ann or another attorney.

(b) Since Ann has a cause of action against Bert for breach (Bert has breached at least part of his promise regardless whether he has "substantially performed"), Ann can recoup the amount of her damages by way of a reduction against the contract price(§ 9.2). Ann's damages are presumably measurable and ascertainable, and Ann can therefore be adequately compensated for the benefit of which she was deprived (§ 9.3). Note that if it were evident that Ann sustained serious damages but those damages were too uncertain for Ann to prove, this factor would weigh heavily against finding substantial performance. This factor (b) causes confusion for many students which can be avoided if one understands the logic behind it. If the non-breaching party (Ann) is able to recover fully for all the harm she suffers as the result of Bert's breach, then forcing her to render her own performance is far less onerous than it would be if she were suffering uncompensable damages which she cannot deduct from the contract price. For example, her damages might be unrecoverable because they are too uncertain or perhaps too unforeseeable.

(c) Bert has rendered significant performance. This is important because of the magnitude of forfeiture that Bert will incur if he is not permitted to enforce Ann's promise. While there is some hardship upon Ann as a result of Bert's breach, it would appear that it would be a greater hardship upon Bert to deny him the right to enforce the contract.

(d) The contract does not provide for future performances, so the fact that Bert is not going to cure is not material.

(e) Bert's breach was willful in the sense that he could have rejected the government position and stayed home to finish the brief. He has knowingly departed from his duty, however, he is probably not acting in bad faith. Because of the nature and importance of the position which Bert accepted, his breach will not likely be found to be a violation of any standard of good faith and fair dealing.

Review §§ 4.11–4.13.a relating to good faith and fair dealing. Consider the alternative approaches to defining these terms and analyze the sense in which "good faith" is being used in Restatement section 241 to determine the materiality of the breach. The First Restatement of Contracts had a slightly different formulation asking whether the breach was "willful" (Restatement First § 275(6)). When that Restatement was adopted in 1932, the phrase "good faith" was not known in contract law.

As analyzed, the factors lead to the conclusion that the breach by Bert was not material and the condition to Ann's duty to pay did substantially occur. Therefore, Bert should be able to recover the contract price minus damages caused to Ann by Bert's breach.

It should be noted that in many cases the analysis of the Restatement factors will result in some points in favor of finding substantial performance and some against. The result is not predicated upon the numerical total of factors favoring and factors opposing a finding of substantial performance. The courts will base their decisions upon the factors that are most critical in the case before it.

§ 8.3 Enforcement of Conditions

Application of the rules set forth in the previous sections produces these examples of the impact of unfilled conditions upon contract rights and duties.

HYPO #1

Assume that Acme Construction and Homer enter a contract to construct a home in conformance with plans and specifications for $200,000. The specifications indicate that pipe manufactured by the Reading Pipe Co. was to be used throughout the house. Acme inadvertently substituted some pipe that had the same physical qualities but was not manufactured by Reading.

There is no express condition in these facts. The contract expressly calls for Reading pipe and Acme expressly promised to use Reading pipe, but there are no express terms of the contract that spell out that the use of Reading pipe is a condition precedent to Homer's duty to pay. While one might development an argument as to implied intentions of the parties, courts would not be expected to find an implied condition here. But the court would construe a condition (thus it would be a constructive condition) concluding that the service portion of the contract must be performed before the owner's duty to pay would arise.

Since building the house is a constructive condition to Homer's duty to pay, Acme need only substantially perform before that duty to pay arises. If Acme uses another brand of pipe of equal quality, this is a breach of contract, but it is clear that Acme has substantially performed (§ 8.2.1). Homer will have a duty to pay the contract price but may deduct recoverable damages resulting from the breach by Acme. As discussed in section 9.2.2 damages in this case would no doubt be based upon diminished value rather than cost to cure and the likely figure is zero.

HYPO #2

Assume that Acme and Homer enter a contract to construct a home in conformance with plans and specifications for $200,000. The specifications indicate that pipe manufactured by the Reading Pipe Co. is to be used throughout. The contract provides in part: "Construction in full compliance with plans and specifications is hereby made an express condition precedent to Homer's duty to pay Acme." As in Hypo #1, the contractor unwittingly substitutes another brand of pipe of equal quality.

Under these revised facts, the parties have made full compliance with plans and specifications an express condition precedent to the owner's duty to pay. Since express conditions ordinarily must fully and literally occur before they are deemed to be fulfilled, there is a serious argument that Acme should go unpaid until it tears the offending pipe out of the walls and replaces it. Forcing such a correction upon the contractor is economically wasteful. To the extent that cure is economically prohibitive, the contractor is going to incur a forfeiture which the common law seeks to avoid in contract law.

Because the substituted pipe is of equal quality and the breach was not wilful and denial of payment would cause a forfeiture, the court is very likely to permit Acme to recover the contract price less whatever recoverable damages Homer has sustained. There are two ways for a court to reach this result:

1) The express condition may be excused as discussed in section 8.6.

2) The express condition may be found not to cover such details or technical violations. The parties' language relating to the condition was rather generic in that it applied to the entire house and treated all details of the plans and specifications with one broad stroke of the brush.

No construction project is completed in exact accordance with every detail specified. Thus, it might be found appropriate to conclude that the express condition language was intended by the parties to apply to departures that involve matters of substance but not to those that are insignificant. (See *Jacob & Youngs v. Kent*, N.Y. 1921.)

HYPO #3

Assume that Acme Construction contracted for a house as in the prior hypos. In this case, the contract language provides:

Construction in full compliance with plans and specifications and in particular the exclusive use of pipe manufactured by the Reading Pipe Co. is hereby made an express condition to Homer's duty to pay.

It is suggested that the parties have left no wiggle-room for the courts. There is no way to avoid the conclusion that use of Reading Pipe throughout is an express condition to Homer's duty to pay. If other brands of pipe are used, the court is faced squarely with the choice of respecting the concept of freedom of contract or party autonomy and enforcing the contract as written or choosing to excuse the condition to avoid a forfeiture. This problem will be continued in section 8.6.6 which deals with excuse of condition to avoid a forfeiture.

§ 8.4 Guidelines to Identify Promises and Different Types of Conditions

No court ever interprets a term of a contract and labels it a promise or a condition without knowing what effect that label will produce. No law student or attorney should attempt to place labels on contract events without considering what results will best carry out the evident intention of the parties and the needs of justice.

Assume the court is interpreting an agricultural lease which contains language indicating that all noxious weeds are to be removed. If the language is interpreted to be an express condition to the tenant's right to remain in possession of the land, then any deviation from the full and literal requirement will create a basis for the landlord contending that the tenant should be evicted. In the case of a multi-year lease, significant investments in long-term crops could be forfeited due to the tenant's failure to remove some of the weeds.

If the language in the lease is interpreted to be a promise, then the failure of the tenant to remove weeds would be a breach of promise for which the landlord could seek damages. Proving the dollar value of damages resulting from having a few weeds on the property would not be a task that the owner's counsel would approach with joy. If the promise to remove weeds is of sufficient importance, it may also be a constructive condition to the tenant's right to remain in possession. In this case, possession could be terminated for a substantial failure of that condition, in other words a substantial breach of the promise to keep the premises weed-free. If removal of weeds is a condition to the tenant's right to continue in possession, finding this to be a constructive condition rather than an express condition would provide a distinct advantage to the tenant.

It would be a mistake to assume that judges interpret contracts however they please to produce whatever results they wish. On the contrary, most judges are deeply concerned with limiting the court's role to carrying out the intention of the parties. But it is quite reasonable to expect that a judge will not wish to read an agricultural lease to provide that removal of weeds is an express condition to the tenant's right to continue in possession. Courts tend to interpret the contract term as language of a promise in such situations. This permits the owner to recover all of the damages that he can prove, and if the situation becomes bad enough, the lease can be terminated because of the substantial failure of a constructive condition to the tenant's right of continued possession (§ 8.2.1).

In the drafting of documents, wise counsel pay particular attention to these issues. If they wish to be able to obtain damages if an event does not occur, then they must make that event a promised performance. If they wish to be able to take or avoid certain action if an event occurs or does not occur, then they must make that event a condition, preferably an express condition. Of course, the same event can be both a promised performance and an express condition. Experienced counsel know, however, that making a certain event a promised performance may provide a court with a ready-made reason not to interpret that same event to be an express condition.

§ 8.4.1 Alternative Vocabulary to "Constructive Conditions"

There is an additional problem with the vocabulary used by courts when discussing conditions. In several jurisdictions including California, courts commonly limit the use of the term "condition" to refer only to what has been described above as an express condition.

Assume a simple contract in which Paul is to paint Mary's house for $10,000. Utilizing the vocabulary discussed in the preceding sections, one would state that there are no express conditions in this contract but that the painting of the house is a constructive condition to Mary's duty to pay and her duty will not arise unless that performance is substantially rendered. If the promise to paint was not fully accomplished, one would then apply the factors set forth in Restatement section 241 to determine whether performance had been substantially rendered and the constructive condition thus substantially fulfilled.

In some jurisdictions, court opinions commonly state that there is no condition present in this contract, but that Mary need not pay if there has been a failure of consideration The logic is that if Paul has not substantially completed the task of painting the house, then the consideration for which Mary bargained has failed and thus Mary has no duty to pay.

The difference is a matter of semantics, not substance. Whether one speaks of substantial failure of consideration or substantial fulfillment of a constructive condition to Mary's duty to perform, the answer will be found by applying the same Restatement section 241 factors to determine whether Paul's duty was substantially performed (§ 8.2.1). If it was, Mary has received substantially the performance to which she was entitled. She has received the consideration for which she bargained and must pay the contract price less any damages for Paul's shortcomings. If Paul's duty to paint was not substantially performed, Mary's duty to pay will not arise because there was a "failure of consideration." Using either vocabulary, Mary's duty does not arise until the duty to paint is substantially fulfilled. If Paul commits a material breach of the contract, Mary's duty will not arise.

§ 8.5 Conditions Subsequent

It is possible to fashion a condition so that it extinguishes an existing duty of performance rather than giving rise to a duty. Such a condition, by definition, occurs after the duty has already arisen, and can therefore be called a condition subsequent. In most situations where conditions are stated in the form of a condition subsequent, they are in substance simply conditions precedent. For example, father (F) contracts with his adult college student son (S) in which F makes a valid enforceable promise to pay S the sum of $500 per month for four years, provided that if S drops out of school, F's duty to make payments will cease. F's duty to make the monthly payments is stated to be an absolute undertaking creating an unconditional duty of performance. It is stated to be subject to being terminated by the occurrence of the event of S leaving college. S's leaving college appears to be a condition the occurrence of which will terminate a duty. It thus might be classified as a condition subsequent.

F's duty to make each monthly payment is actually subject to the condition precedent that S remain in college up to the time the payment is due. While the language of the agreement implies that F's duty is absolute but will be terminated upon the occurrence of the event of S dropping out, in fact there is no duty of immediate performance until the condition of staying in school has occurred. However, because the parties have chosen to use language indicating that the condition was to operate as a condition subsequent, many courts would designate it as such a condition.

Examples of conditions which are truly subsequent in substance rather than merely subsequent in form are not common in contract law. S sells B a tractor. The contract provides that S warrants certain features, that B must give notice of breach at least 120 days before filing suit, and that any action for breach of warranty must be brought within six months following the giving of such notice. Giving notice 120 days before filing suit is a condition precedent to liability. An action cannot be maintained without such notice. Filing an action within six months after giving of notice is a condition subsequent. After notice has been given, S has a present duty owing to B. The failure to file suit within six months will terminate that duty and thus functions as a condition subsequent. True conditions subsequent are encountered with some frequency in the law relating to real property.

Before one gets too confused by the precedent and subsequent classifications, it might be helpful to know that in contract law there is no substantive difference between the two. For purposes of contract analysis, one can simply refer to the cutting of the lawn, the absence of rain on Saturday, or the staying in college as a condition without designating whether it is precedent or subsequent. The result will not be affected by the failure to designate the type of condition. However, in the area of pleading and procedure significance may be placed upon the difference between a condition precedent and subsequent in terms of who has the burden of pleading and proof, the party seeking to enforce the promise usually being required to plead and prove a condition precedent and the party seeking to avoid liability for breach of promise being required to plead and prove the occurrence of the condition subsequent that would terminate the duty.

The definition of "condition" in section 224 of the Restatement (§ 8.1) does not encompass events that terminate a duty of performance. Thus, all "conditions" are precedent in the vocabulary of the Restatement. Events that terminate an obligor's duty of immediate performance are covered in Restatement section 230 and are treated as a grounds for discharge. (See Chapter 6.)

B. EXCUSE OF CONDITIONS
§ 8.6 Excuse of Conditions

Conditions may be fulfilled or excused. A dependent or conditional promise will ripen into a duty of immediate performance if the condition to which it is subject is fulfilled or excused. Thus, even though a condition has not occurred, the duty of the other party to perform may still arise if the condition is legally excused.

Conditions may be legally excused in at least six ways:

(1) by the making of a proper tender which is rejected;

(2) by the failure of a prior condition;

(3) by an anticipatory repudiation of a promise by the other party or voluntary disablement or prospective inability of the other party to perform;

(4) by waiver or estoppel;

(5) by impossibility of performance of the condition; and

(6) to avoid a forfeiture.

§ 8.6.1 Excuse of Condition by Tender

If performance by one party is a condition precedent to the other's duty to perform, then the improper rejection of a tender of performance is a legal excuse for non-occurrence of the condition precedent, and the other party's duty of performance becomes absolute.

This rule is useful when contract performances are concurrently conditioned upon each other. The party who wishes to see the transaction advance must tender his performance in order for the other party's duty to arise (§ 8.1.3). When this is done, the other party may not avoid his obligations simply by rejecting the tender.

A tender of money must be in cash or its equivalent (compare U.C.C. § 2–511(2)). If a personal check is tendered or if a tender is defective for any similar technical reason and the other party does not object on that ground, he will likely be found to have waived the objection (U.C.C. § 2–605). To illustrate, if A agrees to sell a specific automobile to B and B agrees to pay A $10,000, A's refusal to accept B's tender of the money excuses the condition to A's duty, and A's duty to transfer the automobile becomes absolute. Therefore, B could immediately file suit for breach of contract and prevail.

§ 8.6.2 Excuse of Condition by Failure of a Prior Condition

The non-occurrence of a condition may be excused if it is subject to a condition that has failed. Assume that B contracts to build six $80,000 homes on O's land, with O to designate the sites. The contract is entered into in July with construction to begin in September. O fails to designate the sites. Normally, B could not recover from O without proving that he had performed the act of building the houses, thus fulfilling the condition precedent to

O's duty to pay. But O's selection of the sites is an implied condition precedent to B's duty to build. Failure of the condition precedent of designating the sites is a legal excuse for the non-occurrence of B's performance. O's promise to pay has become absolute because of the excuse of the condition precedent that B build the houses. B may recover the profits he would have made on the job. An alternative analysis can be used. If one finds that O had impliedly promised to designate the sites upon which homes would be built, the failure to designate would be a breach of that implied promise.

§ 8.6.3 Excuse of Condition by an Anticipatory Repudiation of a Promise, or by Voluntary Disablement or Prospective Inability to Perform

If before performance of a contract is due a party denies any intention to perform, this constitutes an anticipatory repudiation of a contract. An anticipatory repudiation is often defined as "an unequivocal manifestation of intention not to perform." A statement by a party to the effect that he is encountering difficulties in preparing to perform, that he is not pleased with the bargain, or that he is otherwise uncertain whether performance will be rendered when due, is not sufficient to constitute a repudiation. The words must actually manifest clearly and unequivocally an intent not to perform.

In bilateral contracts, an anticipatory repudiation has the legal effect of excusing the conditions that may have shielded the repudiating party's duty to perform. An anticipatory repudiation may also excuse performance by the other party. The practical effect is that the non-repudiating party may properly suspend his own performance or preparations and has a defense to going forward with contract performance. If the repudiation is properly retracted, the other party will be given additional time in which to perform if that is appropriate in the circumstances.

An anticipatory repudiation may also give rise to an immediate cause of action for breach. In many cases, the innocent party is in a position where action must be taken to mitigate damages if the contract is not going to be performed. Thus it is economically efficient to give the victim the right to react to a repudiation by suspending his own performance or seeking alternative ways to get the return performance that he needs. When this is done, courts generally recognize an immediate right to sue on the contract even though the repudiator's duty to perform may not yet be due under the terms of the contract. Some common law decisions deny an immediate right of action if the innocent party has already fully performed and is simply waiting for the date on which payment will be due. In this latter circumstance, there is no action to be taken to mitigate damages and thus no economic inefficiency to compel the victim to wait until the time that performance was due under the contract.

Prospective inability to perform exists when circumstances indicate that it is highly unlikely that a party will be able to perform. If X contracts to sell Blackacre to Y, the fact that Blackacre now belongs to Z does not constitute prospective inability. X might be able to acquire title from Z thus making performance possible. If it is established that Z is a public utility which needs Blackacre to discharge its utility functions, then it is evident that X will not be able to acquire title and there is a prospective inability to perform.

A voluntary disablement occurs when a party to a contract engages in conduct that destroys or seriously impairs his ability to perform. Assume that on May 20, S contracts to sell and B to buy Blackacre for $100,000 with performance to be on July 1. On June 1, S conveys Blackacre outright to C. By his conduct, S placed his ability to perform beyond his own personal control. This will likely be treated as a voluntary disablement even if C has promised to reconvey to S before July 1.

Repudiation, voluntary disablement and prospective inability give the other party a legal excuse for not fulfilling conditions to the performance that is apparently not going to be rendered. If a party attempts to retract his repudiation or overcomes his inability to perform prior to the time for performance and attempts to reinstate the contract, the contract will be reinstated if the other party has not changed position in reasonable reliance in the interim. In the land sale contract illustration above, if S reacquired title prior to the time for performance and B had not in the meantime purchased another parcel of land or otherwise changed position in reliance, S could enforce the contract. If B had relied by suspending preparations for performance,

B could be given a reasonable extension of time within which to perform.

§ 8.6.3a Prospective Inability, Demand for Assurances, and Repudiation Under the U.C.C.

U.C.C. section 2–609(1) provides:

A contract for sale imposes an obligation on each party that the other's expectation of receiving due performance will not be impaired. When reasonable grounds for insecurity arise with respect to the performance of either party the other may in writing demand adequate assurance of due performance and until he receives such assurance may if commercially reasonable suspend any performance for which he has not already received the agreed return.

This subsection is applicable to a situation involving prospective inability to perform such as might arise when a seller who has agreed to deliver goods on credit acquires information giving rise to doubts as to the buyer's ability to pay. It can also be a very important tool for the party who receives a somewhat ambiguous communication that might be a repudiation. The innocent party may demand assurances as to the other party's intention to perform as well as his ability to perform.

If this procedure were not available, the innocent party would have to make his own determination as to whether the other party had repudiated the contract. This is an unfortunate decision to force upon an innocent party because he may sustain non-compensable damages if he decides incorrectly. For example, if a buyer decided that the seller's message was a repudiation and proceeded to purchase goods elsewhere, the resulting damages would not be recoverable if seller did in fact tender performance and the court found that the message was not a repudiation. On the other hand, if the buyer does not act when the communication is received, a later finding that the message from the seller was a repudiation may cause the court to conclude that buyer should have mitigated by making a cover purchase at that time.

By use of a demand for assurances, the innocent party need not choose at his peril between the alternative routes of mitigating damages by contracting elsewhere or standing by waiting to see whether the other party intends to perform.

Failure to respond within a reasonable period of time to a justified demand for assurances is a repudiation. The Code states that this reasonable time is not to *exceed* 30 days. In appropriate circumstances, the reasonable time in which a response must be given to a demand for assurances could be a very short period of time, even thirty minutes or less.

Under U.C.C. section 2–610, a repudiation with respect to a performance the loss of which will substantially impair the value of the contract, gives the innocent party the right to suspend his own performance and to declare an immediate breach or wait for a commercially reasonable time before treating the contract as breached. This non-breaching party has a defense to going forward with his own performance, and may treat the repudiation as an immediate breach. This is true without regard to whether there is any need to act immediately upon the repudiation.

U.C.C. section 2–611 permits retraction of a repudiation so long as the innocent party has not: (a) canceled, (b) materially changed his position in reliance, or (c) otherwise indicated that he considers the repudiation final.

§ 8.6.3b   Necessity to Demonstrate the Ability to Perform

Where a party is excused from tendering and acquires a cause of action because of an anticipatory breach, he is still ordinarily required to show that he could have performed but for the actions of the guilty party. Thus, if Betty (B) anticipatorily repudiates her promise to hire Jim (J) to sing in B's night club and J thereafter sues for breach of contract, the fact that J became disabled prior to the time for his performance and could not have sung during the period in question would prevent J from recovering. The fact that J committed himself to sing for X after B repudiated is not a bar to J's action because this was a proper effort to mitigate damages which became necessary as a result of the repudiation. The repudiation excused the condition that J remain ready and able to perform (§ 8.6.3).

Assume that after Betty repudiated, her night club was totally destroyed by fire. Unless she set the fire, this would ordinarily excuse her duty to perform on the grounds of impossibility (Chapter 6).

J would have no cause of action against B. (See Restatement section 255 and Illustration #2.)

§ 8.6.4 Excuse of Condition by Waiver or Estoppel

A party whose duty of performance is subject to a condition may communicate to the other party that he will not insist upon the occurrence of that condition. Assume a contract for sale of land to close on December 1, in which time is stated to be of the essence. Seller phones Buyer to advise that it would be more convenient if closing were delayed until the 3rd and Buyer agrees. While this oral agreement may not be a legally enforceable modification of the contract, each party has waived his right to insist on performance on the 1st.

If the condition is not a material part of the bargain and its occurrence does not materially affect the benefit to be received by the promisor, its non-occurrence can be excused by waiver. One may not waive the right to receive a performance that is a significant or material part of the bargain. A material part of the bargain can only be deleted by a contract modification which must be supported by consideration and comply with any other required formalities. Some statutes such as U.C.C. section 2–209 permit modification without consideration but a writing may be required (§ 7.5).

The doctrine of waiver can be used to excuse a condition when the waiving party has indicated by words or conduct a willingness to proceed with the contract without regard to whether the condition is fulfilled. If an insured has failed to file a timely proof of loss which the insurance contract requires within thirty days of the date of the loss as a condition precedent to payment, conduct by the insurer such as continuing to investigate the loss and negotiate a settlement will likely be a waiver of this condition.

Waivers may be withdrawn and the condition reinstated so long as this can be done and is done in a manner which is not unfair or unreasonable to the other party. The critical question will be the extent to which the other party has relied or the extent to which the condition can still be fulfilled.

Waivers of conditions that have already failed are irrevocable when made. If the insured failed to file the proof of loss within the required thirty day period and the insurance company later waived this requirement, that waiver is irrevocable when made because the condition cannot be reinstated in such a manner that the insured could comply with it. Of course, the insured is enjoying the right to enforce his claim which at one point was lost due to failure to comply with the condition. However, this result is deemed more acceptable than allowing the other party to totally defeat the claim by reinstating a condition that it had once waived.

All courts agree that waivers become irrevocable when the other party reasonably relies to the point that the term waived cannot be reasonably reinstated. In many court opinions, this is analyzed as an estoppel. As the terms are being used here, there is no substantive difference between an estoppel and an irrevocable waiver. To illustrate, assume S promises to convey Blackacre to B in exchange for B's promise to pay $150,000 on July 1. Time is made of the essence. B tells S on June 1 that he is having difficulty raising the money, and S states that he will not insist on performance before July 30. If B relies to his detriment on S's statement, by ceasing diligent efforts to raise the money by July 1, S will be estopped from reasserting the condition of performance on July 1. S may be permitted to establish a new date for performance earlier than July 30 if that is reasonable, giving recognition to B's reliance. The same analysis is involved and the same result is reached if one states that S has waived the right to insist on performance on July 1 and this waiver has become irrevocable.

A party who has wrongfully prevented the occurrence of a condition can be estopped from asserting the failure of that condition. If there is a duty to assist or not interfere with the occurrence of a condition, one who fails to cooperate and thereby prevents the fulfillment of the condition cannot rely upon its failure. A condition of party approval can be excused if the party withholds approval wrongfully. Some court opinions will explain these results by stating that the party is estopped from asserting the condition.

§ 8.6.5 Excuse of Condition by Impossibility

Impossibility of performance (or impracticability or frustration of purpose) is often thought of merely as a method of discharge from a contractual duty (Chapter 6). However, if it becomes objectively impossible to fulfill a condition which is not a material part of the agreed exchange, impossibility may excuse the condition. Where a forfeiture could result from requiring the fulfilling of a condition which is only incidental to the bargain, the condition will ordinarily be excused.

Suppose B promises to build a house for O. O promises to pay $175,000, provided B obtains an architect's certificate from a named architect. B builds the house according to specifications, but the architect dies before a certificate can be obtained. The certificate, although an express condition precedent to the right to payment, is only incidental to the basic performance for which the parties bargained, and this condition will be excused by impossibility.

Assume that X agrees to sing at Y's wedding for $500. Thereafter X becomes seriously ill and cannot sing. X's duty to sing will be excused (§ 6.1), but the condition to Y's duty to pay will not be excused. X need not sing, but Y's duty to pay will not arise. This is because the condition, singing, is a material part of the bargain. Even though the duty to sing is properly excused, it would make no sense to require Y to pay. Therefore, the condition to the duty to pay is neither fulfilled nor excused and Y's duty will never arise.

§ 8.6.6 Excuse of Condition to Avoid a Forfeiture

Restatement section 229 provides:

To the extent that the non-occurrence of a condition would cause a disproportionate forfeiture, a court may excuse the non-occurrence of that condition unless its occurrence was a material part of the agreed exchange.

Review the discussion of hypothetical construction contracts in section 8.3. When failure of an express condition leaves one party with a substantial loss due to inability to obtain the anticipated contract benefits, there is a motive to excuse that condition and give the party the benefits of the contract. The contrary position is based on the simple fact that we espouse principles of freedom of contract are we are committed to respect the intention of the parties which in this case includes enforcement of the express condition.

Assume that X, a licensed pilot, purchases a new private jet plane and enrolls with the Carpenter Flying School for lessons to qualify to fly the new jet. At this time, X purchases a new $500,000 life insurance policy from Insurance Co. The policy provides that X is covered while piloting or serving as part of the crew of a piston engine plane, but it expressly provides that until X is fully certified to fly jets, the insurance company will have no duty to pay if he is killed while flying a jet plane unless he is flying with and being instructed by instructor pilot Jane Carpenter.

On a busy Thursday afternoon at the Carpenter School, X is advised that Jane is already flying, but her brother Tom, who is equally credentialed and experienced, can give X his lessons that day. X climbs into the pilot seat with Tom sitting next to him instructing. The plane crashes, X is killed, and the named beneficiary brings action against Insurance Co. for refusal to pay the $500,000. Should the express condition precedent to Insurance Co.'s duty to pay be excused?

Reviewing the specific phrases in Restatement section 229, one finds two critical points that require analysis. There has been a non-occurrence of a condition which would cause a forfeiture of the full policy amount of $500,000. Is that forfeiture "disproportionate?" One might ask, disproportionate to what? The second question is: Was the condition a material part of the agreed exchange?

The unanswered questions cause one to seek further facts. Why was Jane Carpenter named as the one and only instructor pilot whose presence in the plane would fulfill the express condition in the contract? If the agent of the insurance company had told X that the company would only consent to Jane Carpenter because they had experience with her brother Tom whom they consider to be a wild man, then the identity of the instructor pilot becomes quite material. The forfeiture is not "disproportionate" because death while flying with Tom Carpenter was simply not a risk that the insurance company was willing to assume. Conversely, if the agent for Insurance Co. simply told X to write in the name of his instructor pilot and X supplied Jane's name, then the substitution of an equally experienced and qualified instructor would not seem to affect the material terms of the bargain to which Insurance Co. assented. Thus the half-million dollar forfeiture does appear to be disproportionate to the materiality of this contract term and the court could excuse the condition.

§ 8.7 Effect of Severability

A contract to paint a fence for $250 is an "entire" contract. Assuming that painting is a condition to the duty to pay (§ 8.1.3), the painter must substantially perform the entire job before the duty to pay will arise (§ 8.2).

If a painter contracts to paint two separate fences, one for $250 and one for $300, the contract is probably severable. If this is the case, then completion of the first fence will be construed to be a condition to the payment of the $250, and painting the second fence a condition to the $300.

Finding contract performances to be severable has several important results. A painter who receives payment for each job as it is finished will have an easier time with his financial commitments than one who does not get paid until the entire job is completed. The painter who paints one fence and fails to paint the other will be able to enforce a right to payment for the first fence if the contract is severable. He will be liable for such damages as result from his failure to paint the second fence, but he will not find himself unable to assert any right as might be the case if the contract were entire (§ 8.2.1).

The question of severability of contract performance is ultimately resolved by determining the
parties' intentions. Did the parties intend that the
painter was to be paid after each fence was painted
or did they view the contract performance as a
single event? A contract can be severable if:

(a) performance by each party is divisible into
two or more parts that are not inter-dependent
upon each other for their value;

(b) the number of performances due from each
party is the same; and

(c) performance of each part by one party appears to be the agreed exchange for a corresponding part by the other party. The question whether
each part is the agreed exchange for the other
part is a key to a finding of severability.

§ 8.8 The Condition of Approval by a Third Party or by a Principal Party to the Contract

A contract may provide that the duty of a party to
accept and pay for the performance that he is to
receive is subject to the condition that it be approved by a third party. If there is no element of
forfeiture involved, such as in the ordinary contract
for the sale of goods, this express condition is literally enforced and will usually not be excused even
by the death or incapacity of the third party. Fraud
or collusion will excuse the condition, of course, but
the fact that the third party acted unreasonably in
refusing to approve the performance does not constitute grounds for excusing the condition.

When the element of forfeiture is introduced, the standard of conduct required of the third party changes. Consider these factors:

(1) What is the magnitude of the forfeiture involved?

(2) What is the nature of the approval being sought? Is the thing being approved something of utilitarian value with a measurable performance such as an air conditioning system, or is it a matter of aesthetics and taste such as the quality of a nightclub singer? In the latter instance which involves fancy, taste and judgment, the third party will be permitted to exercise a greater degree of latitude and discretion.

(3) How unreasonable is the third party's conduct? Has he refused to inspect at all or refused to inspect thoroughly? Does he give logical reasons for his disapproval or only reasons that are irrational or arbitrary and capricious?

(4) Who is the third party and how was he selected? A renowned expert may be given wider latitude than a run-of-the-mill engineer or other professional.

While some court opinions reject such terminology as "unreasonable," "grossly unreasonable," "arbitrary" and "capricious," it would appear that some classification is helpful. It is worth considering that if the third party is to be held to the standard of acting "reasonably," then the court may be substituting the general standards of the community for the judgment of the person the parties selected. If other architects in town say that a paint job is acceptable, the architect who says it is not will likely be found to have acted unreasonably. Of course, when the parties selected one particular architect, they were not contracting for the judgment of other architects in town.

If it appears that the parties have selected a particular third party to give or withhold approval as to a matter that involves a measure of aesthetics, taste, and fancy, the honest judgment of the third party is unlikely to be disturbed. This is the probable result even in the case where a forfeiture will result.

For example, assume that Art agrees to paint a painting for which Bob promises to pay $15,000 subject to the condition that a particular named art critic give her opinion that the painting is of high quality. If the art critic honestly concludes that the painting is not of high quality, Bob should have no duty to perform.

If a contract requires third party approval but no facts indicate that this particular third party was selected because of any special confidence in his individual skills or judgment, the court will likely excuse the requirement of approval if it is found to have been unreasonably withheld and a forfeiture would result if the condition were enforced. If the performance that is being approved involves a matter of utilitarian function rather that aesthetics or taste, the court will likewise excuse the condition of approval if it is found to have been unreasonably withheld and a forfeiture would result if the condition were enforced.

For example, assume that Connie agrees to rebuild damaged river levees to plans and specifications and the contract provides that Owner's duty to pay is subject to a named local engineer certifying that the levee is properly constructed. If Connie has completed performance but the engineer dies, or refuses to inspect, or unreasonably refuses to certify the levee as properly built, the condition will probably be excused. This result is even more likely to be reached if there are no facts indicating that this engineer was selected because of any special confidence or trust in his personal expertise.

If the duty of a party to perform is subject to that party's own approval or satisfaction, some restrictions must be placed upon the party's discretion if one is to find a contract at all. If the party is totally free to disapprove for any reason, then the promise to perform is illusory, and there is no consideration (§ 2.30). If the approval involves a matter of aesthetics and taste (e.g., a portrait of the promisor's spouse), some courts say that honesty is the standard and honest dissatisfaction is enough to cause the condition to fail and permit rejection of the other's performance. If the performance is one involving utilitarian standards of an objectively measurable nature (e.g., plumbing installed in a mountain cabin), the courts usually imply a duty to act reasonably in exercising the discretion to reject. If approval is unreasonably withheld, the condition of approval will be excused and the duty to perform will arise.

§ 8.8.1 The Condition of Approval; Requiring Good Faith

When contract rights and duties are dependent upon approval of the performance by a third party or by one of the parties to the contract, it is not easy to articulate the standards to which this approving party is to be held. The condition of approval will be excused, or perhaps a new evaluator will be selected, if the person who is to make the decision acts improperly, but the question remains how we are to define improper conduct in this context. One is tempted to try to resolve this problem by stating that the party simply must act in good faith. Unfortunately, that is not a solution.

The terms "good faith" and "good faith and fair dealing" are subject to such a range of interpretation (§§ 4.11–4.13.1) that use of these terms in this situation does nothing to provide guidance to the resolution of the problem. No one will dispute the fact that the party who is to approve or disapprove must act honestly. The critical question is whether there is a higher standard to be applied such as reasonableness. It sounds as though one is making great progress by pronouncing that the approver must "act in good faith" but in fact, one is no closer to a solution. One still must decide whether in this context, good faith involves simply honesty in fact or observance of reasonable standards or reasonable commercial standards (§ 4.12).

The issue is: Is the standard mere honesty or some higher standard relating to reasonableness? Inserting the observation that the approver must act in good faith does not advance the discussion one step toward resolution of that question. It sounds good, but it does not solve any problems. The use of the term "good faith" is actually harmful if the person who uses it thinks that by setting up a good faith standard, further discussion and analysis of the problem is unnecessary,

C. SALE OF GOODS
§ 8.9 Performance of Contracts for the Sale of Goods

If a tender of performance is in some way inadequate, the U.C.C. provides distinctly different rules depending upon whether it is a single lot contract or an installment contract. Therefore, the initial inquiry must be to determine whether section 2–601 (single lot) or section 2–612 (installment contract) is controlling.

Contracts for the sale of goods require tender in a single delivery unless the agreement or the circumstances give either party the right to make or demand delivery in lots (§ 2–307). Section 2–612 defines "installment contract" as "one which requires or authorizes the delivery of goods in separate lots to be separately accepted."

Section 2–601 governs single lot contracts. If the goods or the tender of delivery fail in any respect to conform to the contract, then the buyer may accept the whole tender, reject the whole or accept any commercial unit or units and reject the rest. Literally interpreted, this indicates that the buyer may reject all or part if the tender is one minute late or one widget short. It is difficult to formulate a more "pro-buyer" rule. The buyer's right to reject is subject to the duty of good faith (§ 1–203) that would require that the buyer act honestly (§ 1–201(19)). If the buyer were a merchant, buyer would also be required to observe reasonable commercial standards of fair dealing in the trade (U.C.C. § 2–103(1)(b) and § 8.11).

Section 2–508 gives a seller the right under certain circumstances to cure a defective tender. Section 2–508(1) restates the common law rule that if time for performance has not yet expired, the seller who failed on the first try may try again to make a tender that conforms to the contract. Section 2–508(2) gives the seller additional time to make a conforming tender if the buyer's rejection caught the seller by surprise, that is, if the seller had reasonable grounds to believe the tender would be acceptable.

Under pre-Code law, the buyer had the right to reject a tender if the seller was guilty of a major breach but was forced to accept a tender and be content with his right to damages if the breach was minor. This rule forced the innocent buyer to determine at his peril whether the seller's breach was major or minor, a task from which buyers in single lot contracts have been relieved under section 2–601. Under the Code, the buyer has the right to reject for any defect in tender, but the innocent buyer must still determine at his peril whether the court would conclude that rejection was not in good faith. It has been suggested that if the buyer is honestly dissatisfied with the tender, then a rejection is in good faith. If the buyer is dissatisfied with the bargain rather than with the tender, then rejection would not be an act done in good faith.

If a contract for the sale of goods requires or authorizes delivery in installments, section 2–612 is applicable to determine whether the buyer may reject a non-conforming tender. As section 2–601 is pro-buyer, section 2–612 is pro-seller, and the classification of the contract as single lot or installment will determine the final result in many cases.

Except in the case of defects in the required documents, section 2–612(2) gives the buyer the right to reject an installment only if the nonconformity substantially impairs the value of that installment and cannot be cured. The intent and purpose of section 2–612(2) is explained in comment 5 which provides:

Under subsection (2) an installment delivery must be accepted if the non-conformity is curable and the seller gives adequate assurance of cure. Cure of non-conformity of an installment in the first instance can usually be afforded by an allowance against the price, or in the case of reasonable discrepancies in quantity either by a further delivery or a partial rejection. This Article requires reasonable action by a buyer in regard to

discrepant delivery and good faith requires that
the buyer make any reasonable minor outlay of
time or money necessary to cure an overshipment
by severing out an acceptable percentage thereof.
The seller must take over a cure which involves
any material burden; the buyer's obligation
reaches only to cooperation. Adequate assurance
for purposes of subsection (2) is measured by the
same standards as under the Section on right to
adequate assurance of performance.

The question of the right to declare a breach of
the total contract is covered by section 2–612(3)
which provides:

> Whenever non-conformity or default with respect
> to one or more installments substantially impairs
> the value of the whole contract there is a breach
> of the whole. But the aggrieved party reinstates
> the contract if he accepts a non-conforming in-
> stallment without seasonably notifying of cancel-
> lation or if he brings an action with respect only
> to past installments or demands performance as
> to future installments.

The draftsmen of the Code rejected the terms
major and minor breach. The Code does not define
"substantially impairs the value," but comment 4
to section 2–612 provides in part:

> Substantial impairment of the value of an install-
> ment can turn not only on the quality of the
> goods but also on such factors as time, quantity,
> assortment, and the like. It must be judged in

terms of the normal or specifically known purposes of the contract.

The U.C.C. does not specifically define breach by a buyer, but section 2–703 provides alternative remedies to the seller if the buyer "wrongfully rejects or revokes acceptance of goods or fails to make a payment * * * or repudiates with respect to part of a whole."

Matters related to a buyer's right to reject goods or to revoke acceptance of goods are covered in the chapter on Remedies in section 9.8.

§ 8.10 Warranties Arising From the Sale of Goods and From the Sale of Other Property

There are five distinct warranties that can arise out of the sale of goods.

(1) In all sales of goods the seller warrants that the seller has the right to transfer and is transferring good title and that the goods are not subject to security interests, liens or encumbrances (U.C.C. § 2–312(1) and (2)). This means any breach of warranty of title would occur when the goods are delivered and the period of limitations for the bringing of an action for breach begins to run at that time.

The U.C.C. abolished the common law warranty of "quiet possession." The common law warranty of "quiet possession" assured a buyer that no one would later assert a plausible claim against the goods. The warranty of quiet possession would not be breached until such time as a third party made a claim to the goods, and the period of limitations would run from that date.

Assume that seller is in possession of a stolen painting which seller sells to buyer. Five years later the true owner reclaims the painting. The period for bringing actions under the U.C.C. is four years. Because the warranty of title was breached at the time of delivery, the time to sue the seller has run.

(2) In all sales by a merchant who "regularly deals in goods of that kind," there is a warranty that "the goods shall be delivered free of the rightful claim of any third person by way of infringement or the like * * *" (U.C.C. § 2–312(3)). This warranty would relate to matters such as patent, copyright, or trademark infringement.

(3) There is an express warranty any time a seller of goods creates one by words or conduct. An express warranty is created by affirmations of fact or promise that become part of the basis of the bargain for the sale of goods. A description of the goods or any sample or model that becomes part of the basis of the bargain for the sale of goods also creates an express warranty (U.C.C. § 2–313).

(4) In all sales by a seller who is a "merchant with respect to goods of that kind" there is an implied warranty of merchantability. Among other things, this means that the goods will pass without objection in the trade and are fit for the ordinary purpose for which such goods are used (U.C.C. § 2–314).

(5) U.C.C. section 2–315 concisely defines the implied warranty of fitness for a particular purpose. Several elements must be proven to create this warranty. The buyer must have a particular (out of the ordinary) purpose in mind for the goods and must be looking to the seller and relying upon the seller's skill and judgment to select or furnish goods that are suitable for that particular purpose. In addition, the seller must know both of these facts.

The implied warranty of fitness for a particular purpose is the most difficult warranty to prove because it has several elements and requires proof of the seller's knowledge and state of mind. There is ordinarily no reason to attempt to find an implied warranty of fitness for a particular purpose unless the buyer had some non-ordinary purpose for which the goods as delivered are not suitable. If the goods are not suitable for ordinary purposes, the implied warranty of merchantability should handle the situation. People new to the subject of warranties often attempt to use this implied warranty of fitness for a particular purpose when it is unnecessary.

If a bucket leaks, you need not attempt to prove that your client was buying the bucket to haul water and the seller knew it and knew your client was relying upon the seller to select a bucket that does not leak. Buckets are not supposed to leak, and a leaky bucket will not pass without objection in the trade. It is not fit for the ordinary purpose for which buckets are used. It is not merchantable and the bucket merchant has breached the implied warranty of merchantability.

If a buyer states that she is going camping in cold country and the seller points to a sleeping bag stating "that one is good down to 40 below," we have an express warranty by description and by affirmation of fact. There is no need to attempt to prove who was relying upon whom and who knew it.

Note that the above described warranties arise out of the sale of goods. They do not arise out of a contract and technically they are not a part of contract law. In fact, warranty actions were historically treated as tort cases.

Assume that Bert walks into Sam's Auto Store, selects three quarts of motor oil, and walks to the counter where he sets down the oil. Sam's clerk rings up the sale on the register. The machine indicates a total price of $6.23. Bert pays that amount and walks out with his oil.

A contract requires that at least one party make a promise. Thus, there was no contract between Bert and Sam. There was a sale, but there was no contract. Because Sam is a merchant with respect to goods of this kind, Bert has an implied warranty of merchantability and may have an express warranty based upon package labeling or the like. These warranties arise out of the sale of goods and not out of any contract.

§ 8.10.1 Warranties in Non–Goods Transactions

Warranty of title to real or personal property sold is not new, but warranties of quality were for many centuries confined to sales of goods. In recent years, many courts have found the theory of warranty to be a convenient vehicle for creating and enforcing a buyer's rights with respect to other types of property. For example, some jurisdictions have found a warranty comparable to the implied warranty of merchantability arising out of the sale of new houses. This warranty may be limited to sales by a builder or developer of tract homes or other mass produced housing. As with the warranties associated with the sale of goods, this warranty imposes absolute liability if it is breached. As with all warranty liability, fault is not an issue.

Representations of fact in the sale of real property have been found to create express warranties. If a seller states that the home being sold is thirty feet from the property line this can give rise to an express warranty. If in fact the house is less than thirty feet from the property line, this express warranty has been breached. Because liability is not based upon fault, it matters not whether the seller's misrepresentation of fact was intentional, negligent or innocent. The express warranty is that the house is thirty feet from the property line and if this warranty has been breached, buyer can recover whatever resulting damages buyer can prove.

By finding a warranty and basing an action thereon, the buyer can keep the benefits of the transaction and seek damages for the loss sustained. This may be a better alternative than asserting misrepresentation of fact. Misrepresentation is a defense. Asserting a misrepresentation can provide a basis for avoiding the contract and restoring yourself to the position you were in before the contract was made (§ 5.7). If a buyer has moved in to the new home and is now comfortably situated, asserting misrepresentation and attempting to avoid the contract may not be a satisfactory remedy. Rescission would also require a material or fraudulent misrepresentation to avoid a contract (§ 5.7.1), whereas any breach of warranty that produces measurable damages would give the buyer an action to recover those damages. Further, the breach of warranty action does not require that the buyer surrender the property and thereby give up the benefits of the bargain.

The net effect of these warranty law developments is to allow an action for damages for negligent or innocent misrepresentations of fact that cause damages to a buyer. Some jurisdictions use this terminology, "misrepresentation," rather than describing the action as one for breach of warranty.

Traditional tort law provided an action for fraud if a material misstatement of fact was made knowingly and with the intent to defraud or otherwise cause harm. In some jurisdictions these requirements have been relaxed giving rise to an action in tort for misrepresentations that are not intentional. There is also case law that recognizes a tort for sale by a developer of a defective new house.

The distinction between tort and warranty theories is not as significant as one might expect. Liability for breach of warranty is generally recognized as extending to all harm that was the direct result of the breach. In this aspect, warranty liability is coextensive with tort liability. Most case law indicates that warranty actions are not restricted by *Hadley v. Baxendale (Court of Exchequer 1854)* limitations on liability based upon foreseeability with which the plaintiff must deal in breach of contract cases (§ 9.2.1).

It is important to keep in mind that breach of warranty actions and breach of contract actions are not synonymous. Warranties can arise out of a simple sale in which there was no contract, and the requirements for recovery of damages are different in warranty cases and in contract cases.

§ 8.10.2 Disclaimer of Warranties

U.C.C. section 2–316 deals with disclaimer of warranties. One should study the comments to this section as the subject is quite complex. The code takes the position that warranties may be disclaimed if one does it properly. The code has requirements regarding disclaimers being conspicuous. In some cases the code requires that certain language or alternative language be used. The code requires that words creating express warranties and words of disclaimer be construed as consistent with each other to the extent that such construction is not unreasonable.

Full consideration of this subject requires that one also review section 2–202 and the law relating to the parol evidence rule (§§ 4.5–4.7). Courts must deal with the situation in which the statements made by sales people out on the lot or in the show room are quite different from the language in the written contract. This creates difficult legal issues, particularly in consumer contracts or in other situations in which the buyer may not reasonably be expected to study or understand the detailed language of the written contract.

There is a good deal of public sentiment that sellers should not be permitted to disclaim certain warranties. It is difficult to square this sentiment with the code and perhaps with the needs of the marketplace. There is rather strong public sentiment that a seller who orally represents certain facts or makes certain promises relating to goods should not be able to avoid responsibility for these statements by pointing to the written provisions of the contract of sale. Sections 2–313 and 2–316 and some of the comments to those sections may support this view. All of the policy issues surrounding the parol evidence rule are relevant here.

The U.C.C. does not undertake to provide basic laws for consumer protection. There have been wide variations in the attitudes taken in the different states toward consumer protection. Had the U.C.C. attempted to harmonize these divergent views, it is quite likely that it would not have been as widely adopted as a uniform law as it has. Instead of dealing with consumer protection issues, the U.C.C. applies in conjunction with other state and federal laws dealing with consumer protection. Where they are in conflict, the U.C.C. is subordinated to "any statute regulating sales to consumers, farmers or other specified classes of buyers." (U.C.C. § 2–102). The United States and all states have laws that deal in detail with the subject of warranties and remedies for breach of warranty in the sale of consumer goods. Coverage of these laws is beyond the scope of a course in Contracts.

D.   GOOD FAITH AFFECTING PERFORMANCE

§ 8.11   Good Faith and Contract Performance

The subject of good faith or good faith and fair dealing has been discussed in the chapter dealing with contract interpretation (§§ 4.11–4.13.1). Those materials should be reviewed at this point with consideration given to how these implied contract terms impact upon the performance materials previously covered in this chapter.

In addition to the general obligation to adhere to standards of good faith, Article Two of the U.C.C. has a number of sections that specifically require good faith in some phase of a transaction. For instance, if a contract for the sale of goods permits one party to fix the price, there is an express requirement that this be done in good faith (U.C.C. § 2–305(2)). Other provisions such as U.C.C. section 2–306(2) impose a standard of "best efforts" which is a somewhat higher standard as noted in comment 5 to that section.

Contract law in the United States does not impose a general requirement of good faith in the negotiation stage. The contract is what gives rise to the obligation of good faith and that obligation is applicable to matters relating to the "performance or enforcement" of the contract. An existing contract may impose a requirement of good faith in the negotiation of renewals or the negotiation of contracts concerning related matters.

Some foreign legal systems impose an obligation of good faith in the negotiation process, and there have been significant writings on this subject in American Journals. The German concept of *culpa in contrahendo* imposes significant duties in pre-contract negotiations. The common law, in contrast, imposes primarily negative duties upon parties in the negotiation stage, such as the duty not to misrepresent facts.

A few cases have found liability arising out of pre-contract activities where no contract resulted but most have been based upon a reliance theory. (See *Hoffman v. Red Owl Stores, Inc.* (Wis.1965).) However, it has also been held that a letter of intent imposes upon both parties an obligation to meet and negotiate in good faith in an effort to conclude an enforceable bargain. Refusal to negotiate is a breach of this duty that can produce liability, at least for reliance damages. (See *Channel Home Ctrs. v. Grossman* (3d Cir.1986).)

CHAPTER 9

REMEDIES

A. REMEDIES AVAILABLE AT COMMON LAW

§ 9.1 An Overview of Possible Remedies for Breach of Contract

The subject of remedies is a broad topic. What follows is an introduction to some terms and concepts and a thumbnail description of when different remedies might be available. Most of these remedies relate simply to methods of calculating money damages but a few involve non-monetary relief.

(a) EXPECTATION DAMAGES (Benefit of the bargain damages). The basic remedy for breach of contract in the Anglo–American legal system involves awarding money damages to compensate the injured party for the loss of the benefits which that party would have received had the contract been performed. The formation of a valid enforceable contract creates an expectancy in each party to the contract that the law will protect. The right to the benefits that will be obtained from performance by the other party is in the nature of a property right. When the other party breaches, the victim is entitled to receive a judgment for that amount of money necessary to place the victim, as nearly as possible, in the position the victim would have occupied had the contract been performed. The computation of damages must take into account any amount that the innocent party could reasonably have saved by not having to perform the contract. (§ 9.2).

(b) RELIANCE DAMAGES. If expectation damages cannot be proven or have not been proven, the non-breaching party may recover reliance damages. Reliance damages are measured by the amount of money necessary to compensate the innocent party for expenses or loss incurred in reasonable reliance upon the contract that was breached. Whereas expectation or benefit of the bargain damages are designed to place the victim in the position he would have occupied had the contract been performed, reliance damages are designed to place him in the position he was in before the contract was made. Reliance damages are designed to restore the status quo. The victim is not given any profit or benefit of the contract but is merely being made whole (§ 9.3).

(c) RESTITUTION. Recovery in restitution is designed to require the defendant to disgorge the money value of the benefit that the defendant received from partial performance of the contract. Since restitution is measured by the value of the benefit conferred upon the defendant and not by the damages sustained by the plaintiff, the term "damages" is not accurate when applied to recovery in restitution, but it is often used in that context (§ 9.4 and chapter 10).

The theory used to recover in restitution is not technically a contract theory. When seeking expectation or reliance damages, the plaintiff is asserting the contract and suing for its breach. When seeking recovery in restitution, the plaintiff is asserting that the defendant will be unjustly enriched if not required to disgorge its ill-gotten gain. The existence of a contract that was subsequently breached by the defendant and rescinded by the plaintiff may be a necessary element to establish why the right to restitution exists. But the fact is that the contract has been rescinded and the action is not being brought on the contract.

In some cases, reliance damages and recovery in restitution will produce the same dollar judgment. If X paid $500 as a down payment to Y and Y then breached the contract, in the absence of any additional facts, reliance damages (X's loss incurred in reliance) and restitutionary recovery (Y's unjust enrichment resulting from partial performance prior to breach) will both be $500. However, in many cases the expenses incurred by the innocent party and the value of the benefit enjoyed by the breaching party may be quite different. In that case, the amount recoverable will be different depending upon which theory is applied.

In a restitution action there is ordinarily no legally enforceable contract in existence at the time the suit is brought. There are two typical cases:

(1) The parties had a valid enforceable contract; the wrongdoer committed a material breach

of that contract; and, the innocent party elected to rescind the contract and sue for restitution.

(2) The parties never had an enforceable contract but the plaintiff rendered performance which the defendant accepted and the defendant would be unjustly enriched if permitted to retain these benefits.

(d) STIPULATED DAMAGES (Liquidated damages). At the time the contract is formed, the parties may agree to a fixed sum of money or a formula for ascertaining a sum of money that will be due in the event of a breach of a certain nature. The contract may also expressly provide for certain remedies (such as the right of repair) or limitations on remedies (such as exclusion of any right to recover for consequential damages). When such contract terms are found to be valid and enforceable, the stipulated remedies will supersede whatever remedies might otherwise have been available to the innocent party. The critical question is when are these agreements valid (§ 9.5).

(e) INTEREST. If the contract provides for interest and the sum specified does not violate local laws relating to usury, interest will be calculated in accordance with the contract terms and added to the damages awarded. If there is no express provision in the contract, common law decisions typically allow recovery of interest from the time of the breach if the obligation in question was a "sum certain." For example, if the contract provided for the payment of $5,000 on April 1, and the defendant failed to pay this amount when due, the plaintiff is entitled to interest on $5,000 from April 1 until the date of judgment. Conversely, if the amount owing as a result of the breach of a contract is an unliquidated sum, that is, a sum that cannot be determined precisely until a court makes its findings of fact regarding damages, then the traditional common law rule will deny recovery of prejudgment interest. The logic behind this rule is that when the obligation was a fixed sum of money or a sum that could be determined by mathematical calculation, the defendant should have paid it. However, if the sum is not ascertainable until it is fixed by the court, the defendant could not know how much was owing and could not be expected to have paid it. A growing number of jurisdictions have relaxed this rule. Some jurisdictions permit the trial court to exercise discretion concerning the recovery of interest on unliquidated sums. The percentage rate of interest is usually provided by statute as either a fixed rate or a formula based upon some external index. Some jurisdictions now permit flexibility in fixing prejudgment interest rates.

All jurisdictions provide for interest on judgments from the time they are entered until they are paid. The percentage rate of post-judgment interest is typically fixed by statute.

(f) PUNITIVE DAMAGES (Exemplary damages). Punitive damages are designed to punish the guilty party thereby making an example of him and discouraging similar conduct by him or other parties in the future. In most jurisdictions punitive damages

are available only if the defendant is guilty of repre-
hensible conduct such as fraud, malice or oppression. They are not measured by the loss to the
plaintiff nor the gain to the defendant but rather by
the amount necessary to punish and to deter such
conduct in the future. Thus calculation of the
"proper" amount of punitive damages can include
such matters as the wealth and income of the
defendant.

In most jurisdictions, punitive damages are not
available for breach of contract. However, wrongdoing in a contractual transaction might also involve
the commission of a tort such as fraud in which case
punitive damages might be appropriate.

(g) SPECIFIC ENFORCEMENT. Specific enforcement, also referred to as specific performance
of a contract involves an order of the court compelling the breaching party to complete the contract
performance. In the Anglo–American legal system,
common law courts could not specifically enforce a
contract. Orders compelling a breaching party to
perform could only be decreed by a court of equity
and a court of equity would not act unless the
remedy at law was inadequate. While courts of law
and equity have been merged today, the requirements for obtaining specific performance have not
been substantially changed. Thus specific performance is not available in those contract breaches in
which the money damage remedy at law is completely adequate to place the innocent party in the
position he would have enjoyed had the contract
been performed (§ 9.6).

(h) OTHER REMEDIAL RIGHTS. There are various other remedies that might be available to the innocent party when a contract is breached. As mentioned above, a material breach will permit the other party to invoke the remedy of rescinding the contract. Given appropriate circumstances, a breach or threatened breach will provide grounds for a court order restraining the breaching party from engaging in certain conduct. Certain breaches by a seller will give the buyer the remedy of rejecting goods. Events that create reasonable insecurity may under the U.C.C. give rise to the remedy of being able to demand assurances of due performance by the other party.

§ 9.2 Expectation Damages (Benefit of the Bargain)

When the defendant has breached a valid enforceable contract, the plaintiff is entitled to recover money damages in an amount sufficient to place the plaintiff in the position he would have been in had the contract been performed. This involves compensating the plaintiff for the dollar value of the benefits he would have received had the contract been performed less any savings that plaintiff was reasonably able to make by virtue of not having to perform his own obligations under the contract. In many cases this can be done by relatively easy calculations.

Assume Jane contracts to sell to Bob 1,000 shares of Ajax stock for $50,000. Bob breaches the contract by failing to pay after he has received the stock.

Jane's loss resulting from Bob's failure to perform is $50,000. Her savings are zero as she has fully performed. Damages are $50,000.

Assume that Bob breached by repudiating the contract before Jane delivered the stock. Jane's loss resulting from Bob's failure to perform the contract is $50,000. Her saving is the market value of 1,000 shares of Ajax stock that she did not have to deliver due to Bob's breach. The value of the stock must be reduced to a dollar figure in order to compute money damages.

Since the fair market value of all property varies from time to time, the law must fix a date for determination of that value. There are at least three logical possibilities:

(1) The market value at the time when the stock was to be delivered to Bob (the time of performance).

(2) The market value at the time Jane learned of Bob's breach which in this case would presumably be before the date of performance since Bob repudiated before the time of performance.

(3) The price that Jane actually received when she resold the stock to someone else. This sale will occur sometime after the breach and the price she is able to receive will be dependent upon market conditions at that later time.

Assume that the market price of the stock Jane contracted to sell to Bob fluctuates daily. If Jane resold in a reasonable manner and within a commercially reasonable time, the third alternative in fact is the most accurate measure of the actual harm Jane suffered due to Bob's breach. It measures what Jane did in fact receive for the stock which will be subtracted from the amount she was to receive from Bob.

Common law cases traditionally measured damages based upon market price on the date fixed for performance in the contract (alternative #1 above). Unless Jane was able to resell the stock on that date (the day fixed for delivery), alternative #1 will give Jane damages different from the actual harm she suffered. For transactions in goods, the U.C.C. now provides rules that more accurately reflect the actual harm. If Jane had in fact properly resold the goods (§ 2–706), that resale price will be used to measure her loss (alternative #3). If she did not resell, she receives the difference between contract price and market price at the time and place fixed for tender (§ 2–708). Jane's damages would thus be $50,000 (the amount she should have received from Bob) minus what she actually received from reselling the goods or the market value if they were not sold. Because of the inherent accuracy and fairness of the U.C.C. approach using the actual proceeds of resale to compute damages, modern common law decisions can be expected to adopt this method.

Assume that Harry contracts to build a home for Orpha for $175,000. Before Harry has done any work, Orpha breaches. Harry's damages are the dollar value of the performance he was entitled to receive which is $175,000, minus the savings that he was reasonably able to effect by not having to render his own performance. The latter figure will be established by evidence of what it would have cost Harry to build the house. If that figure is proven to be $160,000, then Harry's damages are $15,000 and that is what he should recover. (Note that Harry's "expectation" under the contract involved making a profit of $15,000 and that is exactly what he will recover.)

Assume that at the time of Orpha's breach Harry had done nothing except to obtain a building permit for which he paid $4,000. Harry's savings resulting from the breach will now be only $156,000 and he is entitled to damages in the sum of $19,000. The formula is simple: How much should Harry have received (175,000) less how much Harry was able to save as a result of the breach (156,000) equals damages (19,000).

If one prefers to do it the hard way, the two step formula gives Harry his profits (175,000 minus 160,000 equals 15,000) plus the amount that he spent or committed to spend on the job before Orpha breached. This two step formula can become tricky if the job was a loser (profits thus being a negative) or if Harry has committed himself to expenses for the construction that now cannot be avoided.

Assume that after Harry has partly performed and Orpha has paid $20,000 of the contract price, Orpha breaches the contract. Harry's damages will be the value of the performance he was yet to receive which is $155,000 (the $175,000 contract price minus $20,000 paid to date), less the dollar value of the savings that he is able to realize by virtue of not having to complete his own performance. Harry will have to produce evidence as to what his savings were. This can be quite complicated in some cases. It may not be simply a matter of adding up what Harry has spent thus far and subtracting that figure from the total anticipated costs. Harry may have already rented equipment for this job for which he has no alternative use. He may have already contracted for specialized labor that cannot be profitably used on other jobs. Such factors will all receive proper consideration if one remembers that the figure to subtract is the actual amount that Harry was reasonably able to save by not having to complete performance. For example, if this figure proves to be $110,000, that sum should be subtracted from $155,000 and Harry's damages are $45,000.

In some situations, special facts may require some common sense modifications of the simple formula discussed above. For example, a breach of contract might leave the victim worse off than simply losing anticipated benefits of the bargain. Assume a contract in which Connie agreed to install new tile in the shower in Bill's home for $3,000. Connie breached the contract by installing defective tiles which will now have to be removed at considerable cost. Bill's loss includes not only the loss of the value of the tiling work (which might be proven by showing the cost of hiring another to do this work) but also the cost of removing the defective tiles. From this total figure Bill must subtract his savings which would be whatever part of the $3,000 he had not yet paid to Connie.

Special facts might also establish some offsetting benefits to the injured party. If Bill was able to resell the tiles that had to be removed for $100 scrap value, this offsetting gain that he was able to realize would have to be deducted from his recovery.

Different types of contracts create different specific problems, but the basic approach is the same. The first step is to establish the dollar value of the performance that the victim should have received but did not. The second step is to determine what deduction should be made for savings that the victim was able to realize by not having to render his own performance.

Assume that Bob is wrongfully discharged from a one-year employment contract. His damages are the wages he should have received that will not now be paid. His savings might include costs such as transportation and parking that can now be avoided because he does not have to go to work. Bob may also avoid damages by taking another job and reducing or eliminating his wage loss in that manner. What sort of employment Bob must accept and how hard he has to look for another job are matters relating to "avoidable consequences" or "mitigation of damages" which are discussed in section 9.2.3.

Loss of the benefit of the bargain can produce other types of damages. Failure of a contractor to complete a movie theater on time will result in loss of use of the theater and the income it could have generated during the delay. Failure to deliver a machine or delivery of a defective machine may result in lost production. The basic rule is one can potentially recover for all damages that result from the breach of contract. Limitations on these types of damages are dealt with in the next sections.

§ 9.2.1 Limitations on Expectation Damages; The Requirements of Certainty and Foreseeability

Damages for breach of contract are not recoverable unless they are proven with a relatively high degree of certainty. When cases are carefully analyzed, it can be seen that courts demand evidence that clearly establishes that some damages of the nature claimed did in fact occur. Once the existence of some damage is proven to have been caused by the breach, the precise amount of damages can be calculated in any reasonable fashion even though some estimation or approximation is required.

Assume that Sara and John contract to enter a partnership for the purpose of operating a restaurant. John is to be the chef and Sara the manager, and they agree to devote full time to the project for at least three years. Before the restaurant is opened, John gets a better offer and breaches his contract with Sara. Sara may be unable to recover any expectation damages or benefit of the bargain damages because the fact that such damages were suffered cannot be established with certainty. A large percentage of new restaurants lose money. It would be quite difficult for Sara to establish that the proposed restaurant would have been profitable. The frequency with which expectation damages are denied to new businesses has led some people to refer to this result as the "new business rule." Most court opinions deny the existence of any such "rule" that a new business cannot recover expectation damages, but it does take strong facts to overcome the problems involved in proving that a new business would in fact have been profitable.

Assume that Sara and John operated their restaurant for one year with John serving as head chef. The business lost $2,000 during the first quarter of operation; broke even during the second quarter; made $6,000 in the third quarter, and made $9,000 during the fourth quarter. John now breaches the three-year contract. Without its chef, the restaurant closes. Sara should be able to prove the fact of damages with certainty. Using evidence of profits and performance of other restaurants plus her own restaurant's history, she should then be able to prove a likely future profit for the remaining two years of their contract. Once the fact of lost profits has been proven with certainty, the law will permit her to recover future profits even though the precise amount of those profits requires some estimation. Sara's damage claim may be defeated or reduced if it is established that she could have replaced John with a comparable chef (§ 9.2.3).

It should be evident that contract law requires greater certainty in the proof of damages than does tort law. There are several possible justifications. We usually select the parties with whom we make contracts and we can plan the transaction including making provision for liquidated damages if appropriate. We do not pick our tortfeasors. There is no opportunity to negotiate a formula or other damage calculation before we are tortiously injured. The law of contracts has strong notions that people negotiating a contract should have an accurate picture of the risks they are assuming including the liability that might result if they are unable to perform. No such policy restrictions on liability have been found appropriate in tort law.

Recovery of contract damages is also limited by the concept of foreseeability. The standards for determining what is foreseeable in contract damages were established in the case of *Hadley v. Baxendale* (Court of Exchequer 1854). This decision with its confused statements of facts was not rendered by a particularly distinguished court nor decided by any noted jurists, but it has had a profound impact upon the law relating to contract damages.

The *Hadley* opinion divides contract damages into two categories: those that arise naturally in the usual course of events from the breach of a contract of the type in question, and those that arise due to special facts and circumstances existing in this particular case. With respect to damages that are the natural and probable result of a breach of this type of contract, the breaching party could contemplate being liable for such damages when the contract was made. These damages have come to be referred to in contract law as "general" damages, and they may be recovered by the plaintiff without any further concerns as to foreseeability.

Damages that occur as a consequence of special facts and circumstances relating to the specific transaction will not be within the contemplation of the breaching party at the time the contract is made unless that person is aware of these special facts and circumstances. These damages have come to be referred to in contract law as "special" or "consequential" damages, and they may be recovered only if it is established that they were foreseeable to the breaching party at the time the contract was made. As used herein, the terms "special" and "consequential" are synonymous. The term "consequential" is preferred.

Assume that Paul has a contract with the Government to deliver military uniforms. The contract provides for certain stipulated damages for each day of delay for late delivery. Paul contracts to pay $15,000 to Dan for delivery by a certain date of materials that Paul plans to use to make the uniforms. Thereafter, shortages of material develop in the marketplace and prices increase. Dan does not deliver. Paul uses reasonable efforts to secure another source of supply and after some delay is able to purchase replacement materials for $20,000. As a direct result of the delay caused by Dan's breach, Paul becomes liable for $12,000 for late delivery of the uniforms to the Government.

Paul has two elements of damage in an action against Dan. He paid $5,000 above the contract price to obtain replacement material and he sustained a $12,000 loss due to the delay that was caused by Dan's breach. The first item is general damages. In a contract for the sale of goods, a natural and probable consequence of breach by the seller is that the buyer may have to pay more for replacement goods. There is no issue whether Dan could foresee this particular increase in price. Price changes of some sort are natural and probable. Paul can obtain judgment for the $5,000 from Dan.

The $12,000 loss constitutes consequential damages because one must prove the special facts of Paul's particular situation to show how and why this loss was caused. Substantial loss on another contract is not a natural and probable result of a breach of a contract for goods. Therefore, Paul's ability to recover for this item is dependent upon showing that Dan was aware of the special facts that caused this loss at the time the Paul–Dan contract was made. Paul probably must show that Dan was aware that Paul had the contract with the Government; that this contract had a clause providing for stipulated damage for delay in delivery, and that delay in receipt of material would result in the inability to perform the Government contract on time. Absent knowledge of any one of these facts, it is unlikely that Dan should have anticipated that a delay would produce damages of this nature.

The distinction between general and consequential damages is important for another reason. Many contracts contain clauses expressly excusing liability for consequential damages. These clauses are generally found to be valid and enforceable (U.C.C. § 2–719) which thus requires the court to determine what damages are consequential and what are general.

Assume that Seller is in the business of producing and selling large computer systems for commercial application. These systems are not compatible with Buyer's existing IBM computer system. After extensive study of Buyer's business operations, Seller contracts to supply a new system for Buyer's business. The contract excludes liability for consequential damages. Seller's equipment fails to perform properly and is ultimately replaced by new IBM equipment. Buyer sues and proves various types of damages including: 1) the cost of converting the IBM records to the new system; 2) the loss of employee time while people sat idle with non-functioning machines; 3) the cost to reconvert all of the records back to IBM after the Seller's system was replaced.

A court found the second item to be general damages. In a contract for the sale of a computer system designed for commercial application, the loss of employee time resulting from the malfunctioning of the computer was viewed as a natural and probable consequence of the breach. No additional special facts need be proven to foresee or explain this loss. The first and third items were found to be consequential damages. They occurred only because of the special fact that Buyer had its existing records on IBM and went back to IBM when Seller's equipment failed. Given the facts of the case, Seller would likely have been liable for these consequential damages because all of the special facts were known to Seller before the contract was made. However, since the contract excluded liability for consequential damages, Buyer could not recover for items 1 and 3. (See *Applied Data Processing, Inc. v. Burroughs Corp.* (D.Conn. 1975).)

A breach of contract can cause emotional distress damages, but ordinarily such damages are not recoverable in a contract action because they are not foreseeable. In commercial transactions, emotional distress is not a natural and probable consequence of a breach nor does the breaching party usually know facts that would cause such damages to result. However, in specialized contracts, emotional distress might be foreseeable. A frequently cited example is a contract with a mortuary for funeral services. In fact, emotional distress is probably the only foreseeable damage resulting from breach of such a contract. One might develop a logical argument that emotional distress damages are also a foreseeable result of breach in such matters as employment contracts, but courts have demonstrated reluctance to permit recovery for this element of damage.

As one considers the issue of foreseeability of damages in contract law, it is hard to avoid comparisons with foreseeability in tort. The concepts are dissimilar. Tort law involves concepts of foreseeability to determine the issue of liability; to decide whether Mrs. Palsgraf is a proper plaintiff. In contract law, one generally knows who is the proper plaintiff. Foreseeability is involved to determine what elements of damage the known plaintiff can include in the recovery. To the extent that the same judge will exhibit more conservative tendencies in a contract case than in a tort case, the factors discussed with respect to required certainty in the fourth paragraph of this section are probably also relevant here.

In some jurisdictions, rules of pleading make distinctions between how special damages and general damages must be set forth in a complaint and how they must be denied in an answer. Rules that determine what damages are special and what are general vary from jurisdiction to jurisdiction. In many cases, these rules are created for the purpose of producing efficiency in pleading and the results are contradictory to the rules of contract law that derive from the *Hadley* case. Confusion is minimized if one uses the term "consequential" instead of "special" when referring to the substantive law that controls contract remedies.

§ 9.2.2 Other Limitations on Expectation Damages

The measure of expectation damages for defective performance may involve measuring the reduction in value of the subject matter of the contract. Assume that a contractor does not fully perform a contract to build a house. If the performance is incomplete rather than being completed in a defective manner, the loss in value will ordinarily be measured by the cost to complete. If a contractor builds a house but fails to install the doors, the loss of value will be measured by the cost to install doors rather than the diminished value of a house that is not habitable because it has no doors. This is a satisfactory remedy because it makes the innocent party "whole" in the sense that the damage recovery will provide an amount sufficient to complete the work called for in the contract.

A different problem arises if the performance is defective rather than incomplete. Ordinarily, one might assume that if a performance is defective, the proper measure of damages should be the cost to correct the defect. However, if a house is built with a load-bearing wall one foot off from where it was supposed to be, the cost to correct this defect may be far greater than the diminution in market value resulting from the error. If correction of the defect would be economically wasteful, the owner will ordinarily be limited to the diminished market value of the structure. If the defect affects the structural integrity of the building or otherwise involves safety of the occupants, then the cost to correct will be recoverable.

Even in the case of incomplete performances, the innocent party may be denied the cost to complete where completion is viewed as economically wasteful. The classic example involves a contract in which one party is to remove material from the earth such as coal or sand and promises to restore the property to its natural grade when the removal is completed. Breach of the promise to restore may result in a situation in which the value of the property is diminished by only a small amount whereas the cost to complete the work is substantial. Assume that the property has a fair market value of $250,000 in its existing condition and would have a fair market value of $300,000 if it were restored to grade. If restoration would cost $450,000, most courts have held that the innocent party is limited to diminished value and can recover only $50,000. There is a split of authority on this issue.

The innocent party may recover the cost to correct rather than the diminished market value if the parties both understood that the contract performance involved highly personalized criteria. It is sometimes stated that anyone has the right to erect a monument to his folly. If the law school contracts for the erection of a statue of the dean in front of the school, construction of a statue that resembles John F. Kennedy rather than the dean should result in damages measured by the cost to correct even though the market value of the property might be more enhanced by Kennedy's likeness than that of the dean.

Expectancy damages can also be denied where they are simply too large in relationship to the contract price. Breach of a contract to perform minor repairs on the furnace in a restaurant before a big weekend might result in very large consequential damages that were quite foreseeable. However, even though the aggrieved party proves substantial damages, recovery may be denied if the amount of damages is out of proportion to the contract price. Where recovery is denied, it is usually based upon the concept that liability for damages of this magnitude was not within the contemplation of the parties at the time the contract was made. Here again the contrast with tort law is significant.

§ 9.2.3 Avoidance of Damages

One cannot recover for damages that could have been avoided with reasonable effort and without undue risk. It is thus stated that the victim of a contract breach is obligated to use reasonable efforts to protect his interests and prevent damages that could reasonably be avoided. For example, a buyer of goods cannot recover consequential damages resulting from non-delivery if there was a readily available source of substitute goods that the buyer could have purchased. This is referred to as a "duty to mitigate" damages. That expression may be inaccurate but it is widely used and accepted.

Interesting avoidance of damage issues can be presented when an employee is wrongfully discharged from a full-time job. The claim for damages for lost wages will be reduced by whatever wages the employee did earn or could reasonably have earned in another job. When the employee does not obtain other employment, the court must determine whether the employee could reasonably have found or should reasonably have accepted another position.

In one famous case (*Parker v. Twentieth Century–Fox Film Corp.* (Cal. 1970)), an actress (Shirley MacLaine) had contracted to perform in a musical movie ("Bloomer Girl") in which she was to have certain artistic control. When the employer breached, she was allowed to recover her lost income even though she had refused the employer's offer to have her perform in another movie for the same salary during the same time period. The substitute movie was entitled "Big Country, Big Man." It was to be filmed in Australia, was not a musical, and MacLaine was to have no artistic control. The court ruled as a matter of law that the substitute employment was both "different" and "inferior."

Generally speaking, courts will not require discharged employees to take positions that are demeaning or beneath their dignity. Courts may also consider the geographic location of the new position, danger posed by the nature of the employment, competence required, impact upon future employment and career, and any other matters that bear upon the question whether this was a reasonable alternative employment for this plaintiff to have accepted.

Parties that earn their living by rendering services may have a flexible capacity. Thus a doctor can always treat one more patient; a lawyer can write one more will; a contractor can build one more house. When such a service provider is the victim of a contract breach, his damages are not mitigated by virtue of the fact that he took on additional work. It is assumed that he could have done both jobs. Distinguish this from the full-time employee who presumably can only work one job; thus when the fired employee takes a second job, his damages are reduced or perhaps eliminated.

§ 9.3 Reliance Damages

Reliance damages are that amount of money necessary to compensate the plaintiff for efforts expended or expenses incurred in reasonable reliance upon the contract. Reliance damages may not exceed benefit of the bargain damages. Thus if benefit of the bargain damages are proven, that amount becomes a ceiling on the recovery. Therefore reliance damages are relevant only when benefit of the bargain or expectation damages are not proven.

Assume that Al contracts to build a commercial building for Mary for $190,000. Shortly after construction commences, Mary's tenant repudiates its lease and Mary repudiates her construction contract with Al. Of course, Al may prove expectation damages and recover the difference between the unpaid contract price and the anticipated costs of completing the work, but this may involve considerable effort and expense. As an alternative, Al may elect to recover reliance damages. This can be accomplished with proof of the expenses reasonably incurred in preparing to perform and performing the construction work prior to the breach by Mary.

Assume that Al's estimator made serious miscalculations in preparing his figures and that the actual cost of construction of Mary's building was going to be $200,000. After Al had spent $6,000 in preparation and performance, Mary breached. Al elected to seek reliance damages of $6,000. If no evidence is introduced as to the total cost of the project, Al will recover $6,000. However, Mary may introduce evidence to prove Al's actual expectation damages which in this case are zero. (His expected benefit of the bargain was $190,000. His savings resulting from not having to complete his own performance were $194,000. Full performance would have resulted in a $10,000 loss to Al, and because Al has spent only $6,000 so far, Mary's breach has in fact saved Al $4,000.) Since reliance damages cannot exceed expectation damages, Al cannot recover in this case. Notice that the burden is on Mary to prove what Al's expectation recovery would be. If Mary does not do so, then Al will recover the $6,000 in reliance damages.

Assume that Jane and Harry contracted to form a partnership to enter the restaurant business. After Jane had incurred expenses in the amount of $3,000 and before the restaurant was opened, Harry breached this contract. Jane may be unable to prove expectation damages because of her inability to establish the requisite certainty (§ 9.2.1), but she can still recover her $3,000 as reliance damages.

§ 9.4 Measuring Recovery in Restitution

Restitutionary recovery is designed to force the defendant to disgorge the economic value of any benefit which was conferred under circumstances where it would be unjust to allow the defendant to retain it. The measure of recovery in restitution is thus the money value of the benefit that the defendant has received (Chapter 10).

§ 9.5 Stipulated Damages (Liquidated Damages)

The parties to a contract may negotiate contract terms providing for specific damages to be paid in the event of breach. Where this is effectively done, the stipulated damages or liquidated damages become the only damages that can be recovered.

The major issue with stipulated damages is whether they constitute a penalty. In the Anglo–American legal system, there is a strong policy that contract damages must be only compensatory and not punitive. Thus, a stipulated damage will be found to be valid only if it reflects an honest effort by the parties to anticipate the probable damage that would result from a breach. If the court concludes that liquidated damages were set at a high figure to compel performance, the provision for liquidated damages will be held to be void. Thus a measure of damages that appears to be punitive will not be enforced. This is in sharp contrast with other legal systems such as those based upon German law which generally permit the parties to negotiate high liquidated damages to compel performance.

The reasonableness of a liquidated damage provision is analyzed on the basis of the facts known to the parties at the time the contract was made. The question is whether the stipulated sum or formula appears to be reasonable based upon what the parties might have anticipated to be the likely result of a given breach. There is also some authority for considering whether the liquidated damage figure is reasonable in relation to the actual harm that resulted (U.C.C. § 2–718(1), and Restatement § 356(1)).

Assume that Bob contracts to build a house for Charles and the contract provides that if the house is not completed within the time fixed in the contract, Bob will pay Charles $10,000 as damages for the delay. This stipulated damage clause is void. It is not an honest effort to estimate damages because it provides for a fixed sum without regard to the duration of the delay.

Assume the same contract with a clause providing for damages in the amount of $1,000 for every day of delay in completion. This clause is also probably void because when compared to the harm that might actually result from a delay in occupying a house, the sum is so large that it appears to be designed as a club to compel timely performance rather than an honest effort to measure anticipated damages. People in the construction industry commonly refer to contract provisions for liquidated damages for delay as "penalty clauses." Attorneys who seek to enforce liquidated damages must be careful not to use the word "penalty" because if the judge decides it is in fact a "penalty clause," it will not be enforced.

Because of the historical preference in our legal system for requiring proof of actual compensatory damages rather than stipulated damages, some jurisdictions have a further limitation upon the validity of such contract terms. These states limit the use of stipulated damages to situations in which at the time the contract is made, it is evident that in the event of breach, damages will be very difficult or impossible to ascertain. Many jurisdictions are moving away from this requirement, but the "difficulty of proof of loss" is still considered in many situations in determining whether a liquidated damage clause should be enforced. U.C.C. section 2–718 permits consideration of this factor in determining whether liquidated damages clauses are valid or void.

Liquidated damage clauses may intentionally underestimate damages. An example is found in contracts for burglar alarm services that typically provide for a rather small sum of damages (perhaps $50) for failure of the system to operate in its intended fashion. Such clauses are generally enforced. They do not raise the problem of being a penalty and are generally subject to attack only on the grounds of unconscionability.

Contract provisions may also limit the remedies available to one party. A seller of goods may insist on a contract term that provides for repair or replacement (usually at the seller's option) as the exclusive remedy in the event the goods do not perform as warranted. Contract terms may exclude some types of damages such as consequential damages. While such limitations may be subject to an unconscionability argument, they are generally found to be valid so long as they do not result in leaving the victim of a breach with no effective remedy. (See U.C.C. § 2–719(2) for a statutory handling of this issue.)

§ 9.6 Specific Enforcement (Specific Performance)

An order compelling a party to perform the contract can be issued only by a court exercising the powers of a court of equity. This remedy is stated to be available only where the "remedy at law" is inadequate. This means that specific performance can be obtained only if the money damage remedies discussed above (the remedies traditionally granted by a court of law as distinguished from a court of equity) will not suffice to provide a sufficient remedy for the victim of a contract breach.

The most common ground for finding that the damage remedy available at law is inadequate is that the subject of the contract is unique. If a contract involves the sale of unique property, then money damages will not place the plaintiff in as good a position as contract performance because the money cannot be used to buy the same property elsewhere.

For reasons that are partly historical, all real property is considered to be unique. In a particular case, goods may also be unique. Such contracts meet the first test for specific performance (that the remedy at law be inadequate). Under U.C.C. section 2–716, specific enforcement of contracts for the sale of goods may be had "where the goods are unique or in other proper circumstances." What constitutes "other proper circumstances" is left for development by case law. Cases in which specific performance has been granted under this section include long term supply contracts for goods that are in short supply. In these cases the goods themselves were not unique (petroleum products for example), but if a seller breaches during a time of shortage, the buyer may be able to prove that no market existed in which the buyer could enter into a comparable long term contract with another party. Thus, the contract obligation might be characterized as unique. The trend in recent years has been to expand upon the circumstances in which contracts may be specifically enforced.

Since specific enforcement decrees are granted by courts exercising the powers of equity, other rules of the law of equity must be considered to determine whether this remedy is available. For example, the plaintiff must establish that the contract when made was fair, just and equitable. The plaintiff must not be guilty of sharp practices in the transaction in question. Full analysis of the requirements imposed by courts of equity is beyond the coverage of the typical Contracts course.

§ 9.7 Remedies Available in Actions Based Upon Promissory Estoppel

Section 90 of the Restatement, First, provided that promises could be enforced when they foreseeably induced reliance of a definite and substantial character (§§ 2.41–2.43). It is clear that Professor Williston was of the opinion that a promise made

enforceable by detrimental reliance would justify
the same remedy as any other legally enforceable
promise. Assume Uncle stated to Nephew: "I will
give you $10,000 to buy a car." In reasonable and
foreseeable reliance, Nephew purchased a car for
$5,000. In Williston's view if Nephew could enforce
Uncle's promise the amount recoverable would be
$10,000. Under this view of the law, persons with
actions based upon section 90 would have the full
range of expectancy of the bargain or reliance damages discussed above. Because Nephew could establish expectation damages of $10,000 he would obvi-
ously choose that alternative and Uncle would not
have the right to limit nephew to a reliance damages.

The Restatement, Second, section 90(1) contains
a revised version of the old section 90. Reliance
under this Restatement need not be of a definite
and substantial character and the recovery may be
less than the full value of the promise. "The remedy
granted for breach may be limited as justice requires." It is evident from this change that the
authors contemplated circumstances in which the
plaintiff may only recover reliance damages. One
might anticipate that today, Nephew would be limited to recovery of only $5,000, the amount actually
spent for the car. In fact, if Nephew could readily
resell the car for $4,000, his reliance damages could
conceivably be limited to $1,000.

Note carefully: If Nephew can prove a bargained
contract with his Uncle, his damages will be $10,-
000 when Uncle breaches his promise to pay that

sum. If Nephew has only a promissory estoppel theory to assert against Uncle, Nephew may get $5,000 (if "justice requires") or perhaps $1,000. Many examination questions in Contracts classes involve situations where Uncle has promised, Nephew has incurred detriment and the facts may or may not be sufficient to find a bargain. If well crafted, these questions can be very difficult to answer. The lazy student notes the consideration issue, decides it is a bit too difficult to worry about, and runs off to the easy task of discussing section 90 and Nephew's reliance. Section 90 is warm and fuzzy, but it may get your client half the promised amount or less. Bargained exchange is tough and unforgiving, but those who master it and find it to be present can get the full $10,000. When you ditch the tough issue to run off to handle the easy one, your professor does notice.

B.   REMEDIES IN SALES OF GOODS
§ 9.8 Buyer's Rejection, Acceptance, and Revocation of Acceptance of Goods

Students should take care in this area and not confuse the terminology in regard to performance of the contract with the identical terminology that is used in connection with the formation of the contract. The materials below are addressing the issue of what the buyer may do when the seller tenders goods under an already-formed contract. The issues relate to the "acceptance, rejection, or revocation of acceptance" **of the goods**, not the "acceptance, rejection or revocation of acceptance" **of an offer**.

(Of course, there is no such concept as "revocation of acceptance of an offer.")

A basic remedy of a buyer of goods under the U.C.C. is the right to reject non-conforming goods. The standard applied in determining if there is a right in the buyer to reject the goods is dependent upon whether the contract calls for delivery of the goods in a single lot or whether the goods are to be delivered in installments. Compare the language of sections 2–307 with that of 2–612(1) for the distinction between a single lot contract and an installment contract. Section 2–307 appears to favor the finding of a single lot contract which obligates the seller to tender all of the goods at one time. However, if there is language or circumstances indicating that the goods can be delivered in separate lots, then 2–612(1) would dictate a finding that it is an installment contract.

If the goods are required to be delivered in a single lot, section 2–601 applies whereas if it is an installment contract section 2–612(2) applies. If there is any defect in tender or delivery of the goods in a single lot contract, section 2–601 gives the buyer the right to reject the whole lot, accept the whole lot, or accept any commercial unit or units and reject the rest. Section 2–601 is frequently referred to as "the perfect tender rule." Its apparent harshness is mitigated significantly by the Seller's right to cure as provided in section 2–508, discussed below. The right to reject for less than perfect tender must also be exercised in good faith and not merely to escape from an unwise bargain.

If the goods are required or authorized to be delivered in installments, then section 2–612(2) applies and the buyer is permitted to reject an installment only if there is a non-conformity which substantially impairs the value of that instalment and cannot be cured. There is no code definition of what constitutes "substantial impairment of value of that installment." This issue will require a detailed factual analysis including some factors addressed below in regard to materiality of breach.

Because it is an installment contract and the buyer cannot reject if the non-conformity can be cured, it is important to determine what might constitute an appropriate cure under 2–612(2). Comment 5 states:

> Under subsection (2) an installment delivery must be accepted if the non-conformity is curable and the seller gives adequate assurances of cure. Cure of non-conformity of an installment in the first instance can usually be afforded by an allowance against the price, or in the case of reasonable discrepancies in quantity either by a further delivery or a partial rejection. This Article requires reasonable action by a buyer in regard to discrepant delivery and good faith requires that the buyer make any reasonable minor outlay of time or money to cure an overshipment by severing out an acceptable percentage thereof. The seller must take over a cure which involves any material burden; the buyer's obligation reaches only to cooperation. * * *

What may be obvious is that the code recognizes in an installment contract that the parties anticipate some sort of ongoing cooperative relationship and there is likely an interest in preserving the relationship despite some minor bumps in the road.

Regardless of whether the contract calls for a single lot delivery or a delivery in installments, any rejection must occur within a reasonable time after delivery or tender of the goods and the rejection will not be effective unless the buyer seasonable notifies the seller of the rejection (§ 2–602(1)). Rejection is possible only so long as the goods have not been accepted. Under section 2–606, acceptance can occur in any one of three ways:

a) after a reasonable opportunity to inspect, the buyer signifies to the seller that the goods are conforming or that he will take or retain the goods in spite of their non-conformity; or,

b) after a reasonable opportunity to inspect, the buyer fails to make an effective rejection; or,

c) the buyer does any act inconsistent with the seller's ownership of the goods.

Assume Connie took delivery of the BMW and retained it for two days without any notification of any kind to the dealer. If one concludes that two days is a sufficient amount of time for Connie to have inspected and discovered the nonconforming sound system, and assuming that the time to give notice had thus begun to run and had also expired, then Connie may be found to have accepted the goods under section 2–606 (b). If Connie had welded trailer hauling equipment onto the frame of the BMW, it is possible to find that she accepted the BMW under section 2–606(c).

When goods have been delivered and the buyer has had reasonable time and opportunity to inspect them, one of two things is going to happen very quickly. The buyer is either going to make an effective rejection of the goods or the buyer will be found to have accepted them. A rejection can be effective even if it is wrongful in the sense that there was no legal or factual basis for rejection under whichever standard (§ 2–601(1) or § 2–612(2)) is applicable. If the buyer wrongfully rejects, the seller will have a remedy against the buyer, but it is a different remedy than would exist if the buyer had accepted the goods. If goods are wrongfully rejected, the seller still has ownership and right to possession of the goods, and ordinarily his claim should be for the difference between the contract price and resale price under section 2–706 or the contract price and market price under section 2–708(1). If the goods are accepted, the buyer now has ownership and right to possession, and the seller has a claim for the contract price under section 2–709.

§ 9.8.1 Legal Affect of Acceptance; Revocation of Acceptance

The legal consequences of a buyer making an acceptance of the goods are significant. As stated in section 2–607, they include the following:

1. The buyer must pay for the accepted goods at the contract rate. Thus Connie would owe the full contract price for the BMW minus whatever amount she could prove by way of damages in not receiving the correct sound system.

2. Once an acceptance occurs, it is to late to reject.

3. The buyer must within a reasonable time give timely notice of any claim for breach or be barred from any remedy.

4. The burden is on the buyer to prove any breach with respect to the goods.

Assume that the BMW as tendered was in complete compliance with the contract requirements but that Connie decided that she wanted a Buick rather than a BMW. Connie has the power to reject the tender of the BMW even though the tender is perfect. Assuming she give notice of rejection in a timely manner, Connie's rejection, though wrongful is still legally effective as a rejection. Connie has breached the contract and may be liable for damages, but she is not stuck with being liable for the contract price of an expensive new car. As is developed in succeeding sections, Dealer will likely have no damages under sections 2–706 or 2–708(1) because contract price, market price and ultimate resale price should all be very similar. Connie is even entitled to restitution of any down payment in excess of $500 (§ 2–718(2)) unless Dealer proves a right to damages, which in this case would probably be the dealer's lost profits under section 2–708(2).

Even after the buyer has accepted the goods, there is still the possibility that this acceptance can be revoked under section 2–608. The legal requirements for revocation of acceptance are quite different from the requirements for rejection.

First, if the buyer had rejected, the seller would have the burden of proving that the tender conformed to the contract. If the buyer is attempting to revoke acceptance, section 2–607(4) places on the buyer the burden of proof as to all the requirements for revocation.

Second, the buyer who is attempting to revoke acceptance must prove an "excuse" for the acceptance of the goods which can be either that he accepted the goods on the reasonable assumption that the non-conformity would be cured and it has not been or that his acceptance was reasonably induced by the difficulty of discovery of the defects or by seller's assurances (§ 2–608(1) (a) and(b).

Third, the buyer must prove that there was a non-conformity in the goods which substantially impairs their value to him (§ 2–608(1)).

And finally, the buyer must give notice of revocation of acceptance within a reasonable time after the buyer discovers or should have discovered the grounds for revocation and before any substantial change in the condition of the goods that is not caused by their own defects (§ 2–608(2)).

Assume that Connie accepted the BMW with the wrong sound system. It is highly unlikely that she can revoke her acceptance. She might be able to prove that she accepted the car with the expectation that the defect would be cured by installing a new sound system, but it would be quite difficult to establish that this non-conformity substantially impairs the value of the BMW to her. If the transmission falls out and Dealer fails to repair it after several efforts, then Connie might be able to revoke her acceptance. Connie likely would not have been able to discover a defect in the transmission until it manifested itself while driving. Therefore if she had made an acceptance of the vehicle, her acceptance was likely induced by the difficulty of discovery. And a defective transmission would likely result in substantial impairment of value to her or any other buyer. The language "to him" in section 2–608(1) is of special significance and you should read comment 2 for the reference to the specific buyer. A person highly allergic to and adversely affected by a minute amount of mold caused by excessive humidity due to an accumulation of moisture in the vehicle (probably in the air conditioning system) should have a right to revoke acceptance of the vehicle even though its market value was not significantly diminished. This buyer would have a right to revoke acceptance even though the seller was unaware of the buyer's particular circumstances at the time of contracting.

Along with the original right to reject, revocation of acceptance is one of the most effective remedies that can be asserted by a buyer such as a consumer. There are other statutes at the federal and state levels that provide additional rights and remedies to buyers of consumer goods as defined by those statutes. Such statutes are not covered in most Contracts courses and are not within the scope of this publication.

If an acceptance is properly revoked, the situation is the same as that which would have existed had the goods been rejected (§ 2–608(3)). (See § 8.9 for a discussion of seller's performance and buyer's right to reject.)

§ 9.9   Seller's Right to Cure After Buyer's Rejection

Section 2–508 provides an important right to a seller who has made a nonconforming tender that was rejected by the buyer. This section allows a seller an opportunity to cure the non-conformity and it provides two different time periods within which a seller may do so.

If the time for performance by the seller has not yet expired, subsection (1) allows the seller to make a conforming tender within the contract time if the seller seasonably notifies the buyer of the intention to do so.

The application of subsection (2) could result in a further reasonable time (beyond the contract time) for the seller to cure if the seller had reason to believe that the nonconforming tender would be accepted with or without a money allowance. As comment 2 indicates, subsection (2) is designed to avoid injustice to a seller as a result of a surprise rejection by the buyer. The "surprise rejection" could be shown if the seller knowingly tendered a slightly lesser quantity of goods or even a greater quantity of goods in the belief that in the former situation the buyer would merely make a deduction in the contract price or in the latter case would accept them without complaint at no additional cost or with a proportionate increase in the contract price. It is also possible to find a "surprise rejection" when the seller tendered goods that may have a significant defect of which the seller was totally unaware. A seller may be "surprised" by the defect and thus would not expect a rejection. For example, the seller tenders electronic components in their factory-sealed box that in fact contains defective goods. Buyer's rejection will be proper but seller may none-the-less have additional time within which to cure under section 2–508(2).

The fact that 2–508 may give the seller time to cure does not mean that the seller is not in breach in regard to the first tender or delivery. If the buyer can establish damages caused by the improper first tender, or damages due to any delay beyond the contract time that would be permitted under subsection (2), the buyer is entitled to recover those damages under the appropriate buyer's remedies sections or deduct those damages from any unpaid contract price (§ 2–717).

Assume that Connie contracts to buy a new BMW from Dealer. The car is delivered to Connie with the wrong sound system. Connie may reject the car. In many cases this initial right to reject is the most effective remedy a consumer may have. As will be discussed below, Connie may also be able to recover any damages due to the improper tender and if the dealer does not timely tender a BMW that conforms to the contract description she may also recover damages for non-delivery as well as being entitled to recover any of the purchase price she may have paid.

§ 9.10   Seller's Remedies for Breach

If the buyer breaches a contract for the sale of goods before the goods have been accepted, the seller may resell. If the resale is made in good faith in a commercially reasonable manner and in compliance with Code requirements such as notice, the seller may recover the difference between the resale price and the contract price plus incidental expenses, less expenses that could be avoided (§§ 2–706 and 2–710). If no resale is made in accordance with section 2–706, the seller may recover the difference between the contract price and the market price at the time and place of tender plus incidental expenses and less expenses which could be avoided (§§ 2–708(1) and 2–710).

If the buyer has accepted the goods or if the goods were destroyed after the risk of loss has passed to the buyer, the seller may maintain an action for the price (§ 2–709(1)(a) and (2)). The seller can also maintain an action for the contract price where the goods are identified to the contract and he is unable, or the circumstances indicate that he will be unable, to resell them at a reasonable price (§ 2–709(1)(b)).

The following hypotheticals demonstrate the impact of these rules.

(a) Sara contracts to sell a new boat to Bert for $21,000. Bert promptly repudiates the contract. After giving proper notice to Bert, Sara can resell the boat in a commercially reasonable fashion. If the boat is resold for $20,000, Sara may recover from Bert $1,000 plus the reasonable costs incurred in reselling less any savings Sara realized. Bert is liable for damages, but Sara cannot force him to pay the contract price and accept the boat.

(b) Assume the same facts but Sara does not resell the boat. If Sara can prove the market price of the boat at the time and place of tender was $20,100, Sara may recover $900 from Bert plus any incidental costs and less any incidental savings.

(c) Sara contracts to sell a new boat to Bert for $21,000. The boat is delivered, Bert accepts it, and Bert has no legal basis to revoke his acceptance. Bert is liable for $21,000, the contract price. The question whether Bert has accepted the boat is pivotal. If Bert has accepted, he is stuck with the boat and must pay the contract price.

(d) Same facts as in (c) except that the boat was destroyed by fire. If the risk of loss has not passed, Bert has no liability and Sara perhaps may be excused from performing on the grounds of impossibility (§ 6.1). If the risk of loss has passed to Bert (§§ 2–509 and 2–510), Bert is liable for the contract price.

(e) Assume that the Sara–Bert contract is for a specially designed boat built to Bert's personal specifications. Bert repudiates the contract after the boat has been built and Sara finds that after reasonable effort, she cannot resell the boat for a reasonable price. Sara may bring an action for the contract price of $21,000. This is an exceptional remedy.

The above mentioned remedies give no adequate relief for breach to the seller who is in a situation where his profits are partly dependent upon the volume of his sales. Consider the Ford dealer who contracts to sell a new car for $31,000. Assume that this price is the fair market value of the car and is $3,000 more than the dealer's cost of buying the car and preparing it for delivery. Before taking delivery, the buyer repudiates the contract.

If the buyer made a deposit before he breached, the dealer could retain $500 of the deposit. The seller can retain $500 or 20% of the contract price, whichever is smaller (§ 2–718(2)(b)). Assuming that no deposit was made or that the dealer is not satisfied with only $500, how should the dealer's damage be ascertained? The dealer cannot maintain an action for the price as the car was not accepted or destroyed nor is the seller unable to resell it for a reasonable price (§ 2–709). The dealer can resell the car and sue for the difference between resale and contract, but assuming he sells it for approximately $31,000, he will have nothing but the incidental damages allowed by section 2–710. He can sue for the difference between contract and market, but this too will be little or nothing. Yet the dealer has sustained damages in the amount of $3,000. At the end of the year he will have sold one less car because of this breach because the person who finally purchases this car would likely have purchased another car from the dealer. One sale was lost, and the dealer's profits for the period in question will be $3,000 less as a result. Even if the business was losing money, the dealer's losses would have been $3,000 less had he made this one additional sale.

The dealer may recover damages in the amount of $3,000 from the buyer under section 2–708(2). This section applies where the other remedies are inadequate. It permits the recovery of the profits, including reasonable overhead, that the seller would have made from full performance by the buyer. It will most frequently be applicable to retailers, wholesalers and manufacturers who are operating at less than full capacity and whose profits are predicated in significant part upon the volume of their sales.

§ 9.11 Buyer's Remedies for Breach

If a contract for the sale of goods is breached by the seller, the buyer may "cover" by making any reasonable purchase of substitute goods in good faith and without unreasonable delay. The buyer may recover the difference between the cost of cover and the contract price together with incidental and consequential damages less any expenses saved (§§ 2–712(1) and (2) and 2–715). If the cover is made in good faith, it does not matter that the price was not in fact the lowest available. Where justified by the circumstances, the goods purchased in substitution need not be identical to those provided for in the contract.

If the buyer does not cover, then the measure of damages is the difference between the market price at the time when the buyer learned of the breach and the contract price, together with incidental and consequential damages less expenses saved (§§ 2–713(1) and 2–715). Note that market price is determined at the time for performance in the case of seller's remedies (§ 2–708(1)). This was the common law rule for both seller's and buyer's damages, but the Code has substituted "the time when the buyer learned of the breach." In many transactions, the seller is to perform by shipping goods to the buyer. If the seller fails to perform, the buyer will not learn of this breach until some time later when the goods fail to arrive. Seller's breaches frequently occur when the market is rising and the difference between the market price when the seller breached and the market price when the buyer learned about it could be significant. In cases of repudiation by the seller, a buyer can learn of breach before the time fixed for performance (§ 2–610). Section 2–713 would appear to provide that this earlier time (when the buyer learned of the breach by virtue of seller's anticipatory repudiation) is also the time to be used to determine market price. (But see section 2–723.)

Market price for buyer's damages is determined by the price at the place of tender except in cases where the goods have been delivered. If the buyer rightfully rejected the goods after arrival or justifiably revoked his acceptance, market price is determined on the basis of prices at the place of arrival.

If the buyer has accepted defective goods and cannot revoke that acceptance, the buyer is stuck with the goods. He may recover damages computed in any reasonable manner. One calculation is the difference, at the time and place of acceptance, between the value of the goods that he accepted and the value that the goods would have had if the goods had conformed to the contract warranties (§ 2–714). Note that this computation does not utilize the contract price. The contract price is not relevant for determining the diminution in value due to the seller's breach.

A buyer may also recover incidental and consequential damages as described in section 2–715. The Code rejects the requirement found in older cases that a party show that the breaching party "tacitly agreed" to assume liability for the particular damages in question (comment 2 to U.C.C. § 2–715), but section 2–715 expressly preserves the common law requirement that damages arise from facts that the breaching party had reason to know at the time the contract was made.

§ 9.11.1 Buyer's Right to the Goods

Common law decisions limited a buyer's right to specific performance to cases in which the goods were unique. The Code incorporates this rule in section 2–716 but adds "or in other proper circumstances." (See § 9.6.)

There are additional circumstances in which the buyer may obtain the goods themselves. This relief may be obtained if the goods have been identified to the contract and the buyer is unable to make a cover purchase (§ 2–716(3)) or, under certain circumstances, where the buyer has made part payment and the seller becomes insolvent (§§ 2–502 and 2–711(2)(a)).

CHAPTER 10

RESTITUTION (UNJUST ENRICHMENT)

§ 10.1 Restitution

Restitution is a separate body of substantive law. It is not part of the law of contracts. Just as an action may be brought in tort or in contract, so can an action be brought in restitution. There is a separate Restatement of Restitution.

Law schools no longer teach restitution as a separate subject. It receives some mention in Contracts classes where restitutionary remedies are included along with contract remedies. There are fundamental differences between the two areas of law, and failure to focus briefly upon these differences can leave students confused and ill-informed. For these reasons, we are including a discussion of restitution in this volume devoted to contracts so that you might be aware of how an action in restitution may arise. You will see how an action for restitution may be available in a fact pattern in which there was a contract or an attempted contract.

The law of restitution provides substantive rights that fill some of the cracks between the law of torts and of contracts. It is frequently labeled "unjust enrichment," an equally appropriate label which is synonymous with restitution. It is also sometimes labeled "quasi contract" but that phrase describes only one aspect of the law of restitution.

To establish a right to restitution, a plaintiff must prove that the defendant was unjustly enriched and that this unjust enrichment was created at the plaintiff's expense or by violating the plaintiff's rights. The notion of what is "unjust" enrichment involves value judgments. If a fence painter quits shortly after he begins, is the owner's retention of the benefit without payment to the fence painter "unjust?" Even the concept of "enrichment" may invoke an analysis of societal standards. Is one who attempts to commit suicide "enriched" by the efforts of a medical team that seeks to revive him and save him? The entire law of restitution is heavily influenced by considerations of policy.

Restitution encompasses a number of subjects that create substantive rights and remedies. Included are quasi-contract, rescission, constructive trust, equitable liens, accounting for profits, subrogation, indemnity and contribution. Some authors also include replevin and ejectment within this subject. Examples are helpful.

§ 10.1.1 Benefits Conferred by Mistake

Assume that P attempts to make a deposit in P's bank account but inadvertently deposits the money to D's account. D is enriched. The enrichment is at P's expense. It is not unjust in the sense that D has committed any wrong but P's conduct is basically blameless and there is no apparent justification for allowing D to keep the gain. By societal standards, the money "should" be returned.

P may maintain an action against D for restitution or unjust enrichment. Note that there is no issue of fault and no tort involved. There is no promise and no contract involved. The measure of recovery is the amount of D's benefit, not the amount of P's loss. If the bank became insolvent after the deposit was made, D's liability would be limited to the amount D could recover from D's account.

Assume that A contracted with X to paint X's house. A painted B's house next door by mistake and without B's knowledge. B, who had previously put the house on the market, sells the mistakenly painted house at a price above what B had sought before the house was painted. B has been enriched. The enrichment is at A's expense, and as in the case of the bank deposit, one might conclude that retention of this gain is unjust. However, policy considerations may lead a court to conclude that there should be no liability for restitution here because of the concerns about permitting people to bestow unwanted "benefits" upon others. On the specific facts given, some courts would permit A to recover from B because the house was being sold and B promptly realized an increased net cash return. The recovery would be equal to the amount by which B was able to increase the price of the house, or if this was more than the cost of the paint job, recovery might be limited to what B would have had to have paid a third-party painter for the same work.

Assume that B was not selling his home and A inadvertently painted it. A's case for restitution is now quite difficult to establish. There are serious problems involved with making people pay for benefits that were foisted upon them in the absence of any emergency or other extenuating circumstance. While B's house may be more valuable, B's financial situation may not make this a good time for B to make this forced investment. B may not like the color. If one changed the facts to assume that A installed a swimming pool while B was away, recovery should clearly be denied. The court cannot assume that B is enriched by the presence of a swimming pool in the backyard.

If A intentionally painted B's house without B's consent, restitution would clearly be denied. A is now an officious intermeddler who is intruding himself into the affairs of others. There is no policy reason to encourage this conduct and denial of recovery would discourage this type of inappropriate conduct. Any windfall to B would be irrelevant. B might even have a cause of action for trespass in tort.

§ 10.1.2   Benefits Derived From the Commission of a Tort

Assume that D Co improperly copies the trademark of P Co. This is a tort for which P can recover whatever damages P can prove. Assume further that P's sales are expanding and it cannot prove with certainty what sales it lost and thus what damages it sustained as the result of D's activity.

However, P could discover and prove how much profit D made while misusing P's trademark.

P can sue in restitution. P can prove the amount by which D has been enriched through its activities. To the extent that those profits were derived from utilizing P's trademark, that enrichment is unjust. Since P cannot prove any losses, P cannot prove that the enrichment was literally obtained at P's expense, but the unjust enrichment resulted from a violation of P's legal rights and that is enough. P can thus recover even though P could prove no loss. The court is requiring D to disgorge its unjust gains. Cases are divided as to whether D can keep the portion of its profits that might reasonably be allocable to managerial and entrepreneurial skills. Some court opinions would even deny to D the right to deduct costs from its gross profits.

P has not proven that it has sustained any losses. There is absolutely no proof of damages. Referring to "recovery of damages in restitution" or recovery of "restitution damages" is thus inaccurate and diverts attention away from the fact that with the exception of punitive damages, restitution is the only area in which we award a money recovery that is unrelated to the damages sustained by the plaintiff.

§ 10.1.3 Rendition of Services

Assume that a man falls unconscious. A good Samaritan (GS) places the man in her car and hauls him to the nearest hospital. In the emergency room a doctor provides medical services while the man remains unconscious. The man dies. There is no tort in this fact situation nor is there any contract. Contracts require a manifestation of assent to be bound and none is present. If any recovery by the hospital or doctor is to be had, it must be in restitution.

The hospital and doctor have provided services that society considers necessary and appropriate. Society wishes to encourage such conduct. Thus, there are policy reasons to provide a legal vehicle to compensate the medical professionals for the services rendered.

The man has been enriched. While he was alive he received treatment intended to save his life. This is something that the law's hypothetical "reasonable person" would want. Had the man been conscious, he presumably would have requested this service. The man received a benefit and was enriched by the treatment even though the treatment was ultimately unsuccessful. Failure to compensate the doctor would make this enrichment unjust. The elements of a cause of action for restitution are present and the doctor will recover.

Compare the actions of the doctor to those of the house painter above. The house painter who intentionally painted B's house without B's consent was branded an "officious intermeddler" and denied recovery. The doctor has intentionally rendered medical services upon an unconscious man who may not have wanted those services. For all the doctor knew, the man may have had religious convictions that would induce him to reject this treatment if he were able. However, the doctor avoids the "officious intermeddler" label for the simple reason that the doctor has engaged in conduct that society wishes to encourage and the house painter has not.

The hospital will recover for the same reasons as the doctor. However, GS will not be so fortunate. There are no facts to establish that GS earns her living running an ambulance service or practicing medicine, and we can conclude that GS did not act with the expectation of compensation. Since she did not render her services with the expectation of payment, she will not recover. The considerations of policy that cause us to want to require payment to ambulance companies, doctors, hospitals and the like does not extend to those who volunteer services with no expectations of compensation. Many court opinions will simply dismiss GS's claim by labeling her a "mere volunteer." The explanation must be more complex than that because had GS been driving her ambulance, saw the man and stopped to take him to the hospital, she would have been no less a "volunteer," yet she (or her company) would have the right to recover for the value of the benefit conferred.

§ 10.1.4 Delivery of Goods

The right to recover in restitution for goods furnished is very similar to the right to recover for services rendered. One who provides goods to another under circumstances where the recipient presumably would, if physically or mentally able, have promised to pay can recover the reasonable value of those goods in restitution.

Restitution actions for services rendered are frequently described as actions for *quantum meruit*. Restitution actions for goods furnished are sometimes described as actions for *quantum valebant*. Both types of actions are often labeled actions for *quasi contract* and in some jurisdictions this label is used as a synonym for restitution or unjust enrichment. Labels are labels and one should be as good as another, but the term *quasi contract* is an unfortunate one because the substantive right that is being discussed has little to do with the law of contract. Restitution involves a liability imposed by society for reasons of public policy and without regard to the will of the defendant. In this sense it is more closely related to the law of torts than to contracts.

Restitution actions arising out of rendition of services or delivery of goods or other furnishing of things of value such as shelter often involve a defendant who was not legally competent at the time the facts arose. The defendant may have been physically absent, unconscious, mentally incompetent, or under age (which is viewed by the law as a form of mental incompetence). There are strong policy reasons to protect the defendant, particularly minors and others who are legally incompetent. But this policy cuts two ways. For example, if there were no way to collect for shelter or other necessities furnished to a minor, the law would be creating a disincentive for people to engage in this activity, and minors would be less likely to receive those necessities in times of distress.

§ 10.1.5 Performance of a Contract or Purported Contract

There are numerous situations in which a party has rendered performance upon a contract or purported contract only to discover that there is no contract remedy. Consider the following possibilities. The negotiation process may fall short of that legally required to form a contract. The partially performed contract may be unenforceable because of failure to comply with some formality such as a writing requirement. The purported contract may have been void from the beginning for a reason such as lack of capacity. An apparently valid contract may have been avoided because of the presence of some defense. Performance of a valid contract may have been excused because of impossibility or frustration of purpose. A valid enforceable contract may have been unilaterally rescinded based upon a material breach by the other party.

In each of these situations, there is no contract on which a suit may be grounded. Even in those instances where there once was a contract, by the time the suit is filed the contract has been rescinded, avoided or excused. Yet partial performance by one party may have enriched the other before the contract was terminated or before it was realized that the contract was not enforceable.

The basis of the action that can be brought in these situations to recover the benefits conferred is restitution. One can ordinarily sue for "breach of contract" and for "rescission and restitution" in the alternative, but ultimately the judgement must be calculated upon one method or the other. The breach of contract action will measure an award by the amount of compensable damages the plaintiff sustained. As developed in the next section, the recovery in restitution will be measured by the benefit conferred upon the defendant.

§ 10.2   Measure of Recovery in Restitution

The proper measure of recovery in restitution cases is the amount by which the defendant was enriched. The measure of recovery is not the plaintiff's loss. This is an easy concept in some situations but a bit tricky in others. The term "damages" is technically inappropriate in a restitution action. "Damages" refers to harm meaning harm to the plaintiff. Restitutionary recovery is not measured by harm to the plaintiff. Harm to the plaintiff is not even a necessary element of the cause of action. Therefore, "damages" is an inappropriate concept here. We will follow the examples used to describe the substantive law of restitution in the previous section.

Some restitution actions simply involve a dollar for dollar transfer of money from plaintiff to defendant. In these cases, the enrichment to the defendant and the harm to the plaintiff are the same and calculation of the proper recovery is obvious. If the plaintiff accidently deposits money to the defendant's account, the amount of the deposit is ordinarily the proper amount of recovery. However, if the bank fails and the defendant loses all or part of the money in the account, plaintiff's recovery will be limited to the defendant's enrichment even though this is less than the plaintiff's loss.

If plaintiff accidently paints defendant's house under circumstances in which recovery in restitution is warranted, recovery will be limited to the enhanced value of defendant's house. Alternatively, defendant's enrichment may be measured by the reasonable cost of hiring a painter because that is what defendant would have had to pay to obtain this service. What plaintiff usually charges may be some evidence of the reasonable cost of hiring painters in this area. But, the measure of recovery is defendant's gain, not plaintiff's costs.

The hypothetical involving the unauthorized (and thus tortious) use of plaintiff's trademark is a good example. In that hypothetical, the court could require defendant to disgorge defendant's entire profits without regard to whether the plaintiff could prove that plaintiff sustained any specific amount of damages.

The physician who rendered necessary emergency treatment to the unconscious man will also recover the amount by which the man was enriched. Since the man died soon after treatment, this benefit appears at first glance to be hard to measure. It is not. Applying societal standards, as distinguished from what we might later learn to have been the personal desires of the man, we assume that reasonable people would want competent medical treatment so long as there is a chance to save them. Since this is an assumed desire, receipt of such services is a benefit. The amount of this benefit is measured by what these services cost in the market place, not by the results achieved. If the man lived, his doctor bill is not measured by the value of his life. If he dies, the proper fee is not zero just because the efforts were not successful.

The man's enrichment should be measured by determining the reasonable value in the community of the medical services that he received. The inquiry is as to how much the patient would have had to pay an ordinary physician for services of this nature. If the plaintiff is an emergency room doctor doing what she does all the time, then her regular fee is what the patient would have had to have paid and this is likely the proper measure of the value of the service received. However, if the doctor is a neurosurgeon who happened to be present giving basic care in the emergency room, the fact that her ordinary fee is $9,000 per procedure would have no relevance in measuring her recovery in restitution.

Finally, one who seeks recovery in restitution for furnishing goods or other property will also recover only the amount by which the defendant was enriched. This should be measured by the value of the benefit conferred. Assume that a minor purchased a used car for $10,000 and neither paid for it nor returned it. Lack of capacity will be a defense to any contract action. Assuming no tort was committed, the seller's only possible recovery will be in restitution. If recovery is permitted, the proper measure of recovery will be the amount by which the minor was unjustly enriched. This should be measured by the value of the car. The $10,000 figure has no relevance. That is only the amount that a person who is legally incompetent agreed to pay and is not relevant to prove value.

CHAPTER 11

THIRD PARTY BENEFICIARIES

A. WHAT PARTIES MAY ASSERT CONTRACT RIGHTS

§ 11.1 Third Party Beneficiary Contracts

Contracts may be formed in which one party's performance is to be rendered directly to a third party or the performance will indirectly confer a benefit upon a third party. Early common law courts had difficulties with the theoretical aspects of permitting a third party, who had no privity with the promisor, and from whom no consideration "flowed," to enforce the contract. Today all American jurisdictions have accepted principles of contract law that allow enforcement of such third party beneficiary contracts.

A third party acquires the right to enforce a contract only if the court finds that the principal parties to the contract intended to create legally enforceable rights in the third party. This test has been expressed using varying terminology in different jurisdictions. Some require a finding that the third party was a "direct" beneficiary, some require that the third party be the "primary" beneficiary, and others inquire whether the contract was made for the "express benefit" of the third party. No matter how articulated, the critical test is whether the third party was intended to have enforceable rights under the contract.

Many contracts are bilateral when formed with two promisors and two promisees. Courts have sometimes indicated a lack of certainty as to which party's intention actually controls in evaluating whether a third party will have enforceable rights under the contract. The third party will typically be seeking to enforce a promise of only one of the parties and it is helpful to identify as the "promisor" that person who made the promise that the third party seeks to enforce. Therefore the other party to the contract will be "the promisee" of that promise. It should be noted that the promise that is being sought to be enforced is not a promise made to the third party himself or herself. It is quite common that the third party will not even have knowledge of the existence of the contract at the time it is formed.

When a purported third party beneficiary seeks to enforce the promise of one of the parties, the focus should be upon the intention of the person to whom that promise was made, that is the promisee of that promise. The question is whether that promisee's manifested intention was to create enforceable rights in the third party. If this is found to be the case, there is nothing unjust, inequitable, or unfair, in requiring the promisor to perform the duty owed to the third party or be liable to the third party for its breach. Therefore, it is the promisee's apparent intention as objectively communicated to the promisor that should control in determining whether enforceable rights were created in the third party. The Restatement, First, reflected the common view that if the promisee's purpose was "to make a gift to the beneficiary or to confer upon him a right against the promisor to some performance" the third party had enforceable rights.

In some jurisdictions, court decisions indicate that both the promisee and the promisor must manifest the intent that the third party be a beneficiary.

§ 11.2   Identification of the Third Party

Historically, third party beneficiaries with enforceable rights have been classified as donee or creditor beneficiaries. A third party without enforceable rights has been identified as an incidental beneficiary to the contract. The distinction between donees and creditors is predicated upon whether the promisee was attempting to confer a gift upon the third party or attempting to discharge an obligation, real or assumed, that was owing to the third party. This classification can be significant for two reasons: (1) it may operate as an aid (not a conclusive test) in determining whether the beneficiary will have enforceable rights at all, and (2) the parties' ability to modify or rescind their contract may be affected because some jurisdictions apply different rules concerning the time the rights of a third party vest (§ 11.5) depending upon their status as a creditor or donee. In addition, a few jurisdictions may still not permit a donee beneficiary to enforce a contract unless a family relationship exists between the donee and the promisee.

The donee/creditor classification is not always clear since there are situations in which both a charitable motive and an attempt to discharge a real or assumed obligation are evident on the part of the promisee. There is also a category of cases, such as employer contracts with persons who are to provide benefits to the employer's employees, in which an attempt to define the motive as charitable or as intending to discharge an obligation is difficult and not really helpful.

The performance of a contract between A and B, in which A agrees to paint B's weather-beaten house, will benefit C, B's neighbor. C will benefit esthetically and perhaps financially if the improvement enhances the marketability of C's property. However, C is nothing more than an incidental beneficiary since there was nothing to indicate to A that B's intention was to confer enforceable rights in C as against A. To use the Restatement, First, classifications, C was neither a creditor nor a donee beneficiary. There was no duty owed by B to C and B did not intend to confer a "gift" upon C.

Assume that there is a contract between A and B in which B agrees to pay money to A in exchange for which A agrees to paint C's house. The performance by A is a direct benefit to C. C is an express beneficiary and the primary purpose of the promisee, B, in entering into such a contract appears to be to confer a benefit upon C. C will be found to be a third party beneficiary, donee or creditor depending upon the motivating force behind B's conduct, and C can acquire enforceable rights under the contract. If B's motives are partly charitable and partly to satisfy an obligation, C will ordinarily be classified as a donee beneficiary in those jurisdictions in which the rights of a donee are superior to those of a creditor.

The Restatement, Second, section 302, does not use the donee/creditor classification but retains the incidental beneficiary terminology as to those beneficiaries who have no enforceable rights. The term "intended beneficiary" is used in the Restatement to describe a third party with enforceable contract rights. To determine if a third party is an "intended beneficiary," an inquiry must first be made into whether "recognition of a right to performance in the beneficiary is appropriate to effectuate the intention of the parties * * * ." Then one must inquire whether:

(a) the performance of the promise will satisfy an obligation of the promisee to pay money to the beneficiary; or

(b) the circumstances indicate that the promisee intends to give the beneficiary the benefit of the promised performance. (Restatement § section 302(1)(a) and (b).)

Section 302 is an interesting one to study. It avoids the traditional classifications of "creditor beneficiary" and "donee beneficiary," yet it refers to the intent to "satisfy an obligation" or to "give

(a) benefit" as the proper inquiries to determine whether a third party has enforceable rights. It refers to "the intention of the parties" (plural) yet it directs us specifically to consider only the promisee when exploring intention to benefit in sub-parts (a) and (b). It is apparent that one may still properly focus upon the intent of the promisee and inquire whether the intent was to satisfy an obligation or to confer a gift.

§ 11.3 Intended Beneficiaries in Special Situations: Government Contracts

Third party beneficiaries can be found to have acquired enforceable rights in situations in which the presence of third party interests is not immediately apparent. Anytime a contract will have the effect of producing a direct benefit for certain individuals or for a class of people, it may become necessary to analyze the question whether the promisee intended that these persons have enforceable rights.

There are many types of contracts that are made between government agencies and private parties or other governmental units for the primary purpose of benefitting a class of citizens. An issue regarding third party rights can exist in contracts providing for such things as job retraining for persons whose employment in the lumber industry was terminated by the creation of a new redwood tree park or replacement housing for persons dislocated by a redevelopment project.

In contracts to which governmental entities are parties, one might assume that the government would prefer to do its own contract enforcing and reserve the right to rescind or modify a contract or determine the manner and extent of enforcement action. Thus one might assume that giving a right of action to a third party beneficiary might not be "appropriate to effectuate the intention of the parties." However, assume that a government contract requires a builder to construct homes to certain minimum standards for a class of buyers such as military veterans. In this circumstance it has been successfully contended that the government did intend to give the home buyers the right to enforce the contract promises. Apartment tenants have been found to be intended beneficiaries of the financing contract between a Federal Agency (HUD) and their landlord (Zigas v. Superior Court of San Francisco (Cal.App. 1981)). Individual beneficiaries would have a direct interest and might be better motivated to pursue the action than a busy government attorney.

Restatement section 302 gives the following illustration:

10. A, the operator of a chicken processing and fertilizer plant, contracts with B, a municipality, to use B's sewage system. With the purpose of preventing harm to landowners downstream from its system, B obtains from A a

promise to remove specified types of waste from its deposits into the system. C, a downstream landowner, is an intended beneficiary under Subsection (1)(b).

§ 11.4 Rights of the Promisee Against the Promisor

If the beneficiary is a creditor beneficiary, the promisee is ordinarily under some duty owing to the beneficiary. When the promisor fails to perform the promise made for the benefit of a creditor beneficiary, the creditor beneficiary may bring action against the promisor or may proceed against the promisee on the original obligation. If the creditor does proceed against the promisee, the promisee will be damaged as a result of the promisor's failure to perform. The promisee may sue the promisor for these damages.

In the case of a donee beneficiary, the promisee is not personally harmed by the promisor's failure to perform. If the donee beneficiary does not take action against the promisor, the promisee has no remedy at law. Some cases permit the promisee to bring an action against the promisor in equity to specifically enforce the contract.

B. PROMISORS' DEFENSES AGAINST THIRD PARTIES' CLAIMS

§ 11.5 Contract Modification or Rescission; Vesting of Third Party's Rights

Vesting of the beneficiary's right is important if and only if the original contracting parties attempt in some manner to modify the contract or rescind the contract in derogation of the already existing rights of the beneficiary. If the beneficiary consents, the promisor and the promisee are generally free to modify the contract to the detriment of the third party or to rescind the contract. However, such modifications or rescissions without the consent of the third party beneficiary will not be effective if they occur after the beneficiary's rights have vested.

Different jurisdictions find third party's rights to have vested upon the occurrence of one of three events. First, there are cases which hold that rights vest immediately at the time the contract is made. This is true even when the beneficiary does not learn of the contract until a later time. Second, a number of cases hold that rights vest at the time the third party acquires knowledge of the contract and agrees to accept the benefits thereof. If the beneficiary learns of the contract and does not expressly reject the benefits, then acceptance is ordinarily presumed. The third and probably the most commonly applied rule requires a change in position by the beneficiary in reliance upon the contract in order for the beneficiary's rights to vest. Ordinarily, only a slight change in position is required, e.g., filing suit against the promisor.

Many states apply different vesting rules to donee and to creditor beneficiaries with the donee beneficiaries' rights usually vesting immediately or when they have knowledge and assent, and the creditor beneficiaries' rights vesting later in time, usually after some reliance. One reason for the distinction is that the creditor will ordinarily have a right of action against his principal debtor, the promisee.

Some states vest the rights of third parties more quickly if the third party is a minor. The inability of a minor to "learn" of his rights and "assent" has led some courts to provide for the immediate vesting of minors' rights upon the making of the contract. Other jurisdictions follow a single rule for vesting without regard to the nature of the beneficiary. Where immediate vesting is applied, it can constitute a trap for the unwary. Assume that A and B enter into a contract in which B agrees to perform a promise for the benefit of C who is totally unaware of what is transpiring. Shortly thereafter, A and B rescind their agreement, possibly to enter a different agreement in which B's promise will be performed for A himself. In a jurisdiction which applies immediate vesting, C acquired an enforceable right against B when the A–B contract was made, and the subsequent A–B rescission does not affect C's right to obtain performance from B.

The Restatement does not distinguish between donee and creditor beneficiaries and has a single rule for vesting. Section 311(3) takes the position that an intended beneficiary's rights vest when the beneficiary "materially changes his position in justifiable reliance on the promise or brings suit on it or manifests assent to it at the request of the promisor or promisee."

§ 11.6 Defenses Assertable Against the Third Party Beneficiary

Because the third party's rights against the promisor are dependent upon the third party beneficiary contract, the third party's rights are subject to defenses which the promisor has in that contract. If no valid contract was formed or if it is not enforceable against the promisor, the promisor may assert this defense against the third party beneficiary. Simply stated, the promisor can assert against the beneficiary any claim or defense arising out of the contract that the promisor could have asserted against the promisee. The sole exception, noted in the preceding section, is that a modification or rescission will not defeat third party rights that had already vested.

Assume that Joe and Mary had a business transaction and that Mary claims that Joe owes her $10,000. Thereafter, Joe entered into a contract with Dan in which Joe promised to render a service for Dan and Dan promised to pay $10,000 to Mary. Now Mary has brought action against Dan for the $10,000.

The promisor can assert against the third party defenses arising under the third party beneficiary contract. Since the sole basis for Mary's action against Dan is the Dan–Joe contract, any defenses which Dan might properly assert under that contract are available against Mary. This would include defenses relating to formation such as misrepresentation or mistake or defenses relating to enforcement such as violation of public policy. It would also include a defense arising out of failure of a condition precedent to Dan's duty to perform such as Joe's failure to perform the service that he agreed to render for Dan.

The only defense that might arise under the Dan–Joe contract that cannot be asserted against Mary would be the defense of modification or rescission that occurred after Mary's rights had vested. If Mary learned of the Dan–Joe contract and changed position in reliance upon her right to recover from Dan, her rights under that contract would be vested no matter which vesting rule the court applied. If Dan and Joe later modified their contract, such as by providing that Dan would pay the $10,000 to Joe instead of to Mary, this modification cannot defeat Mary's vested rights. This is the only significance of vesting. If there has been no attempt to rescind or modify the contract to reduce the third party's rights, then vesting is not an issue and no discussion of that point is required.

A promisor may not assert against a third party defenses that arise out of the transaction between the third party and the promisee. Thus, Dan may not assert against Mary defenses which Joe might have had if Mary had sued Joe. The nature and details of the underlying transaction between Joe and Mary is of no relevance to Dan. Whether Joe actually owed Mary any sum of money or whether Joe had a defense that he could have asserted against Mary is not important. For reasons satisfactory to himself, Joe entered a contract in which he obtained from Dan an agreement to pay $10,000 to

Mary. If the Joe–Dan contract is legally enforceable, it is none of Dan's concern whether Joe was actually obligated to pay Mary.

Assume facts as set forth in the first paragraph of this section except that instead of promising to pay $10,000 to Mary in exchange for Joe's services, Dan promised to "pay whatever amount Joe legally owes to Mary." In this situation, the measure of Dan's obligation is the amount that Joe owes to Mary. For that reason, the details of the Joe–Mary transaction would now be relevant in an action by Mary against Dan, and Dan could properly raise and prove defenses that Joe might have had against Mary. Dan is not being permitted to assert defenses in the Joe–Mary transaction as a defense to his own obligation to perform. Dan is being permitted to prove defenses that Joe might have had against Mary because the amount legally owing from Joe to Mary is the measure of Dan's obligation.

When you have completed your study of this chapter, you may wish to analyze questions 31–32 at the end of this book and compare your analysis with the one given there.

CHAPTER 12

ASSIGNMENT OF RIGHTS AND DELEGATION OF DUTIES

A. ASSIGNMENT OF RIGHTS

§ 12.1 Assignment of Rights; Delegation of Duties Distinguished

Contract rights are akin to property rights in that they can be "owned", and as is the case with most rights, the owner of the right usually has the power and the right to transfer the owner's interest. This is true whether the right be an interest in real property, tangible personal property, an intangible right to collect a debt, or the right to the performance owed under a contract. Like any other transfer of a tangible property right, once a transfer of a contract right has been accomplished, the transferor's interest in the right is usually extinguished and the right becomes the property of the transferee. A transfer of a contract right is called an assignment.

Care must be taken to focus upon what it is that the parties are attempting to "transfer." For example, in a contract in which Painter (P) has promised to paint Owner's (O) house, P has undertaken the duty of painting the house and has acquired the right to payment in accordance with the terms of the contract. If P desires, P can assign (transfer)

508

the right to payment to a third party. P may also desire to arrange to have the work done by the same or another party. If P is attempting to arrange for someone else to perform P's duty of painting, the terminology then would be focused upon whether P is permitted to delegate to the third party P's duty of painting O's house. In other words, should O be required to accept performance from someone with whom O did not contract? If P had merely assigned P's right to the money, it is unlikely that O would be adversely affected by having to pay someone other than P. However, when P delegates the duty of painting O's house to a stranger, O may have a right to object to the delegation. This would be so if O had a significant interest in having P paint the house or if the third party was not qualified.

Duties are not transferable in the sense that rights are. The transfer of a right extinguishes the right in the transferor. Upon assignment by P to X of the right to payment of the money, P's right to payment is extinguished. However, if P delegated to X the duty to paint O's house, P would remain obligated to O for the performance of the painting duties and P would be liable for O's damages if the duty to paint the house is not performed.

Many duties are delegable. However, even though they are delegable and effectively delegated, the delegator remains responsible for their performance. Parties cannot avoid their contractual duties by the simple expedient of delegating their duty of performance. However, if the party to whom the duty is owing (the obligee) agrees to the substitution of the delegatee for the delegator and release of the delegator, a novation results and the delegator is released (§ 13.3).

When P assigns to X the right to payment, P is the assignor and X is the assignee. O would be called the obligor (of the obligation to pay the money). When P delegates to X the duty to paint O's house, P (who is the obligor of the obligation to paint the house) is called the delegator or delegant and X is called the delegatee or delegate.

It is not uncommon to read or hear that one party "assigned the contract" to another. This is an ambiguous expression that must be interpreted by use of surrounding facts and circumstances. The question to be answered is, "Was there only an assignment of the rights, or both an assignment of the rights and delegation of the duties?"

An "assignment of the contract" may mean that the assignor intends to perform the contract duties and manifests an intention only to transfer the contract rights. This is the typical situation if the assignment is made to a bank or other lender as security for a loan. For example, a lender may advance money to a contractor and take an assignment of the right to payment on certain construction contracts. This is done to protect the lender in the event the contractor does not repay the loan. It would be most unlikely that a court would find that the lender has assumed the duty to build the structures.

"Assignment of the contract" may also mean that the assignor manifests an intention to transfer the contract rights and to delegate the contract duties. In this case, the assignee, by consenting to the transaction, impliedly promises to perform the delegated duties. The assignee/delegatee may thus be liable to the other party to the contract or to the assignor/delegator for breach in the event of nonperformance.

It is usually clear from the nature of the transaction between the assignor and assignee whether the parties contemplate that as between the assignor and assignee that the assignor will be expected to perform the contract duties even though the assignee is to receive the performance. However, when the nature of the transaction is such that it is apparent the assignee must perform if he is to receive the contract benefits, there may still be an issue as to whether the assignee has actually promised to perform thereby becoming liable for breach if performance does not occur.

Assume that Henry has contracted to sell 1,000 widgets to Joe for $50,000. Henry then "assigns" this contract to Jane for $500. The U.C.C. (§ 2–210) and the Restatement (§ 328) take the position that the assignee who accepts the assignment under these circumstances becomes bound to perform. There was both an assignment of the right to the payment of $50,000 and a delegation of the duty to Jane to deliver the widgets. When Jane accepted the assignment, Jane will be deemed to have impliedly promised to perform Henry's duty.

As noted in the Restatement, however, in the case of assignment of executory contracts for the purchase and sale of real property, courts generally hold that the assignee does not assume personal liability for the contract performance. In real property transactions, the sale of property which is subject to a mortgage or other encumbrance does not impose upon the buyer personal liability for the payment of the encumbrance unless the buyer expressly assumes that obligation. Some cases expressly consider that analogous situation in holding that an assignee of an executory contract for the purchase of real property does not assume personal liability for payment of the purchase price. An example might be X assigning to Y, for $500 cash, X's rights in a contract for the purchase of Blackacre from S for $400,000. Courts have held that the assignee only acquires the right to the contract performance if he tenders the return performance. While the assignee may not have undertaken a duty to perform, he is not entitled to the return performance unless he does in fact perform.

§ 12.2 What Rights Are Assignable; Effect of Prohibitions Against Assignment

Rights arising from a contract are generally assignable. The other party to the contract, the obligor, may properly object to an assignment of right to receive his performance only if:

(a) his duty is somehow materially changed;

(b) the risk of not receiving the return performance is materially increased; or,

(c) the value of the contract performance is substantially reduced.

Examples might include the attempted assignment by a buyer of his rights under a requirements contract, the rights of a borrower under a loan commitment, or the contract right of a famous person to have her portrait painted. In most of these cases, the problem at least partly involves an attempt to delegate duties that are not properly delegable (§ 12.9).

Most obligors would prefer not to have to deal with assignees, and it is thus not unusual to encounter contract provisions that attempt to prohibit or restrict assignability. Since the assignment of contract rights is a common source of business financing and has other economically beneficial purposes, contract provisions that purport to limit the right to assign have been strictly construed by the courts. Courts may also be influenced by the belief that all rights are alienable and any restrictions or attempted restraint on alienation should be scrutinized taking into account, purpose, necessity and effect.

A contract provision that states that the "contract will not be assigned" has typically been interpreted to prohibit delegation of duties but not assignment of rights. A contract provision to the effect that "rights shall not be assigned" is typically interpreted to constitute a promise not to assign. In that case, an attempted assignment is fully effective and the obligor is left with an action against the assignor for breach of his promise not to assign (for which there will likely be no damages).

Even a contract provision which contains language to the effect that "any attempted assignment of rights is null and void" is usually interpreted as being only for the benefit of the obligor and only having the effect of permitting the obligor to refuse to deal with the assignee. Thus, the assignment can still be valid as between the assignee and the assignor and thus binding upon the assignor's creditors or subsequent assignees.

In addition to the restrictive rules of interpretation of contract provisions which attempt to prohibit assignment, there are various statutes that are designed to preserve freedom to assign rights. The U.C.C. (§ 9–318) prohibits any restriction upon the assignability of the right to receive payment for goods sold or leased, or for services rendered. It also prohibits any restriction upon the assignment for security of any other right to receive money which comes within Article 9 of the Code. In contracts involving transactions in goods, the U.C.C. (§ 2–210) prohibits any restrictions upon assignment of the right to damages for breach of the whole contract or a right arising out of the assignor's full performance of his contract duties. Some common law decisions also interpret contract terms prohibiting assignments so as not to forbid assignment of the right to damages for breach of the entire contract or of the right to payment arising out of the assignor's full performance of his contract obligation. The rationale is that there is no valid business purpose to be served in preventing assignment once the assignor has fully performed, and a debtor who has breached has no valid reason to prevent assignment of a damage claim.

Policy considerations have produced common law and statutory restrictions upon the assignment of certain rights. The assignment of tort claims for personal injuries is prohibited at common law because it violates public policy. It is sometimes stated that public policy considerations preclude the assignment of any type of tort claim, however, the logic of the policy considerations does not necessarily extend to property damage claims, and these can be assigned in some jurisdictions. Most states have statutes that either prohibit or restrict the assignment of contract rights to wages or salary for personal services. Some statutes permit the assignment of all or part of a contract right for wages if the wages have already been earned prior to the time of assignment. Some require written consent by the assignor's spouse.

The Federal Government and many state governments have restrictions on the assignment of claims against the government. These laws are ordinarily interpreted to relieve the government of the duty of dealing with the assignee but do not affect the validity of the assignment as between the assignor and the assignee.

§ 12.3 Requisites of an Assignment

Restatement section 324 provides:

It is essential to an assignment of a right that the obligee manifest an intention to transfer the right

to another person without further action or manifestation of intention by the obligee. The manifestation may be made to the other or to a third
person on his behalf, and, except as provided by
statute or by contract, may be made either orally
or by a writing.

Care must be taken to distinguish between a
manifestation of intent to transfer a right to the
assignee and a statement that identifies a source of
payment or a promise to pay. Attorney X may state
to Attorney Y: "Write the brief and you will get
one-half the fee." This may be a promise of payment and may fix the amount and time when the
payment is due, but it does not appear to manifest
an intent to transfer to Y the present right to
collect the fee or any part of it.

The U.C.C. (§ 1–206) imposes a writing requirement providing that an assignment is not enforceable beyond $5,000 in the absence of a sufficient
writing. Note that this provision is found in U.C.C.
Article 1 and is thus applicable to all assignments,
not just those arising out of transactions in goods.

At one time the common law required that the
contract that created the assigned right had to be in
existence in order to have a valid present assignment. It was not necessary that the right have
already been earned by performance, nor did it
matter that the right was created by an option
contract, but there had to be an existing contractual

relationship from which the assigned right would arise. The logic behind this view was that one could not transfer a property right that did not exist. An attempted assignment of rights that might arise under contracts to be made in the future was treated as a promise to assign.

Recent developments have modified the common law rules in two ways. If there is an existing business or employment relationship, a present attempt to assign a right that will arise out of a future contract anticipated in this existing relationship is now generally recognized as a valid present transfer of the right in question. The other change applies to assignments that come within the coverage of Article 9 of the U.C.C. This article authorizes an agreement between assignor and assignee by which the assignor's rights under future contracts will be effectively assigned the instant these future contracts are made. Technically this does not change the common law rule, but it results in instant assignment of all new contract rights without the necessity of further communication or paperwork between the assignor and the assignee. It also accomplishes the intended purpose of transferring the right in question to the assignee free of any intervening claims of third parties such as creditors of the assignor or parties claiming to be assignees of the same right.

§ 12.4 Assignment of Rights Embodied in a Tangible Object

If there is a tangible thing that represents a right, this tangible thing ordinarily must be transferred from the assignor to the assignee before the latter can effectively enforce the right in question. The right to attend a football game and sit on the 40–yard line is represented by a thing or token which we call a ticket. An attempt to transfer that right to another person without giving that person the ticket will not be sufficient to give the assignee the effective right to gain entrance to the game.

Rights are often evidenced by something such as a written contract. Such a writing does not represent the right. One need not surrender a written contract to enforce a right to payment thereon. There is no requirement that a thing that merely evidences the right be given to the assignee.

Where a token or instrument that represents the right exists, the delivery of that thing is good evidence of the assignor's manifestation of intent to transfer. Such delivery also provides a basis for finding that a gratuitous assignment has been completed and is thus irrevocable (§ 12.5). Failure to deliver the instrument or token that represents the rights may give the obligor a defense to rendering the performance to the assignee because of the assignee's inability to produce the token or instrument. However, the failure to deliver the instrument or token does not necessarily preclude a finding that there has been a valid assignment.

§ 12.5 Revocability of Gratuitous Assignments: Events That Revoke

One anomaly of assignment law is that even though there may have been an effective gratuitous assignment so that the right has been transferred to the assignee, it may be possible for the assignor to revoke the assignment. The reasons for allowing this to occur are in part historical in that an assignment was originally treated as a power of attorney. A power of attorney does not need consideration but unless "coupled with an interest" is terminable any time prior to its exercise. This is no longer the theory used in recognizing the effect of an assignment and the assignee is deemed to be entitled to enforce the right in his or her own name and not as an agent of the assignor. However, the concept of revocability of a gratuitous assignment continues unless there are events or facts that would be tantamount to the completion of a gift of a chattel.

Note that this discussion relates only to the question whether an assignment is revocable. Even if revocable, the assignment is effective and the right can properly be enforced by the assignee up until the time of revocation.

Restatement section 332, provides that a gratuitous assignment is irrevocable if:

(a) the assignment is in a writing either signed or under seal that is delivered by the assignor; or

(b) the assignment is accompanied by delivery of a writing of a type customarily accepted as a symbol or as evidence of the right assigned.

The section goes on to state that the gratuitous assignment ceases to be revocable to the extent that before the assignee's right is terminated he obtains

(a) payment or satisfaction of the obligation, or

(b) judgment against the obligor, or

(c) a new contract of the obligor by novation.

The gratuitous assignment will also become irrevocable if the assignee reasonably and foreseeably changed position in reliance upon the assignment.

Gratuitous revocable assignments may be revoked at will by the assignor and are deemed to be revoked by:

(a) the making of a subsequent assignment of the same right;

(b) demand for performance or acceptance of performance by the assignor from the obligor; or,

(c) death or loss of capacity of the assignor or initiation of bankruptcy proceedings by or against the assignor.

(d) notification from the assignor received by the assignee or the obligor.

Principles of contract law and property law underlie these concepts. Under the law of property, a gift is completed and title to property transferred when a physical object is delivered with donative intent. Thus, the presence of a token, a thing that represents the rights, can be a problem-solver. Delivery of the token can complete the gift. So also can collection of the debt or other enforcement of the right by the assignee.

Cases exist in which an assignor delivered a writing to the assignee which purported to constitute a present transfer of a right. Such deliveries have been found to constitute a valid present assignment and thus, where gratuitous, a completed gift, even where there was a token or instrument representing the right but which was not transferred.

§ 12.6 Partial Assignments

Before the law developed procedures permitting liberal joinder of parties, an obligor was free to ignore a partial assignment of a right because the partial assignment could have the effect of forcing the obligor to defend more than one suit arising out of the single transaction. Partial assignments are now permitted. The obligor is protected from multiple suits by permitting him to force the joinder in one action of all persons holding partial assignments of the same right, including the assignor if the assignor reserves some portion of the right assigned.

§ 12.7 Multiple Assignments of Same Right; Coverage and Impact of U.C.C. Article 9

Assignors with little cash and less morality may find themselves tempted to resell the same right two or more times by assigning it to successive assignees. An assignor who receives value warrants to the assignee that the right assigned actually exists and is subject to no defenses other than those stated. The assignor also warrants that he has no knowledge of any fact that would defeat or impair the value of the assigned right and will do nothing to cause the right to be defeated. Successive assignments of the same right breach this warranty and subject the assignor to liability, but assignors who resell the same right to several people frequently have no visible assets from which to obtain satisfaction of a judgment. Since the obligor only intends to pay his debt once, the issue becomes one of determining which of the successive assignees has priority. Each assignee has parted with value and is innocent of any wrongdoing, yet only one will recover.

Article 9 of the U.C.C. is designed to create a set of rules to facilitate the furnishing of credit secured by personal property. It is a fact that in the United States, most retailers, wholesalers and manufacturers borrow money to operate their businesses. Lending charges are lower if the loans are well secured. One of the most convenient and efficient ways to give security to a lender is to transfer to that lender the right to collect monies due or to become due on the borrower's outstanding contracts. This will be viewed by the lender as good security only if the lender can be satisfied that the borrower has not assigned the same rights to other financial institutions. One clear goal of Article 9 is to provide a way to allow lenders and other interested parties to know whether a party has already assigned its contract rights to others. The solution is to provide a system by which all interested parties will have notice that rights have already been assigned to another person.

Because most assignments of contracts rights have the economic purpose of securing an obligation and because a single set of rules is needed, Article 9 applies to most types of assignments whether they are entered as part of a security transaction or are intended to function as a absolute transfer of the right. Thus while one tends to think of Article 9 as having application only to credit transactions, in fact Article 9 must be consulted if one intends to give value in exchange for the assignment of a contract right.

Article 9 provides specific and definite rules to determine priorities between successive assignees of the same right and between assignees and creditors of the assignor. The common law concept of perfecting a security interest in tangible property by taking possession of that property (a pledge) is preserved. But the principal scheme created by Article 9 is to protect those who obtain signed security agreements from the debtor (assignor) and file in a public office a simple one-page document entitled a "financing statement."

The basic rules are relatively simple. Filing a document (the financing statement) in a public office (usually the Secretary of State) gives notice to all other potential assignees, buyers, lenders and other existing and potential creditors that the contract rights described therein have been assigned or sold. With certain exceptions, priority is given to the person who first filed the financing statement in the public office. There are some significant exceptions where filing is not required. The effect of

Article 9 is to reduce the problem in many cases to determining who first filed a financing statement that covers assignments by the same assignor. Lenders are protected by making certain that they file before money or other valuable property is advanced to the assignor. Of necessity, Article 9 is rather complex, and no one suggests that a student of contract law should know how it works.

In those limited situations in which Article 9 is not controlling, priority among successive assignees is determined by common law rules. The majority rule at common law, the so-called "American rule" provides that the first person who received an irrevocable assignment prevails over all subsequent assignees. The concept is that the assignor transferred the right to the first assignee and had nothing left to transfer to subsequent assignees. An exception or qualification of this rule provides that the first assignee may be estopped from asserting priority if his failure to notify the obligor within a reasonable time resulted in a subsequent assignee being misled. This can occur where the assignor assigned to one assignee who did not give notice to the obligor. Assignor thereafter offers to assign for value to a second assignee who takes the precaution of first checking with the obligor to ascertain that there is a debt that is not yet paid and not yet assigned. If the first assignee's failure to give prompt notice results in the second assignee giving value for the assignment, then estoppel can be raised to preclude the first assignee from asserting his priority. Subsequent assignees have also prevailed when, acting in good faith and without reason to know of a prior assignment, they gave value and obtained payment or a judgment or a new contract in substitution for the assigned obligation or possession of the writing or thing (tokens) that represents the assigned right (§ 12.4)

The minority rule at common law, the so-called "English rule," provides that the first assignee to give notice to the debtor prevails. This rule is based upon the theory that the giving of notice to the debtor is an act that the assignee should perform to perfect his rights as against other assignees or creditors.

§ 12.8 Defenses Available to the Obligor Against the Assignee

An assignment involves a transfer of rights. One basic proposition is that the assignee to whom those rights are transferred can have no better rights than the assignor possessed. This would lead to the general principle that the debtor or obligor can assert against the assignee all of the defenses that the debtor could have asserted against the assignor. However, the Code has created exceptions to this rule.

The basic rule under the Code (§ 9–404) is that a debtor can assert against the assignee:

1) all rights that arise under the contract that created the assigned right, and

2) any other rights that the debtor had against
the assignor so long as these rights were accrued
before the debtor received notice of the assignment.

Application of section 9–404 produces these examples:

Assume that X contracts to paint Y's house for
$6,000. X assigns its right to payment to Bank
which notifies Y and demands that payment be
made directly to Bank.

A) Y may assert against Bank all defenses arising
under the contract, including: X does not paint
the house; X painted the house improperly; X was
an unlicensed contractor; X misrepresented facts
upon which Y relied.

B) Y may assert against Bank all defenses arising
under other transactions provided Y's right to
payment therefore had accrued before notice of
the assignment.

Y may deduct: Y's damages for the tort that X
committed by backing into Y's car before notice of
the assignment; Y's damages for X's failure to pay
Y's fee for legal services rendered by Y for X if this
fee was due and owing before Y received notice of
the assignment.

Y may not deduct: Y's damages for the tort that X
committed by backing into Y's car after Y had
received notice of the assignment to Bank; Y's damages for X's failure to pay Y's fee for legal services

for which Y did not bill until after Y received notice of the assignment.

The defense of payment is available to the debtor so long as payment was made before notice of the assignment and demand for payment by the assignee. After the assignee has demanded that performance be rendered to the assignee, the debtor may no longer make payments to the assignor and claim that the obligation was thereby discharged.

Some common law decisions provided that after notice of assignment, the principal parties to the contract could no longer modify that contract in such a way as to reduce the assignee's rights. U.C.C. section 9–405 expressly changes this rule. Even if there has been an assignment and the assignee has given notice, section 9–405(a) permits modifications that are made in good faith so long as they relate to performances not yet rendered.

Debtors other than consumers may expressly waive defenses against an assignee in the original contract (§ 9–403). When one party to a contract plans to assign rights thereunder (typically a seller of goods or services contemplating assigning the right to payment), that party may seek a contract term in which the buyer waives contract defenses against an assignee. This simple contract term can have far-reaching implications because the buyer can end up paying money to the assignee for defective goods or for goods that were never delivered or services that were never rendered.

B. DELEGATION OF DUTIES
§ 12.9 Delegation of Duties: What Is Delegable

An obligor may properly delegate to another the performance of contract duties so long as the obligee will receive the substantial benefit of the bargain. If the performance to be rendered is one for personal services or otherwise calls for the exercise of skill and discretion, the performance will likely be found to be "too personal" to delegate.

Some performances are of such a nature that they are obviously too personal to delegate, e.g. contracts to teach, to sing or to paint a portrait. Even these duties would be delegable if one were to find that the parties had a contract agreement permitting delegation.

The duty to pay money is delegable. The duty to deliver a fungible good, such as wheat, and similar impersonal activities would also be delegable in the absence of unusual facts that cause the performance to be viewed as personal to the obligor.

Service contracts involving relatively mechanical activities such as painting a house, building a warehouse, or chopping wood would ordinarily be delegable. However, such garden-variety service contracts must be examined in their entirety to determine whether in the particular circumstance the parties contemplated personal performance. Even if one determines that the parties contemplated that the actual performance was to be accomplished by employees, the service may still be too personal to delegate if the duty of supervision is personal to the obligor.

Contracts for professional services such as those of an attorney or a physician are said to involve unique abilities and are thus stated to be non-delegable. However, the retention of the services of an attorney in a law firm would in ordinary circumstances constitute a contract for the services of the firm. Performance by another member of the firm thus does not involve a delegation of duties. A surgeon may properly obtain assistance of another during a lengthy operation and in fact may have an assistant or specialist perform a substantial part of a surgical procedure.

One might assume that contracts with corporations would be delegable in that the corporation would in any event have performance rendered by employees or agents. The parties were no doubt also aware that the ownership and control of the corporation might change during the course of performance of the contract. However, the obligee may have contracted with the corporation in reliance upon the ability and skill of its employees and its supervisors. If this is the case, a delegation by a corporation should be subjected to the usual scrutiny.

The propriety of an attempted delegation of duties in a service contract also involves questions of the skill of the delegatee. A duty that might otherwise be delegable cannot be delegated to one who lacks the capacity or experience to complete the task in a satisfactory manner. For example, a contract to build a cannery to plans and specifications might be delegable to a qualified and experienced cannery builder, but a delegation to one who had no experience in construction of structures of this sort has been found improper, and the attempted performance by the delegatee need not be accepted by the obligee. Conversely, the exceptional qualifications of a particular delegatee may cause the court to find a proper delegation where the delegability of the duty is otherwise questionable. For instance, a delegation by a corporation to its two sole shareholders may not result in any change in the personalities of the parties supervising the performance. A delegation by corporation number one to corporation number two which has purchased the facilities and retained all of the employees of corporation number one has been found not to affect substantially the performance of the contract. In such circumstances, the qualifications of the delegatee may cause the court to find the delegation proper. The ultimate question is whether the obligee can expect to receive substantially the same performance from the delegatee as the obligee had the right to expect from the delegator.

A contract provision that permits delegation will be enforced. Assent by the obligee to a delegation will be enforced if it is given for consideration or if the delegator has changed position in reliance upon the obligee's consent. This might properly be viewed as a waiver of the right to object to the delegation that becomes irrevocable when the other parties rely. (See § 8.6.4.)

A contract provision that prohibits delegation will most likely not be interpreted to prohibit the delegation of a duty that is totally impersonal such as the duty to pay money. However, such a provision expresses the parties' intention to treat the contractual duties as personal to the parties and can make non-delegable a duty that might otherwise have been properly delegated. For example, a contract duty to build a home might ordinarily be delegable, but a provision in that contract requiring performance by the promisor or otherwise expressly prohibiting delegation would likely be enforced. If a duty is delegable, an expression of objection by the obligee after the contract has been made will not prevent a valid delegation nor preclude performance by the delegatee.

§ 12.10 Liability of Delegator and Delegatee

A delegatee does not become liable for the performance of contract duties unless he assumes those duties by expressly or impliedly promising to perform. If the delegatee does assume, the promise to perform creates contract rights in the delegator who may bring an action for its breach. The delegatee's promise to perform also creates contract rights in the obligee who may bring an action as a third party beneficiary of the contract in which the delegatee assumed the duty of performance. Most third party creditor beneficiaries base their rights upon agreements in which a delegatee assumed contract duties (§ 11.2).

A delegator remains liable for the performance of his contract duties despite the fact that the delegatee has assumed them. A denial by the delegator of further obligation under the contract constitutes a repudiation of contract even if the delegatee is competent to perform and expresses willingness to perform.

The obligee may consent to a novation whereby he agrees to accept performance from the delegatee and releases the delegator from further obligation upon the contract. The consideration for the obligee's release of the delegator is the promise of the delegatee to perform (§ 13.3).

If the delegator has repudiated his obligations under the contract, acceptance of performance from the delegatee without an express reservation of rights against the delegator may constitute implied consent by the obligee to a novation. If a duty is non-delegable because of its personal nature, acceptance of performance or part performance with knowledge that it was rendered by a delegatee will constitute a waiver by the obligee of the right to object to the delegation. Other than the above-stated situations, the acceptance by the obligee of performance from the delegatee does not release or waive any rights of the obligee. If a duty is properly delegated, the obligee in fact has no choice but to accept performance by the delegatee. Thus, accepting part performance does not release the delegator from the duty to render the remaining performance. So also, acceptance of goods from a delegatee would not release the delegator from liability for breach of warranty arising from defects in the goods delivered.

When you have completed your study of this chapter, you may wish to analyze questions 33–34 at the end of this book and compare your analysis with the one given there.

CHAPTER 13

DISCHARGE

§ 13.1 Discharge by Performance, Rescission, Release or Contract Not to Sue

The most common manner in which contract duties are discharged is by performance, but there are numerous other methods by which contract obligations can be terminated.

Two parties to a contract may discharge their respective duties by mutually agreeing to rescind their contract so long as a third party's vested rights are not affected. So long as there are executory duties owing on each side, the relinquishment of each party's rights is supported by consideration in the bilateral situation since each is giving up the right to receive performance in exchange for avoiding the duty of performance. Where one party has already fully performed, release of the other by way of "mutual rescission" will raise a consideration issue at common law (§§ 2.24, 2.25, and 2.25.1).

Under the general common law rule, a rescission need be in writing only if the agreement to rescind would produce a transfer of title to land such as the surrender of a long-term lease. With respect to mutual rescissions of leases, real property law must

534

be consulted to determine what is sufficient to constitute the surrender of a leasehold.

An oral rescission is valid even if the statute of frauds requires the contract to be in writing. (See Restatement § 148.) State statutes that provide that a contract in writing can be modified only by another contract in writing, or by an executed oral agreement, have usually been held to apply only to a "modification" and not to rescission. Under common law, a contract can be orally rescinded even though it expressly states it can be modified only by a written document.

The U.C.C. requires that a rescission be in writing if there is a signed agreement which excludes rescission other than by a signed writing. The specific language is in section 2–209(2) which provides:

A signed agreement which excludes modification or rescission except by a signed writing cannot be otherwise modified or rescinded, but except as between merchants such a requirement on a form supplied by the merchant must be separately signed by the other party.

If A has materially breached a contract with B, B has the right to rescind and thereby discharge all rights and duties under the contract. (If B has conferred benefits upon A, B may have an action against A in restitution. See § 10.1.) B also has the right to declare a total breach, thereby relieving himself from the obligation to perform or to accept further performances from A but preserving his right to damages for breach of the entire contract.

If B wishes to preserve the right to collect damages as distinguished from restitution, B should not be seeking to "rescind" the contract. If the victim of a material breach responds by stating that the contract is "rescinded," there is the risk that a court may interpret that term literally and thereby deny the victim any right to recover damages for the breach.

Mutual rescission can also contain a hidden trap. X agrees to harvest 1,000 acres of wheat for Y for a stated price per acre. After X has harvested 50 acres, the contract is "rescinded" by mutual agreement. Under the prevailing common law view, there is no presumption or inference that X has preserved the right to collect at the contract price for the work performed. However, X may still have a right to recover in restitution for the reasonable value of benefits conferred even if the parties did not preserve any rights under the rescinded contract.

The U.C.C. avoids these problems in transactions in goods by providing that when the parties mutually terminate a contract or when either party puts an end to a contract for breach by the other, unless the contrary intention clearly appears, remedies for breach of contract are preserved (§§ 2–106(3) and (4) and 2–720).

The term "release" is used to describe a writing by which a duty owed to the person who signs the writing is discharged. The attempted release of all or part of an obligation without any bargained exchange has been a problem in the common law at least since the case of *Foakes v. Beer* was decided in 1884 (§ 2.27). Some states have provided by statute for the release in writing of all or part of an obligation without consideration. U.C.C. section 1–107 permits a written release without consideration, and this section applies to all matters within any article of the U.C.C. Some states have dispensed with the requirement of consideration by case law if the release is evidenced by a signed writing.

Contracts not to sue are the invention of necessity. Common law decisions hold that a release, rescission or accord and satisfaction that discharges one co-obligor will release other co-obligors whose liability is founded upon a joint duty to perform the obligation in question. The old saying was, "A release of one, was a release of all." To avoid this result, the obligee may enter into a contract not to sue. As the name implies, this involves promising one co-obligor that no action will be maintained against him. This promise is given legal effect, but does not release other persons who might be obligated to perform the same duty. The liability of the other obligors is reduced by the amount paid for the contract not to sue. The Restatement section 295(2) takes the position that words that purport to release or discharge while reserving rights against another co-obligor should be interpreted as a contract not to sue. This would have the effect of preserving the liability of the other obligors in accordance with the stated intention of the person to whom the obligation is owing. Many states have reached the same result by statute. Even where rules have been adopted to protect a creditor in such situations, the law of suretyship will cause the release of a surety in certain circumstances in which the obligee discharges the principal obligor, but, as to negotiable instruments, U.C.C. section 3–605(b) allows the release of a principal to occur without discharge of a surety.

§ 13.2 Discharge by Substitute Contract or by Satisfaction of an Accord Agreement

Substituted contracts and accord agreements look a lot alike. Both involve the situation in which a debtor (the obligor) owes a duty but enters into an agreement with his creditor (the obligee) to perform some different duty instead. A owes B $25 which A has been unable to pay. The parties agree that A will wax B's car instead of paying $25. The only difficult question is determining whether this agreement is a substituted contract (which results in the immediate discharge of the duty to pay $25) or is an accord agreement (in which case there is no immediate discharge of the duty to pay the $25). The difference becomes significant if A fails to wax the car, and B sues A in small claims court. If the agreement to wax the car was a substituted contract, then B must prove the value of one wax job and that is the amount of B's damages. If the agreement to wax the car was only an accord, then the $25 obligation is not yet discharged. The result is that B may choose to enforce either obligation.

In order to determine what the parties intended, it is appropriate to focus upon the results that they apparently sought. If the parties intended that the new agreement would replace the old one, this is a substituted contract resulting in an immediate discharge of the prior obligation. This would be the most likely result if the contract is an executory bilateral contract and both parties' duties are being changed. If the obligee agrees to accept the substituted performance, but does not agree to an immediate discharge, then this is only an accord agreement. This will be the most likely interpretation if the debtor is having difficulty performing or is already in breach and the creditor is apparently accepting the alternative performance in an effort to salvage whatever is possible from the situation. Ultimately, one must look to the entire circumstances and determine whether the parties did or did not intend an immediate discharge of the existing obligation.

Accords are most easily understood with a simple example. Assume that A owes B $700. A offers to give B seven tons of hay in lieu of the $700, and B accepts this offer. On these facts, it would likely be found that no immediate discharge is intended. Therefore, the parties have entered into an accord agreement. The making of this accord does not discharge the duty to pay the $700. (Had the parties manifested the intention that there be an immediate discharge of the duty to pay $700, then their agreement would properly be interpreted to be a substituted contract.)

When A delivers the hay to B, thus performing the accord, this is termed the satisfaction. The satisfaction operates as a discharge of the original obligation to pay $700 as well as a discharge of the obligation to deliver the hay. If the hay is not delivered to B, B has the election to sue on the accord agreement for breach of the promise to deliver the hay or to sue for the $700 which was originally owing since that obligation is not yet discharged.

An agreement to compromise a disputed claim is frequently found to be intended by the parties to operate only as an accord agreement. This accord will be satisfied (and all obligations discharged) when the agreed upon settlement is paid. If no payment is made, the creditor would be free to sue on the accord agreement (for the compromise sum) or bring action for the full amount the creditor claims to be due.

The making of the accord agreement does not discharge the original obligation, but the better rule holds that the making of the accord suspends the original obligation until the obligor has had time to perform.

§ 13.3 Discharge by Novation

A common law novation is a three-party transaction involving the original parties to the contract plus a newcomer. By agreement of the three parties, one of the original parties to the contract is removed from the transaction and the newcomer is substituted in his place.

There are four elements of a valid novation:

(1) There must be a previous obligation;

(2) There must be a mutual agreement of all parties to the old and the new contract;

(3) There must be an apparent intention immediately to extinguish the duties of the parties under the old contract; and,

(4) The new contract must be valid and enforceable.

Assume that Harry has a one-year contract to wash Al's windows once a week for $100. Al sells his store to Betty. Al and Betty meet with Harry and it is agreed that:

(1) Harry will continue to wash the windows for Betty;

(2) Betty will pay $100 per week for this service;

(3) Harry will have no future contract rights against Al; and,

(4) Al will have no future contract rights against Harry.

A novation differs from a simple assignment and delegation in that in a delegation, the delegator (Al in the example) remains liable as a guarantor for the contract performance. In a novation, the original party to the contract (Al) is discharged and has no further rights or liability.

Assume that at the time Al sold the store to Betty, Al introduced Betty to Harry, the window washer. The evidence concerning the precise conversation will probably be vague and contradictory, but Al said something about being happy to be relieved of further concerns about the store and Harry did say something about being pleased to deal with Betty. The problem of interpretation of this transaction will arise if Betty fails to pay Harry for his services.

Assuming that Al was simply informing Harry that Al had assigned his rights and delegated his duties to Betty and Harry was stating that he did not object, then as a delegator, Al remains liable on the contract with Harry. Harry has not manifested his assent to releasing Al from further liability on the contract. Harry would have had no right to object to the assignment and delegation on these facts, but informing Harry of the transaction is an appropriate thing to do.

However, if one can find that Al and Betty were proposing to Harry that Betty would assume liability on the contract if Harry would assent to the release of Al, then Harry's expression of approval would create a novation and Al would have no further rights or duties. Al is discharged because Harry has assented to accept Betty as the sole party responsible for payment for his services. Each of the three parties has incurred a legal detriment and consideration requirements are thus fulfilled. Al has lost his right to have his windows washed, Harry has lost his right to collect from Al, and Betty has become obligated to pay for Harry's services.

Some states including California have statutes that define novation as the substitution of a new obligation for an existing one. As thus defined, the term "novation" is being used to describe a substituted contract and would thus apply to two party transactions (West's Ann. Cal. Civil Code § 1530 et seq.).

§ 13.4   Discharge by Account Stated

An account stated is an agreement by the creditor and debtor to the accuracy of a stated sum as the amount due. If a debtor has purchased items from a creditor or otherwise incurred obligations to a creditor and the creditor sends the debtor a statement of account, the act of keeping the statement for a period of time without objection manifests assent by the debtor to be bound by its terms. The account can also be stated by the debtor or may be reached by mutual efforts of the parties. The creditor can sue upon this "account stated."

Assume that a customer has charged various items at a store on a weekly basis for two years. Periodic payments have been made on this account but the balance has never been reduced to zero. The importance of account stated will be appreciated if one contemplates the evidence that would have to be produced at trial if a merchant sued on the more than 100 contracts which the parties have made. Proof of each sale, of each charge, of each returned item, and of each payment would be cumbersome.

Suit on an account stated permits the case to be established by proving that:

(1) the defendant opened an account and charged some items;

(2) the plaintiff sent periodic statements of this account; and,

(3) the customer impliedly assented to the accuracy of these statements by failing to object.

It is essential that the parties have had at least one previous transaction, i.e., a statement cannot create liability where none previously existed. An account stated cannot supersede a promissory note since such a note is viewed as better evidence of the debt than the account stated.

The statement of an account is not a compromise of a disputed claim. It is an admission by both parties that a certain amount is due. It may be attacked as the product of a mistake or misrepresentation, but the burden of establishing such mistake or misrepresentation is upon the attacking party. The party seeking to enforce the account has the benefit of not having to prove individual items of the obligation.

It has frequently been held that an account stated operates as a discharge of the underlying obligation even though the account has not yet been paid. However, Restatement section 282(2) states: "The account stated does not itself discharge any duty but is an admission by each party of the facts asserted and a promise by the debtor to pay according to its terms." In the Reporter's Note, the Restatement provides: "Whether an agreement has the effect of discharge, formerly attributed to an account stated, is now determined under the rules relating to substituted contracts ... and accords...." (See section 13.2.)

§ 13.5   Miscellaneous Concepts That May Serve as Methods of Discharge

Duties under a voidable contract may be discharged by an exercise of the power of avoidance (Chapter 5).

If a contract deals with an illegal subject matter or has some other aspect of illegality, the defendant can discharge or avoid his liability by asserting illegality as a defense or the court may raise illegality on its own (§ 5.11). (In theory this may be a recognition that no legal duty ever existed rather than the discharge of an existing duty.)

The mere making of a contract for the benefit of a third party creditor beneficiary does not discharge the promisee's duty owed to the creditor, but such a duty is discharged when the promisor renders performance to the creditor beneficiary. Stated another way, the mere delegation of a delegable duty does not extinguish the delegator's duty, but performance by the delegatee will discharge the obligation (§ 12.10). Performance to an assignee also discharges the obligor's duty to the assignor.

If an obligor files a petition in bankruptcy and the trustee does not elect to continue performance, all contractual duties over and above what is paid in the proceedings are discharged.

Under the minority rule, the running of the time set for the bringing of an action for a breach of contract effectively discharges contractual duties, although it is the majority rule that the running of the statute bars only the remedy and does not discharge the debt (§ 2.39.1).

In certain situations, contract obligations may be discharged by the rejection of a valid, unconditional tender. (Compare § 8.6.1 and 8.9.) If the tender is accepted there is, of course, literal performance. The rejection of a proper tender discharges, at least temporarily, the duty of the party who made the tender to perform further, but if time is not of the essence, such a rejection results in only a temporary suspension of the duty of performance, and performance may be demanded within a reasonable time. The tender of money for a consideration not yet received may also provide only a temporary discharge. To illustrate, suppose S contracts to sell a car to B for $12,000. Time for performance is not specified. A tender of payment by B on July 1 only temporarily suspends his duty. B will still have to perform if S, within a reasonable time, tenders performance and gives B time in which to perform. But B's duty to perform would be permanently discharged if performance were due on July 1 and time was found to be of the essence.

If an obligor owes a duty to pay money for a consideration already received, a rejected tender of the payment does not discharge the debt, but it does stop the running of interest. Suppose R owes E $100. On July 1, R tenders E $100 in cash which E rejects. Although the debt is not discharged, E is not entitled to interest after July 1.

The release of a principal releases the surety because a release of the principal tends to militate against the interests of the surety. An actual release is not necessary. Anything that "tends to militate against the interest of the surety" discharges the surety's duties. To illustrate, suppose R owes E $100. R delegates to D the duty to pay E and D assumes the debt. D thereby becomes primarily liable and R becomes a surety. If E were to release D, R would be discharged. However, if there is a negotiable instrument involved, U.C.C. section 3–605 would be applicable and would preclude discharge of the surety.

If a judgment is obtained for breach of a contractual duty, the duty to perform under the contract is "merged" into the judgment and is discharged. A second action on the contractual duty will not lie, and enforcement must proceed on the judgment.

The occurrence of a true condition subsequent (§ 8.5) discharges the existing duty which was subject to that condition.

CHAPTER 14

CONTRACTS QUESTIONS

Most of the following materials are based upon portions of questions taken from bar examinations administered in the United States. The primary function of these questions is to provide practice in issue identification. The commentary answers are neither models nor suggested as required modes of response. If these admonitions are kept in mind, the problems can be valuable in making a determination of your proficiency.

Questions are grouped around subject matter so that they may be analyzed after different blocks of material are completed.

Questions 1 through 10 deal with
offer and acceptance issues
in contract formation.

No. 1

P and D, who were acquainted with each other, resided in communities separated by 100 miles. On February 1, P wrote to D as follows: "Dear D. I have decided to give up my farm, Blackacre, and move to the city. I thought you might consider buying it from me. I would like to get $175,000 out of it. I'll let you have ten days to think about it and talk it over with your spouse. I know both of you would be very happy here. (signed) P." Does this communication constitute a valid offer, and if so, is it irrevocable for a period of 10 days?

An offer must manifest an intention to be presently bound and must create in the offeree the power to form a binding contract by an appropriate acceptance (§§ 2.1 and 2.7). P's letter indicates an intention to sell the farm, but the central question is whether P manifests an intent to be presently bound subject only to acceptance by D. There are no words of promise or commitment to sell to D. There is no direct statement that P considers himself bound to D if D assents, only that P wants to sell to someone and thought D might like to buy. You can test your thinking on this issue by simply considering the question whether you think P should be free to sell his farm to X the next day without having to worry about whether D might have already sent an acceptance. Conditional language ("would" and "thought you might") tends to negate finding an intention to be presently bound.

The most compelling argument in favor of finding an offer is the statement that D will have 10 days to think it over. If P did not intend to give D the power to form a contract by accepting, then there would be no reason to give D a 10 day limit. The ultimate question is what a reasonable person in D's position should understand to be P's intention.

An offer must also be sufficiently definite that when properly accepted, a court will be able to discern what agreement is to be enforced. Traditionally courts require a relatively high degree of certainty for contracts involving an interest in real property. Assuming that "I would like to get $175,-000 out of it," can be interpreted to mean that P is proposing a price of $175,000 (as distinguished from netting $175,000 after costs of sale), the price term is probably sufficient. If "Blackacre" is an identifiable parcel of land known to the parties, the subject matter term is sufficient. The price is implied to be cash payable on delivery of the deed, and these performances are due in a reasonable time. While real property contracts usually cover a multitude of other details, local custom or usage will probably suffice to supply these terms. However, failure to include standard details commonly found in an offer to sell land can have a bearing upon whether one finds that P manifested an intent to be presently bound. Absence of terms may be some indication of intent to have further negotiations.

Promises to hold offers open can be enforceable if made for consideration (§ 2.6.1), but there is no such bargain in the given facts. Promissory estoppel can be utilized to make an offer irrevocable (§§ 2.6.2 and 2.42), but there are no facts indicating a change of position by the offeree in reliance upon the promise not to revoke. Firm offers by merchants to sell goods can be irrevocable pursuant to U.C.C. section 2–205 (§ 2.6.3), but Article 2 does not apply to land transactions. At least one jurisdiction has a statute which enforces promises not to revoke regardless of subject matter, but in the absence of such a statute, the promise not to revoke is not enforceable.

No. 2

S wrote P: "I have in mothballs six milling machines that I have not been able to use for three years. They are in good condition and may be inspected in my shop anytime this month. But I do plan to get rid of them one way or another during that time. Please let me know right away if you are interested at my price of $18,000 for the six." Has S made an offer to P?

Contracts for the sale of goods need not be definite as to all terms (§ 2.2.1), but there must still be a manifestation of intent to be bound to find an offer (§ 2.1). People tend to be less formal in transactions in goods, and intent to be bound is not dependent upon any formal words or phrases, but it still must appear to a reasonable person in the position of P that S has communicated a willingness to be presently bound to sell to P.

S stated that he is going to "get rid of them one way or another during (this month)" which tends to indicate that S may sell them to anyone at any time. This negates an intention to be presently bound to P because that would require that S refrain from selling the goods to another pending P's response. "Please let me know right away if you are interested" also connotes an inquiry. This communication would probably be characterized as a preliminary negotiation or solicitation for an offer. Additional facts regarding prior course of dealing might change this result but one cannot assume such facts as course of dealing or usage of trade unless they are given.

No. 3

X made an offer in writing to B to sell his store for $130,000. B wrote X: "Accept your offer. This contract should be reduced to writing and signed by us." Is there an enforceable contract?

You are given the fact that X made an offer, thus it is established that whatever additional terms that may be needed for the offer were contained in the communication from X. The question to be resolved is whether the parties have manifested an intention to be presently bound or whether one of them has simply manifested a desire to enter into a contract and an intention to be bound as soon as a written contract is prepared and signed. The common source of error in these problems results from failure to place proper emphasis on the need to find an intent to be *presently* bound.

If it is evident that there are further terms to be negotiated or if there is some prospective difficulty in sorting out precisely what has been agreed to in the course of negotiations, then the request that a complete writing be drafted and signed may indicate that a further or final assent to be bound is necessary. In the given facts, the offer is contained in one writing and the offeree's assent is unqualified. Thus it does not appear that there are terms yet to be agreed upon. There could be further details that might be resolved in the process of preparing a formal contract, but none are indicated in the facts. Thus we can find assent to be presently bound, and the signed written contract is intended as a formality. B used language ("accept your offer") that connotes present intent to be bound, and the anticipation of a formal writing does not preclude finding that the parties are already bound to a contract (§§ 2.1 and 2.1.2).

The common law ordinarily denies enforcement of "agreements to agree" where further negotiation of terms is contemplated. The facts are unclear as to whether the subject matter of the contract (his "store") is goods. The U.C.C. provides that parties can effectively assent to be bound prior to completion of their negotiation of terms, however even under the U.C.C. if one found that one of the parties has manifested a desire not to be bound until a formal document is signed, there would be no contract yet.

No. 4

A entered into an agreement with B, an artist, on January 2, whereby B agreed to paint A's portrait. The price was to be mutually arranged by A and B on January 9. On January 7, A repudiated. Is there a contract?

If Article 2 of the U.C.C. applied to this transaction, the sole issue would be whether the parties intended to be bound before the price was fixed. There would be sufficient certainty to enforce a contract because the court could substitute a reasonable price at the time of delivery if the parties failed to agree (§ 2.2.1 and U.C.C. § 2–305). However, since the dominant nature of this transaction appears to be services rather than goods, Article 2 would not apply, and the absence of agreement upon an essential term such as price might prevent finding a contract. The traditional common law approach required that the parties must agree on price (and other terms) or provide a method for fixing the price.

The trend in the common law is now toward following the U.C.C. approach (§ 2.17). Thus if the court finds that the parties manifested to each other an intent to be presently bound before agreeing on price, a court could supply the price term and enforce the contract. Consideration must be given to the practical problem faced by the court. How does one fix the reasonable value of an artist's services? The difficulty of this task might cause a court to note the wisdom of not extending the U.C.C. approach to services of this nature.

No. 5

On January 3, B wrote A that he would paint A's portrait for $3,000. On the same day A, without knowledge of B's letter, wrote B that he would pay $3,000 if B would paint his portrait. Is there a contract?

Identical offers which cross in transmission do not create contracts as neither party is exercising a power to accept (§ 2.4). However, if this involved goods, the U.C.C. provides that a contract can be found even though the moment of its making is undetermined. This principle might be applied by analogy to a service contract. If the facts indicated that the parties had engaged in some further conduct that recognized the existence of a contract, this result would be easier to reach.

No. 6

S sent an offer to B which stated: "Will sell No. 2 winter wheat up to 10,000 tons at $180 a ton for delivery during January." B wrote S: "Would $175 per ton be agreeable for 5,000 tons?" Two days later B changed his mind and wrote: "Send 5,000 tons of wheat at your price." Both messages arrived in regular course of mail. Does B have enforceable rights against S?

Since S's communication is characterized as an offer in the question, this is a given legal conclusion and need not be discussed. It might be noted that where a term such as quantity is left to the offeree, a valid contract can result when the offeree makes the appropriate selection. B's first response inquires whether S would accept a lower price, and the first problem is to determine whether this communication is an acceptance, a counteroffer or a mere inquiry.

To be either an acceptance or a counteroffer, B's first response must manifest an intent to be presently bound to some terms. B's first response uses conditional language ("would") and is in the form of a question. B commits to nothing and is thus not making an expression of acceptance nor making a counteroffer.

Assuming this first response is a mere inquiry, does B's second communication form a contract? This is an unequivocal acceptance within the terms of the offer, thus it forms a contract if the offer is still open. The question is whether the offer lapsed by passage of time. Where no time is stated, offers are open for a reasonable time. The facts do not indicate how S's offer was communicated. If sent by fax or like means, this would be a relevant factor pointing to a very short period of time for acceptance. When dealing with commodities that fluctuate in market price such as grain, the reasonable period for acceptance would be quite short in any event, perhaps a few hours or even a few minutes. We are not given the delay involved in B's first response, but we do know that the second response was "two days later." This would likely be an excessive delay and a court would thus find that S's offer had lapsed before an effective acceptance was made.

If B's first response were found to manifest an intent to be bound, it could operate as an acceptance if it is a definite and seasonable expression of acceptance under 2–207(1). However, it is not likely that a court would find that a response which proposes a reduced price is an "expression of acceptance." This does not indicate that B is attempting to conclude a bargain.

B's first response might be viewed as a counteroffer if one can conclude that B is intending to be bound to buy 5,000 tons at the lower ($175) price. If it is a counteroffer, it would serve to reject S's offer.

B's second response would be another offer and no contract would result.

No. 7

P mailed to D an offer on the 1st and it arrived on the 2nd. On the 10th, P mailed a revocation, which would ordinarily be delivered on the 11th but which was in fact delivered at 2:00 on the 12th. D mailed an acceptance at 1:30 on the 12th. The letter of acceptance was never received. Was a contract formed?

In the absence of a stated time, an offer is effective for a reasonable time. This may or may not extend to 10 days after the receipt of the offer depending upon the nature of the subject matter, the identity and circumstances of the parties and other facts which might affect this determination. Since the offer was sent by mail, it is apparent that the subject matter is not likely something with a volatile market and one might assume in the absence of other facts that a 10 day period for acceptance is not unreasonable. The fact that P thought it appropriate to mail a revocation on the 10th is some indication of an intent that the offer remain open at least to that time (§ 2.5).

With the possible exception of four states (N.D., S.D., MT. and CA.) which adopted the Field Code, revocations are not effective until received by the offeree. There is no basis for placing the risk of delay or loss in transmission upon the offeree; thus, the offer was not effectively revoked prior to the time at which the acceptance was sent. Acceptances are effective upon dispatch if sent by an authorized means (older case law) or by any medium reasonable under the circumstances. Therefore, a contract was formed at 1:30 on the 12th. The fact that the acceptance was never received does not terminate the contract nor preclude its enforcement (§ 2.10). In this case risk of non-delivery or delay in delivery of the acceptance is borne by the offeror because the offeror authorized the means employed for communication or at least failed to specify a different means.

No. 8

A sent to B an offer by letter. B wired acceptance. Is a contract formed when the wire is sent?

The common law rule required that an acceptance be sent by an authorized means, and the means which was used by the offeror would be impliedly authorized. From this it was reasoned by some courts that a method which was faster than that used by the offeror would also be impliedly authorized. Others took the opposite position holding that a mailed offer did not authorize acceptance by wire. The U.C.C. section 2–206 and the Restatement place the emphasis on the reasonableness of the medium used. Assuming that a court were to find that acceptance by wire was reasonable under the circumstances, the contract would be formed when the acceptance is sent. If wire is found to be an unauthorized medium for acceptance, then the acceptance will be effective when the wire is received. Under the Restatement if the wire is received within the time that a letter would have been received, then it becomes operative as of its time of dispatch (§ 2.19 and Restatement § 67).

An analogous problem is created if the offeree accepts by letter entrusted to a private delivery service such as Fed Ex or DHL. Another modern version of this old fact pattern will involve facsimile transmissions, E–Mail, and other methods yet to be invented. To determine when acceptances sent by electronic means are effective, the court should consider the same issues. Use of instantaneous communications will reduce the problems resulting from the ordinary time lapse involved when letters are sent by post. There is still the question of which party should bear whatever risk of delay or risk of non-delivery that is inherent in the method used. The problem might be complicated—or perhaps resolved—in cases in which the delay resulted from equipment failure attributable to one of the parties.

No. 9

The Law Book Co. sent a letter to X, a young attorney: "We are sending you herewith a set of state reports. If you will compile a digest for us of all the workers' compensation decisions therein, you may keep the books free of charge." X promptly began work. Later, after working six months, she received a letter from the Law Book Co. stating: "We have changed our minds about the digest, and so must withdraw our offer. Please return the reports to us at once, or start paying for them." X retained the books and finished the digest two months later. The company refused the digest and instituted suit to recover the price of the books. What result?

X is performing a service for goods, and the U.C.C. can be applied to this transaction (U.C.C. § 2–304(1)). Since there was no communication of an acceptance by X, she will have a contract for research work only if the offer is interpreted as one which permits acceptance by performance rather than requiring a return promise. Where the offeror does not indicate unambiguously how acceptance is to be accomplished, the modern approach is to permit the offeree to accept by either method, thus X may well have chosen an effective means by which to accept (§ 2.9.3). U.C.C. section 2–206 supports this result.

Older common law cases imposed no requirement upon an offeree to notify the offeror that performance had been commenced. There were cases which indicated that the offeree must use reasonable effort to notify the offeror after performance was complete if the offeror had no convenient way of learning this fact (§ 2.10.1). U.C.C. section 2–206(2) would now control this situation. X's failure to notify the offeror within a reasonable period of time permits the offeror to treat the offer as having lapsed before acceptance. If this were treated as a contract for services, Restatement section 54 would be applicable. It provides that the contractual duty of the offeror would be discharged due to lack of notice of the performance unless (a) the offeree exercised reasonable diligence to notify the offeror of acceptance, or (b) the offeror learned of the performance within a reasonable time, or (c) the offer indicated that notification of acceptance was not required.

Since X does not have an enforceable contract for her services as the price of the books, retention of the books with knowledge that Law Book Co. is offering them for a dollar price would manifest assent to pay that price. X would be liable.

No. 10

Jones, a homeowner, wrote to the ABC Air Conditioning Co. asking the price, installed, of ABC's standard unit, the X–12. A salesman at ABC telephoned Jones on September 4, in reply to his letter and said that a special off-season price would be quoted, including installation. Later that day, the sales manager of ABC sent a telegram to Jones which, when received, read as follows: "We would furnish the X–12 delivered to your home for $898. Letter follows."

The letter which followed stated:

"You have been advised of the special price on the X–12, as per our telegram, for your immediate acceptance. Enclosed is a catalog giving full particulars as to our established policies and warranties on our products."

The catalog contained a list price of $1,898 for the X–12 unit and a statement that "all prices quoted are exclusive of installation."

Jones signed and returned the letter by mail the same day with this endorsement: "Accepted. Sept. 6. J.B. Jones. P.S. Shipment must be immediate."

The next day, before the letter was actually received by ABC, the telegraph company advised ABC that, through the telegraph company's mistake, the wire stated a price of $898 instead of $1,498. ABC immediately telephoned Jones and told him that the price quote should have been $1,498; that is, $400 off the regular list price of $1,898 quoted in the catalog.

Discuss the rights of Jones.

This is a transaction in goods, and the communications from ABC appear to manifest the necessary intent and are sufficiently definite to constitute an offer. Jones can properly consider the initial phone call, the telegram, the letter and the catalog to find the manifestation of ABC's intent to be presently bound. While mere price quotes are usually not offers, this was a specific response to an inquiry (§ 2.3), and the specific language "for your immediate acceptance" also indicates that this is more than a price quote. Acceptance by return promise is appropriate.

Jones' reply manifests assent to the offer, but Jones also appears to add the term "immediate shipment." Under U.C.C. section 2–207(1), this expression of acceptance with an additional term would operate as an acceptance. It could also be stated that contracts for sale of goods require delivery within a reasonable time. In the case of an off-the-shelf item, a reasonable time should be rather brief, particularly where the seller is pushing the item as a special and thus presumably has stock on hand. Thus it might be argued that "immediate shipment" is consistent with the terms of ABC's offer and Jones' response is a proper acceptance.

Assuming Jones' response is an acceptance, it would be effective on dispatch assuming that mail is a reasonable medium under these circumstances.

While ABC is usually bound by the communication as delivered despite the error of the telegraph company, a court might reach the conclusion that Jones should have known that $898 was too low even for an off-season special. If Jones knew or should have known that the communication was the product of a mistake, then Jones has no reasonable expectations to protect. Jones cannot snap up a purported offer which he knows to be the product of a mistake (§ 5.5, et seq.).

The ABC salesman orally promised free installation but the catalog stated that prices did not include that service. The telegram also stated the price as "delivered to your home" and in his acceptance, Jones stated: "Shipment (not installation) must be immediate." When there are inconsistencies, later communications ordinarily control over earlier communications. However, Jones can assert that a general statement in a catalog should not supersede an express representation by the ABC salesman and that catalog terms should not apply in any event because this transaction wan an off-season special that varied from catalog terms. While the letter and accompanying catalog that ABC sent and Jones signed is not a complete written integration, the catalog term stating that installation is not included could prevail over the prior oral promise to install. This issue might go either way.

Questions 11–17 deal with consideration
and the alternative of enforcement
based upon reliance.

No. 11

A believed in good faith that he had rights based upon adverse possession of Whiteacre. In fact, Whiteacre belonged to B, and A had no ownership interest in it. A sent a letter to B: "Will sell you my interest in Whiteacre for $10,000. If I do not hear from you within ten days, I will assume that you have accepted." Is a contract formed when B does not respond?

A does not acquire enforceable rights against B under the stated facts because in the absence of special circumstances, silence will not constitute acceptance. There is no course of dealing between the parties and the offeree has not engaged in any conduct from which assent could be implied, thus A cannot enforce any contract against B. B might be able to enforce the contract if B subjectively intended to accept since A's communication expressly authorized this (§ 2.21).

A's release of the invalid claim can be consideration since A had a good faith belief in its validity. The legal detriment can be found in A giving up his right to bring an action to attempt to establish his rights in the property. Some jurisdictions would impose an additional requirement that A's belief be founded upon some credible facts (§ 2.26). If there were any facts indicating, for example, that A had occupied or used Whiteacre, that would satisfy this requirement and consideration could be found if B made any promise to pay.

No. 12

The Rex Co. was under a binding contract with Jones to pay a monthly rent of $10,000 for a drugstore, for three years, beginning January 1, 1999. The Rex Co. paid $10,000 on January 1 and February 1. During the month of February, with permission of Jones, Rex Co. greatly improved the rented premises at its own expense. On February 27, Jones told the Rex Co.: "I am happy about these improvements. They have added to the value of the building. I am going to reduce your rent to $8,000 per month." That same day an agreement was signed by both Jones and the Rex Co. reducing the rent to $8,000. Could Jones later insist on collecting the original $10,000 per month?

The parties have voluntarily agreed to a modification of the lease which is enforceable if the consideration requirement can be satisfied. Consideration involves legal detriment incurred as a bargained exchange for a return promise. Thus, what one did yesterday cannot serve as consideration for a promise made today. As it is sometimes imperfectly stated, "Past consideration is no consideration"

(§ 2.25.1). The improvements made by Rex were not undertaken as part of any bargain, and the promise by Jones to reduce the rent was not made as part of any bargain, thus classical consideration appears to be lacking.

On the facts given, Rex Co. has not made any change of position in reliance upon the promise to reduce the rent, thus promissory estoppel does not provide a basis for enforcing the promise (§ 2.41).

In the absence of a statute which permits modification of contracts without consideration, Rex could remain liable for the full $10,000 per month.

The modern approach is to find a way to enforce contract modifications that are reasonable and are made freely, in good faith, and without duress. The problem presented is to find a theory to justify this result. Alternatives include:

1. In transactions in goods, the U.C.C. enforces modifications without consideration.

2. Some common law decisions enforce modifications by implying a rescission of the old contract and a making of a new one, however, in the case of a lease, it would be quite a fiction to find a surrender of the old lease under these facts.

3. If there are any facts from which one might conclude that the party seeking to enforce the modification had a basis for avoiding the contract or seeking additional compensation for its enforcement, most case law now finds that the party impliedly gave up this right thereby finding a

bargain to support the modification. There are no facts to indicate that Rex Co. had any theory under which it might avoid the original lease.

4. Finally, Restatement section 89 would enforce any modification that is fair and equitable in view of circumstances not anticipated by the parties when the contract was made. This provision is limited to situations in which neither party has fully performed which might make it inapplicable to a lease if one assumes that the landlord's only duty was to give the tenant possession. The facts do not indicate that any unanticipated circumstances have arisen.

Traditional law makes the bare promise to reduce the rent unenforceable, but since most modern commentators consider this to be an inappropriate result, a proper answer would explore every viable theory to enforce the modification, however Rex Co. has a tough case to argue on these facts. This analysis is further developed in the next question.

No. 13

On June 1, O and C entered into a written contract in which C promised to build a road for O according to certain specifications, and O promised to pay C $200,000 upon completion of the job. The written contract included a promise by C to complete the road by January 1. C commenced work immediately, but soon discovered that the roadbed was rockier than he had expected, which fact, together with unusually wet weather, threatened C with considerable additional expense. In August, C called upon O and told O of these circumstances and informed O that he (C) would abandon performance unless a satisfactory adjustment of these difficulties could be made. After some discussion O and C drew up another written agreement, the terms of the new agreement being the same as those of the old except that O promised to pay $290,000. On December 28, C completed the job according to specifications. O has informed C that O will pay only 200,000. What are C's rights against O?

C had a preexisting duty to build the road pursuant to the original C–O contract. O will contend that C was incurring no new detriment and O obtained no new benefit in exchange for O's promise to pay the additional $90,000, and it is unenforceable for lack of consideration. Nor will promissory estoppel apply because by doing what he was already obligated to do, C has not changed position to his detriment.

The facts indicate that C encountered more rocks and bad weather than anticipated and that O's promise was freely made and not induced by duress or bad faith conduct of C. This presents two distinct theories upon which C might rely to find adequate consideration for O's promise.

1) There is case law supporting the proposition that the promise of an owner (or other recipient of a service) to pay extra money is enforceable where the contractor (or other service provider) has encountered unforeseen difficulties. C can establish these

facts. These decisions limit enforcement to additional amounts that are reasonable under the circumstances, and the facts are insufficient to establish whether this requirement could be met by C. Restatement section 89(a) would permit C to enforce the contract modification if that modification is fair and equitable in view of circumstances not anticipated by the parties when the contract was made.

2) If C had a legal excuse from the duty to perform the contract, then giving up the right to avoid the contract could be a legal detriment incurred in exchange for O's promise to pay $290,000. This requires an analysis of the facts to determine whether performance had become impossible or impracticable under the circumstances (§§ 6.1.1 and 6.2). While the facts are incomplete, this result seems unlikely. However, the difficulties need only be of sufficient magnitude to provide a good faith claim of excuse (§ 2.26). Settlement of that good faith claim can be valid consideration. If one has a good faith belief founded upon some facts that he had the right to terminate his performance under a contract, then his agreement to forbear from asserting this right could serve as consideration for O's promise to pay the additional $90,000.

No. 14

C was bound by an enforceable bilateral contractual obligation to build a road for O. After partly performing, C stopped. N, a neighbor of O who would be benefitted by completion of the road, said to C: "If you will finish the job, I'll pay you $5,000."

C agreed and finished the job. What are C's rights against N?

Assuming that N's communication is an offer, it matters not whether it calls for a promise or for performance as C did both. The central question is whether there was consideration for N's promise.

Legal detriment involves doing or promising to do that which one was not previously legally obligated to do. Under the concept of preexisting duty, it can be reasoned that since C already had a legally enforceable obligation to build the road, C incurred no legal detriment in doing so, and thus there is no consideration for N's promise to pay. This is the traditional result even though the duty was owing to O rather than to N.

If C had an opportunity to enter a mutual rescission with O or had some other opportunity (such as impossibility or impracticability) to avoid further duties under the C–O contract, then it could be reasoned that N was making his offer to induce C to forego this opportunity. If one finds that C promised to forebear or did forbear rescinding or avoiding the C–O contract as a bargained exchange for N's promise, then consideration can be found and the promise can be enforced (§ 2.25.1).

There is also authority for limiting the preexisting duty rule to apply only to duties owing to this specific promisor. Since C had no legal duty owing to N, the mutual agreement whereby C would build and N would pay would be supported by consideration under this approach (Restatement § 73, comment d).

No. 15

X, a wealthy lawyer friend of B, promised that if B would attend law school and study a minimum of fifty hours a week, X would pay B $25,000 at the end of each school year. B performed as requested. Does B have rights against X?

It is unlikely that this promisor would want or need a return promise from B. There is nothing to enforce as no foreseeable damages would result from breach. It is likely an offer for an act.

Since B performed the requested acts, the basic elements of a unilateral contract appear to be present, and the issue that will determine B's right to recover is whether there is consideration for X's promise. B stayed in law school and studied fifty hours per week, each of which involved doing an act which B was not legally obligated to do. Thus B did incur a legal detriment, and the question is whether this detriment was incurred as part of a bargain or was merely a condition to a gift. X's position will be that X offered a gift to assist B in her desire to go to law school and study full-time and that remaining in school and studying diligently was simply a condition to the gift. X will analogize this to a promise of an expense-paid trip to Europe in which the promisee must agree to travel, thus incurring what is technically a legal detriment, but that detriment is not part of any bargain. It is merely a necessary act or condition which makes the promisee eligible to receive the gift.

Anytime one notes a situation in which a promise is made with apparent donative intent, it is appropriate to explore the consideration issue very carefully paying particular attention to the question whether there is in fact a bargain. Detriment alone will not suffice because it may simply be a condition to a gift. One analysis which might prove helpful is to ask whether the promisor is benefitting from the act of the promisee which is the asserted consideration. If so, this may be reason to conclude that there is a bargained exchange. A better inquiry might be to ask whether the thing which the promisee is asked to do is simply something which is necessary or appropriate to place the promisee in a position to receive the gift. If the promisee was requested to do more, then there would appear to be a bargain.

A promise to make a gift of $25,000 per year to help a friend through law school would be a gratuitous promise. Requiring that the promisee attend law school might logically be simply a condition of the gift. (One cannot help a friend through law school if the friend does not go to law school.) However, there is no reason why the promisor need demand that the student study fifty hours per week. This is neither necessary or convenient to place B in a position to be able to receive the gift. While there is no indication that X will profit by B's performance, it is most likely more than a mere condition to a gift, and thus a bargain can be found (§ 2.28).

If no consideration is present, B could seek enforcement based upon promissory estoppel. Whether remaining in law school and studying long hours was in fact induced by X's promise and is such action as would make non-enforcement of X's promise an injustice is a question which the authors had best leave to the reader to answer. X's recovery might be limited to the value of the reliance which might be difficult to prove in this case (§§ 2.41 and 9.7).

No. 16

T owned and operated a drugstore on premises owned by L. The lease was due to expire in six months. T signed an agreement in which T agreed to sell the business and the inventory to B for $800,000. B agreed to buy and pay the stated price "upon the condition that B can work out a satisfactory new lease with L." T repudiated the promise to sell, and B sues.

T's promise to sell is not enforceable unless there is consideration to support it. B's promise to pay $800,000 is sufficient legal detriment if B's promise is not illusory. The problem is that B will have no obligation whatever if B does not negotiate a "satisfactory" lease with L. The question is whether B's power to prevent the occurrence of the condition to his duty to pay is so unfettered that B's promise is illusory.

If B has a free way out of the agreement with T, then B's promises are illusory. The agreement by B to the terms of a lease with L does not appear to have any significance to B independent of his purchase of the drugstore. In other words, if B wishes to avoid his obligations to T, B suffers no harm or loss whatever if he simply conducts himself in such a manner that no agreement is reached with L. Thus a court might find that B has made an illusory promise and thus has given no consideration for T's promise to sell.

However, agreements such as that between B and T have commercial utility. It is not uncommon that substantial transactions are negotiated with conditions that will not be fulfilled without action by one or both of the parties. If courts wish to enforce these transactions, the simple approach is to impose upon B an implied promise to use reasonable efforts to obtain a satisfactory lease with L. The court might impose upon B a duty to negotiate with L in good faith in an attempt to conclude a lease. The effect is to create some legal duty in B. B must at least meet and negotiate. Thus there is some bargained legal detriment to B that provides consideration to make the B–T agreement an enforceable contract (§§ 2.24–2.25.1).

No. 17

A owed B $2,000, a debt due on a valid contract. After B's right to enforce payment of the debt was barred by the statute of limitations, A voluntarily delivered to B the following signed writing: "Dear B: Enclosed is $100 of the money I owe you." B received payment on the enclosed check, but A made no further payments. Does B have an enforceable right to another $1,900?

Statutes of limitations set maximum periods of time in which different types of civil actions may be brought. Their purpose is to preclude assertion of stale claims involving forgotten matters. A new promise to pay an obligation which would be enforceable but for the statute of limitations is itself enforceable despite the absence of new consideration. An unqualified acknowledgment of the debt is usually held to be sufficient to imply a promise to pay. Mere part payment has been found in some cases to be sufficient to imply a promise to pay the otherwise unmentioned balance. The communication from A clearly acknowledged that there was an obligation owing in excess of the $100 which was being paid. Many cases would permit the creditor to prove the balance owing by extrinsic evidence and find that A's note impliedly promises to pay that amount. B will likely prevail (§ 2.39.1).

Questions 18 through 22 deal with
the Statute of Frauds.

No. 18

A and B were partners in the shoe manufacturing business. A learned that B personally owed a large sum to X, a distributor of quality shoes. A feared that general knowledge of the financial condition of B would have a serious effect on their business. To prevent disclosure of this information as well as to secure an order for his factories from X, A phoned B and agreed, for lawful consideration, to guarantee payment of his associate's debt to X. May X enforce A's promise?

A has made a promise to guarantee the debt of another, and this obligation would nominally come within the terms of the statute of frauds. However, A's primary purpose or main purpose in making the promise was to secure a benefit or advantage for himself. (Actually there are two such benefits; forestalling bad rumors and obtaining a new order from X.) This is a recognized exception to the statute, and thus the absence of a writing signed by A will not prevent X from enforcing A's promise (§ 3.2.2).

No. 19

On February 26, A paid B $375 in consideration for B's oral promise that on the first day of each month for the next succeeding thirteen months, B would clean and oil certain machinery at A's mine. Is B's promise enforceable?

B's promise is by its terms not capable of full performance within one year and is thus within the statute of frauds. Part performance may affect the enforceability of contracts for the sale of goods or of interests in land, but this doctrine is not ordinarily used to enforce oral contracts which violate the one year provision. However, case law permits contracts not capable of performance within one year to be enforced if one party has fully performed (Restatement § 130(2)).

Alternatively, A has also relied upon the oral contract by making full payment, and A might contend that this reliance provides an alternate basis to make the promise of B enforceable (§ 3.6.4). However, since A is entitled to recover the monies paid on a restitution theory, a court should find that no injustice would result if the oral contract were not enforced (§ 10.1.5).

No. 20

A owned a large tract of timberland in the northern part of the state. B desired to purchase some of the timber, so a portion of the property was marked off by stakes, and it was orally agreed that A would sell and B would buy all the trees standing on the plot for $300,000, with cutting and removal to be completed within two months at B's expense. Pursuant to this agreement, B entered upon the property the following day and cut and removed ten of the trees. Is the contract enforceable?

This is a transaction for the sale of goods under the 1972 amendments to U.C.C. section 2–107. Since the contract is for a price of $500 or more, it is within the writing requirements of U.C.C. section 2–201 which provides in subsection (3)(c) for enforcement "with respect to goods for which payment has been made and accepted or which have been received and accepted." The contract can be enforced for the ten logs which were received and accepted, but this partial performance does not make the entire contract enforceable (§ 3.6.1). Marking a portion of the property with stakes would not appear to constitute receipt and acceptance of goods.

If the party against whom enforcement is sought were to admit the making of the contract "in his pleadings, testimony or otherwise in court," then subsection (3) (b) would permit enforcement to the extent of the quantity admitted.

No. 21

X orally contracts to buy a car from Y for $3,500. X pays Y $25 as a deposit. Is the contract enforceable?

At least some jurisdictions have held that a part-payment in a contract for an indivisible unit of goods makes the entire contract enforceable. A $25 payment on an oral contract for two cars at $4,500 each would presumably make the contract enforceable to the extent of one car (§ 3.6.1).

No. 22

A, a famous painter of biblical characters, invited offers for the purchase of a life-sized picture of Elijah he intended to paint. B's offer of $17,500 was the highest, and A agreed orally with B that he would paint the picture and sell it to B for that price. Is the contract enforceable?

Ordinary service contracts are not within the statute of frauds unless the contract by its terms is incapable of being performed within one year of the date of making. One could enforce an oral contract to build a twin of the Sears Tower or the Grand Coulee Dam. If the A–B contract is for services to be performed by A, the statute of frauds does not apply. If this is viewed as a contract for goods, then the U.C.C. would make the oral contract unenforceable unless further facts bring the case within one of the exceptions found in section 2–201. (§§ 1.3.1).

Since the law is easy and obvious, a good answer to questions of this nature must include careful analysis and characterization of the given facts and the inferences that can be drawn from them. How should a court determine whether B is hiring A to perform a service for B or simply contracting to buy future goods which A will produce? This is not akin to a research and development contract in which the process and work may be more significant than the working model that is to be produced. B is not to control when and how A paints. B's only legitimate concern is with the quality of the goods delivered. If this reasoning were followed, the predominant nature of the contract or the predominant factor involved is a sale of goods and the U.C.C. should apply. Where the artist was to create the painting on a live TV show to be auctioned off at the time of the show, a court found that this was a service contract and not a sale of goods (National Historic Shrines Foundation v. Dali (N.Y.Sup.Ct. 1967).

Question 23 deals with parol
evidence and contract interpretation.

No. 23

S and B executed a written contract pursuant to which S agreed to sell 10,000 rabbits and B agreed to pay $15,000. The written contract specified that delivery was to be at S's ranch on April 1. A dispute arose and the contract was never performed. B sued S and sought to prove the following:

(1) During negotiations, S stated that his hired man would deliver the rabbits to B's ranch.

(2) B told S that B would pay $5,000 down and $10,000 not later than April 15. S assented to this at the time the contract was signed, but thereafter S advised he would demand cash on delivery for the rabbits.

(3) During the negotiations, S stated that he had excess vaccine for a certain rabbit disease and promised to give B enough to vaccinate all of the rabbits. S never tendered any vaccine.

(4) In the industry, "1,000 rabbits" means 100 dozen rabbits. Thus B was entitled to an actual count of 12,000 rabbits under the contract. Which of these items may B prove?

The first question to be resolved by the court is whether the parties intended the writing to be a final expression of at least one or more terms of their agreement. Given the terms contained in the writing, there appears to be no logical reason why one would not conclude that it was a final expression. This final expression of the parties provided for tender of delivery at S's ranch, and this would operate as a discharge of any prior inconsistent agreements. Unless the evidence is being offered to prove mistake or some other defense, B cannot introduce evidence of the promise to deliver the goods to B's ranch as this would contradict an express term of the written contract.

The writing provided for payment of $15,000 for the rabbits and this means cash on delivery under both the common law and the U.C.C. (§ 4.10). Thus B's second item of evidence contradicts an implied term of the written agreement, and S will attempt to exclude it on that basis. While the language commonly used by the courts would appear to support S's position stating that extrinsic evidence cannot contradict implied terms of a writing, the results of many cases do not (e.g., *Masterson v. Sine* (Cal. 1968) and §§ 4.5 and 4.8).

If this credit term is not found to be a contradiction of the terms of the contract, then B can admit this evidence if the writing is found to be only a partial as distinguished from a complete integration. If the writing is complete and exclusive statement of the terms of the agreement, then B cannot introduce evidence which will add the term which provides for credit. This issue will probably be resolved by inquiring whether parties situated in the position of S and B who were entering a contract of this nature would naturally have left this term out of the writing even though they meant it to be a binding part of their final agreement. Since this is a transaction in goods, the court could look to comment 3 of U.C.C. section 2–202 which phrases this question in terms of whether the terms " ... would certainly have been included in the document in the view of the court ..." in which case B would not be permitted to introduce them into evidence. It would not be illogical to conclude that S and B would certainly have included the payment terms in the writing had they intended it to be other than a cash sale, but this is a debatable point.

B's third matter relating to the vaccine is one which does not contradict any express or implied term of the writing and thus can definitely be introduced unless it is found that the writing is a complete integration. This will involve questions similar to those discussed in the preceding paragraph with the answer turning on whether the court finds that this provision would have been included in the writing had the parties intended it to be part of their final agreement. If it would certainly have been included in the agreement, then B cannot present this evidence to the trier of fact. However, the intent to include surplus vaccine in a deal of this nature without mentioning it in the written contract seems quite plausible human conduct, and B thus has a good case to have this evidence admitted.

B's fourth point involves evidence of usage of the trade which is offered to explain the meaning of contract language. Assuming that this method of counting rabbits is observed with such regularity in the rabbit trade in this geographical area that the parties are justified in expecting that it will be observed in the transaction in question, then B will be able to establish that this is a bona fide usage of the trade (U.C.C. section 1–205(2)). (Truth is stranger than fiction. Local custom was found to provide that 1,000 rabbits means 100 dozen rabbits in *Smith v. Wilson* (K.B.1832). In like fashion, "minimum 50% protein" was found to include 49.5% in *Hurst v. W.J. Lake & Co.* (Or. 1932).)

While usage of the trade cannot contradict an express term of the contract (U.C.C. § 2–208(2)), it can be used to explain contract terms. If in fact "1,000 rabbits" means 100 dozen rabbits then proof of this trade usage does not contradict but merely explains. B should be able to get this evidence admitted (§§ 4.3, 4.8).

Questions 24–25 deal primarily
with contract defenses.

No. 24

Prof is a new economics professor at state college. He is new to the area and wishes to pursue his passion for duck hunting. Having been advised to see Jack in Duckville, Prof went to that small town, stopped by the local bar looking for Jack, and encountered Jake. Prof failed to note the difference in name, and Jake did not correct Prof when Prof called him Jack. Prof was most pleased at Jake's glowing reports concerning the number of ducks killed on Jake's pond last year. As Jake poured another drink, he assured Prof a warm bed, good food and fine hunting for $4,500 for the season. Prof read the standard contract form while Jake filled in blanks on another copy. Prof did not dream that the "other copy" was a different form, so he did not bother to "re-read" the actual copy he signed.

Prof actually signed an agreement to pay $6,000. Jake and Jack are two different people, and Jake's beds are cold, as is his food. While Jake's figures concerning last year's kill are probably not too badly exaggerated, last year was the first really good year on Jake's pond in two decades. May Prof successfully disavow any contract obligations to Jake?

Misrepresentation of a material fact upon which Prof reasonably relies is a defense. There is authority for the proposition that intentional misrepresentation of a nonmaterial fact, can also be a defense. If Jake has misrepresented his identity, that should be sufficient. The representations as to last year's kill were made to indicate likely prospects for the ensuing year and are thus "half-truths" which might provide a basis for relief if reliance thereon is reasonable. Representations as to bed and food are probably promises which have not yet been broken. However, if it can be shown that these statements related to past conditions, then they are statements of fact rather than promises and could also be found to be misrepresentations of fact (§ 5.7).

Misrepresentation of the document and the price contained therein is clearly intentional and material, however Prof can anticipate problems showing reasonable reliance. In the alternative this problem can be cast as one of mutual mistake (§§ 5.5, 5.7.1, 5.7.2, 5.7.3).

Lack of capacity based upon voluntary intoxication is not ordinarily the best defense in the

world, but it might have a bearing upon the outcome of a case in which the party pushing the
liquor was obviously attempting to pluck a pigeon
(§§ 5.2, 5.4).

Unconscionability may be available as a defense if
Prof can show procedural and substantive unconscionability. The misrepresentations and paper
switching should establish procedural unconscionability. The facts do not indicate whether the $6,000
price is excessive. If it is clearly excessive, this
would establish substantive unconscionability.
Whether a university economics professor can look
to excessive price to establish substantive unconscionability is an interesting question.

"Bad faith" is a term which might well be mentioned in discussion of this case and might appear
in the court's opinion if Prof prevails. However, the
parties did not owe each other a legally enforceable
duty of good faith prior to the formation of the
contract. Jake's "bad faith" in the dealings between
the parties is not a source of substantive rights for
Prof nor is it a defense which will relieve him from
his contract duties if the other common law defenses discussed above fail. It is therefore in the role of
a supporting argument, but should not be advanced
as the legal basis for rescission of the contract
(§ 4.11).

No. 25

B bought from S a considerable quantity of an
industrial grease known as R–Lube, for 25 cents per

pound. Thereafter, S developed a new lighter-weight grease suitable for some, but not all of the purposes for which R–Lube is suitable, taking great pains to keep the development work secret. By the end of the year, the new product was ready to market and was designated in S's records as "R–Lube Special." On January 2, S mailed to one thousand of his customers a card reading:

> S is now offering for immediate order in any quantity not exceeding 2000 pounds, R–Lube Special at 20 cents per pound. This is an economy product of good quality. Detailed technical specifications will be provided on request.

S knew the new product was not heavy enough for B's operations and did not intend that a card go to B. However, one of the cards was sent to B due to a clerical error in S's office. B at once wrote S: "I am pleased to note the special price on R–Lube. Send me 2000 pounds."

When S received this letter he called B, explained the mistake and advised B that the current price of R–Lube was 28 cents per pound. B nevertheless insisted that he had a contract for 2000 pounds of R–Lube at 20 cents per pound. S consults you. What are his legal relations with B?

Article 2 of the U.C.C. applies to this transaction. The January 2 communication was sent by S's staff and did manifest to B an intent to be bound to sell the product. Despite the fact that it was sent by inadvertence, B has no reason to know of this mistake and it is probably sufficient to constitute an offer (§§ 2.1, 2.1.1, 4.1 and 5.6). The contract price is only $400 and not within the statute of frauds. If it were, the requirement of a writing which specifies quantity should be found to be satisfied (§ 3.3) even though the precise quantity is not determined until there is an acceptance.

The parties have a course of dealing in R–Lube. "R–Lube Special" may sound a bit like a "special" on R–Lube. The message describes the grease as an "economy product" but does not indicate that it is a new or different product. If it can be found that the offer is ambiguous and that S should have known of this ambiguity and B did not have reason to know, then B should be able to enforce a contract on the terms which B understood; that is, a contract for "R–Lube" (§ 4.1). If not, then there is likely a mutual misunderstanding as to the subject matter of the contract and B will lose as no contract was formed (§ 5.6). In the absence of a finding of ambiguity or misunderstanding, B's response would be a counter-offer and rejection at common law (§ 2.12). The U.C.C. should not change this result as B is not manifesting an intention to be bound to buy R–Lube Special which was the subject of S's offer. (§ 2.12.2).

Questions 26 through 30 deal with
contract performance and remedies.

No. 26

B agreed in a binding contract to lend C $3,000, C to execute a negotiable note for that amount with

6% interest, and C to provide for his obligation a surety acceptable to B. C obtained D to act as surety, but B refused to proceed saying that D was not acceptable. Actually B refused D as a surety because he (B) was short of money and did not want to make the loan. Is B liable for breach?

B's obligation to perform was made subject to a condition that is within B's control. This pattern will arise in any situation in which one party is given the right to approve or disapprove of some aspect of the other party's performance.

If B has the unfettered right to disapprove any surety for any reason, then B's promise is illusory (§ 2.30). A court would assume that the parties intended something more than an illusory obligation and would thus qualify B's right of approval by requiring that B act reasonably or in good faith in making the determination. This interpretation is also consistent with the probable intention of the parties.

If B's approval relates to matters of fancy, taste or judgment such as approval of a work of art or music, then B's standard will likely not be measured by that of a reasonable person but only by whether B is acting honestly and in good faith (§§ 8.8 and 8.11). If the performance in question involves utilitarian standards of fitness or economic worth, objective standards are available and B will be required to act reasonably.

The acceptability of a surety could be seen as a matter of economics involving income and net worth, but many lenders view the question whether to loan to an individual as one involving evaluation of personal characteristics. Thus this would be a tough question but for the given fact that B is acting dishonestly. He is dissatisfied with the bargain and not with D. Honesty is the minimum standard for any contract term requiring party approval (§ 8.8). The condition of approval should be excused, and B should be liable for damages.

Many courts discuss these problems in terms of B's obligation to act in good faith. This does not clarify the issue because "good faith" is sometimes defined as requiring only honesty and on other occasions as requiring reasonable conduct or conduct in accord with reasonable commercial standards of the trade. Since the crucial question in party approval cases is often whether the a party should be held to a standard of reasonableness or merely required to be honest, use of an ambiguous term such as good faith does more to hide the issue than to resolve it.

No. 27

Rich, a wealthy man, went to the Custom Shirt Company on September 1st to order a dozen shirts. He let Custom measure him for size, selected the silk to be used in the shirts, and signed a memorandum stating that he would pay $100 for each shirt that Custom would make for him, up to twelve shirts in all.

Custom purchased for $240 the silk for twelve shirts, and cut it into twelve portions to make the cutting of the patterns easier. Custom then started making the first shirt and completed it on September 12th. It tendered the shirt to Rich on that day, but Rich refused it and stated he had decided to cancel the entire order.

Custom realized that it could not dispose of the silk which had been cut for the other eleven shirts because there is no market for cut silk. Custom also knew that if it went ahead and made the shirts and Rich refused to take them, the shirts could be sold to the trade for a price of only $48 per shirt. It would cost $40 for labor to make each shirt.

Custom decided to go ahead and make the eleven shirts after it received Rich's cancellation. When the shirts were completed, they were tendered to Rich, and he refused to accept them. Custom then sold the shirts, but the resale price of the shirts had suddenly dropped, and Custom received only $30 per shirt.

Custom now sues Rich. Is Custom entitled to collect from Rich? If so, how much?

This is a transaction in goods. The memorandum Rich signed manifests an intention to be bound to purchase goods. While it leaves quantity to be determined by the seller, this does not create an insufficiency as to terms (§ 2.2.1).

Custom can accept Rich's offer in any manner reasonable under the circumstances. Since Custom made no promise, acceptance can only be found from the beginning performance which requires notice to Rich within a reasonable time. Custom has cut special ordered silk into twelve pieces for twelve shirts which is likely to be found to be an act sufficiently referable to this contract to be deemed the beginning of performance. The facts do not give the elapsed time, but if the production and tender of the first shirt was accomplished promptly, it would appear that Rich received notice of the fact that performance had begun within a reasonable time. There is nothing about the facts that would create any particular urgency. Thus, one can find a contract for twelve shirts at $100 each (§§ 2.10 and 2.10.1 and U.C.C. §§ 2–206(2) and 2–610).

At the time of Rich's breach one shirt was finished. As to that shirt, Custom would be entitled to recover the difference between the contract price of $100 and the resale price of that shirt, assuming it was resold in compliance with the requirements of U.C.C. section 2–706. If the resale did not comply with the code, Custom may recover the difference between contract and market price at the time and place of tender (§ 9.10 and U.C.C. § 2–708(1)).

As to the other 11 shirts, Custom had a duty to use reasonable commercial judgment with respect to the question whether to complete the shirts or salvage the material (U.C.C. § 2–704(2)). Hindsight discloses that the decision to proceed was unfortunate since $40 labor expense per shirt was incurred and the shirts sold for only $30. However, the facts state that the market price was $48 when the decision to proceed was made. Assuming that it was reasonable to anticipate a sale price of $48 and that the cut material had no market, a court should find the decision to invest $40 to complete was commercially reasonable, and Custom should recover the difference between the contract price ($100) and the resale price ($30) plus incidental costs (such as the cost of resale) less incidental savings, if any. If it were established that $30 was not a reasonable price for the shirts, Custom could have refrained from selling and brought an action under U.C.C. section 2–709 for the contract price holding the shirts as security for the payment of the judgment.

No. 28

Manor, the owner of a certain house and lot, engaged Broker to sell that property under the terms of a signed written agreement which provided, in part:

I, Manor, agree to pay Broker a commission of 6% of the gross sale price of any sale of said property which is arranged by Broker for a consideration of not less than $275,000, such commission to be payable upon consummation of the sale.

Broker procured a buyer, Valley, who offered to purchase the property for $275,000, agreeing to pay $75,000 down and give a note secured by a deed of trust for the balance on certain stated terms. Manor grumbled at these terms, but accepted Valley's offer.

Prior to the time fixed for closing, Manor conveyed the property to Junior, Manor's 22 year old son who wanted to have assets in his name temporarily because he was seeking a performance bond for his new construction business. Valley learned of this conveyance, notified Manor that he was in breach, and purchased a similar parcel of property from Smith. Junior reconveyed title to Manor who tendered title to Valley on the specified day. Valley refused to perform, and Manor thereupon conveyed the property to Junior as a birthday present. What are the rights of Broker against Manor?

(Beware. Respond to the call of the question. The question writer chose not to ask for a discussion of the rights and duties of Valley. Of course, some analysis of the Manor–Valley contract will be required to determine Broker's rights.)

Broker might advance three distinct theories for recovery against Manor. Broker may assert that the language of his contract with Manor provides for payment of a commission when a sale is consummated and that this was accomplished when M and V entered into a valid enforceable contract. There is no obvious answer on this issue although one might reason that the parties logically intended that Manor would pay Broker when Manor got paid and thus "consummation" referred to completion of the transaction. If Broker provided the contract form, the inclination to interpret ambiguous terms of a contract against the draftsman might tip the scales against Broker (§ 4.4).

Broker's second theory for recovery is the contention that Manor's initial conveyance to Junior constituted a form of repudiation that excused Valley from her duty to perform. A party who voluntarily incapacitates himself by committing an act which seriously jeopardizes his ability to perform can be found to have repudiated (§ 8.6.3). Broker's position will be that there is an implied duty of cooperation and certainly an implied duty not to prevent consummation of the sale by breaching (§§ 4.9 and 4.11). Breach of this duty excused the condition precedent (consummation of the sale) to Manor's duty to pay (§ 8.6.2).

If Manor defeats the second theory by establishing that Manor did not breach by conveying title to Junior, then Broker's third theory is that since Manor did not breach, Valley was never excused from performing. Thus the contract with Valley is still enforceable. Recovery on this theory would depend upon whether the court finds that Manor has an implied duty to take legal action to "consummate" the sale with a buyer who will not voluntarily perform. Most court decisions do not impose this burden upon a party who agrees to pay a commission for a completed sale.

No. 29

M, the publisher of a newspaper, contracted with T, the operator of a supermarket, whereby M agreed to publish an advertisement each day for four weeks. T agreed to pay a certain sum in four equal installments at the end of each week. The contract document further recited: "A complete layout of each ad will be delivered to M not later than 10:00 on the day prior to the day on which the ad is to be published."

The first week of performance under the contract has passed, and T promptly paid the first installment. Each day during the week T had been from one to three hours late in submitting her layout to M. M complained to T each day about the delay. On the first day of the second week, T submitted the layout for T's eighth advertisement to M four hours late.

Assume that M consulted you immediately upon receiving this layout, and stated that T's advertising was more of a nuisance than it was worth unless layouts reached M promptly. Indicate, with reasons, your advice to M concerning his legal liability to T if: (1) he refuses to run the eighth advertisement, and (2) he informs T that he will render no further performance under the contract.

The facts stipulate a contract in which M has promised to run T's ads each day for four weeks. Failure to perform that promise would be a breach of contract unless the promise were shielded by a condition which neither occurred nor was excused. If M's promise to print is dependent upon the occurrence of some condition precedent, then the duty will not arise unless the condition was fulfilled or excused.

Under the terms of the contract, T was obligated to deliver ad layouts to M by 10:00 on the day prior to each publication. There was no contract language which explicitly stated that failure to deliver on time would prevent M's duty of performance from arising, thus there is no express condition. However, the delivery was a duty to be performed prior to the time fixed for the duty to print and this is one basis for finding that the delivery is a constructive condition precedent to the duty to print. More specifically, however, the delivery of the copy is clearly an event which T must cause to occur before the printing of the ads can be done. Therefore, timely delivery of the copy could also be viewed as an implied condition of cooperation (§§ 8.1–8.1.3).

M has accepted and run a late copy each day for one week. Despite the fact that M has complained, a court could find that by accepting these late performances and proceeding with the publication, M has waived prompt performance as a condition precedent to his own duty. In the present situation, however, the layouts are being delivered at least one hour later than ever before. Thus even if some waiver might be found, the present failure goes beyond that to which M has acquiesced in the past.

There is at least a partial failure of a condition precedent to M's duty to perform. This is not an express condition, and even if it were labeled an implied condition, it is likely that a court would not enforce a rule requiring full and literal fulfillment or would define the implied condition to require delivery within a reasonable time rather than precisely at 10:00. The test which M's counsel should anticipate being applied is one of substantial performance.

Restatement section 241 states factors to which courts commonly look to determine the presence or absence of substantial performance or substantial occurrence of a condition. Applying these factors to M's case, one finds that M has not given his counsel sufficient facts. We need to know more about M's printing operation and the problems which will result from receiving advertising layouts four hours late. This information is necessary to determine the extent of the harm to M or the extent to which he is being denied the benefits which he could reasonably have anticipated under the bargain. M's harm probably cannot be adequately compensated in damages, because having to hurry and rush an item does not usually produce damages which are measurable or quantifiable in dollars. It would be helpful to know how dependent T is upon advertising, but there is no indication that T is going to suffer any loss in the nature of a forfeiture if one or more ads are not printed. It is too late for T to cure the defect in her performance on this occasion, and the prospects for timely performance in the future are not bright given the record to date. There are insufficient facts from which it can be determined whether T's failure is willful or a violation of standards of good faith and fair dealing, and it seems unlikely that M could prove this on the facts given.

On balance, one might conclude that if the four-hour delay does create sufficient havoc with M's printing routine, M may be justified in his refusal to print this one advertisement on this occasion. Even if the four-hour delay is such that the duty to print this ad does not arise, M's counsel should not advise him to declare a breach of the entire contract.

Particularly in light of the fact that seven prior late performances have been accepted, it would be most unlikely that M could establish that this one, longer delay was a sufficient breach to justify canceling the entire contract. Such action would probably be a repudiation by M which would subject him to liability for such damages as T might be able to establish (§§ 8.2 and 8.6.4).

No. 30

Morel (M) is a large-scale distributor of yogurt. For some years M maintained his own dairy herd to supply part of his milk requirements. When M decided to slow down and devote his time to the yogurt business, he sold his dairy herd and equipment to Toron (T), an experienced dairyman who then owned no other dairy stock. T agreed to pay $875,000 for the cattle and equipment, and M agreed to buy T's output of milk for the next 10 years at the market price at the time of delivery, provided that M would not purchase any quantity in excess of that which M actually required for the production of yogurt.

Two years after this transaction was completed, M was involved in a serious automobile accident which left him unable to continue business activities. Since his only child had gone to law school, M sold his plant and equipment to Borden and retired to Sun City. T has no acceptable alternative market for his milk and sues M for breach of contract. What result?

M agreed to purchase all of T's output of milk up to M's requirements. This is both an output and requirement contract. The quantity would presumably be the same if the parties had provided that M would buy all of his requirements from T provided that M would not demand any quantity greater than that actually produced by T.

At common law, ordinary output contracts and requirements contracts were not found to create an obligation to remain in business and continue to have output or requirements. Liability could be imposed for dishonest avoidance, such as terminating requirements by selling the yogurt business to a child who then hired the father as general manager.

Common law courts recognized that an obligation to remain in business might properly be implied from the other contract terms or circumstances. Thus, in a case where X paid up-front cash for Y's promise to purchase his requirements from X or sell his output to X, the fact that consideration was paid for the executory promise induced some courts to find an implied promise by Y to remain in business. Thus, a court might take evidence to determine whether the $875,000 paid by T was more than the market price for the cattle and equipment without a milk contract in which case it would be concluded that T has paid consideration to M in exchange for M's promise to buy M's requirements of milk from T. From this the court could imply a promise by M to continue in the yogurt business.

U.C.C. section 2–306(1) addresses this general problem and indicates that the measure of the parties obligation is such requirements or output as will occur in good faith. Comment 2 states that a shutdown for lack of orders might be permissible but a shutdown to curtail losses would not. But section 2–306 does not appear to provide any guidance for the resolution of the problem presented. It might be anticipated that a court would fulfill its obligation to analyze section 2–306 and then proceed to find, in accordance with common law cases, that the extra value which M received from T (if such be found) gave rise to a duty upon M to remain in the yogurt business for 10 years.

A conclusion that M was contractually obligated to remain in business does not resolve the case. M's injury prevents M from continuing personally to manage the yogurt business. If the contract is interpreted as limiting the quantity to be purchased to that which M needs in a yogurt business to be managed by M personally, then M's injuries will make performance " * * * impracticable by the occurrence of a contingency the non-occurrence of which was a basic assumption on which the contract was made * * * " (§ 6.1 and U.C.C. § 2–615(a)). In this case, M would be excused from his implied promise to remain in the yogurt business.

Assuming that even a yogurt connoisseur would not claim that the operation of a yogurt business is a duty too personal to delegate, the probable conclusion is that M will not be excused from his implied promise to remain in the yogurt business simply because he is not personally able to manage it.

Questions 31 and 34 deal with third
party beneficiaries and assignment and delegation.

No. 31

A federal agency contracted with a local agency
wherein the federal agency agreed to provide funds
for redevelopment and the local agency promised to
do certain enumerated things. Included was a promise by the local agency to provide "suitable replacement housing" for all persons who would become
obliged to move from their existing residences because of the redevelopment activities. After approximately one-half of the area to be redeveloped had
been vacated and leveled, the federal agency and
the local agency entered into modification of their
agreement pursuant to which the local agency's
obligations with respect to persons uprooted by the
project were rescinded. What are the contract rights
of the affected persons against the federal agency or
local agency?

The first question to be resolved is whether any
persons other than the principal parties to the
contract have legally enforceable rights therein. Restatement section 302 indicates that in order for
these third parties to have enforceable rights one
must find that "recognition of a right to performance in the beneficiary is appropriate to effectuate
the intention of the parties and either (a) the performance of the promise will satisfy an obligation of
the promisee to pay money to the beneficiary; or (b)
the circumstances indicate that the promisee in-

tends to give the beneficiary the benefit of the promised performance."

The promise that would directly benefit the local residents was made by the local agency to the federal agency. Thus the federal agency is the promisee, and the first question becomes: Would recognition of a right to performance in the local citizens be appropriate to effectuate the intention of the parties? It is appropriate to ask whether the federal agency intended to give the local citizens the right to enforce this part of its contract or whether it should reasonably be found to have intended to keep all enforcement powers in its own hands (§ 11.3). If it is determined that the intent was to give the local citizens the right to enforce this part of the contract, then the court should have no particular difficulty finding that Restatement section 302(b) was fulfilled as the federal government could be said to have intended to give these beneficiaries the benefit of this particular promised performance. Because this is a "government contract," Restatement section 313 would not allow recovery against the local agency by a member of the public unless the terms of the contract provided for such liability or "the promisee is subject to liability to the member of the public for damages and a direct action against the promisor is consistent with the terms of the contract and with the policy of the law authorizing the contract and prescribing remedies for its breach."

If one finds that the residents are intended rather than incidental beneficiaries, the next question is whether their rights had vested prior to the time the principal parties to the contract modified it so as to defeat their rights (§ 11.5). This probably requires that the specific persons who are intended beneficiaries be identified which in itself is not an easy task (§ 11.3). There is case law authority for vesting beneficiaries' rights when they rely, or, when they learn of the contract and agree to accept the benefits, or when the contract is made.

The Restatement section 311(3) would terminate the principal parties' power to modify the contract so as to deny benefits to third parties when those third parties have changed position in justifiable reliance or brought suit or manifested assent to it at the request of the promisor or promisee. If the court requires reliance, then the contract modification would defeat the rights of all of the third party beneficiaries except for those who learned of their rights under the contract and detrimentally relied thereon in some manner.

Any contract rights would be against the local agency and not against the federal agency. That federal agency made no promise for their benefit and there is no right of action on any theory such as wrongful rescission.

No. 32

Harry (H) was indebted to Bank for approximately $50,000. The precise amount was disputed by H. H and Mary (M) entered into an agreement whereby M promised to perform H's obligation to Bank.

In the negotiations, H misrepresented certain facts to M. M failed to pay Bank, and Bank sues H and M.

Bank has a right to recover against H. The facts stipulate that H was lawfully indebted to Bank in the amount of $50,000. A debtor cannot relieve himself of liability without the creditor's consent simply by finding someone else who is willing to promise to perform for him. Had M performed, this would have discharged H's obligation to Bank (§ 12.10).

Bank also has the right to recover against M as a third party beneficiary of the H–M contract. M can assert against Bank any defenses which M has on the H–M contract; thus, if the agreement between M and H is not legally enforceable due to H's misrepresentations, Bank has no rights against M (§ 11.6). (Bank and M have no legal relationship other than that arising out of the H–M contract. Thus, if that contract is flawed, Bank's rights are likewise flawed.) M could not ordinarily raise against Bank any defenses which H might have had against Bank. However, in this case, M only promised "to perform H's obligation to Bank." Thus the measure of M's obligation to Bank is the amount which H owed Bank, and defenses available to H could therefore reduce the amount of the obligation which M has assumed.

No. 33

The construction contract between HO and C provided: "C shall not assign any right to payment hereunder." In violation of this term, C, for new value, assigned to Bank its right to receive one progress payment under the contract. May Bank assert valid rights against HO?

Bank may recover from HO under Article Nine of the U.C.C. without regard to common law issues concerning prohibitions against assignment or against partial assignments. U.C.C. section 9–102(1) establishes that Article Nine does apply to this transaction. It provides:

" * * * this Article applies

"(a) to any transaction (regardless of its form) which is intended to create a security interest in personal property or fixtures including goods, documents, instruments, general intangibles, chattel paper or accounts; and also

"(b) to any sale of accounts or chattel paper."

The right to receive payment for services rendered in this fact situation is an "account." (U.C.C. section 9–106.) HO is the party obligated to pay the account and is thus an "account debtor."

Having these definitions in mind, one turns to section 9–318(4) which controls this problem:

"(4) A term in any contract between an account debtor and an assignor is ineffective if it prohibits assignment of an account or prohibits creation of a security interest in a general intangible for money due or to become due or requires the account debtor's consent to such assignment or security interest."

The assignment should be found to be valid (§ 12.2).

No. 34

C entered into a valid contract to build a home for X on X's lot in exchange for $240,000. X sold the lot to Y and assigned and delegated to Y X's rights and duties under the contract. Does C have any immediate rights against X? May C refuse to perform? What will X or Y's rights and duties be if C assigns his contract rights and delegates his contract duties to S, another local contractor?

Contract rights are freely assignable except in unusual situations in which the duties of the promisor would be somehow changed if they were to be rendered to another party. For example, if C promised to build to X's personal satisfaction, X's right might not be assignable. No such problem is presented here, and X may assign to Y the right to receive the services of the contractor.

Contract duties are delegable where the delegation will not deprive the other party to the contract of some significant part of his bargain. X's duty in this case is the duty to pay money which is impersonal. C will not be denied any expected benefits if he is paid by Y rather than by X. Thus the X–Y delegation is proper.

While X remains liable to C on the contract and while C now enjoys the additional right to collect from Y, the practical effect of delegation of duties is that in some cases neither party chooses to pay but rather points to the other party as the appropriate debtor from whom C should collect. Whether C can seek assurance by demanding that X reaffirm his obligations under the contract or that Y acknowledge his new obligation to C probably depends upon the extent to which the court might turn to the U.C.C. for a rule to apply by analogy in this situation (see U.C.C. §§ 2–210(5) and 2–609).

For reasons noted above, C can assign to S his right to payment for the construction work. (See also the discussion of § 9–318(4) in the preceding answer.) The delegation to S of the duty to perform cannot be accomplished without the owner's consent, however, unless C and S can establish that the owner will receive the substantial benefit of his bargain. If the owner will not receive performance substantially equivalent to that which it had the right to expect from C, then this attempted delegation is improper. If C were simply the low bidder in an open bidding process, the delegation would probably be proper assuming that the delegatee, S, is a competent contractor. If X inspected the work of C and other contractors and then selected C to construct his home because of C's acknowledged quality as a homebuilder, the delegation by C to S of the duty to perform would be difficult to sustain (§ 12.9).

Question 35 deals with excuse based upon impossibility or frustration of purpose.

No. 35

On February 1, M brought her daughter to S's dress shop for fittings for a custom made wedding

dress. No agreement was reached as M was examining both the $600 and the $900 models. All parties
understood that the daughter was to be married on
April 5.

On February 2, M wrote to S ordering the $900
wedding dress for delivery by March 20. S received
this note and bought the necessary cloth on her
next trip to the City. S returned to her shop where
S's employees cut the cloth and began to stitch.

On March 10, the daughter's fiancee was killed in
an accident, and M promptly notified S who was
about half finished with the dress. M consults you.
What are her obligations to S?

M's note of February 2 is apparently sufficient to
constitute an offer to buy goods. Assuming it is
signed, it satisfies the minimal requirements of the
statute of frauds for a sale of goods. If unsigned,
section 2–201(3)(a) relating to specially manufactured goods would likely deny use of a statute of
frauds defense to M. Section 2–201(3)(b) would also
apply since your client is not going to lie under
oath.

U.C.C. section 2–206 permits acceptance in any
manner reasonable under the circumstances which
would include beginning performance (§ 2–206(2)
and Restatement § 30(2)). However section 2–
206(2) also permits an offeror to treat an offer as
lapsed if notice of acceptance is not given within a
reasonable time. Therefore, even if beginning performance was an appropriate means of acceptance,
the failure to give notice to M should provide M

with a defense. It might also be effectively argued that the impending wedding created a situation in which M sought and needed an express promise to perform, and thus the circumstances might be found to "unambiguously indicate" that simply beginning performance would not be a reasonable manner of acceptance.

If M did have contractual obligations to S, the death of the groom-to-be does not create a basis for asserting impossibility or impracticability of performance. M can still accept and pay for the dress. Daughter can still wear it. However, the cancellation of the wedding completely frustrates the promisor's purpose in entering into this contract and makes the other party's performance valueless (§ 6.3). The groom's death was an event the nonoccurrence of which was a basic assumption on which the contract was made. There is no reason to assume that M would be found to have assumed this risk, and the frustration occurred without fault on the part of M. Thus M could have established the elements of the defense of frustration of purpose and been excused from her contract promise. Had the wedding been canceled because of a disagreement between the parties, frustration of purpose would probably not be an available defense because this would be an assumed risk.

S should have the right to recover in restitution for materials and the value of the services rendered. (§ 6.4 and 10.1.5). S will likely be denied any "profit" on the contract.

CHAPTER 15

A FRAMEWORK FOR REVIEW

The following sequence of analysis is offered as a suggested approach to a contracts problem.

A. Was a contract formed?

1. Initial analysis looks for manifestation of assent to a bargain by the parties, usually including offer, acceptance and consideration.

a) Was there an offer?

b) Was it accepted?

Did the parties manifest mutual assent in another fashion? (e.g., "A and B signed a written contract." In which case, neither is technically an offeror nor an offeree.)

c) Was there consideration?

2. Alternative analysis (if no sure contract found above) looks for enforcement of a promise based upon promissory estoppel.

a) Was there a promise calculated to induce reliance, etc. (Rest. § 90)

b) Did the other party in fact reasonably rely?

c) To what extent do the circumstances require or justify enforcement of the promise or some lesser remedy?

B. Is the contract within the statute of frauds?

1. If so, is there a sufficient writing?

2. If not, is there another basis for complying with the statute? (e.g., part performance)

3. If not, is the party seeking to rely upon the statute of frauds estopped from doing so?

C. Contract Modification

1. Did the parties mutually agree to modify their contract?

2. Was consideration present or was the requirement of consideration excused by statute or by another established exception? If neither, can promissory estoppel be used to enforce the promise to modify?

3. Was the contract as modified within the statute of frauds and if so, was it satisfied? (See B *supra*).

4. Did the contract contain a writing requirement? Was it waived or satisfied?

5. If the agreement is not enforceable as a modification of the contract, can it still be effective as a waiver of a condition in the contract?

D. Interpretation

1. What are the express terms of the contract?

a) Is one party attempting to add to or modify terms of a writing by use of extrinsic evidence of a prior agreement thereby creating a parol evidence rule issue?

b) Is one party attempting to influence the meaning of terms in a writing by offering evidence as to the parties stated intentions as to the meaning of that term?

c) Apply general rules of interpretation to determine meaning of language in writing.

2. What are the implied terms of the contract?

a) Implied from the parties' course of performance of this contract or course of prior dealings in similar contracts or from general usages of the trade.

b) Implied by parties conduct or implied from other circumstances in the case.

3. What terms will the court construe to be part of the contract without regard to the parties intentions?

a) Constructive conditions.

b) An obligation of good faith or good faith and fair dealing.

E. Defenses

Do the facts indicate the presence of any legitimate issue concerning a possible defense or basis for reforming a contract? (Note that one may have defense issues relating to the original contract and possibly separate defense issues relating to a contract modification.) Defenses for which you should check include:

1. Lack of capacity

2. Duress

3. Undue influence

4. Mistake

5. Misrepresentation

6. Illegality or violation of public policy

7. Unconscionability (procedural and substantive).

8. Bad faith. While included on the list, bad faith is not generally recognized as a defense to contract formation in the absence of some fiduciary relationship. Bad faith is relevant as an issue in contract performance and enforcement where the obligation to act in good faith can impact upon duties of performance and the presence or absence of breach.

F. Third Party Beneficiaries

What parties have rights under the contact? To whom are duties owing? (This should be considered before looking to performance issues.) Consider the special problems that arise because of the nature of the contract as a 3PB contract? These include:

1. The promisor can generally assert against the third party all defenses arising under the contract between the promisor and the promisee, except,

2. Once the rights of the beneficiary have vested, the principal parties to the contract may

not reduce or defeat those vested rights by modifying or rescinding the contract.

G. Assignment of Rights or Delegation of Duties

1. Has any party to a contract assigned his or her rights? If so, was the assignment effective? To whom is the duty now owing? Any special problems raised by this change of the party who holds the right of performance?

2. Has any contract duty been delegated? Was the duty delegable? If so, is the promisee to whom that duty is owing a third party beneficiary of this contract of delegation?

H. Anticipatory Repudiation and Demands for Assurance

1. Has one of the parties manifested an intention not to perform or engaged in conduct that will prevent performance? If there has been a repudiation of future contract duties, what response may the innocent party make? Does the threat of nonperformance require that the other party take steps to mitigate damages? Will the law permit that innocent party to treat the repudiation as a present breach? When is it too late for the "guilty" party to retract the repudiation?

2. If words or circumstances create reasonable doubt about the other party's willingness or ability to perform, do the circumstances justify a demand for assurances? What reasonable demand should the

innocent party be permitted to make? When will an inadequate response be treated as a repudiation?

I. Performance

This is a difficult subject to outline. We prefer to attempt to set forth an approach—a method.

1. Who is suing whom for what? (At the advice stage, before a suit is filed, the question would be who is making a claim or asserting a right against whom for what.) To answer this question, one must find the promise that someone did not perform or fully perform, and identify the person who made that promise. (There is usually more than one promise in a contract. Often both parties make one or several promises. The first step is to sort through and find the promise about which the fight is developing.) Of course, each party may be upset about the failure of the other to perform and you must then analyze both of these promises.

2. Having identified the critical promise or promises, the non-performance of which is causing hard feelings, the next question is whether you are dealing with an independent or unconditional promise or whether the duty of performance was dependent upon the occurrence of some condition. In other words, what were the conditions precedent to the promise?

3. Have the conditions precedent to the promise been fulfilled or excused? If the promise is subject to a condition, the promisor will never have a duty of immediate performance (and will thus never

breach the promise) unless the conditions precedent are fulfilled or excused.

a) What will excuse a condition? Depending upon the nature of the condition, it might be excused for various reasons, e.g. impossibility, by government intervention, or by the failure of the promisor to cooperate as required to permit the condition to occur. A condition of tender may be excused if it would be an idle act. Acts of bad faith might excuse a condition. If it is a condition of satisfaction, it will be excused if the party who was to be satisfied has wrongfully withheld approval. This will require an analysis of the circumstances to determine the level of conduct to which courts will hold the party who was to be satisfied, e.g. reasonableness, honesty, good faith, etc. The bottom line involves using common sense, keeping an eye on what would be a just result, given the contract to which the parties agreed.

b) What will fulfill a condition? If it is a constructive or promissory condition, it is fulfilled by substantial performance. (See Rest. § 241). Another way of phrasing this question is, has there been a material breach? If it is an express condition, full and literal compliance is required, but courts will try to avoid a result that produces a forfeiture.

4. If the conditions to the promise have been fulfilled or excused and the time for performance has arrived, the only remaining issue is whether the

promise has been performed or whether performance has been excused (see part J, below). If the promise has been breached in whole or in part, then the aggrieved party has a right of action for such remedy as the law may allow (see part K, below).

5. In many performance problems, both parties are claiming that the other has breached. Each promise may have been a condition to the other party's promise so that analysis of the position of each is interrelated. This requires an analysis that follows the format above but which considers each party's position. Often they are best analyzed together. Circumstances significant in determining whether a performance failure is material are noted in Restatement section 241. Circumstances significant for determining when an uncured material breach discharges the other party's remaining duties are noted in Restatement section 242.

6. If the transaction involves goods and the problem relates to the tender and acceptance of seller's performance, the first question may be whether this is a single lot or an installment contract (U.C.C. § 2–307). If it is single lot, has there been a defect in tender justifying rejection (2–601)? Has buyer in fact accepted (2–606) or rejected (2–602)? If buyer has rejected, may seller cure (2–508) and re-tender? If buyer has accepted, are facts present that would permit revocation of acceptance (2–608 and 2–607)?

If it is an installment contract, has there been a breach that constitutes a substantial impairment of the value of the installment tendered and cannot be cured (2–612(2))? (If so, buyer may reject that installment.) Has there been such a breach that it substantially impairs the value of the entire contract? (If so, buyer may terminate the entire contract, 2–612(3).)

If the buyer has failed to pay for installments when due or is otherwise in breach, the 2–612(3) analysis is also applied to that breach to determine whether seller can suspend or cancel performances. (If the legal picture is not clear, this is a possible circumstance justifying a demand for assurances— see Part H 2 *supra*.)

J. Excuse of Performance

1. Impracticability

After the contract is formed, the occurrence of an event that makes performance impossible or legally impracticable may excuse performance. To have performance excused, one must prove that the nonoccurrence of this event was a basic assumption on which the contract was made. One must also establish that the risk of this event is not properly allocated to the party seeking relief.

2. Frustration of Purpose

An event that occurs after the contract is made may cause one party's purpose in entering the contract to be substantially frustrated. Performance is not impossible or more difficult, but the value of the return performance for which the party contracted is gone. Other than this distinction, one must ask the same questions and analyze the same factors as with an impracticability defense.

K. Remedies

1. Is there a liquidated damages clause? If it is valid, it controls.

2. If dealing with a common law problem, consider the three alternative remedy approaches including damages measured by benefit of the bargain, measured by reliance upon the contract, and restitution measured by the value of the benefits conferred upon the other party.

a) Benefit of the bargain

Having found a breach, determine what damages were actually caused by the breach. Were these damages foreseeable under *Hadley*: Either as a natural result of a breach of this type of contract (general damages) or as a result of special facts known to the parties when the contract was made (consequential damages)? Is the innocent party able to establish the damages with the requisite certainty? Could the damages have been avoided by reasonable efforts? Are the damages of reasonable magnitude in relationship to the contract?

b) Reliance

If benefit of the bargain damages are not proven, the innocent party may recover damages for the money value of his or her reliance upon the contract. Analyze carefully if attempting to recover for reliance that occurred before the contract was formed.

c) Restitution

Recovery for restitution or unjust enrichment is measured by the money value of the benefit conferred upon the other party. It may be available where the parties never had an enforceable contract or where the contract was rescinded or performance was excused.

3. In dealing with U.C.C. problems, consider whether the problem involves goods that have been accepted (in which case seller's damages will be measured by the contract price and buyer's damages will be measured under 2–714 and possibly 2–715), If the goods have not been accepted, seller's basic damages will most frequently be computed under 2–706 or 2–708(1). A seller who relies on volume may use 2–708(2). In rare cases, the seller may have an action for the price under 2–709. Sellers may also recover incidental damages. Where the goods have not been accepted, buyer's basic damages will be computed under 2–712 or 2–713. Incidentals and consequentials may be available. In exceptional cases, the buyer may have an action to compel delivery of the goods under 2–716.

INDEX

References are to Sections

621